# Economic Analysis of the Law

*B of E*
*clean*
*B. he to Tou county — tailons*
*{ • Situps*
*{ • pushups*

*The Evolution of Conciousness*
*Aseen Ghanma +*
*Waleed Jweinat*
*1-408-984-6429*
*Nzawaydeh@yahoo.com*

*CIIS*

# Economic Analysis of the Law

## Selected Readings

*Edited by*
DONALD A. WITTMAN

**Blackwell**
Publishing

© 2003 by Blackwell Publishers Ltd
a Blackwell Publishing company
except for editorial arrangement and introduction © 2003 by Donald A. Wittman

350 Main Street, Malden, Massachusetts 02148-5018, USA
108 Cowley Road, Oxford OX4 1JF, UK
550 Swanston Street, Carlton, Victoria 3053, Australia
Kurfürstendamm 57, 10707 Berlin, Germany

First published 2003 by Blackwell Publishers Ltd

*Library of Congress Cataloging-in-Publication Data*

Economic analysis of the law : selected readings / edited by Donald A. Wittman.
    p. cm.
Includes bibliographical references and index.
   ISBN 0–631–23157–9 (hbk : alk. paper) — ISBN 0–631–23158–7 (pbk : alk. paper)
1. Law—Economic aspects.   I. Wittman, Donald A.
   K487.E3 E26 2003
   330—DC21

                                                                    2002001969


A catalogue record for this title is available from the British Library.

Set in 10 on 12 pt Garamond
by Ace Filmsetting Ltd, Frome, Somerset
Printed and bound in the United Kingdom
by TJ International, Padstow, Cornwall

For further information on
Blackwell Publishing, visit our website:
http://www.blackwellpublishing.com

# Contents

Jan
30,

Jan 27

DONE

# Preface

The guiding principle for this collection of articles is to provide the reader with a solid grounding in the economic analysis of law. I have chosen articles that are both intuitive and interesting to the novice.

Most published articles are written for fellow academics. This means that economic articles are typically filled with formal mathematics, something only a fellow academic economist could love. In this reader, I have generally eschewed such articles. And I have deleted the mathematics in the few exceptions where I included articles that originally contained mathematical formulae. As a substitute for mathematics, the articles in the collection provide considerable economic intuition. In this way, the reader can apply the intuition to other areas not covered in the book. In addition, I have shortened the original articles by about 75 percent. This not only allows the book to be about one-quarter the price, but also allows the reader to focus on the essentials. I have found that when articles are too long students tend to skim readings rather than try for a deeper understanding. The original articles were generally directed to a different audience – researchers in the field. I have tried to cut the articles in such a way that they are more directed to the student.

For the economics major, this collection offers a respite from the dry theory presented in intermediate microeconomics texts. The theory presented here is much more alive than the endless drill on isocost curves and the like.

For the law student, this collection creates a unified vision of the law. This is in contrast to law school, where torts, contracts, and corporate law, etc., are treated as completely separate fields, each with their own logic.

For each article, I have provided the background and context in which the article was written. In this way, the collection is not merely a string of articles with no apparent connection, but a more cohesive offering. For motivation, I have included a number of articles on controversial topics.

Introductory readings in the economic analysis of law typically have a large dose of readings that are antagonistic to the enterprise. This collection does not. Presumably, a person reads this book in order to see what economic analysis can explain about the law rather than hear some hackneyed arguments against economic theory.

This collection contains work by two Nobel prize-winning authors and work by others who have been very influential in the economic analysis of law. I hope that everyone learns a great deal from these articles. Certainly I have.

I thank Cheryl Van de Veer and Zoe Sodja for all their Herculean effort in converting the original articles into text format. Even with the aid of optical readers, this was not an easy task.

# Acknowledgments

The editor and publishers gratefully acknowledge the following for permission to reproduce copyright material.

Coase, Ronald (1960) "The Problem of Social Cost," 3 *Journal of Law and Economics*, 2–144. © 1960 by The University of Chicago.

Cooter, Robert (1982) "The Cost of Coase," 11 *Journal of Legal Studies* 1–29. © 1982 by The University of Chicago.

Calabresi, Guido and A. Douglas Melamed (1972) "Property Rules, Liability Rules, and Inalienability: One View of the Cathedral," 85 *Harvard Law Review* 1089–1128. © 1972 by the Harvard Law Review Association.

Brown, John P. (1998) "Economic Theory of Liability Rules," in Peter Newman (ed.) *The New Palgrave Dictionary of Economics and the Law*, Palgrave Macmillan: London. Reproduced with permission of Palgrave.

Cooter, Robert (1985) "Unity in Tort, Contract, and Property: The Model of Precaution," 73 *California Law Review* 1–45. © 1985 by the California Law Review, Inc. Reprinted by permission of the University of California, Berkeley.

Wittman, Donald (1998) "Coming to the Nuisance" in Peter Newman (ed.) *The New Palgrave Dictionary of Economics and Law*, Palgrave Macmillan: London. Reproduced with permission of Palgrave.

Shavell, Steven (1984) "Liability for Harm versus Regulation of Safety," 13 *Journal of Legal Studies* 357–374. © 1984 by The University of Chicago.

Kronman, Anthony T. (1978) "Mistake, Disclosure, Information, and the Law of Contracts," 7 *Journal of Legal Studies* 35–64. © 1978 by The University of Chicago.

Landes, William M. and Richard Posner (1989) "An Economic Analysis of Copyright Law," 18 *Journal of Legal Studies* 325–363. © 1989 by The University of Chicago.

Hansmann, Henry and Marina Santilli (1997) "Authors' and Artists' Moral Rights: A Comparative Legal and Economic Analysis," 26 *Journal of Legal Studies* 95–143. © 1997 by The University of Chicago.

Priest, George L. (1981) "A Theory of the Consumer Product Warranty," 90 *Yale Law Journal* 1297–1352. Reprinted by permission of The Yale Law Journal Company and William S. Hein Company.

Polinsky, A. Mitchell (1987) "Fixed Price versus Spot Price Contracts: A Study in Risk Allocation," 3 *Journal of Law, Economics and Organization* 27–46. Reprinted by permission of Oxford University Press.

Rubin, Paul H. (1978) "The Theory of the Firm and the Structure of the Franchise Contract," 21 *Journal of Law and Economics* 223–233. © 1978 by The University of Chicago.

Klein, Benjamin (1980) "Transaction Cost Determination of 'Unfair' Contractual Arrangements," 70 *American Economic Association Papers and Proceedings*, 356–362. Reprinted by permission of the American Economic Association.

Woodward, Susan E. (1985) "Limited Liability in the Theory of the Firm," 141 *Journal of Institutional and Theoretical Economics* 601–611.

Jensen, Michael C. and William H. Meckling (1976) "Theory of the Firm: Managerial Behavior, Agency Costs, and Ownership Structure," 3 *Journal of Financial Economics* 305–360. Reprinted with permission from Elsevier Science.

Winter, Ralph K., Jr. (1977) "State Law, Shareholder Protection, and the Theory of the Corporation," 6 *Journal of Legal Studies* 251. © 1977 by The University of Chicago.

Easterbrook, Frank H. and Daniel R. Fischel (1981) "The Proper Role of a Target's Management in Responding to a Tender Offer," 94 *Harvard Law Review* 1161–1204. © 1981 by the Harvard Law Review Association.

Carlton, Dennis W. and Daniel R. Fischel (1983) "The Regulation of Insider Trading," 35 *Stanford Law Review*, 857–895. Permission conveyed through Copyright Clearance Center, Inc.

Baird, Douglas G. and Thomas H. Jackson (1984) "Corporate Reorganizations and the Treatment of Diverse Ownership Interests: A Comment on Adequate Protection of Secured Creditors in Bankruptcy," 51 *University of Chicago Law Review* 97–130. Reprinted with permission.

Landes, Elisabeth M. and Richard A. Posner (1978) "The Economics of the Baby Shortage," 7 *Journal of Legal Studies* 323–348. © 1978 by The University of Chicago.

Prichard, J. Robert S. (1984) "A Market for Babies," 34 *University of Toronto Law Journal* 341–357. Reprinted by permission of University of Toronto Press Incorporated.

Cohen, Lloyd (1987) "Marriage, Divorce and Quasi-rents: Or, "I Gave Him the Best Years of My Life," 16 *Journal of Legal Studies* 267–303. © 1987 by The University of Chicago.

Becker, Gary S. (1968) "Crime and Punishment: An Economic Approach," 76 *Journal of Political Economy* 169–217. © 1968 by The University of Chicago.

Posner, Richard A. (1993) "Blackmail, Privacy, and Freedom of Contract," 141 *University of Pennsylvania Law Review* 1817–1848. Reprinted with permission.

Baily, Martin J. (1992) "Approximate Optimality of Aboriginal Property Rights," 35 *Journal of Law and Economics* 183–198. © 1992 by The University of Chicago.

Ellickson, Robert C. (1993) "Property in Land," 102 *Yale Law Journal* 1315–1400. Reprinted by permission of The Yale Law Journal Company and William S. Hein Company.

Wittman, Donald (1982) "Efficient Rules of Thumb in Highway Safety and Sports Activity," 72 *American Economic Review* 78–90. Reprinted by permission of the American Economic Association.

Brinig, Margaret F. (1990) "Rings and Promises," 6 *Journal of Law, Economics, and Organization* 203–215. Reprinted by permission of Oxford University Press.

The publishers apologize for any errors or omissions in the above list and would be grateful to be notified of any corrections that should be incorporated in the next edition or reprint of this book.

# Part I

## Coase Theorem

# 1

# The Problem of Social Cost

## *Ronald H. Coase*

### EDITOR'S INTRODUCTION

It is fitting that we start the collection of readings with "The Problem of Social Cost." This article is the foundation for much of what follows in the economic analysis of law. It is also the most cited article in economics and the basis for Ronald Coase receiving the Nobel Prize in economics. The article is remarkable in a number of ways. First, it made people realize that both the injurer and injured were inputs into the production of damage. Before the publication of Coase's article, the solution to an externality problem (e.g., sparks from a train igniting farmers' crops planted near the railroad) was to change the behavior of the injurer (e.g., put in a spark arrestor). After Coase's article, one also had to consider changing the behavior of the injured (e.g., planting crops that were more fire-resistant). Second, the article demonstrated that the private market could solve problems that economists had heretofore believed were solvable only by government. Before "The Problem of Social Cost," people believed that if a rancher was not liable for the damage from his cows trampling his neighbor's corn field, then there would be too much damage and a "Pigovian" tax on the production of cows would be needed. After publication of this article, people realized that the neighboring farmer would pay the rancher to stop his cows from harming the corn if the reduction in damage to the farmer was greater than the cost to the rancher of preventing his cows from damaging the corn. Furthermore, Coase showed that in the absence of transaction costs (e.g., haggling and monitoring of agreements), the amount of damage would be the same whether the farmer had the right to no harm or the rancher had the right to harm. This became the basis of the "Coase theorem." But Coase was more interested in the opposite situation. He argued that the existence of transaction costs determined the optimal institutions and laws.

## I. The Problem to be Examined

This paper is concerned with those actions of business firms which have harmful effects on others. The standard example is that of a factory the smoke from which has harmful effects on those occupying neighbouring properties. The economic analysis of such a situation has usually proceeded in terms of a divergence between the private and social product of the factory, in which economists have largely followed the treatment of Pigou in *The Economics of Welfare*. The conclusions to which this kind of analysis seems to have led most economists is that it would be desirable to make the owner of the factory liable for the damage caused to those injured by the smoke, or alternatively, to place a tax on the factory owner varying with the amount of smoke produced and equivalent in money terms to the damage it would cause, or finally, to exclude the factory from residential districts (and presumably from other areas in which the emission of smoke would have harmful effects on others). It is my contention that the suggested courses of action are inappropriate, in that they lead to results which are not necessarily, or even usually, desirable.

## II. The Reciprocal Nature of the Problem

The traditional approach has tended to obscure the nature of the choice that has to be made. The question is commonly thought of as one in which A inflicts harm on B and what has to be decided is: how should we restrain A? But this is wrong. We are dealing with a problem of a reciprocal nature. To avoid the harm to B would inflict harm on A. The real question that has to be decided is: should A be allowed to harm B or should B be allowed to harm A? The problem is to avoid the more serious harm. . . . [Consider] the [true] case of a confectioner the noise and vibrations from whose machinery disturbed a doctor in his work. To avoid harming the doctor would inflict harm on the confectioner. The problem posed by this case was essentially whether it was worth while, as a result of restricting the methods of production which could be used by the confectioner, to secure more doctoring at the cost of a reduced supply of confectionery products. Another example is afforded by the problem of straying cattle which destroy crops on neighbouring land. If it is inevitable that some cattle will stray, an increase in the supply of meat can only be obtained at the expense of a decrease in the supply of crops. The nature of the choice is clear: meat or crops. What answer should be given is, of course, not clear unless we know the value of what is obtained as well as the value of what is sacrificed to obtain it. To give another example, . . . [consider] the contamination of a stream. If we assume that the harmful effect of the pollution is that it kills the fish, the question to be decided is: is the value of the fish lost greater or less than the value of the product which the contamination of the stream makes possible. It goes almost  without saying that this problem has to be looked at in total *and* at the margin.

## III. The Pricing System with Liability for Damage

I propose to start my analysis by examining a case in which most economists would presumably agree that the problem would be solved in a completely satisfactory manner: when the damaging business has to pay for all damage caused *and* the pricing system works smoothly (strictly this means that the operation of a pricing system is without cost).

A good example of the problem under discussion is afforded by the case of straying cattle which destroy crops growing on neighbouring land. Let us suppose that a farmer and a cattle-raiser are operating on neighbouring properties. Let us further suppose that, without any fencing between the properties, an increase in the size of the cattle-raiser's herd increases the total damage to the farmer's crops. What happens to the marginal damage as the size of the herd increases is another matter. This depends on whether the cattle tend to follow one another or to roam side by side, on whether they tend to be more or less restless as the size of the herd increases and on other similar factors. For my immediate purpose, it is immaterial what assumption is made about marginal damage as the size of the herd increases.

To simplify the argument, I propose to use an arithmetical example. I shall assume that the annual cost of fencing the farmer's property is $9 and that the price of the crop is $1 per ton. Also, I assume that the relation between the number of cattle in the herd and the annual crop loss is as follows:

| Number in herd (Steers) | Annual crop loss (Tons) | Crop loss per additional steer (Tons) |
|---|---|---|
| 1 | 1 | 1 |
| 2 | 3 | 2 |
| 3 | 6 | 3 |
| 4 | 10 | 4 |

Given that the cattle-raiser is liable for the damage caused, the additional annual cost imposed on the cattle-raiser if he increased his herd from, say, two to three steers is $3 and in deciding on the size of the herd, he will take this into account along with his other costs. That is, he will not increase the size of the herd unless the value of the additional meat produced (assuming that the cattle-raiser slaughters the cattle), is greater than the additional costs that this will entail, including the value of the additional crops destroyed. Of course, if, by the employment of dogs, herdsmen, aeroplanes, mobile radio, and other means, the amount of damage can be reduced, these means will be adopted when their cost is less than the value of the crop which they prevent being lost. Given that the annual cost of fencing is $9, the cattle-raiser who wished to have a herd with four steers or more would pay for fencing to be erected and maintained, assuming that other means of attaining the same end would not do so more cheaply. When the fence is erected, the marginal cost due to the liability for damage becomes zero, except to the extent that an increase in the size of the herd necessitates a stronger and therefore more expensive fence because more steers are liable to lean against it at the same time. But, of course, it may be cheaper for the cattle-raiser not to fence and to pay for the damaged crops, as in my arithmetical example, with three or fewer steers.

It might be thought that the fact that the cattle-raiser would pay for all crops damaged would lead the farmer to increase his planting if a cattle-raiser came to occupy the neighbouring property. But this is not so. If the crop was previously sold in conditions of perfect competition, marginal cost was equal to price for the amount of planting undertaken and any expansion would have reduced the profits of the farmer. In the new situation, the existence of crop damage would mean that the farmer would sell less on the open market but his receipts for a given production would remain the same, since the cattle-raiser would pay the market price for any crop damaged. Of course, if cattle-raising commonly involved the destruction of crops, the coming into existence of a cattle-raising industry might raise the price of the crops involved and farmers would then extend their planting. But I wish to confine my attention to the individual farmer.

I have said that the occupation of a neighbouring property by a cattle-raiser would not cause the amount of production, or perhaps more exactly the amount of planting, by the farmer to increase. In fact, if the cattle-raising has any effect, it will be to decrease the amount of planting. The reason for this is that, for any given tract of land, if the value of the crop damaged is so great that the receipts from the sale of the undamaged crop are less than the total costs of cultivating that tract of land, it will be profitable for the farmer and the cattle-raiser to make a bargain whereby that tract of land is left uncultivated. This can be made clear by means of an arithmetical example. Assume initially that the value of the crop obtained from cultivating a given tract of land is $12 and that the cost incurred in cultivating this tract of land is $10, the net gain from cultivating the land being $2. 1 assume for purposes of simplicity that the farmer owns the land. Now assume that the cattle-raiser starts operations on the neighbouring property and that the value of the crops damaged is $1. In this case $11 is obtained by the farmer from sale on the market and $1 is obtained from the cattle-raiser for damage suffered and the net gain remains $2. Now suppose that the cattle-raiser finds it profitable to increase the size of his herd, even though the amount of damage rises to $3; which means that the value of the additional meat production is greater than the additional costs, including the additional $2 payment for damage. But the total payment for damage is now $3. The net gain to the farmer from cultivating the land is still $2. The cattle-raiser would be better off if the farmer would agree not to cultivate his land for any payment less than $3. The farmer would be agreeable to not cultivating the land for any payment greater than $2. There is clearly room for a mutually satisfactory bargain which would lead to the abandonment of cultivation. . . .

I think it is clear that if the cattle-raiser is liable for damage caused and the pricing system works smoothly, the reduction in the value of production elsewhere will be taken into account in computing the additional cost involved in increasing the size of the herd. This cost will be weighed against the value of the additional meat production and, given perfect competition in the cattle industry, the allocation of resources in cattle-raising will be optimal. What needs to be emphasised is that the fall in the value of production elsewhere which would be taken into account in the costs of the cattle-raiser may well be less than the damage which the cattle would cause to the crops in the ordinary course of events. This is because it is possible, as a result of market transactions, to discontinue cultivation of the land. This is desirable in all cases in which the damage that the cattle would cause, and for which the cattle-raiser would be willing to pay, exceeds the amount which the farmer would pay for use of the land. In conditions of perfect competition, the amount which the farmer would pay for the use of the land is equal to the difference between the value of the total production when the factors are employed on this land and the value of the additional product yielded in their next best use (which would be what the farmer would have to pay for the factors). If damage exceeds the amount the farmer would pay for the use of the land, the value of the additional product of the factors employed elsewhere would exceed the value of the total product in this use after damage is taken into account. It follows that it would be desirable to abandon cultivation of the land and to release the factors employed for production elsewhere. . . . Given the possibility of market transactions, a situation in which damage to crops exceeded the rent of the land would not endure. Whether the cattle-raiser pays the farmer to leave the land uncultivated or himself rents the land by paying the land-owner an amount slightly greater than the farmer would pay (if the farmer was himself renting the land), the final result would be the same and would maximise the value of production. Even when the farmer is induced to plant crops which it would not be profitable to cultivate for sale on the market, this will be a purely short-term phenomenon and may be expected to lead to an agreement under which the planting will cease. The cattle-raiser will remain in that location and the marginal cost of meat production will be the same as before, thus having no long-run effect on the allocation of resources.

## IV. The Pricing System with No Liability for Damage

I now turn to the case in which, although the pricing system is assumed to work smoothly (that is, costlessly), the damaging business is not liable for any of the damage which it causes. This business does not have to make a payment to those damaged by its actions. I propose to show that the allocation of resources will be the same in this case as it was when the damaging business was liable for damage caused. As I showed in the previous case that the allocation of resources was optimal, it will not be necessary to repeat this part of the argument.

I return to the case of the farmer and the cattle-raiser. The farmer would suffer increased damage to his crop as the size of the herd increased. Suppose that the size of the cattle-raiser's herd is three steers (and that this is the size of the herd that would be maintained if crop damage was not taken into account). Then the farmer would be willing to pay up to $3 if the cattle-raiser would reduce his herd to two steers, up to $5 if the herd were reduced to one steer and would pay up to $6 if cattle-raising was abandoned. The cattle-raiser would therefore receive $3 from the farmer if he kept two steers instead of three. This $3 foregone is therefore part of the cost incurred in keeping the third steer. Whether the $3 is a payment which the cattle-raiser has to make if he adds the third steer to his herd (which it would be if the cattle-raiser was liable to the farmer for damage caused to the crop) or whether it is a sum of money which he would have received if he did not keep a third steer (which it would be if the cattle-raiser was not liable to the farmer for damage caused to the crop) does not affect the final result. In both cases $3 is part of the cost of adding a third steer, to be included along with the other costs. If the increase in the value of production in cattle-raising through increasing the size of the herd from two to three is greater than the additional costs that have to be incurred (including the $3 damage to crops), the size of the herd will be increased. Otherwise, it will not. The size of the herd will be the same whether the cattle-raiser is liable for damage caused to the crop or not.

It may be argued that the assumed starting point – a herd of three steers – was arbitrary. And this is true. But the farmer would not wish to pay to avoid crop damage which the cattle-raiser would not be able to cause. For example, the maximum annual payment which the farmer could be induced to pay could not exceed $9, the annual cost of fencing. And the farmer would only be willing to pay this sum if it did not reduce his earnings to a level that would cause him to abandon cultivation of this particular tract of land. Furthermore, the farmer would only be willing to pay this amount if he believed that, in the absence of any payment by him, the size of the herd maintained by the cattle-raiser would be four or more steers. Let us assume that this is the case. Then the farmer would be willing to pay up to $3 if the cattle-raiser would reduce his herd to three steers, up to $6 if the herd were reduced to two steers, up to $8 if one steer only were kept and up to $9 if cattle-raising were abandoned. It will be noticed that the change in the starting point has not altered the amount which would accrue to the cattle-raiser if he reduced the size of his herd by any given amount. It is still true that the cattle-raiser could receive an additional $3 from the farmer if he agreed to reduce his herd from three steers to two and that the $3 represents the value of the crop that would be destroyed by adding the third steer to the herd. Although a different belief on the part of the farmer (whether justified or not) about the size of the herd that the cattle-raiser would maintain in the absence of payments from him may affect the total payment he can be induced to pay, it is not true that this different belief would have any effect on the size of the herd that the cattle-raiser will actually keep. This will be the same as it would be if the cattle-raiser had to pay for damage caused by his cattle, since a receipt foregone of a given amount is the equivalent of a payment of the same amount.

It might be thought that it would pay the cattle-raiser to increase his herd above the size that he would wish to maintain once a bargain had been made, in order to induce the farmer to make a larger total payment. And this may be true. It is similar in nature to the action of the farmer (when the cattle-raiser was liable for damage) in cultivating land on which, as a result of an agreement with the cattle-raiser, planting would subsequently be abandoned (including land which would not be cultivated at all in the absence of cattle-raising). But such manoeuvres are preliminaries to an agreement and do not affect the long-run equilibrium position, which is the same whether or not the cattle-raiser is held responsible for the crop damage brought about by his cattle.

It is necessary to know whether the damaging business is liable or not for damage caused since without the establishment of this initial delimitation of rights there can be no market transactions to transfer and recombine them. But the ultimate result (which maximises the value of production) is independent of the legal position if the pricing system is assumed to work without cost.

## V. The Problem Illustrated Anew

The harmful effects of the activities of a business can assume a wide variety of forms. . . . A recent case in Florida concerned a building which cast a shadow on the cabana, swimming pool, and sunbathing areas of a neighbouring hotel. The problem of straying cattle and the damaging of crops, which was the subject of detailed examination in the two preceding sections, although it may have appeared to be rather a special case, is in fact but one example of a problem which arises in many different guises. To clarify the nature of my argument and to demonstrate its general applicability, I propose to illustrate it anew by reference to. . . [an] actual case.

Let us . . . consider the case of *Sturges v. Bridgman.*[1] . . . In this case, a confectioner (in Wigmore Street) used two mortars and pestles in connection with his business (one had been in operation in the same position for more than 60 years and the other for more than 26 years). A doctor then came to occupy neighbouring premises (in Wimpole Street). The confectioner's machinery caused the doctor no harm until, eight years after he had first occupied the premises, he built a consulting room at the end of his garden right against the confectioner's kitchen. It was then found that the noise and vibration caused by the confectioner's machinery made it difficult for the doctor to use his new consulting room. "In particular . . . the noise prevented him from examining his patients by auscultation for diseases of the chest. He also found it impossible to engage with effect in any occupation which required thought and attention." The doctor therefore brought a legal action to force the confectioner to stop using his machinery. The courts had little difficulty in granting the doctor the injunction he sought. . . .

The court's decision established that the doctor had the right to prevent the confectioner from using his machinery. But, of course, it would have been possible to modify the arrangements envisaged in the legal ruling by means of a bargain between the parties. The doctor would have been willing to waive his right and allow the machinery to continue in operation if the confectioner would have paid him a sum of money which was greater than the loss of income which he would suffer from having to move to a more costly or less convenient location or from having to curtail his activities at this location or, as was suggested as a possibility, from having to build a separate wall which would deaden the noise and vibration. The confectioner would have been willing to do this if the amount he would have to pay the doctor was less than the fall in income he would suffer if he had to change his mode of operation at this location, abandon his operation, or move his confectionery business to some other location. The solution of the problem depends essentially on whether the continued use of the machinery adds more to the confectioner's income than it subtracts from the doctor's. But now consider the situation if the confectioner had won the case. The confectioner would then have had the right to continue operating his noise and vibration-generating machinery without having to pay anything to the doctor. The boot would have been on the other foot: the doctor would have had to pay the confectioner to induce him to stop using the machinery. If the doctor's income would have fallen more through continuance of the use of this machinery than it added to the income of the confectioner, there would clearly be room for a bargain whereby the doctor paid the confectioner to stop using the machinery. That is to say, the circumstances in which it would not pay the confectioner to continue to use the machinery and to compensate the doctor for the losses that this would bring (if the doctor had the right to prevent the confectioner's using his machinery) would be those in which it would be in the interest of the doctor to make a payment to the confectioner which would induce him to discontinue the use of the machinery (if the confectioner had the right to operate the machinery). The basic conditions are exactly the same in this case as they were in the example of the cattle which destroyed crops. With costless market transactions, the decision of the courts concerning liability for damage would be without effect on the allocation of resources. . . .

  . . .

Judges have to decide on legal liability but this should not confuse economists about the nature of the economic problem involved. In the case of the cattle and the crops, it is true that there would be no crop damage without the cattle. It is equally true that there would be no crop damage without the crops. The doctor's work would not have been disturbed if the confectioner had not worked his machinery; but the machinery would have disturbed no one if the doctor had not set up his consulting room in that particular place. . . . If we are to discuss the problem in terms of causation, both parties cause the damage. If we are to attain an optimum allocation of resources, it is therefore desirable that both parties should take the harmful effect (the nuisance) into account in deciding on their course of action. It is one of the beauties of a smoothly operating pricing system that, as has already been explained, the fall in the value of production due to the harmful effect would be a cost for both parties.

  . . .

The reasoning employed by the courts in determining legal rights will often seem strange to an economist because many of the factors on which the decision turns are, to an economist, irrelevant. Because of this, situations which are, from an economic point of view, identical will be treated quite differently by the courts. The economic problem in all cases of harmful effects is how to maximise the value of production. . . . But it has to be remembered that the immediate question faced by the courts *is not* what shall be done by whom *but* who has the legal right to do what. It is always possible to modify by transactions on the market the initial legal delimitation of rights. And, of course, if such market transactions are costless, such a rearrangement of rights will always take place if it would lead to an increase in the value of production.

## VI. The Cost of Market Transactions Taken into Account

The argument has proceeded up to this point on the assumption (explicit in Sections III and IV and tacit in Section V) that there were no costs involved in carrying out market transactions. This is, of course, a very unrealistic assumption. In order to carry out a market transaction it is necessary to discover who it is that one wishes to deal with, to inform people that one wishes to deal and on what terms, to conduct negotiations leading up to a bargain, to draw up the contract, to undertake the inspection needed to make sure that the terms of the contract are being observed, and so on. These operations are often extremely costly, sufficiently costly at any rate to prevent many transactions that would be carried out in a world in which the pricing system worked without cost.

In earlier sections, when dealing with the problem of the rearrangement of legal rights through the market, it was argued that such a rearrangement would be made through the market whenever this would lead to an increase in the value of production. But this assumed costless market transactions. Once the costs of carrying out market transactions are taken into account it is clear that such a rearrangement of rights will only be undertaken when the increase in the value of production consequent upon the rearrangement is greater than the costs which would be involved in bringing it about. When it is less, the granting of an injunction (or the knowledge that it would be granted) or the liability to pay damages may result in an activity being discontinued (or may prevent its being started) which would be undertaken if market transactions were costless. In these conditions the initial delimitation of legal rights does have an effect on the efficiency with which the economic system operates. One arrangement of rights may bring about a greater value of production than any other. But unless this is the arrangement of rights established by the legal system, the costs of reaching the same result by altering and combining rights through the market may be so great that this optimal arrangement of rights, and the greater value of production which it would bring, may never be achieved. . . .

It is clear that an alternative form of economic organisation, which could achieve the same result at less cost than would be incurred by using the market, would enable the value of production to be raised. As I explained many years ago, the firm represents such an alternative to organising production through market transactions. Within the firm individual bargains between the various co-operating factors of production are eliminated and for a market transaction is substituted an administrative decision. The rearrangement of production then takes place without the need for bargains between the owners of the factors of production. A landowner who has control of a large tract of land may devote his land to various uses taking into account the effect that the interrelations of the various activities will have on the net return of the land, thus rendering unnecessary bargains between those undertaking the various activities. Owners of a large building or of several adjoining properties in a given area may act in much the same way. In effect, using our earlier terminology, the firm would acquire the legal rights of all the parties and the rearrangement of activities would not follow on a rearrangement of rights by contract, but as a result of an administrative decision as to how the rights should be used.

It does not, of course, follow that the administrative costs of organising a transaction through a firm are inevitably less than the costs of the market transactions which are superseded. But where contracts are peculiarly difficult to draw up and an attempt to describe what the parties have agreed to do or not to do (e.g. the amount and kind of a smell or noise that they may make or will not make) would necessitate a lengthy and highly involved document, and, where, as is probable, a long-term contract would be desirable; it would be hardly surprising if the emergence of a firm or the extension of the activities of an existing firm was not the solution adopted on many occasions to deal with the problem of harmful effects. This solution would be adopted whenever the administrative costs of the firm were less than the costs of the market transactions that it supersedes and the gains which would result from the rearrangement of activities greater than the firm's costs of organising them.

But the firm is not the only possible answer to this problem. The administrative costs of organising transactions within the firm may also be high, and particularly so when many diverse activities are brought within the control of a single organisation. In the standard case of a smoke nuisance, which may affect a vast number of people engaged in a wide variety of activities, the administrative costs might well be so high as to make any attempt to deal with the problem within the confines of a single firm impossible. An alternative solution is direct government regulation. Instead of instituting a legal system of rights which can be modified by transactions on the market, the government may impose regulations which state what people must or must not do and which have to be obeyed. Thus, the government (by statute or perhaps more likely through an administrative agency) may, to deal with the problem of smoke nuisance, decree that certain methods of production should or should not be used (e.g. that smoke-preventing devices should be installed or that coal or oil should not be burned) or may confine certain types of business to certain districts (zoning regulations).

The government is, in a sense, a super-firm (but of a very special kind) since it is able to influence the use of factors of production by administrative decision. But the ordinary firm is subject to checks in its operations because of the competition of other firms, which might administer the same activities at lower cost and also because there is always the alternative of market transactions as against organisation within the firm if the administrative costs become too great. The government is able, if it wishes, to avoid the market altogether, which a firm can never do. The firm has to make market agreements with the owners of the factors of production that it uses. Just as the government can conscript or seize property, so it can decree that factors of production should only be used in such-and-such a way. Such authoritarian methods save a lot of trouble (for those doing the organising). Furthermore, the government has at its disposal the police and the other law enforcement agencies to make sure that its regulations are carried out.

It is clear that the government has powers which might enable it to get some things done at a lower cost than could a private organisation (or at any rate one without special governmental powers). But the governmental administrative machine is not itself costless. It can, in fact, on occasion be extremely costly. Furthermore, there is no reason to suppose that the restrictive and zoning regulations, made by a fallible administration subject to political pressures and operating without any competitive check, will necessarily always be those which increase the efficiency with which the economic system operates. Furthermore, such general regulations which must apply to a wide variety of cases will be enforced in some cases in which they are clearly inappropriate. From these considerations it follows that direct governmental regulation will not necessarily give better results than leaving the problem to be solved by the market or the firm. But equally there is no reason why, on occasion, such governmental administrative regulation should not lead to an improvement in economic efficiency. This would seem particularly likely when, as is normally the case with the smoke nuisance, a large number of people are involved and in which therefore the costs of handling the problem through the market or the firm may be high.

There is, of course, a further alternative, which is to do nothing about the problem at all. And given that the costs involved in solving the problem by regulations issued by the governmental administrative machine will often be heavy (particularly if the costs are interpreted to include all the consequences which follow from the government engaging in this kind of activity), it will no doubt be commonly the case that the gain which would come from regulating the actions which give rise to the harmful effects will be less than the costs involved in government regulation.

The discussion of the problem of harmful effects in this section (when the costs of market transactions are taken into account) is extremely inadequate. But at least it has made clear that the problem is one of choosing the appropriate social arrangement for dealing with the harmful effects. All solutions have costs and there is no reason to suppose that government regulation is called for simply because the problem is not well handled by the market or the firm. Satisfactory views on policy can only come from a patient study of how, in practice, the market, firms and governments handle the problem of harmful effects. Economists need to study the work of the broker in bringing parties together, the effectiveness of restrictive covenants, the problems of the large-scale real-estate development company, the operation of government zoning and other regulating activities. It is my belief that economists, and policy-makers generally, have tended to over-estimate the advantages which come from governmental regulation. But this belief, even if justified, does not do more than suggest that government regulation should be curtailed. It does not tell us where the boundary line should be drawn. This, it seems to me, has to come from a detailed investigation of the actual results of handling the problem in different ways. But it would be unfortunate if this investigation were undertaken with the aid of a faulty economic analysis. The aim of this article is to indicate what the economic approach to the problem should be.

## VII. The Legal Delimitation of Rights and the Economic Problem

The discussion in Section V not only served to illustrate the argument but also afforded a glimpse at the legal approach to the problem of harmful effects. . . . Of course, if market transactions were costless, all that matters (questions of equity apart) is that the rights of the various parties should be well defined and the results of legal actions easy to forecast. But as we have seen, the situation is quite different when market transactions are so costly as to make it difficult to change the arrangement of rights established by the law. In such cases, the courts directly influence economic activity. It would therefore seem desirable that the courts should understand the economic consequences of their decisions and should, insofar as this is possible without creating too much uncertainty about the legal position itself, take these consequences into account when making their decisions. Even when it is possible to change the legal delimitation of rights through market transactions, it is obviously desirable to reduce the need for such transactions and thus reduce the employment of resources in carrying them out.

. . .

## Note

1.   Ch. D. 852 (1879).

# 2

## The Cost of Coase

### *Robert Cooter*

## EDITOR'S INTRODUCTION

Ronald Coase argued that bargaining can overcome the problem of externalities when trans-action costs are zero. And hence from an efficiency point of view it does not make any difference whether a farmer has the right to non-damage from cows or his rancher neighbor has the right to have his cows damage the farmer's land. Either way, the outcome is the same. Robert Cooter shows that bargaining inherently involves strategic behavior whereby each side is willing to trade off some probability of a agreement in return for a greater surplus from the agreement should it be made. The possibility of a failed bargain means that even when transaction costs are zero, the assignment of rights does make a difference since the status quo has a privileged position. In a nutshell, Cooter shows that the so-called "Coase theorem" is not a theorem, but rather a conjecture on how people will behave. Cooter then stands the Coase theorem on its head and produces the Hobbes theorem – society may want to limit the kinds of strategic behavior available to the parties since threats, especially if they are carried out, are costly.

## Introduction

The publication of "The Problem of Social Cost" in 1960 by Ronald Coase brought together two powerful intellectual currents, namely, the economic theory of externalities and the common-law tradition concerning torts and nuisance. The sea is fertile but rough where two ocean currents meet, and the same can be said of the disputes provoked by Coase. Coase developed his argument through a series of concrete examples, such as the rancher and the farmer, the railroad sparks and the corn crops, etc. He steadfastly refused to articulate the general truths underlying the examples; for example, the famous "Coase theorem" is ab-stracted from the paper but not stated in it. After two decades of debate the generalizations underlying the examples are still disputed.

. . .

Coase gave his name to a fundamental theorem on externalities and tort law, but he left to others the job of stating exactly what the theorem says. The basic idea of the theorem is that the structure of the law which assigns property rights and liability does not matter so long as transaction costs are nil, bargaining will result in an efficient outcome no matter who bears the burden of liability. The conclusion may be drawn that the structure of law should be chosen so that transaction costs are minimized, because this will conserve resources used up by the bargaining process and also promote efficient outcomes in the bargaining itself.

. . .

We shall argue that the central version of the Coase theorem cannot be deduced from economic assumptions. The widespread belief to the contrary is symptomatic of confusion about bargaining. This confusion results in blindness toward certain outcomes of policy. We shall try to restore accurate vision by explaining the relations among liability law, bargaining, and the economic assumptions of rational behavior.

## Bargaining problem

. . .

. . . Polinsky has offered this compact statement of Coase's theorem: "If transaction costs are zero the structure of the law does not matter because efficiency will result in any case."[1] The transaction costs of bargaining refer to the cost of communicating among the parties (including the value of time used up in sending messages), making side payments (the cost of the transaction, not the value of what is exchanged), and the cost of excluding people from sharing in the benefits exchanged by the parties. In the case of contingent commodities, the cost of obtaining information on the actions of the players is also treated as a transaction cost, so the inefficiencies from moral hazard and adverse selection are swept under the blanket of transaction costs. . . .

The mechanism for achieving efficiency in the absence of competitive markets is bargaining. For example, Calabresi formulated the Coase theorem as follows: "If one assumes rationality, no transaction costs, and no legal impediments to bargaining, *all* misallocation of resources would be fully cured in the market by bargains."[2] This formulation apparently presupposes a general proposition about bargaining, namely, . . . [b]argaining games with zero transaction costs reach efficient solutions. . . .

In order to evaluate this interpretation of Coase, we must explain the place of bargaining in game theory. A zero-sum game is a game in which total winnings minus total losses equals zero. Poker is an example. A zero-sum game is a game of pure redistribution, because nothing is created or destroyed. By contrast, a coordination game is a game in which the players have the same goal. For example, if a phone conversation is cut off, then the callers face a coordination problem. The connection cannot be restored unless someone dials, but the call will not go through if both dial at once. The players win or lose as a team, and winning is productive, so coordination games are games of pure production.

A bargaining game involves distribution and production. Typically, there is something to be divided called the stakes. For example, one person may have a car to sell and the other may have money to spend. The stakes are the money and the car. If the players can agree upon a price for the car, then both of them will benefit. The surplus is the joint benefits from cooperation, for example, consumer's surplus plus seller's surplus in our example of the car. If the players cannot agree upon how to divide the stakes, then the surplus will be lost. In brief, bargaining games are games in which production is contingent upon agreement about distribution.

The bargaining version of the Coase theorem takes an optimistic attitude toward the ability of people to solve this problem of distribution. The obstacles to cooperation are portrayed as the cost of communicating, the time spent negotiating, the cost of enforcing agreements, etc. These obstacles can all be described as transaction costs of bargaining. Obviously, we can conceive of a bargaining game in which these costs are nil.

A pessimistic approach assumes that people cannot solve the distribution problem, even if there are no costs to bargaining. According to this view, there is no reason why rationally self-interested players should agree about how to divide the stakes. The distribution problem is unsolvable by rational players. To eliminate the possibility of noncooperation, we would have to eliminate the problem of distribution, that is, to convert the bargaining game into a coordination game. But it makes no sense to speak about a bargaining game without a problem of distribution.

Our example of selling a car illustrates the collision of these two viewpoints. The costs of communicating, writing a contract, and enforcing its terms are the transaction costs of buying or selling a car. These costs sometimes constitute an obstacle to exchange. However, there is another obstacle of an entirely different kind, namely the absence of a competitive price. The parties must haggle over the price until they can agree upon how to distribute the gains from trade. There is no guarantee that the rational pursuit of self-interest will permit agreement. If we interpret zero transaction costs to mean that there is no dispute over price, then we have dissolved the bargaining game.

The polar opposite of the optimistic bargaining theorem can be stated as follows: "Bargaining games have noncooperative outcomes even when the bargaining process is costless." This line of thought suggests the polar opposite of the Coase theorem: "Private bargaining to redistribute external costs will not achieve efficiency unless there is an institutional mechanism to dictate the terms of the contract." [O]ne institutional mechanism to achieve efficiency . . . [is] a competitive market, which eliminates the power of parties to threaten each other. Another such institution is compulsory arbitration.

The conception of law which is the polar opposite to Coase is articulated in Hobbes and is probably much older. It is based upon the belief that people will exercise their worst threats against each other unless there is a third party to coerce both of them. The third party for Hobbes is the prince or leviathan – we would say dictatorial government – who has unlimited power relative to the bargainers. Without his coercive threats, life would be "nasty, brutish, and short."[3] We shall refer to the polar opposite of the Coase theorem as the Hobbes theorem.

The Coase theorem identifies the problem of externalities with the cost of the bargaining process, whereas the Hobbes theorem identifies the problem with the absence of an authoritative distribution of the stakes. We shall argue that both theorems are false. However, they are illuminating falsehoods because they offer a guide to structuring law in the interest of efficiency.

In real situations faced by policymakers, transaction costs are positive. The Coase theorem suggests that the role of law is to assign entitlements to the party who values them the most, so that the costly process of exchanging the entitlement is unnecessary. There are many similar versions of this proposition, for example, liability for accidents should be assigned to the party who can prevent them at lowest cost, or the cost of breach of contract should be assigned to the party who is the best insurer against nonperformance. If the party who values the entitlement the most cannot be identified, then it should be assigned to the party who can initiate an exchange at the least cost.

The Hobbes theorem suggests that the role of law is to minimize the inefficiency that results when bargaining fails, by restricting the threats which the parties can make against each other. In the jargon of game theory, law increases the value of the noncooperative solution by eliminating elements of the payoff matrix with low value. This function is obvious in criminal law, where threats of violence against property or persons are punished. This function of law is also apparent in regulation of collective bargaining and strike activity. We claim that the same principle is at work where the threat is, say, to pollute a stream, to not perform on a contract, or to not take precautions against accidents.

For example, suppose that efficiency requires both the injurer and the victim to take precautions against accidents. According to the Hobbes theorem, liability should be assigned to the party whose lack of precaution is most destructive. Put technically, liability should be assigned to the party for whom the excess of joint benefits over the private costs of precaution is largest. Alternatively, consider the problem of nonperformance on a contract by the promisor. According to the Hobbes theorem, liability should be assigned to the promisee if excessive reliance by the promisee results in more net damage than insufficient precaution by the promisor against the events causing nonperformance. . . .

The Coase theorem and the Hobbes theorem have contradictory implications for the size of government. We can see this point most clearly by considering the policy implications in the ideal world of zero transaction costs. According to the Coase theorem, there is no continuing need for government under these conditions. Like the deist god, the government retires from the scene after creating some rights over externalities, and efficiency is achieved regardless of what rights were created. According to the Hobbes theorem, the coercive threats of government or some similar institution are needed to achieve efficiency when externalities create bargaining situations, even though bargaining is costless. Like the theist god, the government continuously monitors private bargaining to insure its success.

The Coase theorem represents extreme optimism about private cooperation and the Hobbes theorem represents extreme pessimism. Perhaps the Coase theorem is more accurate than the Hobbes theorem in the sense that gains from trade in bargaining situations are more often realized than not, or perhaps the Hobbes theorem is more accurate from the perspective of lawyers who must pick up the pieces when cooperation fails. We shall not attempt an allocation of truth. The strategic considerations are not normally insurmountable, as suggested by Hobbes, or inconsequential, as suggested by Coase. An informed policy choice must balance the Coase theorem against the Hobbes theorem in light of the ability of the parties to cooperate. Our next task is to develop a theory of bargaining, based upon standard economic assumptions, which facilitates thinking about the obstacles to cooperation.

The error in the bargaining version of the Coase theorem is to suppose that the obstacle to cooperation is the cost of communicating, rather than the strategic nature of the situation. Bargainers remain uncertain about what their opponents will do, not because it costs too much to broadcast one's intentions, but because strategy requires that true intentions be "disguised." The error in the Hobbes theorem is to suppose that bargainers increase their demands without regard to the reduction in probability of settlement. In equilibrium when expectations are rational, players do not adopt strategies which always lead to noncooperation, nor do they adopt strategies which always lead to cooperation.

. . .

# Conclusion

"The Problem of Social Cost" brought together two divergent intellectual traditions, and its poignant examples continue to be a valuable instrument for teaching the economic analysis of law. But this classic has its costs. . . .

We . . . considered the bargaining interpretation of the Coase theorem, which states that externalities will be cured by private bargains, even in the absence of competitive prices, provided that there are no obstacles to the bargaining process. Inspired by Hobbes, we formulated the polar-opposite theorem: Externalities will not be cured by private bargains unless someone coerces the parties to agree about the price. The Coase theorem and the Hobbes theorem are illuminating falsehoods. The Coase theorem is false because the final obstacle to private noncompetitive bargains is the absence of a rule for dividing the surplus, not the cost of bargaining. In fact, it is cheaper to engage in strategic behavior when communication is inexpensive. The Hobbes theorem is false because bargainers moderate their demands in order to increase the likelihood of agreement. The Coase theorem is illuminating because it suggests that liability rights should be allocated by the court in the way that they would be if cooperative agreements were always achieved. The Hobbes theorem is illuminating because it suggests that legal rights should be structured to eliminate the most destructive noncooperative outcomes. . . .

. . . [S]trategic behavior sometimes results in noncooperative outcomes. . . . [T]he equilibrium is rational in the sense that every individual is maximizing his expected utility, and everyone's expectations are accurate, but noncooperative outcomes still occur. Noncooperative outcomes occur because each player's strategy is best against opponents on average, but not best against every individual opponent. Reducing the transaction costs of bargaining . . . does not generally increase the probability of cooperation.

Coase created a new field out of poignant examples. After twenty years we ought to get clear about the underlying generalizations.

## Notes

1.  A. Mitchell Polinsky, "Economic Analysis as a Potentially Defective Product: A Buyer's Guide to Posner's Economic Analysis of Law", 87 *Harv. L. Rev.* 1165 (1974).
2.  Guido Calabresis, "Transaction Costs, Resource Allocation, and Liability Rules – A Comment," 11 *J. Law & Econ.* 68 (1968)
3.  Thomas Hobbes, *Leviathan* 100 (Collier-MacMillan ed. 1973).

# Part II

---

## Property Rights, Liability Rules, and Regulation

# 3

*entitlements* (handwritten)

# Property Rules, Liability Rules, and Inalienability: One View of the Cathedral

## Guido Calabresi and A. Douglas Melamed

### EDITOR'S INTRODUCTION

An entitlement, such as the right to be free of smoke, can be protected by a property right (the person may give up the right voluntarily, but presumably this will occur only if the price paid compensates for the loss of the right), by a liability rule (the right can be involuntarily taken away, but a third party determines the value of the loss), or by inalienability (the right cannot be taken away). In the absence of transaction costs, the "Coase theorem" suggests that it would not make any difference whether an entitlement was protected by a property right or a liability rule or which side had the entitlement in the first place. Guido Calabresi and Douglas Melamed take the opposite perspective – the high transaction cost case. They first show how the relative costs of markets and courts determine whether a liability rule, property right, or rule of inalienability is used to protect an entitlement. Essentially, property rights are preferred over liability rules when market transaction costs are low in comparison to court transaction costs; the reverse holds when market transaction costs are relatively high. Calabresi and Melamed then consider the four combinations that arise from the two possible entitlements (e.g., the polluter has the right to pollute or the pollutee has the right to no pollution) and the first two means of protection of the entitlement (liability or property right) and show why one method is chosen over the others even though in the absence of transaction costs all four would yield identical results. The paper is important because it first shows the inherent symmetry of various methods to control externalities and then provides an insightful explanation for why one of the methods is chosen over the others. Finally, it demonstrates the unity of the law by showing how the same considerations arise in areas of the law that are ostensibly different (e.g., criminal, property, and tort law).

## I. Introduction

Only rarely are Property and Torts approached from a unified perspective. Recent writings by lawyers concerned with economics and by economists concerned with law suggest, however, that an attempt at integrating the various legal relationships treated by these subjects would be useful both for the beginning student and the sophisticated scholar. By articulating a concept of "entitlements" which are protected by property, liability, or inalienability rules, we present one framework for such an approach. We then analyze aspects of the pollution problem and of criminal sanctions in order to demonstrate how the model enables us to perceive relationships which have been ignored by writers in those fields.

The first issue which must be faced by any legal system is one we call the problem of "entitlement." Whenever a state is presented with the conflicting interests of two or more people, or two or more groups of people, it must decide which side to favor. Absent such a decision, access to goods, services, and life itself will be decided on the basis of "might makes right" – whoever is stronger or shrewder will win. Hence the fundamental thing that law does is to decide which of the conflicting parties will be entitled to prevail. The entitlement to make noise versus the entitlement to have silence, the entitlement to pollute versus the entitlement to breathe clean air, the entitlement to have children versus the entitlement to forbid them – these are the first order of legal decisions.

Having made its initial choice, society must enforce that choice. Simply setting the entitlement does not avoid the problem of "might makes right"; a minimum of state intervention is always necessary. Our conventional notions make this easy to comprehend with respect to private property. If Taney owns a cabbage patch and Marshall, who is bigger, wants a cabbage, he will get it unless the state intervenes. But it is not so obvious that the state must also intervene if it chooses the opposite entitlement, communal property. If large Marshall has grown some communal cabbages and chooses to deny them to small Taney, it will take state action to enforce Taney's entitlement to the communal cabbages. The same symmetry applies with respect to bodily integrity. Consider the plight of the unwilling ninety-eight-pound weakling in a state which nominally entitles him to bodily integrity but will not intervene to enforce the entitlement against a lustful Juno. Consider then the plight – absent state intervention – of the ninety-eight-pounder who desires an unwilling Juno in a state which nominally entitles everyone to use everyone else's body. The need for intervention applies in a slightly more complicated way to injuries. When a loss is left where it falls in an auto accident, it is not because God so ordained it. Rather it is because the state has granted the injurer an entitlement to be free of liability and will intervene to prevent the victim's friends, if they are stronger, from taking compensation from the injurer. The loss is shifted in other cases because the state has granted an entitlement to compensation and will intervene to prevent the stronger injurer from rebuffing the victim's requests for compensation.

The state not only has to decide whom to entitle, but it must also simultaneously make a series of equally difficult second order decisions. These decisions go to the manner in which entitlements are protected and to whether an individual is allowed to sell or trade the entitlement. In any given dispute, for example, the state must decide not only which side wins but also the kind of protection to grant. It is with the latter decisions, decisions which shape the subsequent relationship between the winner and the loser, that this article is primarily concerned. We shall consider three types of entitlements – entitlements protected by property rules, entitlements protected by liability rules, and inalienable entitlements. The categories are not, of course, absolutely distinct; but the categorization is useful since it reveals some of the reasons which lead us to protect certain entitlements in certain ways.

An entitlement is protected by a property rule to the extent that someone who wishes to remove the entitlement from its holder must buy it from him in a voluntary transaction in which the value of the entitlement is agreed upon by the seller. It is the form of entitlement which gives rise to the least amount of state intervention: once the original entitlement is decided upon, the state does not try to decide its value. It lets each of the parties say how much the entitlement is worth to him, and gives the seller a veto if the buyer does not offer enough. Property rules involve a collective decision as to who is to be given an initial entitlement but not as to the value of the entitlement.

Whenever someone may destroy the initial entitlement if he is willing to pay an objectively determined value for it, an entitlement is protected by a liability rule. This value may be what it is thought the original holder of the entitlement would have sold it for. But the holder's complaint that he would have demanded more will not avail him once the objectively determined value is set. Obviously, liability rules involve an additional stage of state intervention: not only are entitlements protected, but their transfer or destruction is allowed on the basis of a value determined by some organ of the state rather than by the parties themselves.

An entitlement is inalienable to the extent that its transfer is not permitted between a willing buyer and a willing seller. The state intervenes not only to determine who is initially entitled and to determine the compensation that must be paid if the entitlement is taken or destroyed, but also to forbid its sale under some or all circumstances. Inalienability rules are thus quite different from property and liability rules. Unlike those rules, rules of inalienability not only "protect" the entitlement; they may also be viewed as limiting or regulating the grant of the entitlement itself.

It should be clear that most entitlements to most goods are mixed. Taney's house may be protected by a property rule in situations where Marshall wishes to purchase it, by a liability rule where the government decides to take it by eminent domain, and by a rule of inalienability in situations where Taney is drunk or incompetent. This article will explore two primary questions: (1) In what circumstances should we grant a particular entitlement? and (2) In what circumstances should we decide to protect that entitlement by using a property, liability, or inalienability rule?

## II. The Setting of Entitlements

What are the reasons for deciding to entitle people to pollute or to entitle people to forbid pollution, to have children freely or to limit procreation, to own property or to share property? They can be grouped under three headings: economic efficiency, distributional preferences, and other justice considerations. [Here, we focus on economic efficiency].

### . . . ECONOMIC EFFICIENCY

Perhaps the simplest reason for a particular entitlement is to minimize the administrative costs of enforcement. This was the reason Holmes gave for letting the costs lie where they fall in accidents unless some clear societal benefit is achieved by shifting them.[1] By itself this reason will never justify any result except that of letting the stronger win, for obviously that result minimizes enforcement costs. Nevertheless, administrative efficiency may be relevant to choosing entitlements when other reasons are taken into account. This may occur when the reasons accepted are indifferent between conflicting entitlements and one entitlement is cheaper to enforce than the others. It may also occur when the reasons are not indifferent but lead us only slightly to prefer one over another and the first is considerably more expensive to enforce than the second.

But administrative efficiency is just one aspect of the broader concept of economic efficiency. Economic efficiency asks that we choose the set of entitlements which would lead to that allocation of resources which could not be improved in the sense that a further change would not so improve the condition of those who gained by it that they could compensate those who lost from it and still be better off than before. This is often called Pareto optimality. To give two examples, economic efficiency asks for that combination of entitlements to engage in risky activities and to be free from harm from risky activities which will most likely lead to the lowest sum of accident costs and of costs of avoiding accidents. It asks for that form of property, private or communal, which leads to the highest product for the effort of producing.

Recently it has been argued that on certain assumptions, usually termed the absence of transaction costs, Pareto optimality or economic efficiency will occur regardless of the initial entitlement. For this to hold, "no transaction costs" must be understood extremely broadly as involving both perfect knowledge and the absence of any impediments or costs of negotiating. Negotiation costs include, for example, the cost of excluding would-be freeloaders from the fruits of market bargains. In such a frictionless society, transactions would occur until no one could be made better off as a result of further transactions without making someone else worse off. This, we would suggest, is a necessary, indeed a tautological, result of the definitions of Pareto optimality and of transaction costs which we have given.

Such a result would not mean, however, that the same allocation of resources would exist regardless of the initial set of entitlements. Taney's willingness to pay for the right to make noise may depend on how rich he is; Marshall's willingness to pay for silence may depend on his wealth. In a society which entitles Taney to make noise and which forces Marshall to buy silence from Taney, Taney is wealthier and Marshall poorer than each would be in a society which had the converse set of entitlements. Depending on how Marshall's desire for silence and Taney's for noise vary with their wealth, an entitlement to noise will result in negotiations which will lead to a different quantum of noise than would an entitlement to silence. This variation in the quantity of noise and silence can be viewed as no more than an instance of the well-accepted proposition that what is a Pareto optimal, or economically efficient, solution varies with the starting distribution of wealth. Pareto optimality is optimal *given* a distribution of wealth, but different distributions of wealth imply their own Pareto optimal allocation of resources.

All this suggests why distributions of wealth may affect a society's choice of entitlements. It does not suggest why *economic efficiency* should affect the choice, if we assume an absence of any transaction costs. But no one makes an assumption of no transaction costs in practice. Like the physicist's assumption of no friction or Say's law in macro-economics, the assumption of no transaction costs may be a useful starting point, a device which helps us see how, as different elements which may be termed transaction costs become important, the goal of economic efficiency starts to prefer one allocation of entitlements over another.

. . .

## III. Rules for Protecting and Regulating Entitlements

Whenever society chooses an initial entitlement it must also determine whether to protect the entitlement by property rules, by liability rules, or by rules of inalienability. In our

framework, much of what is generally called private property can be viewed as an entitle-  *def*
ment which is protected by a property rule. No one can take the entitlement to private  *no monhot*
property from the holder unless the holder sells it willingly and at the price at which he
subjectively values the property. Yet a nuisance with sufficient public utility to avoid injunc-  *def*
tion has, in effect, the right to take property with compensation. In such a circumstance the  *def*
entitlement to the property is protected only by what we call a liability rule: an external,
objective standard of value is used to facilitate the transfer of the entitlement from the
holder to the nuisance. Finally, in some instances we will not allow the sale of the property
at all, that is, we will occasionally make the entitlement inalienable.

This section will consider the circumstances in which society will employ these three rules
to solve situations of conflict. Because the property rule and the liability rule are closely
related and depend for their application on the shortcomings of each other, we treat them
together. We discuss inalienability separately.

## A. Property and liability rules

Why cannot a society simply decide on the basis of the already mentioned criteria who
should receive any given entitlement, and then let its transfer occur only through a voluntary
negotiation? Why, in other words, cannot society limit itself to the property rule? To do this
it would need only to protect and enforce the initial entitlements from all attacks, perhaps
through criminal sanctions, and to enforce voluntary contracts for their transfer. Why do we
need liability rules at all?

In terms of economic efficiency the reason is easy enough to see. Often the cost of  *a why*
establishing the value of an initial entitlement by negotiation is so great that even though a  *liability*
transfer of the entitlement would benefit all concerned, such a transfer will not occur. If a  *rules*
collective determination of the value were available instead, the beneficial transfer would
quickly come about.

Eminent domain is a good example. A park where Guidacres, a tract of land owned by  *ex*
1,000 owners in 1,000 parcels, now sits would, let us assume, benefit a neighboring town
enough so that the 100,000 citizens of the town would each be willing to pay an average of
$100 to have it. The park is Pareto desirable if the owners of the tracts of land in Guidacres
actually value their entitlements at less than $10,000,000 or an average of $10,000 a tract. Let
us assume that in fact the parcels are all the same and all the owners value them at $8,000.
On this assumption, the park is, in economic efficiency terms, desirable – in values foregone  *EX*
it costs $8,000,000 and is worth $10,000,000 to the buyers. And yet it may well not be
established. If enough of the owners hold out for more than $10,000 in order to get a share
of the $2,000,000 that they guess the buyers are willing to pay over the value which the
sellers in actuality attach, the price demanded will be more than $10,000,000 and no park will
result. The sellers have an incentive to hide their true valuation and the market will not
succeed in establishing it.

An equally valid example could be made on the buying side. Suppose the sellers of
Guidacres have agreed to a sales price of $8,000,000 (they are all relatives and at a family
banquet decided that trying to hold out would leave them all losers). It does not follow that
the buyers can raise that much even though each of 100,000 citizens *in fact* values the park
at $100. Some citizens may try to freeload and say the park is only worth $50 or even

nothing to them, hoping that enough others will admit to a higher desire and make up the $8,000,000 price. Again there is no reason to believe that a market, a decentralized system of valuing, will cause people to express their true valuations and hence yield results which all would *in fact* agree are desirable.

Whenever this is the case an argument can readily be made for moving from a property rule to a liability rule. If society can remove from the market the valuation of each tract of land, decide the value collectively, and impose it, then the holdout problem is gone. Similarly, if society can value collectively each individual citizen's desire to have a park and charge him a "benefits" tax based upon it, the freeloader problem is gone. If the sum of the taxes is greater than the sum of the compensation awards, the park will result.

Of course, one can conceive of situations where it might be cheap to exclude all the freeloaders from the park, or to ration the park's use in accordance with original willingness to pay. In such cases the incentive to freeload might be eliminated. But such exclusions, even if possible, are usually not cheap. And the same may be the case for market methods which might avoid the holdout problem on the seller side.

Moreover, even if holdout and freeloader problems can be met feasibly by the market, an argument may remain for employing a liability rule. Assume that in our hypothetical, freeloaders can be excluded at the cost of $1,000,000 and that all owners of tracts in Guidacres can be convinced, by the use of $500,000 worth of advertising and cocktail parties, that a sale will only occur if they reveal their true land valuations. Since $8,000,000 plus $1,500,000 is less than $10,000,000, the park will be established. But if collective valuation of the tracts and of the benefits of the prospective park would have cost less than $1,500,000, it would have been inefficient to establish the park through the market – a market which was not worth having would have been paid for.

Of course, the problems with liability rules are equally real. We cannot be at all sure that landowner Taney is lying or holding out when he says his land is worth $12,000 to him. The fact that several neighbors sold identical tracts for $10,000 does not help us very much; Taney may be sentimentally attached to his land. As a result, eminent domain may grossly undervalue what Taney would actually sell for, even if it sought to give him his true valuation of his tract. In practice, it is so hard to determine Taney's true valuation that eminent domain simply gives him what the land is worth "objectively," in the full knowledge that this may result in over or under compensation. The same is true on the buyer side. "Benefits" taxes rarely attempt, let alone succeed, in gauging the individual citizen's relative desire for the alleged benefit. They are justified because, even if they do not accurately measure each individual's desire for the benefit, the market alternative seems worse. For example, fifty different households may place different values on a new sidewalk that is to abut all the properties. Nevertheless, because it is too difficult, even if possible, to gauge each household's valuation, we usually tax each household an equal amount.

The example of eminent domain is simply one of numerous instances in which society uses liability rules. Accidents is another. If we were to give victims a property entitlement not to be accidentally injured we would have to require all who engage in activities that may injure individuals to negotiate with them before an accident, and to buy the right to knock off an arm or a leg. Such pre-accident negotiations would be extremely expensive, often prohibitively so. To require them would thus preclude many activities that might, in fact, be worth having. And, after an accident, the loser of the arm or leg can always very plausibly deny that he would have sold it at the price the buyer would have offered. Indeed, where negotiations after an accident do occur – for instance pretrial settlements – it is largely because the alternative is the collective valuation of the damages.

It is not our object here to outline all the theoretical, let alone the practical, situations where markets may be too expensive or fail and where collective valuations seem more desirable. . . . It is enough for our purposes to note that a very common reason, perhaps the most common one, for employing a liability rule rather than a property rule to protect an entitlement is that market valuation of the entitlement is deemed inefficient, that is, it is either unavailable or too expensive compared to a collective valuation.

. . .

## B. Inalienable entitlements

Thus far we have focused on the questions of when society should protect an entitlement by property or liability rules. However, there remain many entitlements which involve a still greater degree of societal intervention: the law not only decides who is to own something and what price is to be paid for it if it is taken or destroyed, but also regulates its sale – by, for example, prescribing preconditions for a valid sale or forbidding a sale altogether. Although these rules of inalienability are substantially different from the property and liability rules, their use can be analyzed in terms of the same efficiency and distributional goals that underlie the use of the other two rules.

While at first glance efficiency objectives may seem undermined by limitations on the ability to engage in transactions, closer analysis suggests that there are instances, perhaps many, in which economic efficiency is more closely approximated by such limitations. This might occur when a transaction would create significant externalities – costs to third parties.

For instance, if Taney were allowed to sell his land to Chase, a polluter, he would injure his neighbor Marshall by lowering the value of Marshall's land. Conceivably, Marshall could pay Taney not to sell his land; but, because there are many injured Marshalls, freeloader and information costs make such transactions practically impossible. The state could protect the Marshalls and yet facilitate the sale of the land by giving the Marshalls an entitlement to prevent Taney's sale to Chase but only protecting the entitlement by a liability rule. It might, for instance, charge an excise tax on all sales of land to polluters equal to its estimate of the external cost to the Marshalls of the sale. But where there are so many injured Marshalls that the price required under the liability rule is likely to be high enough so that no one would be willing to pay it, then setting up the machinery for collective valuation will be wasteful. Barring the sale to polluters will be the most efficient result because it is clear that avoiding pollution is cheaper than paying its costs – including its costs to the Marshalls.

Another instance in which external costs may justify inalienability occurs when . . . [there are] moralisms.

If Taney is allowed to sell himself into slavery, or to take undue risks of becoming penniless, or to sell a kidney, Marshall may be harmed, simply because Marshall is a sensitive man who is made unhappy by seeing slaves, paupers, or persons who die because they have sold a kidney. Again Marshall could pay Taney not to sell his freedom to Chase the slaveowner; but again, because Marshall is not one but many individuals, freeloader and information costs make such transactions practically impossible. . . . . The state must, therefore, either ignore the external costs to Marshall, or if it judges them great enough, forbid the transaction that gave rise to them by making Taney's freedom inalienable.

. . .

. . . [Paternalism is another] efficiency reason for forbidding the sale of entitlements under certain circumstances . . . [For] example, the prohibitions on a whole range of activities by minors. . . . Paternalism is based on the notion that at least in some situations the Marshalls know better than Taney what will make Taney better off. Here we are not talking about the offense to Marshall from Taney's choosing to read pornography, or selling himself into slavery, but rather the judgment that Taney was not in the position to choose best for himself when he made the choice for erotica or servitude. The first concept we called a moralism and is a frequent and important ground for inalienability. . . .

. . .

## IV. The Framework and Pollution Control Rules

Nuisance or pollution is one of the most interesting areas where the question of who will be given an entitlement, and how it will be protected, is in frequent issue. . . . First, Taney may not pollute unless his neighbor (his only neighbor let us assume), Marshall, allows it (Marshall may enjoin Taney's nuisance). Second, Taney may pollute but must compensate Marshall for damages caused (nuisance is found but the remedy is limited to damages). Third, Taney may pollute at will and can only be stopped by Marshall if Marshall pays him off (Taney's pollution is not held to be a nuisance to Marshall). In our terminology rules one and two (nuisance with injunction, and with damages only) are entitlements to Marshall. The first is an entitlement to be free from pollution and is protected by a property rule; the second is also an entitlement to be free from pollution but is protected only by a liability rule. Rule three (no nuisance) is instead an entitlement to Taney protected by a property rule, for only by buying Taney out at Taney's price can Marshall end the pollution.

The very statement of these rules in the context of our framework suggests that something is missing. Missing is a fourth rule representing an entitlement in Taney to pollute, but an entitlement which is protected only by a liability rule. The fourth rule, really a kind of partial eminent domain coupled with a benefits tax, can be stated as follows: Marshall may stop Taney from polluting, but if he does he must compensate Taney.

As a practical matter it will be easy to see why even legal writers . . . have ignored this rule. Unlike the first three it does not often lend itself to judicial imposition for a number of good legal process reasons. For example, even if Taney's injuries could practicably be measured, apportionment of the duty of compensation among many Marshalls would present problems for which courts are not well suited. If only those Marshalls who voluntarily asserted the right to enjoin Taney's pollution were required to pay the compensation, there would be insuperable freeloader problems. If, on the other hand, the liability rule entitled one of the Marshalls alone to enjoin the pollution and required all the benefited Marshalls to pay their share of the compensation, the courts would be faced with the immensely difficult task of determining who was benefited how much and imposing a benefits tax accordingly, all the while observing procedural limits within which courts are expected to function.

The fourth rule is thus not part of the cases legal scholars read when they study nuisance law, and is therefore easily ignored by them. But it is available, and may sometimes make more sense than any of the three competing approaches. Indeed, in one form or another, it may well be the most frequent device employed. To appreciate the utility of the fourth rule and to compare it with the other three rules, we will examine why we might choose any of the given rules.

We would employ rule one (entitlement to be free from pollution protected by a property rule) from an economic efficiency point of view if we believed that the polluter, Taney, could avoid or reduce the costs of pollution more cheaply than the pollutee, Marshall. Or to put it another way, Taney would be enjoinable if he were in a better position to balance the costs of polluting against the costs of not polluting. We would employ rule three (entitlement to pollute protected by a property rule) again solely from an economic efficiency standpoint, if we made the converse judgment on who could best balance the harm of pollution against its avoidance costs. If we were wrong in our judgments and if transactions between Marshall and Taney were costless or even very cheap, the entitlement under rules one or three would be traded and an economically efficient result would occur in either case. If we entitled Taney to pollute and Marshall valued clean air more than Taney valued the pollution, Marshall would pay Taney to stop polluting even though no nuisance was found. If we entitled Marshall to enjoin the pollution and the right to pollute was worth more to Taney than freedom from pollution was to Marshall, Taney would pay Marshall not to seek an injunction or would buy Marshall's land and sell it to someone who would agree not to seek an injunction. As we have assumed no one else was hurt by the pollution, Taney could now pollute even though the initial entitlement, based on a wrong guess of who was the cheapest avoider of the costs involved, allowed the pollution to be enjoined. Wherever transactions between Taney and Marshall are easy, and wherever economic efficiency is our goal, we could employ entitlements protected by property rules even though we would not be sure that the entitlement chosen was the right one. Transactions as described above would cure the error. While the entitlement might have important distributional effects, it would not substantially undercut economic efficiency.

The moment we assume, however, that transactions are not cheap, the situation changes dramatically. Assume we enjoin Taney and there are 10,000 injured Marshalls. Now *even if* the right to pollute is worth more to Taney than the right to be free from pollution is to the sum of the Marshalls, the injunction will probably stand. The cost of buying out all the Marshalls, given holdout problems, is likely to be too great, and an equivalent of eminent domain in Taney would be needed to alter the initial injunction. Conversely, if we denied a nuisance remedy, the 10,000 Marshalls could only with enormous difficulty, given freeloader problems, get together to buy out even one Taney and prevent the pollution. This would be so even if the pollution harm was greater than the value to Taney of the right to pollute.

If, however, transaction costs are not symmetrical, we may still be able to use the property rule. Assume that Taney can buy the Marshalls' entitlements easily because holdouts are for some reason absent, but that the Marshalls have great freeloader problems in buying out Taney. In this situation the entitlement should be granted to the Marshalls unless we are sure the Marshalls are the cheapest avoiders of pollution costs. Where we do not know the identity of the cheapest cost avoider it is better to entitle the Marshalls to be free of pollution because, even if we are wrong in our initial placement of the entitlement, that is, even if the Marshalls are the cheapest cost avoiders, Taney will buy out the Marshalls and economic efficiency will be achieved. Had we chosen the converse entitlement and been wrong, the Marshalls could not have bought out Taney. Unfortunately, transaction costs are often high on both sides and an initial entitlement, though incorrect in terms of economic efficiency, will not be altered in the market place.

Under these circumstances – and they are normal ones in the pollution area – we are likely to turn to liability rules whenever we are uncertain whether the polluter or the pollutees can most cheaply avoid the cost of pollution. We are only likely to use liability rules where we are uncertain because, if we are certain, the costs of liability rules – essentially the costs of collectively valuing the damages to all concerned plus the cost in coercion to those who would not sell at the collectively determined figure – are unnecessary. They are unnecessary because transaction costs and bargaining barriers become irrelevant when we are certain who is the cheapest cost avoider; economic efficiency will be attained without transactions by making the correct initial entitlement.

As a practical matter we often are uncertain who the cheapest cost avoider is. In such cases, traditional legal doctrine tends to find a nuisance but imposes only damages on Taney payable to the Marshalls. This way, if the amount of damages Taney is made to pay is close to the injury caused, economic efficiency will have had its due; if he cannot make a go of it, the nuisance was not worth its costs. The entitlement to the Marshalls to be free from pollution unless compensated, however, will have been given *not* because it was thought that polluting was probably worth less to Taney than freedom from pollution was worth to the Marshalls, nor even because on some distributional basis we preferred to charge the cost to Taney rather than to the Marshalls. It was so placed *simply because we did not know* whether Taney desired to pollute more than the Marshalls desired to be free from pollution, and the only way we thought we could test out the value of the pollution was by the only liability rule we thought we had. This was rule two, the imposition of nuisance damages on Taney. At least this would be the position of a court concerned with economic efficiency which believed itself limited to rules one, two, and three.

Rule four gives at least the possibility that the opposite entitlement may also lead to economic efficiency in a situation of uncertainty. Suppose for the moment that a mechanism exists for collectively assessing the damage resulting to Taney from being stopped from polluting by the Marshalls, and a mechanism also exists for collectively assessing the benefit to each of the Marshalls from such cessation. Then – assuming the same degree of accuracy in collective valuation as exists in rule two (the nuisance damage rule) – the Marshalls would stop the pollution if it harmed them more than it benefited Taney. If this is possible, then even if we thought it necessary to use a liability rule, we would still be free to give the entitlement to Taney or Marshall for whatever reasons, efficiency or distributional, we desired.

Actually, the issue is still somewhat more complicated. For just as transaction costs are not necessarily symmetrical under the two converse property rule entitlements, so also the liability rule equivalents of transaction costs – the cost of valuing collectively and of coercing compliance with that valuation – may not be symmetrical under the two converse liability rules. Nuisance damages may be very hard to value, and the costs of informing all the injured of their rights and getting them into court may be prohibitive. Instead, the assessment of the objective damage to Taney from foregoing his pollution may be cheap and so might the assessment of the relative benefits to all Marshalls of such freedom from pollution. But the opposite may also be the case. As a result, just as the choice of which property entitlement may be based on the asymmetry of transaction costs and hence on the greater amenability of one property entitlement to market corrections, so might the choice between liability entitlements be based on the asymmetry of the costs of collective determination.

. . .

The problems of coercion may as a practical matter be extremely severe under rule four. How do the homeowners decide to stop the factory's use of low-grade coal? How do we assess the damages and their proportional allocation in terms of benefits to the homeowners? But equivalent problems may often be as great for rule two. How do we value the damages to each of the many homeowners? How do we inform the homeowners of their rights to damages? How do we evaluate and limit the administrative expenses of the court actions this solution implies?

The seriousness of the problem depends under each of the liability rules on the number of people whose "benefits" or "damages" one is assessing and the expense and likelihood of error in such assessment. A judgment on these questions is necessary to an evaluation of the possible economic efficiency benefits of employing one rule rather than another. The relative ease of making such assessments through different institutions may explain why we often employ the courts for rule two and get to rule four – when we do get there – only through political bodies which may, for example, prohibit pollution, or "take" the entitlement to build a supersonic plane by a kind of eminent domain, paying compensation to those injured by these decisions. But all this does not, in any sense, diminish the importance of the fact that an awareness of the possibility of an entitlement to pollute, but one protected only by a liability rule, may in some instances allow us best to combine our distributional and efficiency goals.

. . .

Thus far in this section we have ignored the possibility of employing rules of inalienability to solve pollution problems. A general policy of barring pollution does seem unrealistic. But rules of inalienability can appropriately be used to limit the levels of pollution and to control the levels of activities which cause pollution.

One argument for inalienability may be the widespread existence of moralisms against pollution. Thus it may hurt the Marshalls – gentleman farmers – to see Taney, a smoke-choked city dweller, sell his entitlement to be free of pollution. A different kind of externality or moralism may be even more important. The Marshalls may be hurt by the expectation that, while the present generation might withstand present pollution levels with no serious health dangers, future generations may well face a despoiled, hazardous environmental condition which they are powerless to reverse. . . . Finally, society might restrict alienability on paternalistic grounds. The Marshalls might feel that although Taney himself does not know it, Taney will be better off if he really can see the stars at night, or if he can breathe smogless air.

. . .

## V. The Framework and Criminal Sanctions

Obviously we cannot canvass the relevance of our approach through many areas of the law. But we do think it beneficial to examine one further area, that of crimes against property and bodily integrity. The application of the framework to the use of criminal sanctions in cases of theft or violations of bodily integrity is useful in that it may aid in understanding the previous material, especially as it helps us to distinguish different kinds of legal problems and to identify the different modes of resolving those problems.

Beginning students, when first acquainted with economic efficiency notions, sometimes ask why ought not a robber be simply charged with the value of the thing robbed. And the same question is sometimes posed by legal philosophers. If it is worth more to the robber than to the owner, is not economic efficiency served by such a penalty? Our answers to such a question tend to move quickly into very high sounding and undoubtedly relevant moral considerations. But these considerations are often not very helpful to the questioner because they depend on the existence of obligations on individuals not to rob for a fixed price and the original question was why we should impose such obligations at all.

One simple answer to the question would be that thieves do not get caught every time they rob and therefore the costs to the thief must at least take the unlikelihood of capture into account. But that would not fully answer the problem, for even if thieves were caught every time, the penalty we would wish to impose would be greater than the objective damages to the person robbed.

A possible broader explanation lies in a consideration of the difference between property entitlements and liability entitlements. For us to charge the thief with a penalty equal to an objectively determined value of the property stolen would be to convert all property rule entitlements into liability rule entitlements.

The question remains, however, why *not* convert all property rules into liability rules? The answer is, of course, obvious. Liability rules represent only an approximation of the value of the object to its original owner and willingness to pay such an approximate value is no indication that it is worth more to the thief than to the owner. In other words, quite apart from the expense of arriving collectively at such an objective valuation, it is no guarantee of the economic efficiency of the transfer. If this is so with property, it is all the more so with bodily integrity, and we would not presume collectively and objectively to value the cost of a rape to the victim against the benefit to the rapist even if economic efficiency is our sole motive. Indeed when we approach bodily integrity we are getting close to areas where we do not let the entitlement be sold at all and where economic efficiency enters in, if at all, in a more complex way. But even where the items taken or destroyed are things we do allow to be sold, we will not without special reasons impose an objective selling price on the vendor.

Once we reach the conclusion that we will not simply have liability rules, but that often, even just on economic efficiency grounds, property rules are desirable, an answer to the beginning student's question becomes clear. The thief not only harms the victim, he undermines rules and distinctions of significance beyond the specific case. Thus even if in a given case we can be sure that the value of the item stolen was no more than X dollars, and even if the thief has been caught and is prepared to compensate, we would not be content simply to charge the thief X dollars. Since in the majority of cases we cannot be sure of the economic efficiency of the transfer by theft, we must add to each case an undefinable kicker which represents society's need to keep all property rules from being changed at will into liability rules. In other words, we impose criminal sanctions as a means of deterring future attempts to convert property rules into liability rules.

The first-year student might push on, however, and ask why we treat the thief or the rapist differently from the injurer in an auto accident or the polluter in a nuisance case. Why do we allow liability rules there? In a sense, we have already answered the question. The only level at which, before the accident, the driver can negotiate for the value of what he might take from his potential victim is one at which transactions are too costly. The thief or rapist, on the other hand, could have negotiated without undue expense (at least if the good was one which we allowed to be sold at all) because we assume he knew what he was going to do and to whom he would do it. The case of the accident is different because knowledge exists only at the level of deciding to drive or perhaps to drive fast, and at that level negotiations with potential victims are usually not feasible.

The case of nuisance seems different, however. There the polluter knows what he will do and, often, whom it will hurt. But as we have already pointed out, freeloader or holdout problems may often preclude any successful negotiations between the polluter and the victims of pollution; additionally, we are often uncertain who is the cheapest avoider of pollution costs. In these circumstances a liability rule, which at least allowed the economic efficiency of a proposed transfer of entitlements to be tested, seemed appropriate, even though it permitted the nonaccidental and unconsented taking of an entitlement. It should be emphasized, however, that where transaction costs do not bar negotiations between polluter and victim, or where we are sufficiently certain who the cheapest cost avoider is, there are no efficiency reasons for allowing intentional takings, and property rules, supported by injunctions or criminal sanctions, are appropriate.

## Note

1.   See O.W. Holmes, Jr., *The Common Law* 76–77 (Howe, ed. 1963).

# 4

# Economic Theory of Liability Rules

## *John P. Brown*

### EDITOR'S INTRODUCTION

The following contribution by John Brown is a less formal version of an earlier article. Brown considers situations with high market transaction costs, a prominent example being automobile accidents. Clearly, it is impossible to contract with all potential victims before driving one's car across town. With high transaction costs, the choice of liability rule does make a difference on the outcome.

Brown first shows that the problem of minimizing the cost of accidents and accident prevention is identical to the standard production problem of choosing the optimal amount of capital and labor. Prevention by the potential injurer (injured) should be undertaken until the last dollar spent on prevention reduces damages by an additional dollar. This is the efficient or optimal point. Optimality requires that, in general, both the injurer and the injured undertake preventative measures.

Efficiency cannot be achieved by either a regime of strict liability by the injurer or a regime of no liability by the injurer. Instead, a negligence rule is required, whereby one side is made liable if that party is negligent (that is, acting less than optimally). If one side is liable only if negligent, then that side will have the incentive to undertake the efficient amount of precaution. Then the other side is fully liable and will thus take the optimal level of precaution, as well. Negligence-type rules are the standard rules when accidents are involved, and the economic calculus had already been derived in a famous appellate court decision by Judge Learned Hand (*United States v. Carroll Rowing Co.*, 159 F2d 169), thus demonstrating the economic foundation of tort law.

The economic theory of liability rules is a body of analysis of the economic consequences of tort liability rules. Since tortious harm can be avoided to some degree by taking precautions, the economic theory of liability is grounded in the economics of precautions. Tort law governs relations between strangers who hurt one another. The strangers are not dealing with one another in organized markets nor have they contracted with one another. It is not an analysis of organized markets. Instead, it is an analysis of economic behavior in the face of accidents that might or might not happen, where costly precautions may or may not be put to use, and where, if an accident happens, a potential injurer may have to pay damages, or a potential victim may not be able to collect damages.

## Scope: Economics Applied to Tort Law rather than Contract Law

Legal rules of liability for torts have an impact on economic behavior. Whether the impact is socially beneficial or perverse, whether the rules have a large or a small impact, these are the subject of the economic theory of liability.

A tort is any wrongful act, other than a breach of contract, for which a civil lawsuit may be brought by a private person. Our discussion will be limited to cases where the parties are strangers to each other, in the sense that they have not had or taken the opportunity to enter into agreements or contracts with each other about the consequences of potential harm caused by one to the other.

Liability rules describe the circumstances under which a court will grant damages for injuries to oneself or one's resources. Liability rules are distinct from property rights, which allow one to exclude all others from the use of that resource. I may not be able to prevent you from hitting my car, but through the application of liability rules, I can get a court to force you to pay damages to me for hitting my car.

The economic behavior at issue is the extent to which parties take costly precautions which can protect others or themselves from harm.

The economic theory of contracts and contract enforcement involves very different considerations and is beyond the scope of this essay. Still, it should be pointed out that where parties have a contract with each other, but the contract does not cover a contingency that in fact occurs, then the parties might be considered as strangers, and often tort law concepts can provide structure and background to any analysis, whether legal or economic.

## The Economics of Precautions

### THE PRODUCTION OF PRECAUTIONS

The economics of precautions is, in part, an exercise in the standard economic theory of production. Here, the good produced is a level of accident avoidance which is best expressed as a probability of the accident being avoided (one minus the probability of the accident). In the standard case, production of a level of accident avoidance requires amounts of two inputs or precautions. Later we shall let one of the precautions be under the control of the injurer and one under the control of the victim. The standard neoclassical production theory is usually developed under the assumptions of positive and declining marginal products for each input and the inputs are available at fixed prices. One can determine efficient combinations of the two inputs to produce any particular level of accident avoidance. In the simplest case, when both precautions and the cost of the accident are simply denominated in dollars, and the cost of the accident is fixed, one can easily identify the least cost combination of precautions and accident probability. See figure overleaf for a standard representation of production where the product is accident avoidance, increasing upward to the right. Standard isoquants show different combinations of precautions that jointly produce equal levels of accident avoidance, and the straight lines represent equal cost combinations of precautions. The optimal combination, the combination that would be chosen if both precautions and the cost of the accident were under common control, will be where the isoquant and isocost lines are tangent. Of the many tangencies, that will be chosen where the marginal cost of increased production is the same as the marginal benefit of accident avoidance.

As the economist would have it, at the best combination of precautions the marginal cost of each precaution is equal to the value of its marginal product of accident probability reduction. At less than the optimal level of either precaution, the marginal benefits of increased precaution are greater than the marginal cost of the precaution. Whenever less than appropriate levels of precautions are being taken, it can be said that there are further precautions that can be taken, should be taken, but are not being taken.

In general, of course, the least cost level of accidents, or probability of accidents, is not zero, and requires some positive level of both precautions. Of course, there are simpler cases, where one of the precautions is unnecessary, or the least cost solution is to use enough precautions to avoid the accident altogether. These corner solutions are easily dealt with, but we shall ignore them here.

## Centralized Control over Precautions

The classic tort case during the nineteenth century was a fire in ricks of flax stacked near the railroad tracks awaiting shipment to market, and the fire was caused by sparks flying from a

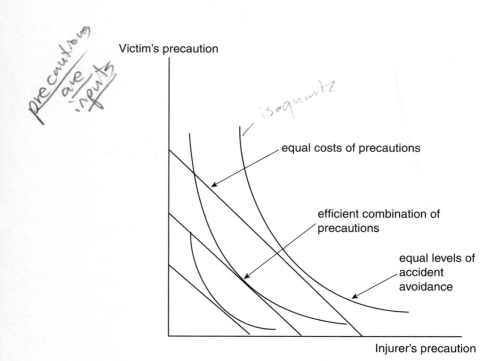

passing train. In these cases there are two available precautions: arrest more of the sparks before they leave the engine by adding an expensive spark arrester, or move the flax to a less convenient location farther from the tracks. If, as was occasionally the case, the train and the land were both owned by the same party, say the Union Pacific, then there would be no lawsuit after a fire.

Where both precautions are in the control of the same person or firm – the Union Pacific – and the accident costs are borne by them, then the Union Pacific has every incentive to choose the optimal level of each precaution and hence the optimal level of accident avoidance. If something other than the best combination of precautions were taken, the Union Pacific would reduce its costs by changing the level of precautions toward the best level. If the marginal benefits of the precaution were greater than their marginal costs, the owner would increase the precaution, whether by moving the flax farther from the tracks or by using a more effective spark arrester.

This centralized solution is the standard for testing the efficiency of legal rules. The legal rules play out in the same technology under the same costs, but the harm and one of the critical precautions are under separate control by people who are strangers unless they meet in court after an accident.

Coase in his classic "The Problem of Social Cost" (1960) took Pigou to task for what Coase considered a misunderstanding of these and other railroad accidents. . . .

## Decentralization to Two Parties with Liability Rules

With this background in hand, we can now turn to the analysis of liability. In the context of a tort case, the precautions are controlled by two strangers rather than one person or company. The strangers have typically not communicated at all prior to the accident, let alone negotiated about joint precautions. They now come together in court, and their case is decided according to the rules of liability to be applied. It is the tradition of the economic analysis of liability rules to ignore many of the important complexities and costs incurred in the courts to focus on the rules themselves. So courts are typically assumed to act without mistake and without cost. It is a further simplification to assume that damages, if awarded by the court, are the same as the full cost of the accident to the victim. See Calfee and Craswell (1984) for the effects of uncertainty in the courts on the incentives to take precautions.

This analysis is carried out under the assumption that the lack of precaution by the injurer caused the accident that harmed the victim. Causation itself is a complex area that has received significant attention by economists as well as legal scholars.

## Liability Rules

It is useful to separate liability rules into two groups, rules based on negligence by one party or the other, and two simpler rules, strict liability for the injurer and no liability for the injurer. We treat the simple rules first, then describe negligence and finally treat the negligence-based rules.

## The simple rules

There are two very simple liability rules that require no judgment on the part of the court, except to decide if the rule applies. They are no liability and strict liability. No liability simply means that a victim cannot collect damages from an injurer.

Under strict liability, the injured plaintiff need only present the case to the court in order to collect damages from the injurer. This rule is the symmetric opposite of no liability.

## Equilibrium under the simple rules

Equilibrium under these simple rules is equally simple. Under a rule of no liability, the injurer has no incentives to take precautions to avoid the accident, and the victim will take the most cost-effective precautions under her control, operating under the assumption that the injurer will take no precautions. Of course, this is not the same solution as if there were a single owner. Typically, the injurer will take too few precautions, and the victim will take too many, and the result will be too many accidents. The rule is inefficient.

Under a strict liability rule, where the injurer will fully reimburse the victim for the full cost of the accident, the victim has no incentive to take any precautions and the injurer will take the most cost-effective precautions under the assumption that the victim will take none. Again, as compared to the centralized decision, the rule will be inefficient. The injurer will take too many precautions and the victim will take too few. Again, injuries will be higher, as well.

## Negligence, the standard of care, and efficient precautions

Negligence is a central concept in the common law and in the economic theory of liability. Following an accident or tort, a party is negligent if the fact-finder determines that he or she did not meet the appropriate standard of care, or as it is sometimes said, did not use due care. Or equivalently, a party is negligent if there is a precaution that the party could have taken, should have taken, and did not take.

The central result of the economic theory of liability is that, under circumstances that economists consider usual, if the standard of care of the negligence rule is the same as the amount of care that would be taken under centralized control, then a negligence rule will lead to efficient choice of precautions by both injurer and victim. . .

## The negligence-based rules

It is possible to distinguish a number of negligence-based rules. . . . This discussion is limited to . . . the negligence rule and the negligence rule with a contributory negligence defense.

### Negligence rule

Under the negligence rule the victim cannot collect from the injurer unless the injurer is found negligent.

## *Negligence rule with a contributory negligence defense*

Under the negligence rule with a contributory negligence defense, the injurer is liable if he is negligent *and* the victim is not.

One of the earliest cases in American tort law that laid out the rule of negligence with a contributory negligence defense was the 1850 Massachusetts case of *Brown v. Kendall,* where the defendant or injurer took up a stick to separate fighting dogs belonging to the plaintiff – the victim – and the defendant. In the course of beating the dogs the defendant accidentally hit the plaintiff in the eye, injuring him severely. Chief Justice Shaw laid down the rule:

> if both plaintiff and defendant at the time of the blow were using ordinary care, or if at that time the defendant was using ordinary care, and the plaintiff was not, or if at that time, both the defendant and the plaintiff were not using ordinary care, then the plaintiff could not recover. [60 Mass. (6 Cush.) 292 (1850)]

## *Other rules*

The analytical structure that is applied to the simple rules and the negligence-based rules can be applied to any well-defined liability rule. The huge literature in the economic theory of tort liability is, to a large degree, the application of this structure to an amazing variety of issues.

## EQUILIBRIUM UNDER NEGLIGENCE-BASED RULES

It is the essence of a precaution that the level of precaution is chosen prior to the accident, typically prior even to knowing that the accident would happen or knowing who the other party would be. Because of the jointness of production between the precautions of the two parties, the efficacy of the precaution I take depends on the amount of precautions you take, whoever you may be. That decision is certainly one made under uncertainty and is usefully thought of as a strategy in a two-person non-cooperative game. Then, the outcome of the game can be considered with the tools of game theory. The economic theory of liability is traditionally a study of the properties of the non-cooperative equilibria of these games. An equilibrium for a game is a pair of choices of precautions by the two parties such that, given the choice by the other party, neither party has an incentive to change his or her own choice.

To construct an equilibrium, we first construct response functions for each party like those in Cournot's analysis of duopoly. A response function shows the least cost response of one party to a particular level of precaution taken by the other. Where those response functions intersect is the equilibrium to the game. The cost of a response takes into account both the cost of the precaution taken and the cost of the liability for the accident. To make the discussion symmetric, we shall say that the victim is liable for the accident if he or she cannot collect in court from the injurer, and we shall abstract from differences between the judgment and the cost of the accident by assuming them to be the same.

To prepare the way, consider the simpler response functions assuming that each party would bear the full costs of the accident. . . . The injurer's response function shows his cost-minimizing response to any given level of precaution by the victim, assuming that he will bear the full cost of the accident. In turn, the victim's response function shows her cost-minimizing response to any given level of precaution by the injurer, assuming that she will bear the full cost of the accident. The full-cost response functions are equivalent to the first order conditions of minimization of the total cost of the accident and its precautions. As a result they intersect at the joint level of precautions which minimizes the total cost, the combination that would have been chosen if there were centralized joint control over both precautions. Thus it is the case that if both the injurer and the victim were forced to bear the full cost of the accident, their incentives would lead them to choose the most efficient combination of precautions. But, of course, such double jeopardy does not conform to the legal rules in any real jurisdiction.

From these full-cost reaction functions, we can construct reaction functions for the various rules. Under a negligence rule with a contributory negligence defense, the victim will pay the full cost of the accident, unless the defendant injurer is negligent and the victim is not, in which case the victim will collect the full cost of the accident from the injurer. That is, if the injurer uses less care than the standard of care would call for and the victim meets the standard of care, the victim will not pay for the accident, and will have no incentive to take any precautions beyond meeting the standard of care. If the injurer meets the standard of care, the victim will bear the full cost of the accident and has the full incentive to take precautions, depending on the level of precautions of the injurer. But once the injurer has met the standard of care he has no further incentive to take more care because he bears no further responsibility for the cost of the accident. . . .

For the negligence rule without a contributory negligence defense, the same methods can be used to show that the efficient combination of precautions is again the unique equilibrium under this rule. . . .

Indeed, the equilibrium will be efficient as long as the rule requires that the injurer pays when the injurer is negligent and the victim is not, and that the victim pays when the victim is negligent and the injurer is not. Efficiency is not affected by shifts in liability either when both parties have met the standard of care or when neither has met the standard of care.

*Efficiency.* The standard of efficiency is the standard provided by centralized control: what precautions would be taken if all precautions were taken by, and all harm was borne by, a single person.

## Changing the Amount of the Activity

In some situations the parties to potential accidents control not only the level of precautions that they take, but also the amount of the potentially dangerous activity, as well. One can choose how carefully to drive and how much to drive. Just as decisions about care should take into account the risks imposed on others, so should decisions about the amount of the risky activity to be undertaken. It would be best if liability rules provided incentives for the proper level of activity, as well as the proper level of care. Unfortunately, as Shavell (1980) has shown, there is no liability rule that simultaneously provides appropriate incentives for both injurer and victim to take the appropriate level of care and choose the appropriate amount of activity. This negative result may go too far; if a court can consider negligence in terms of both care and amount of activity, the original analysis can apply.

. . .

## Other Comments

The analysis of liability rules has been carried out at a high level of abstraction. This is a frequent source of frustration or irritation for lawyers steeped in the common law. Liability rules apply to a bewildering variety of situations. Tort cases are nothing if they are not concrete, and are won by careful analysis of particular facts. That high level of abstraction is probably appropriate given the extraordinary variety of cases in which the rules are applied. It is the general rules that are the subject of analysis, not the particular cases. It is general rules that can inform people's choices of levels of care before accidents do – or usually do not – occur.

These common-law notions are very robust under changes in technology, unlike many statutory or regulatory rules. Negligence is a meaningful concept where due care is meaningful. The rule has been applied to separating fighting dogs, but it can be just as sensibly applied to accidents that take place electronically or on the World Wide Web, or in the control room of a nuclear reactor.

It is an interesting aspect of negligence rules that the courts do not more and more carefully set out what appropriate precautions might be. Indeed that is typically the role of the jury, not the judge. We do not find courts setting out particular standards, which are then refined by later litigation. Instead, the jury determines if a party met the standard of due care or not, and reports that judgment, without identifying what the standard might be.

A theory of negligence is helpful in thinking about decisions among liability rules. It is only part of any analysis of the choice between liability rules and other forms of control, such as regulation or taxation of potentially dangerous behavior. One must also have a theory of regulation or taxation in order to avoid the obvious pitfalls of comparing a carefully analyzed system found flawed with a stylized and apparently perfect alternative. Then decisions might be made on the basis of the extent of the analysis, rather than on the merits of the alternatives.

## Bibliography

*Brown v. Kendall,* 60 Mass. (6 Cush.) 292 (1850).

Calfee, J. and Craswell, R. 1984. Some effects of uncertainty on compliance with legal standards. *Virginia Law Review* 70: 965–1003.

Coase, R. 1960. The problem of social cost. *Journal of Law and Economics* 3: 1–44.

Shavell, S. 1980. Strict liability versus negligence. *Journal of Legal Studies* 9: 1–25.

# 5

## Unity in Tort, Contract, and Property: The Model of Precaution

### *Robert Cooter*

## EDITOR'S INTRODUCTION

Tort, contract, and property law all allocate the cost of harm. As Coase and Brown have shown, for many types of harm, efficiency requires precaution by both injurer and victim. Incentives for precaution are efficient when both parties are responsible for the harm caused by their marginal reductions in precaution. This is what Robert Cooter labels double responsibility at the margin. An absolute rule, such as strict liability, erodes the victim's incentives for precaution. Conversely, a rule of no liability erodes the injurer's incentives for precaution. Cooter considers three mechanisms in the common law that combine compensation and incentives for efficient precaution.

The first mechanism is the fault rule. When an injurer satisfies the legal standard of care, a small reduction in his precaution will make him negligent. Thus, he is liable for the harm resulting from marginal reductions in his precaution. Furthermore, when the injurer satisfies the legal standard of care, the victim bears residual responsibility and is responsible for harm resulting from any reduction in her own precaution. Thus, as Brown showed earlier, the injurer takes efficient precaution to avoid legal responsibility and the victim takes efficient precaution because she bears residual responsibility. In Cooter's analysis, this is the first method of creating double responsibility at the margin.

The second common-law mechanism that Cooter considers is invariant damages, as exemplified by liquidation of damages provisions in the law of contracts. A liquidation clause stipulates a dollar amount to be paid as compensation in the event of breach. When damages are liquidated, the breaching party is responsible for the stipulated damages and the victim of the breach is responsible for actual damages. Thus, invariant damages encourage double responsibility at the margin - the promisor balances the cost of precaution against the stipulated damages and the victim balances the benefits of reliance against the potential loss.

The third mechanism that Cooter considers is the coercive order from a court, such as an injunction against a nuisance. Economists are unenthusiastic about coercive orders for reasons that are developed at length in the economic critique of regulation. However, the right to an injunction may have desirable economic effects if it is used as a bargaining chip rather than actually exercised. Unlike coercive orders, bargaining solutions have desirable economic properties. The right to obtain an injunction may enable nuisance victims to achieve adequate compensation by private agreement with the injurer, and the parties to the bargain will desire to make its terms efficient.

Much of the common law is concerned with allocating the costs of the harm such as the harm caused by accidents, nuisances, breaches of contract, or government takings of private property. There are at least two distinct goals for adopting allocative cost rules: the *equity* goal of compensating victims and the *efficiency* goal of minimizing costs to society as a whole. These goals in turn can be formulated as two principles: the compensation principle and the marginal principle. The compensation principle states that victims should be compensated for harm caused by others. The marginal principle states that social costs should be minimized by equating the incremental benefit of each precautionary activity to its incremental cost.

Is the common law primarily concerned with the justice of compensation or the efficiency of cost minimization? Presented this way, the two principles appear to be rival theories of law. This article, however, poses a different question: How does the common law combine the goal of compensation with the goal of minimizing social costs? The two principles now appear as complementary, rather than rival, explanations. As a result, this article assumes that there are circumstances in which compensation is required for reasons of justice and examines mechanisms that attempt to provide compensation, without undermining incentives for efficient behavior.

In addition to direct costs, there are many indirect social costs of harm, such as the cost of precautions against harm, the cost of bearing the risk of harm, the cost of obtaining information about risk, and the cost of settling disputes. Analyzing all of these costs thoroughly, however, is impossible in an article of modest length. Consequently, this article selects two types of cost for detailed analysis, the direct cost of harm and the cost of precautions against it. The "model of precaution" is my label for an account of the relationship between these two types of costs.

. . . [This] article shows that the model of precaution is similar in structure for torts, contracts, and property. Thus the theme of the article is the unity of the common law at the simplest level of economic analysis.

. . .

# The Model of Precaution

## A. FORMS OF PRECAUTION

Even when necessary or unavoidable, an accident, breach of contract, taking, or nuisance causes harm. The affected parties, however, can usually take steps to reduce the probability or magnitude of the harm. The parties to a tortious accident can take precautions to reduce the frequency or destructiveness of accidents. In contract, the promisor can take steps to avoid breach, and the promisee, by placing less reliance on the promise, can reduce the harm caused by the promisor's breach. Similarly, for governmental takings of private property, the condemnor can conserve on its need for private property, while property owners can reduce the harm they suffer by avoiding improvements whose value would be destroyed by the taking. Finally, the party responsible for a nuisance can abate; furthermore, the victim can reduce his exposure to harm by avoiding the nuisance.

Generalizing these behaviors, I extend the ordinary meaning of the word "precaution" and use it as a term of art in this article to refer to any action that reduces harm. Thus the term "precaution" includes, for example, prevention of breach and reduced reliance on promises, conservation of the public need for private property and limited improvement of private property exposed to the risk of a taking, and abatement and avoidance of nuisances. These examples are, of course, illustrative, not exhaustive.

## B. THE PARADOX OF COMPENSATION

When each individual bears the full benefits and costs of his precaution, economists say that social value is internalized. When an individual bears part of the benefits or part of the costs of his precaution, economists say that some social value is externalized. The advantage of internalization is that the individual sweeps all of the values affected by his actions into his calculus of self-interest, so that self-interest compels him to balance all the costs and benefits of his actions. According to the marginal principle, social efficiency is achieved by balancing all costs and benefits. Thus, the incentives of private individuals are socially efficient when costs and benefits are fully internalized, whereas incentives are inefficient when some costs and benefits are externalized.

In situations when both the injurer and the victim can take precaution against the harm, the internalization of costs requires both parties to bear the full cost of the harm. To illustrate, suppose that smoke from a factory soils the wash at a commercial laundry, and the parties fail to solve the problem by private negotiation. One solution is to impose a pollution tax equal to the harm caused by the smoke. The factory will bear the tax and the laundry will bear the smoke, so pollution costs will be internalized by both of them, as required for social efficiency. In general, when precaution is bilateral, the marginal principle requires both parties to be fully responsible for the harm. The efficiency condition is called double responsibility at the margin.

One problem with the combination of justice and efficiency, however, is that compensation in its simplest form is inconsistent with double responsibility at the margin. In the preceding example, justice may require the factory not only to pay for harm caused by the smoke, but also to compensate the laundry for that harm. Compensation, however, permits the laundry to externalize costs, thereby compromising efficiency. Thus, a paradox results: If the factory can pollute with impunity, harm is externalized by the factory; if the factory must pay full compensation, harm is externalized by the laundry; if compensation is partial, harm is partly externalized by the factory and partly externalized by the laundry. Assigning full responsibility for the injury to one party or parceling it out between the parties cannot fully internalize costs for both of them. Thus, there is no level of compensation that achieves double responsibility at the margin. In technical terms, when efficiency requires bilateral precaution, strict liability for any fraction of the harm, from zero percent to 100 percent, is inefficient.

Rules that combine compensation for harm with incentives for efficient precaution are therefore patently difficult to formulate. The problem confronted in this ... article is to explain how the law combines compensation with double responsibility at the margin. The law has evolved three distinct mechanisms for achieving this end, which I will sketch by reference to the law of torts, contracts, and property.

## 1. Accidents

Assume that Xavier and Yvonne are engaged in activities that sometimes result in accidents. If an accident occurs, Yvonne's property is damaged and Xavier's is not. For this reason I will call Xavier the injurer and Yvonne the victim, regardless of who is at fault. The probability that an accident will occur depends on the precautions taken by both of them, which are costly. The relationship between harm and precaution is easy to visualize in concrete cases. . . . Suppose that Xavier operates a railroad train that emits sparks that sometimes set fire to Yvonne's cornfield. Xavier can reduce the harm to the corn by installing spark arresters, by running the trains more slowly, or by running fewer trains. In a like manner, Yvonne can reduce the harm by planting her corn farther from the tracks, by planting cabbage instead of corn, or by leaving the fields fallow.

There are two rules that assign liability without regard to fault. The first of these is a rule of no liability, which means that courts will not redistribute the cost of accidents. Under such a rule, the victim bears the full cost of accidents. The second rule is strict liability, which means that the injurer must compensate the victim whenever an accident occurs. The rule used by the courts for allocating accident costs will determine Xavier's and Yvonne's incentives for precaution.

As noted by Professor Coase, the rule of law makes no difference from the viewpoint of social efficiency if Xavier and Yvonne can bargain with each other and agree on the reallocation of social costs. Therefore, in order for the rule of law to make a difference, one must assume that obstacles prevent potential injurers and victims from bargaining together. The conclusions that follow from this assumption can be stated briefly. If the rule of law is no liability, the injurer has no economic incentive to take precaution and so will minimize his expenditure on precaution by taking none. If the rule of law is strict liability with perfect compensation, the victim is indifferent to whether or not an accident occurs. Since she has no economic incentive to take precaution, she will minimize her expenditure on precaution by not taking any. Thus, no liability and strict liability with perfect compensation are symmetrical opposites.[1]

The desirability of no liability or strict liability can be evaluated from the viewpoint of economic efficiency. The measure of social costs in the simple model of precaution is the sum of the parties' costs of precaution and the expected cost of harm. Efficient levels of precaution minimize the social costs of accidents. For most accidents, precaution is bilateral in the sense that social efficiency requires both injurer and victim to take at least some precaution. The rule of no liability and the rule of strict liability with perfect compensation both lack incentives for one of the parties to take precaution, so these rules cannot be efficient for accidents that are bilateral in this sense.

. . .

This is an instance of the paradox of compensation. Nonetheless, the paradox can be resolved by adopting fault rules that assign responsibility for harm according to the fault of the parties. To illustrate, a simple negligence rule requires the victim to be compensated by the injurer if, and only if, the latter is at fault. Under a simple negligence rule, Xavier will satisfy the legal standard in order to avoid liability. Thus, if the legal standard corresponds to the efficient level of precaution, Xavier's precaution will be efficient. Since Yvonne knows that she bears residual responsibility, she internalizes the costs and benefits of precaution; therefore, her incentives are efficient. Thus, if the legal standard of fault corresponds to the efficient level of care, both parties will take efficient precaution.[2]

Like the tax solution, a simple negligence rule creates a condition in which each party bears the cost of the harm caused by a small decrease in his precaution. The injurer responds by minimally fulfilling the legal standard of care, so that even a small reduction in his care will cause him to be liable. Absent that reduction in care by the injurer, however, the victim will be responsible. Thus, each party bears the full cost of the increase in harm caused by the decrease in his precaution. This is double responsibility at the margin.

The same method of reasoning can be used to show that efficient incentives for precaution are created by fault rules other than simple negligence, such as negligence with contributory negligence, strict liability with contributory negligence, or comparative negligence. Under any fault rule, the injurer can escape responsibility by satisfying the legal standard, so an efficient legal standard will cause his behavior to be efficient. Similarly, the victim's precaution will be efficient because he bears residual responsibility and thus internalizes the costs and benefits of precaution. So long as the legal standards correspond to efficient precaution, all such rules create double responsibility at the margin. Thus the particular rule can be chosen that best accords with the requirements of just compensation.

The reader may raise some objections to this analysis of torts. After all, expensive legal fees may make no-fault rules more efficient than negligence rules and, in certain situations, precaution by only one party may be more efficient than bilateral precaution. The savings in legal fees mentioned in the first objection are omitted from the simple model of precaution by assuming away the costs of dispute resolution. Furthermore, upon close examination, the second objection is incorrect unless some odd assumptions are made about the technology of precaution.

. . . .

## 2. Breach of contract

Yvonne and Xavier enter into a contract in which Yvonne pays for Xavier's promise to deliver a product in the future. There are certain obstacles to Xavier's performance that might arise, and if severe obstacles materialize, Xavier will not be able to deliver the product as promised. The probability of timely performance depends in part on Xavier's efforts to prevent such obstacles from arising. These efforts are costly.

One purpose of contracting is to give Yvonne confidence that Xavier's promise will be performed, so that she can rely upon his promise. Reliance on the contract increases the value to Yvonne of Xavier's performance. However, reliance also increases the loss suffered in the event of breach. The more the promisee relies, therefore, the greater the benefit from performance and the greater the harm caused by breach.

To make this description concrete, suppose that Xavier is a builder who signs a contract to construct a store for Yvonne by the first of September. Many events could jeopardize timely completion of the building; for example, the plumbers union may strike, the city's inspectors may be recalcitrant, or the weather may be inclement. Xavier can increase the probability of timely completion by taking costly measures, such as having the plumbers work overtime before their union contract expires, badgering the inspectors to finish on time, or rescheduling work to complete the roof before the rainy season arrives. Yvonne, on the other hand, must order merchandise for her new store in advance if she is to open with a full line on the first of September. If she orders many items for September delivery and the store is not ready for occupancy, she will have to place the goods in storage, which is costly. The more merchandise she orders, the larger her profit will be in the event of performance, and the larger her loss in the event of nonperformance.

As thus described, the structure of the contractual model is similar to the model developed for tortious accidents. The precaution taken by the potential tortfeasor against accidents parallels the steps taken by the promisor to avoid obstacles to performance. The parallel between the victim and the promisee, however, is more subtle. *More* precaution by the tort victim is like less reliance by the contract promisee, because each action reduces the harm caused by an accident or a breach. Therefore, the tort victim's precaution against accidents and the contract promisee's reliance upon the contract are inversely symmetrical.

If Xavier does not perform, then a court must decide whether a breach has occurred or whether nonperformance is excused by circumstances. Among the excuses that the law recognizes are: that the quality of assent to the contract was too low due to mistake, incapacity, duress, or fraud; that the terms of the contract were unconscionable; or that performance was impossible or commercially impractical. If the court narrowly construes excuses, usually finding nonperformance to be a breach, then Xavier will usually be liable. If the court construes excuses broadly, usually finding nonperformance to be justified, then Xavier will seldom be liable.

The incentive effects of a broader or narrower construction of excuses are similar to the effects of strict liability and no-liability rules in tort. If defenses are narrowly construed and perfect expectation damages are awarded for breach, the promisee will rely as if performance were certain. Specifically, Yvonne will order a full line of merchandise as if the store were certain to open on the first of September. A promisee's reliance to the same extent as if performance were certain corresponds to a tort victim's failure to take precaution against harm.

A broad construction of excuses has the symmetrically opposite effect: the promisor expects to escape liability for harm caused by his breach, so he will not undertake costly precautions to avoid nonperformance. Specifically, if Xavier is unconcerned about his reputation or the possibility of future business with Yvonne, and if nonperformance due to a plumber's strike, recalcitrant inspectors, or inclement weather will be excused, say, on grounds of impossibility, then Xavier will not take costly precautions against these events. The promisor's lack of precaution against possible obstacles to performance corresponds to the injurer's lack of precaution against tortious accidents.

As explained, the narrow and broad constructions of excuses for breach of contract affect behavior in ways that parallel no liability and strict liability in tort. Furthermore, the effects of these constructions on cost internalization and efficiency are also parallel. Specifically, if excuses are broadly construed, allowing the promisor to avoid responsibility for breach regardless of his precaution level, the promisor will externalize some of the costs of breach. As a result, his incentives to take precaution against the events that cause him to breach are insufficient relative to the efficient level. If, on the other hand, excuses are narrowly construed and full compensation is available for breach, the promisee can externalize some of the costs of reliance. Insofar as the promisee can transfer the risk of reliance to the promisor, her incentives are insufficient to provide efficient reliance and, therefore, reliance will be excessive.

To illustrate, social efficiency requires Xavier to hire the plumbers to work overtime if the additional cost is less than the increase in Yvonne's expected profits caused by the higher probability of timely completion. Suppose, however, that there are circumstances in which tardiness will be excused regardless of whether or not Xavier hired the plumbers to work overtime. Suppose for example that inclement weather excuses tardiness on grounds of impossibility. In the event inclement weather provides Xavier with an excuse, the extra cost of hiring the plumbers to work overtime, which is valuable to Yvonne, has no value to Xavier. Anticipating this eventuality, Xavier may not hire the plumbers to work overtime, even though social efficiency may require him to do so.

Social efficiency also requires Yvonne to restrain her reliance in light of the objective probability of breach. To be more precise, social efficiency requires her to order additional merchandise until the resulting increase in profit from anticipated sales in the new store, discounted by the probability that Xavier will finish the store on time, equals the cost of storing the goods, discounted by the probability that Xavier will finish the new store late. Suppose, however, that Xavier must compensate Yvonne for her storage costs in the event that the goods must be stored. From a self-interested perspective, Yvonne has no incentive to restrain her reliance in these circumstances. Anticipating this possibility, instead of weighting the cost of storage by the objective probability of breach, Yvonne will weight it by the probability of breach without compensation. Since in this example the probability of breach is greater than the probability of breach without compensation, the weight Yvonne gives to the possibility of storage cost is too small. Therefore, her reliance will be excessive and thus inefficient.

In general, the possibility of successful excuses may externalize the costs of not taking precaution, so that the promisor takes too little precaution and the probability of breach is excessive. Similarly, the possibility of compensation may externalize the costs of reliance, so the promisee relies too heavily and the harm that materializes in the event of breach is excessive. This is an aspect of the paradox of compensation that arises in tort with respect to no liability and strict liability. As with tort law, contract law has a solution to the paradox, but the contract solution is different from the tort solution. To illustrate the characteristic remedy in contracts, consider the liquidation of damages. If the contract stipulates damages for breach requiring Xavier to remit, say, $200 per day for late completion, then the promisor will have a material incentive to prevent breach. Specifically, Xavier may find that paying the plumbers to work overtime is cheaper than running the risk of late completion. If the promisee receives the stipulated damages as compensation, then the level of her compensation is independent of her level of reliance, so she has a material incentive to restrain her reliance. Specifically, if Yvonne receives $200 per day in damages for late completion whether or not she orders the bulky merchandise, she may avoid the risk of bearing storage costs by not ordering it.

Like a negligence rule in tort, liquidation of damages in a contract imposes double responsibility at the margin: the promisor is responsible for the stipulated damages and the victim is responsible for the actual harm. By adjusting the level of stipulated damages, efficient incentives can be achieved for both parties. Stipulated damages are efficient when they equal the loss that the victim would suffer from breach if her reliance were efficient. To illustrate, assume that efficient reliance requires Yvonne to order the compact merchandise and not the bulky merchandise. Furthermore, assume that if Yvonne orders the compact merchandise she will lose $200 in profits for each day that Xavier is late in completing the new store. Under these assumptions, liquidating damages at $200 per day for late completion provides efficient incentives for both Xavier and Yvonne.

Under the stated assumptions, stipulating damages at $200 per day will cause Yvonne to order the compact merchandise and not the bulky merchandise. Consequently, the actual harm that Yvonne will suffer in the event of breach is $200 per day. Thus the stipulation of damages at the efficient level is a self-fulfilling prophecy: the stipulation of *efficient* damages causes the actual damages to equal the stipulation. Since Xavier internalizes the actual harm caused by breach, and Yvonne bears the risk of marginal reliance, there is double responsibility at the margin as required for efficiency.

Since liquidation of damages provides an immediate solution to the problem of over reliance, it would seem that liquidation clauses should be found in contracts where efficiency requires restraints on reliance. In fact, rather than liquidating damages, most contracts leave the computation of damages until after the breach has occurred. When damages are not liquidated in the contract and restraint of reliance is required by efficiency, various legal doctrines are available that can accomplish the same end as liquidation of damages. Liquidated damages restrain reliance by making damages invariant with respect to reliance. Courts restrain reliance by applying other legal doctrines that make damages similarly invariant.

To illustrate, the goods supplied by different firms in a perfectly competitive market are, by the definition of perfect competition, perfect substitutes. When the promisor fails to perform in a competitive market, damages are ordinarily set equal to the cost of replacing the promised performance with a close substitute (the replacement-price formula). Specifically, if the seller breaches his promise to supply a good at a specified price, the damages paid to the buyer may include the additional cost of purchasing the good from someone else. In technical terms, damages in such a case will equal the difference between the spot price and the contract price for that particular good. In a competitive market, no single buyer or seller can influence these prices. Consequently, damages computed by the replacement-price formula are invariant with respect to the level of the promisee's reliance. Thus, replacement-price damages in a competitive market have the same efficiency characteristics as liquidated damages.

For noncompetitive markets, doctrinal alternatives are available to reduce or eliminate the effects of variations in damages due to reliance. To illustrate, recovery may be limited to damages that were foreseeable at the time the promise was made. It is but a short step to argue that reliance that is excessive in efficiency terms is also unforeseeable. Thus, the foreseeability doctrine can be used to avoid compensation for excessive reliance.

There are other doctrinal approaches to damages that have similar effects. For example, suppose that Xavier fails to complete the building on the first of September as promised, and Yvonne has to rent temporary space elsewhere. The court might award damages based in part on the additional rent, if it finds Yvonne's calculation of lost profits too speculative. If damages are based on the additional rent, and if the additional rent varies less than Yvonne's profits with respect to her reliance, then her incentive to over rely is reduced. As another example, failure to perform on a franchise agreement may result in an award of damages equal to the profit of similar franchise establishments, but not the "speculative profits" lost by the particular plaintiff. The general point of these two examples is that if compensation is restricted to nonspeculative damages, and if nonspeculative damages vary less with respect to reliance than the actual harm, then restricting compensation to nonspeculative damages reduces the incentive to over rely.

. . .

## [3]. Nuisance

In discussing tortious accidents, my example was a railroad train emitting sparks that some-times burned a farmer's fields. Instead of describing such fires as tortious accidents, how-ever, the farmer might have described the sparks as a nuisance. The choice of description has no effect on the nonlegal aspects of the situation, such as the need for bilateral precau-tion, but there is a difference in the legal remedy. The traditional remedy for tortious accidents is compensatory damages, while the traditional remedy for nuisance in property law is injunctive relief.

When the remedy is injunctive, and not compensatory, the paradox of compensation does not arise. Nonetheless, injunctions do give rise to efficiency problems. An injunction is a coercive order issued by a court. Assuming a failure in private negotiations by the disputants, if a coercive order is to be efficient, it must demand efficient behavior. However, the authorities who issue the order may be too remote from the facts to know what behavior is efficient, or they may not be motivated to demand it.

The preceding argument recapitulates the economists' critique of regulation. A regulation is a coercive order issued by a government agency. People subject to a regulation are likely to possess information that the regulator needs to identify the correct command, but it may be difficult for the regulator to obtain this information. This is so because the cost of gathering such information is high, and because the people who possess such information have incentives not to divulge it. The economists' critique of "command and control" regulation is that it requires too much information, as well as disinterestedness, on the part of regulators.

Economists therefore urge regulators to adopt methods that alter incentives and redirect information instead of issuing commands, so that affected parties can work out the best course of action among themselves. This approach suggests viewing nuisances as a subject for private bargaining, a view that has been developed at length in the continuing com-mentary on the Coase theorem. The central conclusion of this literature is that private bargaining among a small number of people with well-defined rights usually has an efficient outcome. . . .

These conditions – small numbers of bargainers and well-defined rights – are often satisfied in property disputes. In economic terms, a nuisance is external harm imposed by one property's use upon another. The externality often is limited to contiguous pieces of real estate, which limits the number of affected property owners. To illustrate, noise, foul odors, and pollution diminish rapidly with distance from the source. The owners of property contiguous to the nuisance, who are the ones substantially harmed by it, are thus often few in number.

For some kinds of nuisance the rights are well defined, and contiguity keeps the number of affected parties small, suggesting a presumption of efficient private bargaining. The cen-tral claim of the Coase theorem is that private bargaining will achieve efficiency regardless of who is assigned the well-defined rights, because the rights will be bought and sold until the final owner values them more than anyone else. It does not matter from an efficiency perspective whether the injurer has the right to make a nuisance or the victim has the right to enjoin it. To illustrate, if the law gives the injurer the right to create a nuisance, and the victim values freedom from the nuisance more than the injurer values his right to create the nuisance, then the victim can always buy the right from the injurer. Conversely, if the law gives the victim the right to enjoin a nuisance, and the injurer values the ability to make a nuisance more than the victim values being free from it, then the injurer can always buy the right from the victim.

One purpose of the remedy of injunctive relief in nuisance cases is to strengthen the bargaining position of victims. The right to an injunction enables victims to bargain from a position of strength. If victims have the right to enjoin a nuisance, they will not accept an injurer's settlement offer unless it involves a combination of abatement and compensation that the victims prefer to an injunction. In economic jargon, the right to injunctive relief establishes the victims' threat point in bargaining; the injurer cannot induce the victims to settle unless the terms of the cooperative solution benefit the victims more than the advantage they derive from exercising their threat.

Because of private bargaining, the right to injunctive relief against nuisances offers the potential for combining compensation with efficiency. However, these two goals are usually not achieved unless the parties settle. Exercising the right to an injunction usually indicates a breakdown in the bargaining process. When bargaining breaks down, an injunction cannot cause efficient behavior unless the coercive order prescribes it, which is unlikely given the court's limited information. Consequently, from an efficiency perspective, injunction is an appropriate remedy for classes of cases in which settlement is usual and trials are rare. From this perspective, therefore, injunctive rights are socially desirable creations in inverse proportion to the frequency with which they are exercised.

. . .

## Summary and Conclusion

Economic theory is unified because its theorems are derived from its axioms. Consequently, the economic analysis of law must be capable of being unified insofar as it is an application of economic theory. Identifying unity in the economic analysis of law is a matter of finding the correct order in which to make simplifying assumptions. The starting point in contracts, torts, and property is the relationship between precaution against injuries and the allocation of the cost of injuries. The analysis of this interaction is called the model of precaution.

The usual situation is one in which injurers and victims can both influence the harm suffered by victims. The injurer can reduce harm by taking precautions against accidents, preventing the events that cause breaches of contract, conserving on land taken for public purposes, or abating nuisances. Similarly, the victim can reduce the cost of injury by taking precaution against accidents, relying less upon contracts, restraining investment to improve property that is likely to be taken, or avoiding nuisances.

Efficiency requires both parties to balance the cost of further precaution against the consequent reduction in harm and to act accordingly. Incentives to act in this way exist when each party is responsible for the cost of the harm. To put it succinctly, efficiency requires double responsibility at the margin.

Courts often construe justice as requiring the party at fault to compensate the innocent party, but compensation changes the incentives of the victim and injurer. If the foreseeable cost of harm is reduced, the victim may be encouraged to take too little precaution and rely instead on compensation to make him whole. Thus, combining justice with efficient incentives is difficult. Torts and contracts each have a characteristic solution to this problem. The tort solution conditions the responsibility of one of the parties on reasonable precaution. A negligence rule induces reasonable precaution by one of the parties by offering an escape from further responsibility, and by the other party because of her residual responsibility.

The contract solution sets damages at an invariant level with respect to the victim's reliance. Invariant damages are exemplified by liquidated damages, but other legal doctrines for computing damages often have the same effect. Liquidated damages make the injurer liable for the stipulated damages and the victim responsible for the actual damage. This contract remedy is also applicable to takings when the government purchases an option entitling it to buy property at a stipulated price. If the property is subsequently taken, the government is liable for the stipulated price, and the property owner is responsible for the actual loss. Stipulating damages or stipulating the purchase price creates double responsibility since the injurer bears the stipulated cost and the victim bears the actual loss.

There are many simplifications in this model. For example, dispute resolution is assumed to be costless, decision makers are assumed to be risk neutral, and all parties are assumed to have the same information. Notwithstanding these simplifications, the model can explain the economic purpose of many features of law.

. . .

# Notes

1.  This is the standard conclusion, first proved by Brown, "Toward an Economic Theory of Liability," 2. *J. Legal Stud.*, 323, 328 (1973).
2.  . . . For a proof of this result see Brown, supra note 1.

# 6

## Coming to the Nuisance

### *Donald Wittman*

**EDITOR'S INTRODUCTION**

After Coase (1968) and Brown (1973) it was well understood that both the polluter and the polluttee were inputs into the production of damage and that courts should undertake a cost-benefit analysis to determine whether one or the other should leave or both remain in the area with each mitigating optimally. But what if either the polluter or the polluttee were in the area first? Should this affect the cost-benefit calculations? This is the question that I answer. I show when being first should and should not be considered, and demonstrates that the law of nuisance reflects the economic thinking on the subject.

> If my neighbour makes a tan-yard, so as to annoy and render less salubrious the air of my house or gardens, the law will furnish me with a remedy; but if he is first in possession of the air, and I fix my habitation near him, the nuisance is of my own seeking, and must continue.
>
> (Blackstone 1766: 402–403)[1]

For Blackstone, being first is everything: when the plaintiff comes to the nuisance, then the nuisance has the right to continue; when the nuisance comes to the plaintiff, then the plaintiff has the right. This rule has the benefit of simplicity, but economic logic suggests that the unalloyed application of this rule must be inefficient. Allocation on the basis of being first entails costs associated with getting "there" first and staying there. Giving free tickets to a rock concert to the first ten people in line on Monday morning may result in people camping out in line over the whole weekend. With regard to land use, unnecessary or inappropriate timing of investment (in tanneries or homes) may occur in order to establish prior rights.

On the other hand, intuition suggests that "being first is nothing" is not a satisfactory rule, either. The truth lies somewhere in between, and, as will be shown below, it is economic logic that clarifies the contingencies when being first counts and the doctrine of coming to the nuisance should be invoked.

The analysis is in two separate steps. The first step is to determine the optimal outcome and the second step is to design rules that lead to that outcome.

We start with the first step. For convenience we will characterize the problem as a conflict between a nuisance (say a cattle feedlot or smoking factory) and homeowners. The basic insight is to view the problem as an issue of resource allocation over time and to ask which sequence is optimal. That is, the determination of who should have the right depends on the costs and benefits of the entire income stream, not just on those costs and benefits after the second party came.

We consider the following six scenarios as candidates for efficient allocation over time. (1) The nuisance comes first, the residences come second, and the nuisance leaves; (2) the nuisance comes first, the residences come second, and both remain with each mitigating the damage optimally given that the other is there; (3) the nuisance comes first and the residences never come to the area; (4) the residences come first and the nuisance never comes; (5) the residences come first, the nuisance comes second with each mitigating the damage optimally given that the other is there; and (6) the residences come first, the nuisance comes second, and the residences leave.

Note that we do not consider all possible scenarios. For example, we do not consider the following sequence, the nuisance comes second and then immediately leaves, since this is clearly inefficient.

Having determined the optimal sequence for a particular set of circumstances, the next step is to determine the liability rule or property right that promotes the efficient sequence. Strategic behavior by the participants trying to be first and thereby gaining extra consideration is avoided by granting extra consideration to the side which *should* have been first instead of to the side who was actually first. The extra consideration is the inclusion of moving costs by the side who should have been first into the cost-benefit calculations. As can be seen from the six possible efficient scenarios, moving costs of the other party are not part of the cost-benefit calculations, because no efficient sequence would have the second party move in and then move out again.

But how do we determine who should have been first? Some areas, even before either the nuisance or the houses are present, are clearly inappropriate for one or the other use; in such cases, the right goes to the appropriate use regardless of who was there first. Other areas have no distinguishing characteristics and it is the first use that creates the character of the area. In such cases, it is the first that gains the right. Finally, the optimal character of a place may change over time. In such cases, the moving costs of the party that was there first and should have been there first are considered in the calculations. The details will become clearer as we consider these possibilities in turn.

## 1. Character of the Area Predetermined

Parties should anticipate the future, especially when the future is easy to see. In *Gau v. Ley*, 38 Ohio C.C. 235 (1916) the nuisance came to the residents. The court held that the plaintiff was not entitled to relief from the noise arising from the operation of the defendant's plant, which was built after the plaintiff constructed his home. Two railroads were operating on tracks nearby long before the plaintiff and others located their homes in the vicinity. "[I]t was not reasonable to presume that plaintiff, in the presence of all these facts, could not *have foreseen* that in the large and growing city of Cincinnati, the march of business would sooner or later follow the line of these railroads and convert the adjacent strip of land into business uses." Even though the residential area was there first, the residents should have foreseen that the location was ideally suited for the nuisance. Consequently, the residents should not have been there first and their moving costs should not be included in weighing the costs and benefits of alternative land use (while it is appropriate to include the costs of moving the businesses in the cost-benefit analysis). Of course, even if the cost of moving the homes were included, the balance would have been against the homeowners. In this case, it is more efficient that the homes were built elsewhere in the first place than having the appropriately located business mitigate the damage to the inappropriately located houses. Therefore the burden of mitigation was left entirely to the homeowners. The court's judgment in *Gau v. Ley* is neither unusual nor controversial. The logic is mirrored in *Bove v. Donner-Hanna Coke Corp.*, 258 N.Y.S. 229 (1932) where the court stated: "It is true that the appellant was a resident of this locality for several years before defendant came on the scene . . . and that when the plaintiff built her house, the land on which these coke ovens now stand was a hickory grove. This region was never fitted for a residential district (low land, river, seven railroads)."

Notice that, in comparing the costs and benefits of the polluter versus the pollutee it is inappropriate to consider the costs of the pollutee rebuilding since the pollutee should not have been there in the first place. A judicial outcome granting the property rights to the polluter serves as a precedent. Potential residents facing a similar set of costs and benefits in the future will choose to be in an appropriate location in the first place. We can also ask which party would end up with the right if transaction costs were zero. The trick here is to know when the question should be asked. It should be asked before the residents have built their homes (more generally, before either side has made an investment).

The logic can be applied equally well to a nuisance that inappropriately builds in an area most suitable for residential housing.

## 2. Character of the Place Determined by its First Use

Swamps and railroad tracks are appropriate locations for heavy industry and inappropriate for housing; hill-tops in urban areas are appropriate for housing and inappropriate for heavy industry. But sometimes large expanses of land are featureless, and the first use of the land establishes its character.

This was the case in *Mahlstadt v. City of Indianola*, 100 N.W. 2d 189 (1959). Mahlstadt, a housing developer, had enjoined the operation of the city dump. The appellate court overruled the lower court and ruled in favor of the defendant. There was nothing peculiar to the location making it particularly appropriate or inappropriate for housing or for a dump. Therefore the first activity determined the character of the location. The court held that the dump's "prior operation at that place should be given substantial weight in determining the character of the locality and the reasonableness or unreasonableness of operating it there." City dumps need to be located near cities – the cost of transporting garbage is very high. The long-run stream of costs and benefits made it appropriate for the dump to be located there initially and to maintain operation as the area became more residential. However, if the residents were there first, it would have been inefficient to locate a dump next to them and the courts would have ruled in favor of the plaintiffs. In a nutshell, when the character of the place is determined by the first user, the doctrine of coming to the nuisance and its converse are invoked.

Suppose that developers could collect damages or force dumps to move. Would developers or homeowners be better off in the long run? Surprisingly, the answer is no. Consider the case where homeowners receive $10,000 per house for being next to a pre-existing city dump. Then they would be willing to pay $10,000 more for their homes; the same holds for the developer. So in this situation, a system of compensation does not make homeowners or developers better off. The only person that is affected by the rule is the original owner of the undeveloped property.

## 3. Character of the Place Determined by the Second Use

There are many situations where the first party should have been there first, yet the second party creates the dominating character of the place. Cities often expand into rural areas. Rural areas are appropriate for animal husbandry, but cities and cattle feedlots do not mix very well. Of the three possibilities, cities leap-frog around cattle feedlots, urban housing and businesses border cattle feedlots, and feedlots relocate, the last is clearly the most efficient. And the law unambiguously reflects this economic logic.

In such situations, the law is unlikely to compensate for the costs of relocation even though the party was there first and should have been there first. There are several reasons for such a policy. First, alternative land uses are likely to be more profitable, so that the feedlot owner would benefit from relocating. Second, over time, the owner of the property could have let the property depreciate rather than undertake repairs and upgrades. Third, a system of compensation would be costly since in the absence of compensation the outcome (shutting down the feedlot) is the same and a court case is rarely needed. And fourth, a system of compensating feedlots for moving would encourage owners to hold on to their businesses in order to collect damages (the problems that arise in the absence of compensation, too few feedlots in period one or too much expansion of the urban area in period two are less likely except at the very margin).

The taking away of a property right without compensation might appear to violate some basic notions of the inviolability of property. But this paradox is resolved if we realize that all property rights are contingent in space and time. For example, I have the right to dig holes on my land, but not to throw dirt at people passing by. Similarly, people have the right to have a cattle feedlot on their property but not if the area is urban. That is, when the city grows around the cattle feedlot, and the feedlot is forced to move without compensation, the owner of the feedlot is not losing his property rights since the owner never had the right to have a feedlot within an urban area.

Even though, the cost of relocation of feedlots is factored in, it is easy to see that the efficient outcome is for the feedlots to move as the city expands. For other kinds of activity, where there are more substantial moving costs and smaller negative externalities, the stream of benefits may make it economically efficient to give rights to an activity when it should have been first even if the activity would have been outlawed if it had not been first. Thus there is "nonconforming land use" for those activities that should have been there first and should remain while initiation of similar activities are prevented because the cost-benefit stream dictates that they should be undertaken elsewhere.

> There is a very marked distinction to be observed in reason and equity between the case of a business long established in a particular locality, which has become a nuisance from the growth of population and the erection of dwellings in proximity to it, and that of a new erection or business threatened in such vicinity; and it requires a much clearer case to justify a court of

equity in interfering by injunction to compel a person to remove an establishment in which he has invested his capital and been carrying on business for a long period of time than would be required to prevent the establishment of an objectionable business by one who comes into the neighborhood proposing to establish such a business for the first time, and is met at the threshold of his enterprise by a remonstrance of the inhabitants.

> *Barth v. Christian Psychopathic Hospital Association*, 163 N.W. 62 (1917)

Once again, the doctrine of coming to the nuisance and its converse are invoked in a more modified form than used by Blackstone.

The role of sequence in allowing for nonconforming land use is very evident when there is severe damage to the nonconforming structure due to fire, earthquake, etc. Then the prior use is no longer prior, and cannot be reinstated.

> With the improvement substantially destroyed, the land on which it is located will presumably have approximately as much value for use in conformity with the ordinance as otherwise and the public interest in conformity with the ordinance will be served if he is not permitted to continue the nonconforming land use.
>
> *O'Mara v. Council of the City of Newark*, 238 CA2d 836, 838 (1965)

Sometimes the nonconforming land use is allowed a certain amortization period. Consistent with our economic analysis, such a scheme must be reasonable in character and commensurate with the investment involved. The relevant factors include remaining useful life, the harm to the public if the structure remains standing beyond the prescribed amortization period and cost of moving. See *United Business Com. v. City of San Diego*, 91 CA3d 156, 189 (1979) and *City of Los Angeles v. Gage*, 127 Cal. App. 2d 442 (1954).

Note that the analysis makes no difference whether it is a government regulation or a private suit in a court of law.

## 4. The Character of the Place is Determined by the Second Use, but the Second Use Should Not Have Been There

We now come to the most complicated situation, which is also the most enlightening. It is possible that the second use creates the character of the area, yet the second use should not have been there in the first place.

In *Spur Industries v. Del E. Webb Development Co.*, 494 P. 2d 700 (1972) the defendant commenced cattle-feeding operations in an agricultural area well outside the boundaries of any city and subsequently a real-estate developer purchased land nearby and began to develop an extensive retirement community. The court held that the developer was entitled to enjoin the cattle-feeding operation as a nuisance but was required to *indemnify* the cattle feeder for the reasonable cost of moving or shutting down. The novel solution in this case reflects the fact that the cattle-feeding operator could not have reasonably foreseen the development of a retirement community nearby and therefore should be compensated for all costs associated with moving his business.

If the court had not questioned whether the developer should have been there in the first place, the court would have ruled for the feedlot to move without compensation as it was cheaper to move the feedlot than to move the residents. But without compensation an inefficient precedent would have been established. Developers would choose areas inappropriate from a social cost-benefit analysis because the developers would not incur the costs to the adjacent nuisance of moving away. In future situations, even if it were cheaper for the builder to develop elsewhere than to make the feedlot move, the developer might move near the feedlot (if he did not have to compensate the feedlot owner). Thus courts are encouraging individuals to make efficient decisions by anticipating the future and considering the *whole* stream of costs and benefits and not just those costs and benefits which arise after both parties are located in the area.

# 5. Extensions

Sequence is important in other areas of law, as well. For example, the doctrine of last clear chance in accident law puts extra burden on the second party to mitigate damages even if the first party acted inefficiently; the analysis is parallel to *Spur Industries v. Del Webb*. In other areas, being first confers special advantages. For example, at a four-way stop, the car that has come to the stop first has the right of way; this is roughly parallel to *Mahlstadt v. Indianola*.

## Note

1.   Blackstone, William, 1766. *Commentaries on the Laws of England* vol. 2 (1st ed.) University of Chicago facsimile of Vol. 2 (1979, A.W.B. Simpson, ed.) Chicago.

# 7

## Liability for Harm versus Regulation of Safety

### *Steven Shavell*

### EDITOR'S INTRODUCTION

So far the analysis has implicitly assumed that the administrative costs of a liability rule system Pigovian taxes, and regulation are zero. In this article, Steven Shavell explicitly considers such costs, which enables him to analyze the choice between prior regulation and post liability. The main problem with a system of liability is that the injurer may be judgment-proof. When the injurer's liability exceeds his assets, greater degreed of liability does not have an additional deterrent effect. Prior regulation tends to have two problems: It is more costly to administer since it is used even when there is not an injury and it is harder to tailor to the specifics of the situation — a speed limit may be unnecessarily restrictive for skilled drivers and insufficiently restrictive for unskilled drivers. Shavell's analysis demonstrates that regulation and liability are both used, but in proportions appropriate to their strengths and weaknesses.

## 1. Introduction

Liability in tort and the regulation of safety represent two very different approaches for controlling activities that create risks of harm to others. Tort liability is private in nature and works not by social command but rather indirectly, through the deterrent effect of damage actions that may be brought once harm occurs. Standards, prohibitions, and other forms of safety regulation, in contrast, are public in character and modify behavior in an immediate way through requirements that are imposed before, or at least independently of, the actual occurrence of harm.

   As a matter of simple description, it is apparent that liability and safety regulation are employed with an emphasis that varies considerably with the nature of the activity that is governed. Whether I run to catch a bus and thereby collide with another pedestrian will be influenced more by the possibility of my tort liability than by any prior regulation of my behavior (informal social sanctions and risk to self aside). Similarly, whether I cut down a tree that might fall on my neighbor's roof will be affected more by the prospect of a tort suit than by direct regulation. But other decisions — whether I drive my truck through a tunnel when it is loaded with explosives or mark the fire exits in my store, or whether an electric utility incorporates certain safety features in its nuclear power plant – are apt to be determined substantially, although not entirely, by safety regulation. There are also intermediate cases, of course; consider, for instance, the behavior of ordinary drivers on the road and the effects of tort sanctions and regulation of automobile use.

What has led society to adopt this varying pattern of liability and safety regulation? What is the socially desirable way to employ the two means of alleviating risks? These are the questions to be addressed here, and in answering them I use an instrumentalist economic method of analysis, whereby the effects of liability rules and direct regulation are compared and then evaluated on a utilitarian basis, given the assumption that individual actors can normally be expected to act in their own interest. In making this evaluation, I have not counted compensation of injured parties as an independent factor on the grounds that first-party insurance (augmented if necessary by a public insurance program) can discharge the compensatory function no matter what the mix of liability and regulation. Likewise, for simplicity, I ignore the complications that would be introduced by considering interest group theories of regulation. Also, I do not make an explicit attempt to determine the extent to which the conclusions reached may be separately attributable to either of the two dimensions in which liability and safety regulation differ: employed only after harm is done versus beforehand; employed only at the initiative of private parties versus a public authority.

Subject to these caveats and assumptions, this article first discusses four general determinants of the relative desirability of liability and regulation. It then argues in light of the determinants that the actual, observed use of the two methods of reducing risks may be viewed as socially desirable, or roughly so. The article concludes with several qualifying remarks and with comments on how the analysis could be extended to incorporate additional means of social control including the fine and the injunction.

## II. Theoretical Determinants of the Relative Desirability of Liability and Safety Regulation

To identify and assess the factors determining the social desirability of liability and regulation, it is necessary to set out a measure of social welfare; and here that measure is assumed to equal the benefits parties derive from engaging in their activities, less the sum of the costs of precautions, the harms done, and the administrative expenses associated with the means of social control. The formal problem is to employ the means of control to maximize the measure of welfare.

We can now examine four determinants that influence the solution to this problem. The first determinant is the possibility of a *difference in knowledge about risky activities* as between private parties and a regulatory authority. This difference could relate to the benefits of activities, the costs of reducing risks, or the probability or severity of the risks.

Where private parties have superior knowledge of these elements, it would be better for them to decide about the control of risks, indicating an advantage of liability rules, other things being equal. Consider, for instance, the situation where private parties possess perfect information about risky activities of which a regulator has poor knowledge. Then to vest in the regulator the power of control would create a great chance of error. If the regulator overestimates the potential for harm, its standard will be too stringent, and the same will be the case if it underestimates the value of the activity or the cost of reducing risk. If the regulator makes the reverse mistakes, moreover, it will announce standards that are lax.

Under liability, however, the outcome would likely be better. This is clear enough under a system of strict liability – whereby parties have to pay damages regardless of their negligence – for then they are motivated to balance the true costs of reducing risks against the expected savings in losses caused. Now assume that the form of liability is the negligence rule – according to which parties are held responsible for harm done only if their care falls short of a prescribed level of "due" care – and suppose further that once harm occurs, the courts could acquire enough information about the underlying event to formulate the appropriate level of due care. Then parties, anticipating this, would be led in principle to exercise due care. The situation is altered for the worse if the courts are unable to acquire sufficient information to determine the best level of due care; but the outcome would still be superior to that achievable under regulation if the information obtained ex post at trial would be better than that which a regulator could acquire and act upon ex ante.

These conclusions are reversed, of course, if the information possessed by a regulator is superior to private parties' and the courts'; converse reasoning then shows that the use of direct regulation would be more attractive than liability.

The question that remains, therefore, is when we can expect significant differences in information between private parties and regulators to exist. And the answer is that private parties should generally enjoy an inherent advantage in knowledge. They, after all, are the ones who are engaging in and deriving benefits from their activities; in consequence, they are in a naturally superior position to estimate these benefits and normally are in at least as good a position to estimate the nature of the risks created and the costs of their reduction. For a regulator to obtain comparable information would often require virtually continuous observation of parties' behavior, and thus would be a practical impossibility. Similarly, the courts – when called upon under a negligence system – should have an advantage, though a less decisive one, over a regulator. One would indeed expect courts to adjust the due care level to take into account the facts presented by litigating parties more easily than a regulator could individualize its prior standards or modify them to reflect changed conditions.

Yet this is not to say that private parties or the courts will necessarily possess information superior to that held by a regulatory authority. In certain contexts information about risk will not be an obvious by-product of engaging in risky activities but rather will require effort to develop or special expertise to evaluate. In these contexts a regulator might obtain information by committing social resources to the task, while private parties would have an insufficient incentive to do this for familiar reasons: A party who generates information will be unable to capture its full value if others can learn of the information without paying for it. For parties to undertake individually to acquire information might result in wasteful, duplicative expenditures, and a cooperative venture by parties might be stymied by the usual problems of inducing all to lend their support.

Continuing, once a regulator obtains information, it may find the information difficult to communicate to private parties because of its technical nature or because the parties are hard to identify or are too numerous. Thus we can point to contexts where regulators might possess better information than private parties to whom it cannot easily be transmitted, even if the usual expectation would be for these parties to possess the superior information.

The second of the determinants of the relative desirability of liability and regulation is that *private parties might be incapable of paying for the full magnitude of harm done*. Where this is the case, liability would not furnish adequate incentives to control risk, because private parties would treat losses caused that exceed their assets as imposing liabilities only equal to their assets. But under regulation inability to pay for harm done would be irrelevant, assuming that parties would be made to take steps to reduce risk as a precondition for engaging in their activities.

In assessing the importance of this argument favoring regulation over liability, one factor that obviously needs to be taken into account is the size of parties' assets in relation to the probability distribution of the magnitude of harm; the greater the likelihood of harm much larger than assets, the greater the appeal of regulation.

Another factor of relevance concerns liability insurance. Here the first point to make is that a party's motive to purchase liability insurance against damage judgments exceeding his assets will be a diminished one, as the protection will in part be for losses that the party would not otherwise have to bear. A party with assets of $20,000 might not be eager to purchase coverage against a potential liability of $100,000, as four-fifths of the premium would be in payment for the $80,000 amount that he would not bear if he did not buy coverage. Hence, it might be rational for the party not to insure against the $100,000 risk. If this is the case, then the assertion that liability does not create an adequate motive to reduce risk is clearly unrebutted.

Suppose, however, that the party does choose to purchase liability insurance covering losses substantially exceeding his assets or is required by statute to do so. What then is his incentive to take care? The answer depends on whether insurers can easily determine risk-reducing behavior – so that they can link the premium charged or the other terms or conditions of coverage to the party's precautions. Where this linkage can be established, the party's incentive to take care should be tolerably good. But if insurers find it too costly to verify insureds' efforts at risk reduction, then their incentives to take care may be insufficient; plausibly, they could be lower than if no insurance coverage had been obtained. Consider a requirement that the party facing a $100,000 risk purchase full coverage against it and assume that the insurer cannot observe anything about the party's exercise of care. Then as the party would not have to pay a higher premium or be otherwise penalized for failure to take proper care, he would have no reason to do this. Yet if he had not owned the liability coverage, at least his $20,000 assets would have been at risk, supplying him with some motive to take care. Thus, it appears that the problem of inadequacy of incentives to take care which arises when parties' assets are less than potential harms can either be mitigated or exacerbated by the (mandatory or voluntary) purchase of liability insurance, depending on insurers' ability to monitor insureds.

. . . .

Let us turn next to the third of the four general determinants, the chance that *parties would not face the threat of suit for harm done.* Like incapacity to pay for harm, such a possibility results in a dilution of the incentives to reduce risk created by liability, but it is of no import under regulation.

The weight to be attached to this factor depends in part upon the reasons why suit might not be brought. One reason that a defendant can escape tort liability is that the harms he generates are widely dispersed, making it unattractive for any victim individually to initiate legal action. This danger can be offset to a degree if victims are allowed to maintain class actions, whose application has problematic features, however. A second cause of failure to sue is the passage of a long period of time before harm manifests itself. This raises the possibility that by the time suit is contemplated, the evidence necessary for a successful action will be stale or the responsible parties out of business. A third reason for failure to sue is difficulty in attributing harm to the parties who are in fact responsible for producing it. This problem could arise from simple ignorance that a given harm or disease was caused by a human agency (as opposed to being "natural" in origin) or from inability to identify which one or several out of many parties was the cause of harm.

The last of the determinants is the magnitude of the *administrative costs incurred by private parties and by the public* in using the tort system or direct regulation. Of course, the costs of the tort system must be broadly defined to include the time, effort, and legal expenses borne by private parties in the course of litigation or in coming to settlements, as well as the public expenses of conducting trials, employing judges, empaneling juries, and the like. Similarly, the administrative costs of regulation include the public expense of maintaining the regulatory establishment and the private costs of compliance.

With respect to these costs, there seems to be an underlying advantage in favor of liability, for most of its administrative costs are incurred only if harm occurs. As this will usually be infrequent, administrative costs will be low. Indeed, in the extreme case where the prospect of liability induces parties to take proper care and this happens to remove all possibility of harm, there would be no suits whatever and thus no administrative costs (other than certain fixed costs). Moreover, there are two reasons to believe that even when harm occurs administrative costs should not always be large. First, under a well-functioning negligence rule, defendants should in principle generally have been induced to take due care; injured parties should generally recognize this and thus should not bring suit. Second, suits should usually be capable of being settled cheaply by comparison to the cost of a trial. A final cost advantage of the liability system is that under it resources are naturally focused on controlling the behavior of the subgroup of parties most likely to cause harm; for because they are most likely to cause harm (and presumably most likely to be negligent), they are most likely to be sued.

Under regulation, unlike under liability, administrative costs are incurred whether or not harm occurs; even if the risk of a harm is eliminated by regulation, administrative costs will have been borne in the process. Also, in the absence of special knowledge about parties' categories of risk, there is no tendency for administrative costs to be focused on those most likely to cause harm, again because these costs are incurred before harm occurs. On the other hand, a savings in administrative costs can typically be achieved through the use of probabilistic means of enforcement. But there is a limit to these savings because there is some minimum frequency of verification necessary to insure adherence to regulatory requirements.

## JOINT USE OF LIABILITY AND REGULATION

Examination of the four determinants has thus shown that two generally favor liability – administrative costs and differential knowledge – and the other two favor regulation – incapacity to pay for harm done and escaping suit. This suggests not only that neither tort liability nor regulation could uniformly dominate the other as a solution to the problem of controlling risks, but also that they should not be viewed as mutually exclusive solutions to it. A complete solution to the problem of the control of risk evidently should involve the joint use of liability and regulation, with the balance between them reflecting the importance of the determinants.

If, then, some combination of liability and regulation is likely to be advantageous, two questions immediately arise: Should a party's adherence to regulation relieve him of liability in the event that harm comes to pass? On the other hand, should a party's failure to satisfy regulatory requirements result necessarily in his liability? Our theory suggests a negative answer to both questions.

As to the first, if compliance with regulation were to protect parties from liability, then none would do more than to meet the regulatory requirements. Yet since these requirements will be based on less than perfect knowledge of parties' situations, there will clearly be some parties who ought to do more than meet the requirements - because they present an above-average risk of doing harm, can take extra precautions more easily than most, or can take precautions not covered by regulation. As liability will induce many of these parties to take beneficial precautions beyond the required ones, its use as a supplement to regulation will be advantageous. At the same time, just because this is true, regulatory requirements need not be as rigorous as if regulation were the sole means of controlling risks.

A similar analysis is appropriate for the second question. If failure to satisfy regulatory requirements necessarily resulted in a finding of negligence, then some parties would be undesirably led to comply with them when they would not otherwise have done so. In particular, there will be some parties (a) who ought not to meet regulatory requirements because they face higher than usual costs of care or because they pose lower risks than normal and (b) who will not have been forced to satisfy regulatory requirements due to flaws in or probabilistic methods of enforcement. By allowing these parties to escape liability in view of their circumstances, the possibility that they would still be led to take the wasteful precautions can be avoided.

To illustrate, suppose that a $500 expenditure is desirable for typical firms to make to prevent $1,000 in losses, but for atypical firms, an additional $500 expenditure will prevent another $1,000 in losses. If the regulator is unable to tell the atypical firms apart and tailor regulations to them, then only through the deterrent of liability will these firms be led to make the extra $500 expenditure. Note, however, that use of liability alone would not be desirable, as then firms with low assets or ones likely to escape suit might not make even the first $500 expenditure.

## III. Activities Controlled Mainly by Liability: The Typical Tort

In this section and the next I will attempt to show that the theoretically desirable uses of tort liability and regulation correlate roughly with their uses in fact. In speaking first about activities controlled primarily by liability rules, I will for concreteness make reference to two activities mentioned earlier - to my chopping down a tree that might fall on my neighbor's home and to my running to catch a bus and possibly colliding with another person. A consideration of the relevance of the four determinants to activities such as these will suggest strong advantages of the liability system and acute drawbacks of regulation.

As regards the first determinant, there is ample reason to believe that private parties would possess much better information about risks and whether and how to reduce them than would a regulator. Because I would know the precise position of my tree and of my neighbor's home, I would likely have superior insight into the chance of an accident and the opportunity to lower it by use of guy wires, or by cutting down the tree in stages. Likewise, I would presumably be better able to determine whether I should do the work myself or hire an independent contractor to do it. Similarly, my knowledge of the probability of knocking someone down when running for a bus at that particular corner under these particular conditions of visibility and weather would be better than a regulator's, and I would surely know more about the importance of catching the bus.

In these situations private parties possess the better information because they apparently do obtain it as an ordinary by-product of their activities and can take into account the changes in circumstance that influence the risks and the value of their activities. Consequently, parties should make reasonably satisfactory decisions under liability, while costly mistakes would be unavoidable under regulation. Were the regulatory authority to set forth rules on the felling of trees or the pursuit of buses, it is a certainty that the rules would sometimes be too restrictive, imposing needless precautions that would not be taken due to a concern only over liability; conversely, the rules would fail to identify desirable precautions that parties would obviously be motivated to take to avoid liability.

Turning next to the ability to pay for harm done, there is admittedly a potential problem, but sometimes not one of great magnitude. The damage to my neighbor's roof, for example, will probably be limited in scope, and I am likely to have assets plus liability insurance sufficient to cover it whether I own or rent my house. While inability to pay for harm counts as a weakness of liability in respect to the typical tort, it does not stand out as a problem of unusual dimension, at least by comparison to many of the situations to be discussed in the next part of the article.

The likelihood that suit would be brought against a liable defendant, moreover, appears to be relatively high for the typical tort, as none of the reasons for failure to bring suit seems to apply. Harms generally will not be dispersed among victims; my tree will fall on one, not many, roofs; I will collide with one or at most several pedestrians. Harms will not take a long period of time to manifest themselves; rather, any injury that I cause to a pedestrian or any damage to my neighbor's roof will be an immediate and direct consequence of my behavior. Further, harms will normally be readily attributed to responsible parties; there will be no mystery over whose tree damaged my neighbor's roof or over how the damage came about. There is thus no argument favoring regulation for fear that proper defendants would systematically escape suit.

Finally, liability should enjoy a significant administrative cost advantage over regulation in controlling the risks of typical torts. One does have the impression that it should be much less costly for society to incur administrative costs only when falling trees happen to descend on neighbors' homes and only when individuals chasing buses happen to collide with pedestrians, fairly unlikely events, than for society to formulate and enforce regulations on when and how trees may be cut down and on when individuals may be allowed to hurry after a bus. Indeed, virtually all our routine activities – walking, mowing a lawn, playing catch – are perfectly innocuous in the overwhelming majority of instances, so that the savings achieved by limiting the bearing of administrative costs to those few occasions when harm occurs must be great.

The notion of effective regulation of the activities of everyday life even seems fanciful to contemplate, particularly because it would necessitate the use of extremely frequent and intrusive verification procedures. This is because what would usually need to be determined by a regulatory authority are aspects of modifiable behavior rather than "fixed" physical objects. While it may be enough to inspect elevator cables annually, because their condition will change little over that period, effective regulation of ordinary behavior such as whether I chase after buses clearly requires much more frequent monitoring.

Also of importance is the tendency for administrative costs to be incurred primarily in controlling the parties most likely to cause harm. Because those who fail to prevent their trees from falling on their neighbors' roofs must be a disproportionately awkward group, it is a good thing that the liability system's costs be concerned only with them; it would be a waste for society to incur costs to monitor the majority of careful individuals whose trees fall safely to the ground; yet that is just what the regulatory approach requires.

Let us now summarize our discussion. Of the four determinants, differential knowledge and the size of administrative costs pointed strongly in favor of use of liability to reduce the risk of the typical tort, while inability to pay for harm done worked with only moderate force against it, and the possibility of escaping suit did not constitute an argument against it. Thus, the use in practice of liability to control the familiar category of risks known as torts seems to be the theoretically preferred solution to the problem.

## IV. Activities Subject to Significant Regulation

This section will argue that it is desirable that society resort to safety regulation where it generally does – in controlling the risks of fire, the production and sale of many foods and drugs, the generation of pollutants, and the transport and use of explosives and other dangerous materials. A consideration of the four determinants in these areas will lead to the conclusion that substantial regulation is not a coincidence but rather is needed, both because liability alone would not adequately reduce risks and because the usual disadvantages of regulation are not as serious as in the tort context.

First, what typifies much of regulation in the areas of concern is that its requirements can be justified by common knowledge or something close to it. Presumably most of us would agree that it is well worthwhile for explosives to be transported over designated routes that avoid the drastic risks of explosions in tunnels or in densely populated locations; that expenditures on very strong elevator cables are warranted by the resulting reduction in the probability of fatal accidents; that milk should be pasteurized to decrease the chances of bacterial contamination. In these and similar cases, the regulatory authority can be reasonably confident that its requirements are justified in the great majority of situations. To be sure, they will not always be justified; there will be some occasions when milk will be consumed soon enough that failure to pasteurize it would lead to no significant risk. But these occasions will be few in number, and the error due to inappropriate regulation will be small.

Furthermore, even where the proper design of regulation must be based on much more than common knowledge, the regulatory authority may not suffer an informational disadvantage, but instead may enjoy a positive advantage relative to private parties. Notably, in dealing with many health-related and environmental risks, a regulatory agency may have better access to, or a superior ability to evaluate, relevant medical, epidemiological, and ecological knowledge. A small fumigating company, for example, might know little about, and have limited ability to understand, the nature of the risks that the chemicals it uses create. The same might be true of a large producer of pesticides; it may be uneconomical for the producer to develop and maintain expert knowledge about the dangerous properties of pesticides, especially where there are economies of scale in acquiring this knowledge and where it would benefit others.

Consideration of the determinant concerning inability to pay for harm done also suggests why we regulate the activities that we do. A fire at a nightclub or hotel could harm a large number of individuals and create losses greater than the worth of the owner. The harm caused by mass consumption of spoiled food or by inoculation with vaccines with adverse side-effects could easily exhaust the holdings of even a large corporation, and so too with the losses resulting from explosions, oil spills, or the release of toxic agents or radioactive substances. Clearly, in many areas of regulation, potential liability could exceed the assets of the firms involved (certainly of their employees), and the deterrent effect of tort law is therefore diluted.

Deterrence is similarly diluted by the likelihood that responsible parties would not be sued for a wide class of environmental and health-related harms. Many of these harms are sufficiently dispersed that individual victims do not find it worth their while to bring suit. In addition, these harms often become apparent only after the passage of years, either because ecological damage or the disease process itself is slow (as with asbestosis) or because the substance generating the risk retains its potency for a long period (as with the anthrax bacillus or radioactive wastes). In consequence, it may be difficult for victims to assemble the evidence necessary to succeed in a suit, the responsible individuals may have retired or died, or the firms themselves may have gone out of business. Last, it is frequently hard to trace environmental and health-related harms to particular causes and then to particular firms. Many different substances may combine to produce a given type of harm, and the mechanism that links cause to effect may be complex and incompletely understood. There are, then, a variety of reasons to believe that parties responsible for environmental and health-related harms would not be sued, and hence to find the use of regulation attractive.

Finally, regarding administrative costs, several factors may offset the underlying advantage of liability in the major regulated areas. First, what regulation often requires is the presence of particular safety devices – fire extinguishers, guard rails, lifeboats – making enforcement less costly than if regulation demanded particular modes of behavior. And where regulation does demand a type of behavior, there may be features of the situation making lack of compliance hard to conceal. How easy would it be for a dairy to keep secret its failure to pasteurize milk when samples can be tested at low cost and when numbers of employees would be aware of the violation? Second, probabilistic methods of enforcement of regulation are often employed; firms are subject to spot visits by regulatory authorities; products and services are randomly selected and examined. Thus, the administrative costs of verifying adherence to regulatory requirements appear sometimes to be low per party, while other times some savings are realized by verifying compliance on a probabilistic basis.

We conclude that the importance of the four determinants is different for the major regulated areas from what it is for the typical tort. In the regulated areas, there is a larger likelihood that responsible parties will be unable to pay for or will escape detection and suit for harms that they bring about; and the disadvantages of regulation involving administrative costs and differential knowledge are less troublesome. Of course, the relative weights of these determinants will change from one case to the next – the possibility of escaping suit, for example, is of significant concern for harms due to pesticides although of little concern for damage caused by fire. But the overall balance of the determinants in the various cases should indicate the desirability of substantial regulation.

This general claim of theoretical consistency is further supported by considering the "second-order" choices society has made over which aspects of an activity to regulate given the initial choice that the activity is one that should be subject to important controls. While fire regulations will often contain requirements concerning the installation of smoke alarms and sprinkler systems, they inevitably will not cover many routine practices, such as whether to store flammable furniture polish in a closet through which a heating pipe passes. Regulating these practices would usually be very expensive (closets would have to be checked frequently) or require a highly contextual sort of knowledge (type of polish and of heating pipe). It therefore appears that the two disadvantages of regulation – the magnitude of administrative costs and the regulator's inferior information about risk – help explain what aspects of a regulated activity are left unregulated.

The claim of theoretical consistency is also confirmed by the observed interrelationship between regulation and imposition of liability, especially in the basic rule that compliance with regulation does not necessarily relieve a party of liability. Moreover, the cases often say that it is "unusual circumstances" or "increased danger" that makes additional precautions desirable, which is exactly what our theory suggested ought to give rise to liability despite satisfaction of regulation. Similarly, the failure to conform to regulation does not in fact automatically result in liability. And the explanation that is furnished here – that a party's "violation of the [statutory] law" does not imply his negligence if the special circumstances justify the apparent disobedience – again comports with the theory.

## V. Concluding Comments

The basic purpose of the last two sections of this article has been to demonstrate how the observed use of liability and regulation can be explained by looking to the four determinants discussed at the outset. As would be true of any simple theory, however, the fit between the theory presented here and reality is only approximate.

Indeed, we often encounter the view that major mistakes have been made in the use of liability and regulation. On the one hand, it may be asserted that regulation has proved inadequate, as for instance in controlling the disposal of toxic wastes. This particular claim may well have merit, for until recently toxic wastes were little regulated, while the threat of tort liability probably provided an insufficient deterrent against improper disposal – due to manifold problems faced by victims in establishing causation and to the possibility that responsible parties would be unable to pay for harm done. Conversely, there are frequent charges that certain regulations are too restrictive, as in complaints that various OSHA requirements and antipollution standards are unduly constraining or impose excessive costs on industry.

That there are such examples of apparent social irrationality is to be expected, for the choices actually made about regulation and liability are obviously influenced by factors lying outside the framework of this analysis, and in any event often will not reflect a conscious, careful use of a cost-benefit calculus. Moreover, the complexity of the relationship between liability and regulation and the many unanswered empirical questions also afford ready explanations for differences between observed and ideal results.

. . .

# Part III

## Intellectual Property

# 8

## Mistake, Disclosure, Information, and the Law of Contracts

### Anthony T. Kronman

**EDITOR'S INTRODUCTION**

Property rights in information encourage the gathering of information, but may discourage the dissemination of information at the time of a transaction. When do individuals have a duty to disclose information and when can they keep the information private? Anthony Kronman's answer is that the person has a property right to information when it is costly to gain such information, but the person does not have a property right and therefore cannot take advantage of his information when the information is obtained at very low cost. Thus when a petroleum engineer purchases land, he does not have to tell the seller that the land has petroleum deposits underneath. If he were forced to do so, his incentive to gain the information in the first place would be greatly diminished. On the other hand, the seller of a house is obligated to tell the future buyer about its latent defects. As the owner of the house, the seller is likely to know the latent defects as a by-product of ownership (that is, no extra cost is involved in obtaining the information); in contrast, it would be costly for the buyer on her own to discover the defects before purchase.

This article is placed under the heading of intellectual property, because the property right is in knowledge and the ideas are closely related to the other papers in this heading. Obviously, it could be considered part of the law of contracts, as well. For similar reasons, Richard Posner's article on blackmail, which is presented under the crime heading, could have been included in this section on intellectual property.

. . .

## Introduction

This paper attempts to explain an apparent inconsistency in the law of contracts. On the one hand, there are many contract cases – generally classified under the rubric of unilateral mistake – which hold that a promisor is excused from his obligation to either perform or pay damages when he is mistaken about some important fact and his error is known (or should be known) to the other party. On the other hand, cases may also be found which state that in some circumstances one party to a contract is entitled to withhold information he knows the other party lacks. These latter cases typically rest upon the proposition that the party with knowledge does not owe the other party a "duty of disclosure."

Although these two lines of cases employ different doctrinal techniques, they both address essentially the same question: if one party to a contract knows or has reason to know that the other party is mistaken about a particular fact, does the knowledgeable party have a duty to speak up or may he remain silent and capitalize on the other party's error? The aim of this paper is to provide a theory which will explain why some contract cases impose such a duty and others do not.

The paper is divided into three parts. In the first part, I discuss the problem of unilateral mistake and offer an economic justification for the rule that a unilaterally mistaken promisor is excused when his error is known or should be known to the other party. In the second part of the paper, I propose a distinction between two kinds of information – information which is the result of a deliberate search and information which has been casually acquired. I argue that a legal privilege of nondisclosure is in effect a property right and attempt to show that where special knowledge or information is the fruit of a deliberate search the assignment of a property right of this sort is required in order to ensure production of the information at a socially desirable level. I then attempt to show that a distinction between deliberately and casually acquired information is useful in explaining why disclosure is required in some contract cases but not in others.

In the third, and concluding, part of the paper, I return briefly to the problem of unilateral mistake, in order to reconcile the apparent conflict between the two lines of cases described above. I argue that this apparent conflict disappears when the unilateral mistake cases are viewed from the perspective developed in the second part of the paper.

# I. Mistake and Allocation of Risk

Every contractual agreement is predicated upon a number of factual assumptions about the world. Some of these assumptions are shared by the parties to the contract and some are not. It is always possible that a particular factual assumption is mistaken. From an economic point of view, the risk of such a mistake (whether it be the mistake of only one party or both) represents a cost. It is a cost to the contracting parties themselves and to society as a whole since the actual occurrence of a mistake always (potentially) increases the resources which must be devoted to the process of allocating goods to their highest-valuing users.

There are basically two ways in which this particular cost can be reduced to an optimal level. First, one or both of the parties can take steps to prevent the mistake from occurring. Second, to the extent a mistake cannot be prevented, either party (or both) can insure against the risk of its occurrence by purchasing insurance from a professional insurer or by self-insuring.

In what follows, I shall be concerned exclusively with the prevention of mistakes. Although this limitation might appear arbitrary, it is warranted by the fact that most mistake cases involve errors which can be prevented at a reasonable cost. Where a risk cannot be prevented at a reasonable cost – which is true of many of the risks associated with what the law calls "supervening impossibilities" – insurance is the only effective means of risk reduction. (This is why the concept of insurance unavoidably plays a more prominent role in the treatment of impossibility than it does in the analysis of mistake.)

Information is the antidote to mistake. Although information is costly to produce, one individual may be able to obtain relevant information more cheaply than another. If the parties to a contract are acting rationally, they will minimize the joint costs of a potential mistake by assigning the risk of its occurrence to the party who is the better (cheaper) information-gatherer. Where the parties have actually assigned the risk – whether explicitly, or implicitly through their adherence to trade custom and past patterns of dealing – their own allocation must be respected. Where they have not – and there is a resulting gap in the contract – a court concerned with economic efficiency should impose the risk on the better information-gatherer. This is so for familiar reasons: by allocating the risk in this way, an efficiency-minded court reduces the transaction costs of the contracting process itself.

The most important doctrinal distinction in the law of mistake is the one drawn between "mutual" and "unilateral" mistakes. Traditionally, courts have been more reluctant to excuse a mistaken promisor where he alone is mistaken than where the other party is mistaken as to the same fact. Although relief for unilateral mistake has been liberalized during the last half-century (to the point where some commentators have questioned the utility of the distinction between unilateral and mutual mistake and a few have even urged its abolition), it is still "black-letter" law that a promisor whose mistake is not shared by the other party is less likely to be relieved of his duty to perform than a promisor whose mistake happens to be mutual.

Viewed broadly, the distinction between mutual and unilateral mistake makes sense from an economic point of view. Where both parties to a contract are mistaken about the same fact or state of affairs, deciding which of them would have been better able to prevent the mistake may well require a detailed inquiry regarding the nature of the mistake and the (economic) role or position of each of the parties involved. But where only one party is mistaken, it is reasonable to assume that he is in a better position than the other party to prevent his own error. As we shall see, this is not true in every case, but it provides a useful beginning point for analysis and helps to explain the generic difference between mutual and unilateral mistakes.

. . .

In the past, it was often asserted that, absent fraud or misrepresentation, a unilateral mistake never justifies excusing the mistaken party from his duty to perform or pay damages. This is certainly no longer the law [if it ever was]. . . . One well-established exception protects the unilaterally mistaken promisor whose error is known or reasonably should be known to the other party. Relief has long been available in this case despite the fact that the promisor's mistake is not shared by the other party to the contract.

For example, if a bidder submits a bid containing a clerical error or miscalculation, and the mistake is either evident on the face of the bid or may reasonably be inferred from a discrepancy between it and other bids, the bidder will typically be permitted to withdraw the bid without having to pay damages (even after the bid has been accepted and in some cases relied upon by the other party). Or, to take another example, suppose that A submits a proposed contract in writing to B and knows that B has misread the document. If B accepts the proposed contract, upon discovering his error, he may avoid his obligations under the contract and has no duty to compensate A for A's lost expectation. A closely related situation involves the offer which is "too good to be true." One receiving such an offer cannot "snap it up"; if he does so, the offeror may withdraw the offer despite the fact that it has been accepted.

In each of the cases just described, one party is mistaken and the other has actual knowledge or reason to know of his mistake. The mistaken party in each case is excused from meeting any contractual obligations owed to the party with knowledge.

A rule of this sort is a sensible one. While it is true that in each of the cases just described the mistaken party is likely to be the one best able to prevent the mistake from occurring in the first place (by exercising care in preparing his bid or in reading the proposed contract which has been submitted to him), the other party may be able to rectify the mistake more cheaply in the interim between its occurrence and the formation of the contract. At one moment in time the mistaken party is the better mistake-preventer (information-gatherer). At some subsequent moment, however, the other party may be the better preventer because of his superior access to relevant information that will disclose the mistake and thus allow its correction. This may be so, for example, if he has other bids to compare with the mistaken one since this will provide him with information which the bidder himself lacks. Of course, if the mistake is one which cannot reasonably be known by the non-mistaken party (that is, if he would have to incur substantial costs in order to discover it), there is no reason to assume that the non-mistaken party is the better (more efficient) mistake-preventer at the time the contract is executed. But if the mistake is actually known or could be discovered at a very slight cost, the principle of efficiency is best served by a compound liability rule which imposes initial responsibility for the mistake on the mistaken party but shifts liability to the other party if he has actual knowledge or reason to know of the error. Compound liability rules of this sort are familiar in other areas of the law: the tort doctrine of "last clear chance" is one example.

The cases in which relief is granted to a unilaterally mistaken promisor on the grounds that his mistake was known or reasonably knowable by the other party appear, however, to conflict sharply with another line of cases. These cases deal with the related problems of fraud and disclosure: if one party to a contract knows that the other is mistaken as to some material fact, is it fraud for the party with knowledge to fail to disclose the error and may the mistaken party avoid the contract on the theory that he was owed a duty of disclosure? This question is not always answered in the same way. In some cases, courts typically find a duty to disclose and in others they do not. It is the latter group of cases – those not requiring disclosure – which appear to conflict with the rule that a unilateral mistake will excuse if the other party knows or has reason to know of its existence.

In the cases not requiring disclosure, one party is mistaken and the other party knows or has reason to know it. Can these cases be reconciled with those which stand for the proposition that a unilateral mistake plus knowledge or reason to know will excuse the mistaken party? More particularly, can the apparent divergence between these two lines of cases be explained on economic grounds?

The rest of this paper is devoted to answering these two questions. In brief, the answer I propose is as follows. Where nondisclosure is permitted (or put differently, where the knowledgeable party's contract rights are enforced despite his failure to disclose a known mistake), the knowledge involved is typically the product of a costly search. A rule permitting nondisclosure is the only effective way of providing an incentive to invest in the production of such knowledge. By contrast, in the cases requiring disclosure, and in those excusing a unilaterally mistaken promisor because the other party knew or had reason to know of his error, the knowledgeable party's special information is typically not the fruit of a deliberate search. Although information of this sort is socially useful as well, a disclosure requirement will not cause a sharp reduction in the amount of such information which is actually pro-duced. If one takes into account the investment costs incurred in the deliberate production of information, the two apparently divergent lines of cases described above may both be seen as conforming (roughly) to the principle of efficiency, which requires that the risk of a unilateral mistake be placed on the most effective risk-preventer.

## II. The Production of Information and the Duty to Disclose

### A. General considerations

It is appropriate to begin a discussion of fraud and nondisclosure in contract law with the celebrated case of *Laidlaw v. Organ*.[1] Organ was a New Orleans commission merchant engaged in the purchase and sale of tobacco. Early on the morning of February 19, 1815, he was informed by a Mr. Shepherd that a peace treaty had been signed at Ghent by American and British officers, formally ending the War of 1812. Mr. Shepherd (who was himself interested in the profits of the transaction involved in *Laidlaw v. Organ*) had obtained information regarding the treaty from his brother who, along with two other gentlemen, brought the news from the British Fleet. . . .

   Knowledge of the treaty was made public in a handbill circulated around eight o'clock on the morning of the nineteenth. However, before the treaty's existence had been publicized . . . , Organ, knowing of the treaty, called on a representative of the Laidlaw firm and entered into a contract for the purchase of 111 hogsheads of tobacco. Before agreeing to sell the tobacco, the Laidlaw representative "asked if there was any news which was calculated to enhance the price or value of the article about to be purchased." It is unclear what response, if any, Organ made to this inquiry.

   As a result of the news of the treaty – which signaled an end to the naval blockade of New Orleans – the market price of tobacco quickly rose by 30 to 50 percent. Laidlaw refused to deliver the tobacco as he had originally promised. Organ subsequently brought suit to recover damages and to block Laidlaw from otherwise disposing of the goods in controversy. Although the report of the case is unclear, it appears that the trial judge directed a verdict in Organ's favor. The case was appealed to the United States Supreme Court, which in an opinion by Chief Justice Marshall remanded with directions for a new trial. The Court concluded that the question "whether any imposition was practiced by the vendee upon the vendor ought to have been submitted to the jury" and that as a result "the absolute instruction of the judge was erroneous." Marshall's opinion is more famous, however, for its dictum than for its holding:

> The question in this case is, whether the intelligence of extrinsic circumstances, which might influence the price of the commodity, and which was exclusively within the knowledge of the vendee, ought to have been communicated by him to the vendor? The court is of opinion that he was not bound to communicate it. It would be difficult to circumscribe the contrary doctrine within proper limits, where the means of intelligence are equally accessible to both parties. But at the same time, each party must take care not to say or do anything tending to impose upon the other.

Although Marshall's dictum in *Laidlaw v. Organ* has been sharply criticized, it is still generally regarded as an accurate statement of the law (when properly interpreted). The

*invisible hand,*
*not separate*

broad rule which Marshall endorses has usually been justified on three related grounds: that it conforms to the legitimate expectations of commercial parties and thus accurately reflects the (harsh) morality of the marketplace; that in a contract for the sale of goods each party takes the risk that his own evaluation of the worth of the goods may be erroneous; or finally, that it justly rewards the intelligence and industry of the party with special knowledge (in this case, the buyer). . . .

From a social point of view, it is desirable that information which reveals a change in circumstances affecting the relative value of commodities reach the market as quickly as possible (or put differently, that the time between the change itself and its comprehension and assessment be minimized). If a farmer who would have planted tobacco had he known of the change plants peanuts instead, he will have to choose between either uprooting one crop and substituting another (which may be prohibitively expensive and will in any case be costly), or devoting his land to a nonoptimal use. In either case, both the individual farmer and society as a whole will be worse off than if he had planted tobacco to begin with. The sooner information of the change reaches the farmer, the less likely it is that social resources will be wasted.

. . .

Allocative efficiency is promoted by getting information of changed circumstances to the market as quickly as possible. Of course, the information doesn't just "get" there. Like everything else, it is supplied by individuals (either directly, by being publicized, or indirectly, when it is signaled by an individual's market behavior).

In some cases, the individuals who supply information have obtained it by a deliberate search; in other cases, their information has been acquired casually. A securities analyst, for example, acquires information about a particular corporation in a deliberate fashion - by carefully studying evidence of its economic performance. By contrast, a businessman who acquires a valuable piece of information when he accidentally overhears a conversation on a bus acquires the information casually.

As it is used here, the term "deliberately acquired information" means information whose acquisition entails costs which would not have been incurred but for the likelihood, however great, that the information in question would actually be produced. These costs may include, of course, not only direct search costs (the cost of examining the corporation's annual statement) but the costs of developing an initial expertise as well (for example, the cost of attending business school). If the costs incurred in acquiring the information (the cost of the bus ticket in the second example) would have been incurred in any case – that is, whether or not the information was forthcoming – the information may be said to have been casually acquired. The distinction between deliberately and casually acquired information is a shorthand way of expressing this economic difference. Although in reality it may be difficult to determine whether any particular item of information has been acquired in one way or the other, the distinction between these two types of information has – as I hope to show – considerable analytical usefulness.

If information has been deliberately acquired (in the sense defined above), and its possessor is denied the benefits of having and using it, he will have an incentive to reduce (or curtail entirely) his production of such information in the future. This is in fact merely a consequence of defining deliberately acquired information in the way that I have, since one who acquires information of this sort will by definition have incurred costs which he would have avoided had it not been for the prospect of the benefits he has now been denied. By being denied the same benefits, one who has casually acquired information will not be discouraged from doing what – for independent reasons – he would have done in any case.

. . . . Strictly speaking, casually acquired information (as I have used the term up to this point) represents the ideal limit of a continuum – the case in which the change in magnitude that results from eliminating one of the benefits of possessing certain information is zero. In any real case there will be incentive effects – which fall somewhere along the continuum. However, where the decline in the production of a certain kind of information which is caused by denying its possessor the right to appropriate the information for his own benefit is small, it is likely to be more than offset by the corresponding social gain that results from the avoidance of mistakes. In the argument that follows, I shall use the term "casually acquired information" in a somewhat looser sense than I have used it so far to refer to information of this sort.

One effective way of insuring that an individual will benefit from the possession of information (or anything else for that matter) is to assign him a property right in the information itself – a right or entitlement to invoke the coercive machinery of the state in order to exclude others from its use and enjoyment. The benefits of possession become secure only when the state transforms the possessor of information into an owner by investing him with a legally enforceable property right of some sort or other. The assignment of property rights in information is a familiar feature of our legal system. The legal protection accorded patented inventions and certain trade secrets are two obvious examples.

One (seldom noticed) way in which the legal system can establish property rights in information is by permitting an informed party to enter – and enforce – contracts which his information suggests are profitable, without disclosing the information to the other party. Imposing a duty to disclose upon the knowledgeable party deprives him of a private advantage which the information would otherwise afford. A duty to disclose is tantamount to a requirement that the benefit of the information be publicly shared and is thus antithetical to the notion of a property right which – whatever else it may entail – always requires the legal protection of private appropriation. Of course, different sorts of property rights may be better suited for protecting possessory interests in different sorts of information. It is unlikely, for example, that information of the kind involved in *Laidlaw v. Organ* could be effectively protected by a patent system. The only feasible way of assigning property rights in short-lived market information is to permit those with such information to contract freely without disclosing what they know. It is unclear, from the report of the case, whether the buyer in *Laidlaw* casually acquired his information or made a deliberate investment in seeking it out (for example, by cultivating a network of valuable commercial "friendships"). If we assume the buyer casually acquired his knowledge of the treaty, requiring him to disclose the information to his seller (that is, denying him a property right in the information) will have no significant effect on his future behavior. Since one who casually acquires information makes no investment in its acquisition, subjecting him to a duty to disclose is not likely to reduce the amount of socially useful information which he actually generates. Of course, if the buyer in *Laidlaw* acquired his knowledge of the treaty as the result of a deliberate and costly search, a disclosure requirement will deprive him of any private benefit which he might otherwise realize from possession of the information and should discourage him from making similar investments in the future.

In addition, since it would enable the seller to appropriate the buyer's information without cost and would eliminate the danger of his being lured unwittingly into a losing contract by one possessing superior knowledge, a disclosure requirement will also reduce the seller's incentive to search. Denying the buyer a property right in deliberately acquired information will therefore discourage both buyers and sellers from investing in the development of expertise and in the actual search for information. The assignment of such a right will not only protect the investment of the party possessing the special knowledge, it will also impose an opportunity cost on the other party and thus give him an incentive to undertake a (cost-justified) search of his own.

If we assume that courts can easily discriminate between those who have acquired information casually and those who have acquired it deliberately, plausible economic considerations might well justify imposing a duty to disclose on a case-by-case basis (imposing it where the information has been casually acquired, refusing to impose it where the information is the fruit of a deliberate search). A party who has casually acquired information is, at the time of the transaction, likely to be a better (cheaper) mistake-preventer than the mistaken party with whom he deals – regardless of the fact that both parties initially had equal access to the information in question. One who has deliberately acquired information is also in a position to prevent the other party's error. But in determining the cost to the knowledgeable party of preventing the mistake (by disclosure), we must include whatever investment he has made in acquiring the information in the first place. This investment will represent a loss to him if the other party can avoid the contract on the grounds that the party with the information owes him a duty of disclosure.

If we take this cost into account, it is no longer clear that the party with knowledge is the cheaper mistake-preventer when his knowledge has been deliberately acquired. Indeed, the opposite conclusion seems more plausible. In this case, therefore, a rule permitting nondisclosure (which has the effect of imposing the risk of a mistake on the mistaken party) corresponds to the arrangement the parties themselves would have been likely to adopt if they had negotiated an explicit allocation of the risk at the time they entered the contract. The parties to a contract are always free to allocate this particular risk by including an appropriate disclaimer in the terms of their agreement. Where they have failed to do so, however, the object of the law of contracts should be (as it is elsewhere) to reduce transaction costs by providing a legal rule which approximates the arrangement the parties would have chosen for themselves if they had deliberately addressed the problem. This consideration, coupled with the reduction in the production of socially useful information which is likely to follow from subjecting him to a disclosure requirement, suggests that allocative efficiency is best served by permitting one who possesses deliberately acquired information to enter and enforce favorable bargains without disclosing what he knows.

A rule which calls for case-by-case application of a disclosure requirement is likely, however, to involve factual issues that will be difficult (and expensive) to resolve. *Laidlaw* itself illustrates this point nicely. On the facts of the case, as we have them, it is impossible to determine whether the buyer actually made a deliberate investment in acquiring information regarding the treaty. The cost of administering a disclosure requirement on a case-by-case basis is likely to be substantial.

As an alternative, one might uniformly apply a blanket rule (of disclosure or nondisclosure) across each class of cases involving the same sort of information (for example, information about market conditions or about defects in property held for sale). In determining the appropriate blanket rule for a particular class of cases, it would first be necessary to decide whether the kind of information involved is (on the whole) more likely to be generated by chance or by deliberate searching. The greater the likelihood that such information will be deliberately produced rather than casually discovered, the more plausible the assumption becomes that a blanket rule permitting nondisclosure will have benefits that outweigh its costs.

In *Laidlaw*, for example, the information involved concerned market conditions. The results in that case may be justified (from the more general perspective just described) on the grounds that information regarding the state of the market is typically (although not in every case) the product of a deliberate search. The large number of individuals who are actually engaged in the production of such information lends some empirical support to this proposition.

## B. THE CASE LAW

The distinction between deliberately and casually acquired information helps us to understand the pattern exhibited by the cases in which a duty to disclose is asserted by one party or the other. By and large, the cases requiring disclosure involve information which is likely to have been casually acquired (in the sense defined above). The cases permitting nondisclosure, on the other hand, involve information which, on the whole, is likely to have been deliberately produced. Taken as a group, the disclosure cases give at least the appearance of promoting allocative efficiency by limiting the assignment of property rights to those types of information which are likely to be the fruit of a deliberate investment (either in the development of expertise or in actual searching).

The economic rationale for permitting nondisclosure is nicely illustrated . . .[in] cases involving the purchase of real estate where the buyer had reason to believe in the existence of a subsurface oil or mineral deposit unknown to the seller. For example, in *Neill v. Shamburg*,[2] the parties were cotenants of an oil lease on a 200-acre tract. The buyer (Shamburg) bought his cotenant's interest in the tract for $550 (with a provision for an additional $100 in case a well producing six or more barrels of oil a day should be found). At the time of the sale, Shamburg was operating several wells on an adjacent tract of land. One of the wells was quite valuable. Shamburg "directed his employees not to give information on this subject" and said nothing to his cotenant regarding the well when he purchased her interest in the 200-acre tract. The court held that Shamburg did not owe Neill any duty of disclosure and refused to set aside the sale of her half interest in the oil lease. The court supported its conclusion with the following argument:

> . . . [U]nless there is some exceptional circumstance to put on him the duty to speak, it is the right of every man to keep his business to himself. . . . We do not find in the acts of Shamburg, under the circumstances, anything more than a positive intention and effort to reap the benefit of his enterprise, by keeping the knowledge of its results to himself, and we agree with the master that this "falls far short of establishing fraud."

. . . .

Information pertaining to the likelihood of a subsurface oil or mineral deposit will often be the fruit of a deliberate investment either in actual exploration or in the development of geological expertise. In order to encourage the production of such information, our legal system generally permits its possessor to take advantage of the ignorance of others by trading without disclosure.

. . . .

With regard to *latent* defects, the older authorities are equivocal. Some cases state that a seller who is aware of such a defect must disclose it to his buyer or forgo the bargain. Others state that the seller is privileged to remain silent if he wishes. In the last twenty-five years, however, there has been a marked expansion of the duty to disclose latent defects. One particularly dramatic illustration involves the sale of a home infested with termites. A seller of a house in Massachusetts in 1942 was held to have no legal duty to disclose the existence of a termite infestation of which the buyer was ignorant. . . .

Eighteen years later, in *Obde v. Schlemeyer*,[3] a Washington seller was held to have a duty to disclose under identical circumstances. The Washington court concluded that the seller had a duty to speak up, "regardless of the [buyer's] failure to ask any questions relative to the possibility of termites," since the condition was "clearly latent - not readily observable upon reasonable inspection." . . .

. . . [T]he disclosure of latent defects makes good sense from the . . . perspective offered here. In the first place, it is likely to be expensive for the buyer to discover such defects; the discovery of a latent defect will almost always require something more than an ordinary search. Even where neither party has knowledge of the defect, it may be efficient to allocate to the seller the risk of a mistaken belief that no defect exists, on the grounds that of the two parties he is likely to be the cheapest mistake-preventer.

Where the seller actually knows of the defect, and the buyer does not, the seller is clearly the party best able to avoid the buyer's mistake at least cost – unless the seller has made a deliberate investment in acquiring his knowledge which he would not have made had he known he would be required to disclose to purchasers of the property any defects he discovered. A seller, of course, may make a substantial investment in acquiring information concerning a particular defect: for example, he may hire exterminators to check his property for termites. But even so, it is unlikely that his principal aim in acquiring such information is to obtain an advantage over potential purchasers. Typically, homeowners conduct investigations of this sort in order to protect their own investments. In most cases, a homeowner will have an adequate incentive to check for termites even if the law requires him to disclose what he discovers; furthermore, many termite infestations are discovered by simply living in the house - something the owner will do in any event. A disclosure requirement is unlikely to have a substantial effect on the level of investment by homeowners in the detection of termites: the point is not that information regarding termites is costless (it isn't), but that a disclosure requirement would not be likely to reduce the production of such information. This represents an important distinction between cases like *Obde*, on the one hand, and those like *Laidlaw* and *Shamburg* . . . , on the other.

. . .

## C. THE DUTY TO DISCLOSE AND THE RESTATEMENTS

In addition to generating a substantial case law, the problem of disclosure in bargain transactions has also been addressed by the draftsmen of three different restatements. It is instructive to compare the treatment which the problem of disclosure has received at the hands of the restaters. . . .

. . .

Section 551(2)(e) is illustrated with the following example.

A is a violin expert. He pays a casual visit to B's shop where second-hand musical instruments are sold. He finds a violin which, by reason of his expert knowledge and experience, he immediately recognizes as a genuine Stradivarius, in good condition, and worth at least $50,000. The violin is priced for sale at $100. Without disclosing his information or his identity, A buys the violin from B for $100. A is not liable to B.

Although A's visit to B's shop is described as "casual," A has certainly incurred costs in building up his knowledge of musical instruments and one of his anticipated benefits may have been the discovery of an undervalued masterpiece. . . . .

Locating valuable instruments which have been incorrectly identified by their owners serves a useful social purpose: after the Stradivarius has been discovered, it will undoubtedly find its way into the hands of a higher-valuing user (for example, a concert violinist or a university with a collection of rare instruments). An undiscovered Stradivarius is almost certainly misallocated. By bringing it to light, a bargain-hunting expert in musical instruments promotes the efficiency with which society's scarce resources are allocated. If he has in-curred costs in doing so (and the development of expertise is one – perhaps the most important – of these costs), the bargain hunter will be discouraged from future searching if he is not given a property right in whatever information he acquires (in the form of a privilege to deal without disclosing).

By the same token, since it enables him to benefit (costlessly) from the other party's special information and eliminates the risk that he will be unable to recover an undervalued masterpiece which he sells by mistake, a disclosure requirement also reduces the owner's incentive to search (that is, to correctly identify the attributes of his own property). Because it reduces the incentive of both the owner and the bargain-hunter to undertake a deliberate search, a disclosure requirement increases the likelihood that the instrument will remain undiscovered and therefore misallocated.

. . . .

## III. Unilateral Mistake and the Duty to Disclose

The rule that a unilaterally mistaken promisor will be excused when his mistake is known or should be known to the other party is typified by the mistaken bid cases and by those in which the mistaken party's error is the result of his having misread a particular document (usually, the proposed contract itself). In both instances, the special knowledge of the non-mistaken party (his knowledge of the other party's error) is unlikely to be the fruit of a deliberate search. Put differently, a rule requiring him to disclose what he knows will not cause him to alter his behavior in such a way that the production of information of this sort will be reduced.

A contractor receiving a mistaken bid, for example, usually becomes aware of the mistake (if he does at all) by comparing the mistaken bid with others that have been submitted, or by noting an error which is evident on the face of the bid itself. In either case, his knowledge of the mistake arises in the course of a routine examination of the bids which he would undertake in any event. The party receiving the bid has an independent incentive to scruti-nize carefully each of the bids which are submitted to him: the profitability of his own enterprise requires that he do so. It is of course true that the recipient's expertise may make it easier for him to identify certain sorts of errors in bids that have been submitted. But the detection of clerical mistakes and errors in calculation is not likely to be one of the principal reasons for his becoming an expert in the first place. A rule requiring the disclosure of mistakes of this kind is almost certain not to discourage investment in developing the sort of general expertise which facilitates the detection of such mistakes.

. . . .

## Conclusion

In this paper, I have emphasized the way in which one branch of the law of contracts promotes efficiency by encouraging the deliberate search for socially useful information. It does so, I have argued, by giving the possessor of such information the right to deal with others without disclosing what he knows. This right is in essence a property right, and I have tried to show that the law tends to recognize a right of this sort where the information is the result of a deliberate and costly search and not to recognize it where the information has been casually acquired. This basic distinction between two kinds of information (and the theory of property rights which is based upon it) introduces order into the disclosure cases and eliminates the apparent conflict between those cases which permit nondisclosure and the well-established rule that a unilaterally mistaken promisor will be excused if his error is or reasonably should be known by the other party.

Although I have confined my discussion to contract law – indeed, to one rather small part of it – the theoretical approach developed in the second part of the paper may prove to be useful in analyzing related problems in other areas of the law. For example, to what extent can the disclosure requirements in our securities laws which are aimed at frustrating insider trading be said to rest upon (and to be justified by) the idea that inside information is more likely to be casually discovered than deliberately produced? If this is in fact one of the principal assumptions underlying the various disclosure requirements imposed by our securities laws, what conclusions – if any – can be drawn regarding the proper scope of these requirements? For example, how much should a tender offeror have to publicly disclose concerning his plans for the corporation he hopes to acquire? Does the analysis offered in this paper throw any light on the requirement of "non-obviousness" in patent law? (Is this perhaps a legal device for discriminating between information which is the result of a deliberate search and information which is not?) Do the distinctions suggested here help us to understand the proliferation of disclosure requirements in the consumer products field and to form a more considered judgment as to their desirability? A legal theory which provided a common framework for the analysis of these and other questions would have considerable appeal.

## Notes

1. Laidlaw *v.* Organ, 15 U.S. (2 Wheat.) 178.
2. Neill *v.* Shamburg, 158 PA. 263, 27 Atl 992 (1893).
3. Obde *v.* Schlemeyer, 56 Wash. 2d 449, 353 P.2d 672 (1960). . . . .

# 9

## An Economic Analysis of Copyright Law

### William M. Landes and Richard Posner

**EDITOR'S INTRODUCTION**

With the rise and (possibly temporary) demise of Napster (registered trademark), intellectual property issues have made newspaper headlines. With intellectual property, the marginal cost of spreading an idea, record, or book is very low, especially in comparison to the cost of producing the first copy. Just think how expensive it is to produce the first copy of Microsoft Word (trademark) and how cheap it is to reproduce. Intellectual property rights are protected by copyright, patents, and trade secrets. William Landes and Richard Posner discuss the optimal protection of intellectual property rights given the costs and benefits inherent in the particular situation.

  If there are no intellectual property rights, then the incentive to produce the song. book, etc. is greatly reduced but the intellectual property that is produced will be spread optimally. Subject to certain caveats, greater protection of intellectual property rights will increase the production of intellectual property, but will result in less than an optimal distribution. an important caveat is that if copyright protection were too expansive, say ideas were copyrightable, then the production of new ideas could be reduced because of greatly increased transaction costs (negotiation with the original holder of the idea or litigation in court to determine whether the new idea was really new). Not surprisingly then, ideas, plots, and book titles cannot be copyrighted. Landes and Posner not only consider the general outlines of copyright protection, but also explain many details (e.g., why music copyright is stronger then the copyright for books, why copyright holds for a particular length of time after an author's death, and why there is a fair use doctrine).

Intellectual property is a natural field for economic analysis of law, and copyright is an important form of intellectual property. Yet while there are good introductions to the economics of copyright law, and a number of excellent articles on the economics of copying (as distinct from copyright *law*), no article examines the field of copyright as a whole, discussing the evolution and major doctrines in the law from an economic standpoint. This article. . . tries to fill this gap – although the field is so vast that our analysis cannot be exhaustive. As in most of our work, we are particularly interested in positive analysis, and specifically in the question to what extent copyright law can be explained as a means for promoting efficient allocation of resources.

A distinguishing characteristic of intellectual property is its "public good" aspect. While the cost of creating a work subject to copyright protection – for example, a book, movie, song, ballet, lithograph, map, business directory, or computer software program – is often high, the cost of reproducing the work, whether by the creator or by those to whom he has made it available, is often low. And once copies are available to others, it is often inexpensive for these users to make additional copies. If the copies made by the creator of the work are priced at or close to marginal cost, others may be discouraged from making copies, but the creator's total revenues may not be sufficient to cover the cost of creating the work. Copyright protection – the right of the copyright's owner to prevent others from making copies – trades off the costs of limiting access to a work against the benefits of providing incentives to create the work in the first place. Striking the correct balance between access and incentives is the central problem in copyright law. For copyright law to promote economic efficiency, its principal legal doctrines must, at least approximately, maximize the benefits from creating additional works minus both the losses from limiting access and the costs of administering copyright protection.

Section I develops the basic economic model of copyright protection, including an analysis of the optimal degree of that protection. Section II applies the model to the principal doctrines of copyright law. It considers such questions as the originality requirement for copyright protection, . . . the protection of derivative works, and issues of fair use.

# I. The Basic Economics of Copyright

We begin with the factors – including, of course, copyright protection – that determine the number of works created. Then we examine the exploitation of the created work – the number of copies and the price per copy.

## A. NUMBER OF WORKS AS A FUNCTION OF COPYRIGHT AND OTHER FACTORS

### 1. General considerations

The cost of producing a book or other copyrightable work (we start by talking just about books and later branch out to other forms of expression) has two components. The first is the cost of creating the work. We assume that it does not vary with the number of copies produced or sold, since it consists primarily of the author's time and effort plus the cost to the publisher of soliciting and editing the manuscript and setting it in type. Consistent with copyright usage we call the sum of these costs the "cost of expression."

To simplify the analysis, we ignore any distinction between costs incurred by authors and by publishers, and therefore use the term "author" (or "creator") to mean both author and publisher. In doing this we elide a number of interesting questions involving the relation between author and publisher. For example, do such principles as *droit moral*, entitling authors to reclaim copyright from assignees after a fixed period of years or entitling artists to royalties on resales of their art by initial (or subsequent) purchasers, increase or reduce the incentive to create new works? . . .

The second component of the cost of producing a work increases with the number of copies produced, for it is the cost of printing, binding, and distributing individual copies. The cost of expression does not enter into the making of copies because, once the work is created, the author's efforts can be incorporated into another copy virtually without cost.

For a new work to be created, the expected return – typically, and we shall assume exclusively, from the sale of copies – must exceed the expected cost. The demand curve for copies of a given book is, we assume, negatively sloped because there are good but not perfect substitutes for a given book. The creator will make copies up to the point where the marginal cost of one more copy equals its expected marginal revenue. The resulting difference between price and marginal cost, summed over the number of copies sold, will generate revenues to offset the cost of expression. Since the decision to create the work must be made before the demand for copies is known, the work will be created only if the difference between expected revenues and the cost of making copies equals or exceeds the cost of expression. If we assume that the cost of creating (equivalent) works differs among authors, the number of works created will increase until the returns from the last work created just covers the (increasing) cost of expression.

Two qualifications should be noted. First, for many types of intellectual property some price discrimination may be possible because individual works are not perfect substitutes and arbitrage is preventable. Thus, a book publisher will commonly charge higher prices for hardcover editions and later reduce the price for persons willing to wait for the paperback edition to appear. Similarly, the prices charged by exhibitors for first-run movies will generally be higher than the prices in the aftermarket (cable viewing, video cassettes, and network television). Price discrimination increases revenue and thus the number of works produced, though it may not increase the number of copies of each work. Second, the demand for copies of a given work depends not only on the number of copies but on the number of (competing) works as well. The greater the number of such works (past and present), the lower the demand for any given work. Thus, the number of works and the number of copies per work will be determined simultaneously, and the net effect of this interaction will be to reduce the number of works created.

This description of the market for copies and the number of works created assumes the existence of copyright protection. In its absence anyone can buy a copy of the book when it first appears and make and sell copies of it. The market price of the book will eventually be bid down to the marginal cost of copying, with the unfortunate result that the book probably will not be produced in the first place, because the author and publisher will not be able to recover their costs of creating the work. The problem is magnified by the fact that the author's cost of creating the work, and many publishing costs (for example, editing costs), are incurred before it is known what the demand for the work will be. Uncertainty about demand is a particularly serious problem with respect to artistic works, such as books, plays, movies, and recordings. Even with copyright protection, sales may be insufficient to cover the cost of expression and may not even cover the variable cost of making copies. Thus, the difference between the price and marginal cost of the successful work must not only cover the cost of expression but also compensate for the risk of failure. If a copier can defer making copies until he knows whether the work is a success, the potential gains from free riding on expression will be even greater, because the difference between the price and marginal cost of the original work will rise to compensate for the uncertainty of demand, thus creating a bigger profit potential for copies. So uncertainty generates an additional disincentive to create works in the absence of copyright protection.

Practical obstacles limit copying the original works of others even in the absence of any copyright protection. But these obstacles, while serious in some cases, can easily be exaggerated. When fully analyzed, they do not make a persuasive case for eliminating copyright protection.

1. *The copy maybe of inferior quality, and hence not a perfect substitute for the original.* In the case of books and other printed matter, the copier may not be able to match the quality of paper or binding of the original or the crispness of the printing, and there may be errors in transcription. None of these is an important impediment to good copies any longer, but in the case of works of art – such as a painting by a famous artist – a copy, however accurate, may be such a poor substitute in the market that it will have no negative effects on the price of the artist's work. Indeed, the copy may have a positive effect on that price, by serving as advertising for his works. On the other hand, it may also deprive him of income from selling derivative works – the copies of his paintings – himself. (More on derivative works shortly.) To generalize, when either the cost of making equivalent copies is higher for the copier than for the creator or the copier's product is a poor substitute for the original, the originator will be able to charge a price greater than his marginal cost, even without legal protection. And, obviously, the greater the difference in the costs of making copies and in the quality of copies between creator and copier (assuming the latter's cost is higher or quality lower), the less need there is for copyright protection.

2. *Copying may itself involve some original expression – as when the copy is not a literal copy but involves paraphrasing, deletions, marginal notes, and so on – and so a positive cost of expression.* The copier may incur fixed costs as well, for example costs of rekeying the words from the copy he bought or of photographing them. Still, we would expect the copier's average cost to be lower than the creator's because it will not include the author's time or the cost of soliciting and editing the original manuscript. Nevertheless, when the copier cannot take a completely free ride on the creator's investment in expression and his other fixed costs, the need for copyright protection is reduced.

Between the literal copier and the author who makes no use whatever of previous works, three additional types of producer can be distinguished. One is the author who makes at least some, but perhaps modest, use of previous works; most authors are of this type. Next is the author of a derivative work, that is, a work that draws very heavily on previous works, though the derivative work involves some original elements. Third is the unoriginal copier who nevertheless tries to complicate the author's task of proving infringement by differentiating the copied work from the original in minor ways. Derivative works and infringement are discussed in Section II; the author who makes some use of previous works figures prominently in our . . . analysis, along with the literal copier.

3. *Copying takes time, so there will be an interval during which the original publisher will not face competition.* This point, which is related to the first because generally the cost of production is inverse to time, has two implications for the analysis of copyright law. First, because modern technology has reduced the time it takes to make copies as well as enabled more perfect copies to be made at low cost, the need for copyright protection has increased over time. Second, for works that are faddish – where demand is initially strong but falls sharply after a brief period – copyright protection may not be as necessary in order to give the creator of the work a fully compensatory return.

4. *There are contractual alternatives to copyright protection for limiting copying.* One is licensing the original work on condition that the licensee not make copies of it or disclose it to others in

a way that would enable them to make copies. But contractual prohibitions on copying may, like trade secrets, be costly to enforce and feasible only if there an few licensees. Where widespread distribution is necessary to generate an adequate return to the author or where the work is resold or publicly performed, contractual prohibitions may not prevent widespread copying. Thus, the greater the potential market for a work, the greater the need for copyright protection. The development of radio, television, and the phonograph has expanded the market for copies and thereby increased the value of copyright protection.

5. *Since a copier normally must have access to a copy in order to make copies, the creator may be able to capture some of the value of copies made by others by charging a high price for the copies he makes and sells.* For example, a publisher of academic journals may be able to capture part of the value that individuals obtain from copying articles by charging a higher price for the journal – especially to libraries; or a record company may be able to charge a higher price because of home taping. Although this possibility limits the need for copyright protection, it does not eliminate it. If one can make many copies of the first copy, and many copies of subsequent copies, the price of copies will be driven down to marginal cost and the creator will not be able to charge a sufficiently higher price for his copy to capture its value in allowing others to make more copies; no one (except the first copier and the most impatient reader) will buy from him rather than from a copier.

6. *Many authors derive substantial benefits from publication that are over and beyond any royalties.* This is true not only in terms of prestige and other nonpecuniary income but also pecuniary income in such forms as a higher salary for a professor who publishes than for one who does not, or greater consulting income. Publishing is an effective method of self-advertisement and self-promotion. The norms against plagiarism (that is against copying without giving the author credit) reinforce the conferral of prestige by publishing; to the extent that those norms are effective, they ensure that the author will obtain recognition, if not always royalties, from the works he publishes.

Such points have convinced some students of copyright law that there is no need for copyright protection. Legal rights are costly to enforce – rights in intangibles especially so – and the costs may outweigh the social gains in particular settings. Perhaps copyright in books is one of them. After all, the first copyright law in England dates from 1710 (and gave much less protection than modern copyright law), yet publishing had flourished for hundreds of years in England despite censorship and widespread illiteracy. The point is a little misleading, however. In the old days, the costs of making copies were a higher fraction of total cost than they are today, so the problem of appropriability was less acute. . . . Finally, while it may be difficult to determine whether, on balance, copyright is a good thing, it is easy to note particular distortions that a copyright law corrects. Without copyright protection, authors, publishers, and copiers would have inefficient incentives with regard to the timing of various decisions. Publishers, to lengthen their head start, would have a disincentive to engage in prepublication advertising and even to announce publication dates in advance, and copiers would have an incentive to install excessively speedy production lines. There would be increased incentives to create faddish, ephemeral, and otherwise transitory works because the gains from being first in the market for such works would be likely to exceed the losses from absence of copyright protection. There would be a shift toward the production of works that are difficult to copy; authors would be more likely to circulate their works privately rather than widely, to lessen the risk of copying; and contractual restrictions on copying would multiply.

. . . [B]eyond some level copyright protection may actually be counterproductive by raising the cost of expression. . . . Creating a new work typically involves borrowing or building on material from a prior body of works, as well as adding original expression to it. A new work of fiction, for example, will contain the author's expressive contribution but also characters, situations, plot details, and so on, invented by previous authors. Similarly, a new work of music may borrow tempo changes and chord progressions from earlier works. The less extensive copyright protection is, the more an author, composer, or other creator can borrow from previous works without infringing copyright and the lower, therefore, the costs of creating a new work. Of course, even if copyright protection effectively prevented all unauthorized copying from a copyrighted work, authors would still copy. But they would copy works, whose copyright protection had run out, or they would disguise their copying, engage in costly searches to avoid copying protected works, or, incur licensing and other transaction costs to obtain permission to copy such works. The effect would be to raise the cost of creating new works – the cost of expression, broadly defined – and thus, paradoxically, perhaps lower the number of works created.

Copyright holders might, therefore, find it in their self-interest, ex ante, to limit copyright protection. To the extent that a later author is free to borrow material from an earlier one, the later author's cost of expression is reduced; and, from an ex ante viewpoint, every author is both an earlier author from whom a later author might want to borrow material and the later author himself. In the former role, he desires maximum copyright protection for works he creates; in the latter, he prefers minimum protection for works created earlier by others. In principle, there is a level of copyright protection that balances these two competing interests optimally – although notice that the first generation of authors, having no one to borrow from, will have less incentive to strike the optimal balance than later ones. We shall see in Section II that various doctrines of copyright law, such as . . . the fair use doctrine, can be understood as attempts to promote economic efficiency by balancing the effect of greater copyright protection – in encouraging the creation of new works by reducing copying – against the effect of less protection – in encouraging the creation of new works by reducing the cost of creating them.

. . .

# II. Applications

## A. THE NATURE OF COPYRIGHT PROTECTION

Our task now is to . . . explain the principal features of copyright law. We begin with the nature of the protection that a copyright gives its owner. In contrast to a patent, a copyright merely gives protection against copying; independent (that is, accidental) duplication of the copyrighted work is not actionable as such. In speaking of "independent (accidental, inadvertent) duplication" we are addressing only the problem of an independent *recreation* of the original copyrighted work. The accidental *use* of someone else's work might be thought of as duplication, but in that context liability for infringement is strict, much as it is for the trespass on a neighbor's land made by a person who thinks that he owns it.

The more difficult question is to explain why duplication in the sense of independent recreation is not actionable. Our analysis suggests two possible explanations. The first is the added cost to the author of checking countless numbers of copyrighted works to avoid inadvertent duplication. The costs (if actually incurred – a qualification whose significance will become apparent shortly) would . . . lower social welfare because both net welfare per work . . . and the number of works created would fall. True, the author's gross revenues might rise if the reduction in the amount of accidental duplication raised the demand for copies or made that demand less elastic. But since accidental duplication of copyrighted works is rare (except in the area of popular music, discussed below), the net effect of making it unlawful would be to lower social welfare.

In contrast to copyright, accidental infringements of patents are actionable, and the difference makes economic sense. A patent is issued only after a search by the applicant and by the Patent Office of prior patented inventions. This procedure is feasible because it is possible to describe an invention compactly and to establish relatively small classes of related inventions beyond which the searchers need not go. The procedure makes it relatively easy for an inventor to avoid accidentally duplicating an existing patent.

No effort is made by the Copyright Office to search copyrighted works before issuing a copyright, so copyright is not issued but is simply asserted by the author or publisher. There are billions of pages of copyrighted material, any one page of which might contain a sentence or paragraph that a later writer might, by pure coincidence, duplicate so closely that he would be considered an infringer if he had actually copied the words in question or if copying were not required for liability. What is infeasible for the Copyright Office is also infeasible for the author. He cannot read all the copyrighted literature in existence (in all languages, and including unpublished works!) in order to make sure that he has not accidentally duplicated some copyrighted material.

The cost of preventing accidental duplication would be so great, and the benefits in terms of higher revenues (and so the amount of damages if such duplication were actionable) so slight because such duplication is rare, that even if it were actionable no writer or publisher would make much effort to avoid accidental duplication, so the increase in the cost of expression would probably be slight. . . .

The second reason we expect accidental duplication not to be made unlawful derives from the economic rationale for copyright protection, which is to prevent free riding on the author's expression. Accidental duplication does not involve free riding. Since the second work is independently created, its author incurs the full cost of expression. If the works are completely identical – a remote possibility, to say the least – competition between the two works could drive the price of copies down to marginal cost and prevent either author from recovering his cost of creating the work. It is more likely that significant differences between the two works will remain, so that both authors may be able to earn enough to cover their respective costs of expression – particularly if neither author is the marginal author, whose gross revenues would just cover the cost of expression in the absence of accidental duplication.

Although for simplicity our analysis focuses on copyright protection for literature and other written works, it is applicable, mutatis mutandis, to other forms of expression as well. A significant difference between literary and musical copyright is that courts hold that accidental duplication may infringe a songwriter's copyright if his song has been widely performed. Since most popular songs have simple melodies and the number of melodic variations is limited, the possibility of accidental duplication of several bars is significant. Widespread playing of these songs on the radio makes it likely that the second composer will have had access to the original work, which both increases the likelihood of accidental duplication and reduces the cost of avoiding it. If proof of intentional duplication were required for infringement, composers of popular songs would have little copyright protection and social welfare would fall.

This result may appear to show that musical copyright follows the pattern of patent law rather than of literary copyright, but the appearance is deceptive. Two forms of "accidental" duplication of a copyrighted work must be distinguished. The first is independent creation: the duplicator makes no use, direct or indirect, of the copyrighted work. Such a duplicator is never an infringer. The second is unconscious borrowing. Unlike the independent creator, the unconscious borrower is a free rider, and is therefore properly deemed an infringer. Musical copyright is special only in that unconscious borrowing is more likely in the musical than in the literary realm.

To distinguish between copying and independent duplication, the courts use an implicit indifference-curve analysis in which access is traded off against similarity. Where there is a strong showing of similarity, it is more likely that the original work was copied and less likely that it was independently created (particularly for complicated works, in contrast to, say, a few bars of a popular melody). In such a case, the copyright owner can prevail even if he presents only weak evidence that the defendant had access to the original work. On the other hand, where the differences between the original work and its "copy" are substantial, the copyright owner will. normally have to provide strong evidence of access to rebut the defense of independent creation.

## B. THE SCOPE OF PROTECTION

The most difficult economic questions about copyright law have to do with the scope of legal protection. We shall discuss these under the headings of (1) idea versus expression, (2) derivative works, and (3) fair use.

### 1. Idea versus expression

*i) The economic rationale for not protecting ideas.* A copyright protects expression but not ideas. . . . [W]e offer several reasons for the difference in treatment.

a) Suppose that . . . $N$ works . . . express the same idea differently; for example, each work might be a different novel about a romance between young people who belong to different social classes or religious faiths and whose parents are feuding. If copyright protected the first author's idea, the cost of expression to each of the remaining $N-1$ authors would increase, because each would have to invest time and effort in coming up with an original idea for his work, or to substitute additional expression for the part of his idea that overlapped the first author's, or to incur licensing and other transaction costs to obtain the right to use the first author's idea. The net effect of protection would be to reduce the number of works created. . . .

The traditional explanation for protecting only expression emphasizes the welfare losses from monopoly of an idea. We emphasize the increase in the cost of creating works and the reduction in the number of works rather than the higher price (per copy) that is normally associated with monopoly. . . .

b) The author is both a user of ideas developed by others and a creator of new ideas. Suppose our $N$ authors did not know which one would be the first to come up with an idea that the other $N-1$ authors would use. Since . . . the costs involved in coming up with the kind of new idea normally embodied in an expressive work usually are low relative to the costs in time and effort of expressing the idea, and since the originator of the idea will probably obtain a normal return in one form or another from being first in the market even without receiving copyright protection, the $N$ authors, behind a veil of ignorance, probably would agree unanimously (or nearly so) to a rule that protected expression but not ideas. If so, then that rule would be Pareto optimal.

. . .

[c]) A final concern is with the administrative costs involved in defining rights in ideas. Courts would have to define each idea, set its boundaries, determine its overlap with other ideas, and, most difficult of all, identify the idea in the work of the alleged infringer.

. . .

## 2. Derivative works

A derivative work is a translation into a different language or medium. Illustrations include a German translation of an English play, the movie version of a play, photographs of a painting, a wind-up Mickey Mouse doll, and a porcelain plate with scenes taken from a movie. The owner of a copyrighted work has a right to prevent the making of a derivative work and thus can sue the maker of an unauthorized derivative work for infringement of the original. He can also copyright the derivative work. Thus he has a monopoly of works derived from his copyrighted work. If, however, the original work is in the public domain, the creator of the derivative work can obtain a copyright of the derivative work, though not, of course, of the original.

The case for giving the owner of a copyrighted work a monopoly of its derivative works as well is a subtle one. It is not, as it might seem to be, to enable the original author, publisher, and so on, to recoup his fixed costs. By definition, the derivative work is an imperfect substitute; often it is no substitute at all. A person who is in the market for an original painting priced at \$20,000 will not be interested in a \$50 photograph of the painting. A German who cannot read English will not buy the English original if there is no German translation. There are exceptions, of course; for example, a movie based on a book might reduce or, more likely, expand the demand for the book. Even where there is no element of substitution or complementarity – that is, where the derivative work is not part of the copiers' supply curve . . . , so that the demand faced by the author for the original is independent of the demand for the derivative work – giving the original author the exclusive right over derivative works will enhance his income. But the conferral of the right is not necessary in order to prevent his sales from being driven to zero. And since it is not certain that any copyright protection is necessary to enable authors and publishers to recover their fixed costs, it would be speculative to conclude that without control over derivative works authors and publishers would not be able to cover the fixed costs of the original work – though no doubt some works would not be created without the expectation of revenues from derivative works, just as some products would not be produced if producers were forbidden to price discriminate.

To understand the best economic case for giving the owner of the original control over derivative works, even if the demand for the work is unrelated to the demand for the original, one must first consider why derivative works should be copyrightable. Imagine the situation of the translator who was not permitted to obtain copyright protection for his contribution to the derivative work, viewed as the joint product of him and the original author. To translate *The Brothers Karamazov* into English is an enormously time-consuming task. If the translator could not obtain a copyright of the translation, he might be unable to recover the cost of his time; for anyone would be free to copy the translation without having incurred that cost and could undersell him at a profit.

This analysis may seem to imply that the derivative, not original, author should be allowed to copyright the derivative work. Not so. Such a rule could distort the timing of publication of both the original and derivative works. The original author, eager to maximize his income from the work, would have an incentive to delay publication of the original work until he had created the derivative work as well (or arranged for its creation by licensees), in order to gain a head start on any would-be author of such a work.

Another reason for giving the original author a monopoly of derivative works is to reduce transaction costs. Suppose Dostoevsky's heir owned the copyright on the original Russian version of *The Brothers Karamazov,* but some American owned the copyright on the English translation. A publisher who wanted to bring out a new edition of that translation would have to deal with two copyright holders. Transaction costs would be reduced if one person owned both copyrights. Of course, even if they were separately owned to begin with, one of the owners could buy the other's copyright. But this transaction, with its attendant costs, can be avoided if the law places the power to obtain both copyrights in the same person to begin with – and that is, in effect, what the law does.

   . . .

## 3. Fair use

"Fair use" is a doctrine that allows some copying of a copyrighted work without deeming the copier an infringer, even though the copyright holder has not authorized the copying. The conventional view is that no general theory can explain the cases that invoke the doctrine. Such a view is reinforced by Section 107 of the Copyright Act, which codified the fair use doctrine for the first time. Section 107 identifies a series of factors – drawn from prior judicial decisions – to be considered, such as purpose and character of use, nature of copyrighted work, amount and substitutability of portion used, and effect on potential market for copyrighted work, but leaves open the question of their relative importance and how one uses them to determine whether a use is fair. Our economic model, however, explains the major applications of the fair use principle.

i) *The high-transaction-cost case.* Suppose that the costs of a voluntary exchange are so high relative to the benefits that no such exchange is feasible between a user of a copyrighted work and its owner. User A might be willing to pay B (the copyright holder) a sum that B would gladly accept to consent to the use of the work, but the cost of negotiating such a license may be prohibitive if, for example, all A wants to do is quote a brief passage from B's work. A fair use privilege creates a clear benefit to A but does not harm B. The copier here is neither a firm selling copies nor a potential purchaser of copies, so his projected use affects neither the supply of copies nor the demand for them.

. . . [Q]ualifications are in order. . . .

[F]air use, if too broadly interpreted, might sap the incentive to develop innovative market mechanisms that reduce transaction costs and make economic exchanges between copyright holders and users feasible. The American Society for Composers, Authors, and Publishers (ASCAP) (or Broadcast Music, Inc. [BMI], the other performing-rights organization) is an illustrative market response to copyright problems caused by high transaction costs. The number of users (radio and TV stations, nightclubs, and so on) of copyrighted music makes individual negotiations with copyright holders to acquire performance rights infeasible. This problem is eliminated when ASCAP acquires nonexclusive rights from copyright holders and offers a blanket license to users for an annual fee; this allows users to perform any songs in ASCAP's repertory. Since performance distributions from ASCAP are an important part of composers' incomes, a fair use exception for performance would greatly reduce the pecuniary incentive to compose music.

. . .

These are not arguments against the fair use doctrine. They are arguments for construing it narrowly. Only if the benefits of the use exceed the costs of copyrighted protection – as they do *not* in the performing-rights case, given the economical method of conferring copyright through performing-rights organizations, and possibly not in the chapter photocopying case as well – is the no right/no liability solution of fair use defensible on pure transaction-cost grounds.

ii) *Book reviews.* A standard example of fair use is the book review that quotes brief passages from the book being reviewed. Conventional legal analysis conceives the doctrine as striking a balance between the author's interest in royalties and the interest of the reviewer and his readers in free access to limited portions of the work. The first stage of economic analysis reconceives the doctrine as economizing on transaction costs, though they need not be prohibitive as in our previous discussion. Since book reviews are a substitute for advertising, the publisher presumably would "license" reviewers to quote brief passages from the book for free. By giving reviewers, in effect, an automatic license, the fair use doctrine avoids the costs of explicit transactions between publishers and reviewers that would yield the identical outcome. This is the theory by which "time-shifting" home video recordings of copyrighted television programs were held in the *Betamax* case to be protected by the fair use doctrine.

. . .

iii) *Parody.* One stage beyond the review is the parody, which copies the distinctive features of the original work in order to recall it to the reader. The reminding function is essential; without the reader's awareness of the original, the parody will not be recognized as such and so will fall flat. One could view the parody as a derivative work, and give the author of the original work control over it, but this would enable the author of the original work to stifle what is often a particularly effective form of criticism – ridicule.

A difficult case is that of the noncritical parody, perhaps better described as "burlesque" and well illustrated by Jack Benny's famous burlesque of *Gas Light*. Benny was not attacking *Gas Light* any more than Abbott and Costello were attacking *Frankenstein* in *Abbott and Costello Meet Frankenstein.* Humorous but not ridiculing versions of the original, these burlesques are derivative works in a pure form, and modern copyright law gives the copyright holder the exclusive right to make such works. A derivative work is a substitute, though an imperfect one, for the original; it may therefore siphon revenues from the original work not by disparaging that work but by satisfying part of the demand for it. So maybe the law should try to distinguish between parody and burlesque and treat the latter but not the former as infringing. The difficulty of doing this should be obvious. Yet the law may already be doing it implicitly by the emphasis it places on whether the allegedly infringing work is fulfilling the demand for the original work (which a parody does not do); if so it is a derivative work and infringing.

iv) *Reducing the cost of creating works.* The question of fair use arises in another setting involving the permissible use that later authors can make of earlier works: deciding whether an allegedly infringing work is "substantially similar" to the work which it is said to infringe. Answering this question requires a court to sort out the contribution to the new product of the original copyright holder and the alleged infringer. The inputs into a work of fiction (including movies, television plays, and so on) include characters, situations, plot details, and so on, invented by previous authors and not yet so standard or hackneyed that they are considered part of the elementary repertory of stock characters and situations on which all authors should be free to draw. When "substantial similarity" is defined, narrowly, the later author will be allowed to use these inventions without having to negotiate with the copyright holder. Courts refer to this, as a *productive* fair use, as distinct from simply a *reproductive* use. A productive use is one that lowers the cost of expression and tends to increase the number of works, while a reproductive one simply increases the number of "copies" of a given work, reduces the gross profits of the author, and reduces the incentives to create works. Not surprisingly, a fair use defense for a productive use is looked on more favorably than such a defense for a reproductive use.

Striking the right balance [is] a critical . . . if all borrowing from previously copyrighted works were deemed infringement, the number of new works ($N$) might fall. Whether the law has struck the right balance is not readily determinable, but the fact that the law denies protection for ideas and requires substantial, rather than some, similarity for infringement is evidence of implicit awareness of the problem.

## C. THE OPTIMAL TERM OF A COPYRIGHT

The usual economic argument for limiting the duration of a right in intellectual property is twofold. First, such a limitation reduces the potential monopoly profits (hence, rent seeking and resource misallocation) from ownership of such a right. Second, it reduces tracing costs. Both reasons loom large in the patent area, which is why patents expire much sooner than either copyrights or trademarks. Patents confer larger potential gains than copyrights or trademarks, and (a related point) patented inventions are hard to keep track of over a long period of time because an invention (for example, the wheel) may eventually become embodied in a vast range of different products. Trademarks rarely confer any monopoly power. And they pose no tracing problem, because to be valid a trademark must be used in conjunction with a specific product that is actually being sold in the market; hence the term of a trademark is indefinite (that is, until abandonment – just as with real property and other tangible products).

Copyrights, too, rarely confer monopoly power, but there are two types of tracing problem, though neither is serious. First, it is hard to keep track of heirs over many generations. This is a potential problem with real estate as well, but is solved by having a registry of land titles. A similar system could be instituted for copyrights. Second, books may go out of print and older works in general may not be easily available. But this problem is solved by having a registry – the Copyright Office – which retains copies of all copyrighted works. . . . Nevertheless, since the tracing cost is positive and grows with the amount of time that has elapsed since the publication of the copyrighted work, there is an argument for limiting the term of a copyright to the point at which the incentive effects of copyright become negligible because of the time value of money. Income prospects that lie twenty-five years in the future have little effect on present decisions, though not zero since people do make provisions for retirement more than twenty-five years in advance. The prospect of royalties in one hundred years, however, would have no effect on most authors' incentives.

. . .

If we are right that copyrights should be time-limited to save on tracing costs, it might seem to follow that all property rights should similarly be limited. But this is wrong. Even one hundred years from now it will be desirable to have a given parcel of land owned by someone, in order to prevent overuse – and why not the heirs of the present owner unless they sell it before then? There is no congestion externality in the case of information, including the text of a book, and hence no benefit (yet potentially substantial costs) in perpetuating ownership beyond the period necessary to enable the author or publisher to recoup the fixed costs of creating the work. After that, it is fine to dump the copyrighted work into the public domain. As we do not intend land ever to be in the public domain, we cannot economize on the costs of administering property rights by placing a time limit on these rights in land.

This point can be sharpened by contrasting the copyright situation with that of "publicity rights" (rights to the commercial exploitation of a person's name or likeness), where there is a congestion externality. Suppose an insurance company wants to use a picture of George Washington in its logo and an heir of George Washington appears and objects, claiming that the right of publicity is a descendible right. The heir could not argue that the recognition of such a right almost two hundred years after the death of a public figure is necessary to recoup the investment in becoming a public figure, but he could argue that, unless there is a property right in the public figure's name and likeness, there may be congestion, resulting in a loss of value. This is the economic insight behind the growing movement toward making publicity rights inheritable and also behind state antidilution statutes. The advertising value of a name and likeness may be shed if anyone can use them. That is not a problem with books, art works, and other copyrighted items.

The current length of a copyright is the author's lifetime plus fifty years.[1] This reflects a long trend toward lengthening the term of copyright as well as expanding its scope . . . which in this country has gone from twenty-eight years in 1790 (a fourteen-year initial term renewable for another fourteen years) . . . to the present term in 1976. This trend is consistent with the fact that the cost of copying has fallen over this period, for we showed earlier that the lower the cost of copying the greater the optimal scope of copyright protection.

The present term may seem both too long – the author who publishes a work at age thirty and dies at age eighty has one hundred years of copyright protection, and even in the unlikely event that the work will still generate a substantial income in the one hundredth year, the present value of that expectation will be virtually zero – and arbitrary in making the term of the copyright depend on the author's longevity. But maybe the term is neither too long nor arbitrary. A point stressed in the legislative history of the 1976 act is that, by making the death of the author the determining date for copyright protection, "all of a particular author's works, including successive revisions of them, would fall into the public domain at the same time, thus avoiding the present problems of determining a multitude of publication dates and of distinguishing 'old' and 'new' matter in later editions." . . .

## Note

1.   Since the original article was written, copyright law has been changed again. For works created after January 1978 copyright runs for a term of 70 years after the death of the author or last surviving author, and it can run for longer for "works for hire".

# 10

# Authors' and Artists' Moral Rights: A Comparative Legal and Economic Analysis

*Henry Hansmann and Marina Santilli*

### EDITOR'S INTRODUCTION

In recent years the United States has followed other common-law jurisdictions, as well as most of the civil-law jurisdictions of western Europe, in adopting legislation recognizing artists' "moral rights." Moral rights include the ability of an artist to prevent changes to his/her art regardless of how many times the art has been sold and resold before the present owner's threat of alteration. For example, moral rights can prevent a purchaser from cutting up a painting into four separate paintings. In contrast, a seller of an automobile or other object can put no servitude on the use of the object by those who purchase from the first purchaser (this is known as privity of contract). Henry Hansmann and Marina Santilli provide an economic explanation for moral rights for art but not for other objects. Because the value of art depends on the artist's oeuvre, the alteration of an artist's work has a reputational externality (typically negative). By granting the artist a moral right to protect his/her reputation, this benefits, not just the individual artist, but other owners of the artist's work, as well. Hansmann and Santilli discusses the importance of copyright doctrine in performing a similar role, and consider many other details of the law, including inalienability of artist rights and why it is often legal to destroy a work of art but not to alter it.

## I. Introduction

In many nations, including most of western Europe, the law has long recognized interests of authors and artists in their work that are separate from copyright and that can be retained by an author or artist even after he has transferred his copyright to another person or persons and (in the case of visual arts, such as painting or sculpture) has also parted with the physical work of art itself. Principal among these legally recognized interests are four distinct rights that are commonly referred to collectively as authors' and artists' "moral rights": the right of *integrity,* under which the artist can prevent alterations in his work; the right of *attribution* or *paternity,* under which the artist can insist that his work be distributed or displayed only if his name is connected with it; the right of *disclosure,* under which the artist can refuse to expose his work to the public before he feels it is satisfactory; and the right of *retraction* or *withdrawal,* under which the artist can withdraw his work even after it has left his hands. Most countries that recognize these rights make them, to a greater or lesser degree, inalienable.

In contrast, the common-law countries, including conspicuously the United States, historically not only have failed to make explicit provision for such continuing rights of artists in their work but have legal regimes that effectively render unenforceable any effort by an individual artist to craft and retain such rights in his own creations after he has transferred the other elements of ownership. Thus, patterns of rights that are mandatory under the civil-law regimes of Europe have been forbidden by the common law. This is in strong contrast to the usual relationship between these two legal systems: in general, the common law is far more hospitable to the creation of divided property rights than is the civil law.

These differing views of authors' and artists' rights are often presented as a basic distinction between the intellectual property law regimes found in the civil-law countries and those found in the common-law countries. They have long been a subject of considerable debate and controversy, and increasingly so in recent years as the United States and the European Community have struggled to determine whose policies concerning intellectual property will dominate the international legal order. One important focus of this controversy has been the Berne Convention on Copyright, originally drafted in 1886, which requires that signatory countries provide protection for moral rights, including particularly the rights of paternity and integrity. For more than 100 years the United States refused to sign the Berne Convention, in part because of objections to the moral rights clause. Then, in 1989, the United States reversed its position and signed, claiming that U.S. law had evolved to the point where it could be construed, as a whole, to provide the minimal protection for artists' moral rights required by the Convention – and noting further that, even if U.S. law did not provide this minimum protection, other signatory countries were also not in compliance, yet nobody had ever objected.

Many commentators have long argued that, to bring the United States more closely into compliance with the Berne Convention, to establish greater harmony between U.S. law and that of the European Community, and to improve the status of authors and artists, the law in the United States should be reformed to provide greater protection for authors' and artists' moral rights. Partly in response to these pressures, various laws extending these rights have been enacted over the past two decades. At least 11 states now explicitly recognize moral rights in greater or lesser degree, and in 1989 Congress enacted the federal Visual Artists Rights Act (VARA), which makes provision for the rights of integrity and attribution. Moreover, even in the absence of specific legislation, American courts have at times offered protection for interests analogous to moral rights through extension of common-law rights or through expansive interpretation of particular statutory rights, such as the trademark laws. Still, it is often argued that more should be done.

Interest in this subject is also high outside the United States. The scope of artists' moral rights varies considerably from one European country to another – with France being generally the most expansive – thus leading to debates as to which regime is superior and to difficulties in harmonizing law among the member states of the European Union. Moreover, within individual European countries there is often considerable controversy about the precise interpretation to be given existing statutory and decisional law concerning artists' moral rights.

Although there already exists an extensive legal literature on moral rights, that literature largely lacks systematic analysis from an economic point of view. In this essay we seek to fill that gap. Our principal objective is not to advance specific normative proposals but rather to clarify debate on the subject, exploring the functions served by moral rights and illuminating the pros and cons of various doctrinal alternatives. We also seek, more broadly, to offer insight into the general functions served by copyright doctrine and into the character and role of the general rules of law, found in all jurisdictions, that severely limit the possibilities for creating divided property rights.

. . .

. . . . We begin [our discussion] with the right of integrity, which is both the most important of the moral rights from a practical standpoint and the one that best illustrates the issues raised by moral rights in general. For economy of expression, we shall generally use the term "artists" throughout to refer collectively to both visual artists (such as painters and sculptors) and to authors of literary works.

## II. The Right of Integrity

The right of integrity is described in the Berne Convention as follows: "Independently of the author's economic rights, and even after the transfer of said rights, the author shall have the right . . . to object to any distortion, mutilation, or other modification of, or other derogatory action in relation to, the said work, which would be prejudicial to his honor or reputation."

A prototypical, and famous, application of the right of integrity involved a refrigerator that was painted by the French artist Bernard Buffet and contributed by him to a charity auction. The individual who purchased the refrigerator proceeded to cut it into six panels that he intended to sell separately, evidently to increase its resale value. Buffet sued the purchaser of the refrigerator to prevent the selling of his dismembered work, invoking his right of integrity under French law, and won his case.

Similar protection was not generally available under American law prior to the recent state and federal enactments. A prominent example involves a massive mobile by Alexander Calder that was purchased at an exhibition by a private collector and then donated to the Pittsburgh airport. The airport repainted the black and white sculpture in green and gold – the colors of Allegheny County – and also, over Calder's protests, altered the orientation of the sculpture's elements and soldered them to prevent movement. For the remaining 18 years of his life, Calder sought to have the work restored to its original state but was unsuccessful.

In the civil-law countries, the right of integrity applies not just to painting, sculpture, and the other visual arts but also to literary works. This is in contrast to the United States, where recent federal and state legislation recognizing moral rights has generally been confined to the visual arts. In the discussion that follows, we focus largely on the application of the right of integrity to the visual arts, and particularly to painting, sculpture, and other forms of artistic expression in which the work of art is primarily embodied in a single unique object rather than (as in the case of movies) in multiple reproductions. We have chosen this focus because unique works of art illustrate most clearly the functions served by the right of integrity and because for literary works . . . copyright doctrine serves (at least in the United States) many of the same functions that might otherwise be served by the right of integrity. Most of our analysis, however, applies to literary works as well as to the visual arts.

## A. CREATING DIVIDED PROPERTY RIGHTS

Jurisdictions that recognize the right of integrity give artists continuing property rights in their work. Thus, even after a painter has sold one of his paintings, and that painting has subsequently been resold again several times over, the artist can still take legal action directly against the current owner if that owner seeks to alter the painting in ways inconsistent with the artist's right of integrity. Absent the doctrine of moral rights, it would not be possible, in general, for an artist to retain such a continuing interest in his work after its sale. Under both European and American contract law, a seller of a chattel generally cannot reserve rights in the chattel, of either an affirmative or a negative character, that are enforceable against subsequent purchasers even if those purchasers have notice of the initial seller's intention to reserve such rights. (Of course, by means of contract, a seller can retain rights against the initial purchaser, with whom he is in privity of contract.) Moral rights legislation changes this rule in the case of works of art, permitting the artist, in effect, to maintain a continuing negative servitude in his work, analogous to the servitudes that can be created in real property in both civil-law and common-law systems.

The law's general prohibition on servitudes in chattels is not difficult to rationalize on efficiency grounds. It seems unlikely that such servitudes would often be valuable: sellers of objects do not generally have important interests, separate from and stronger than those of other persons, that could be affected by the use of the object in the hands of subsequent owners. At the same time, servitudes can seriously impede the use and transferability of property, since they impose on owners the burden of keeping track of any servitudes and, when a use inconsistent with a servitude seems worthwhile, of locating and negotiating with the owner of the servitude to seek permission.

The law's willingness to enforce easements, covenants, and equitable servitudes on real property, where the benefit of the servitude "touches and concerns" neighboring property, presumably reflects (1) the potentially large advantages in coordinating the uses of parcels of property that are, by their nature, bound in a spatial relationship to each other regardless of their separate ownership, (2) the relatively low costs to the owner of the burdened parcel of remaining informed of the burden, and (3) the ease of obtaining release when that is desirable. Similarly, the few special cases in which the law permits the enforcement of servitudes on chattels – such as security interests in personal property or resale price maintenance – arguably involve circumstances in which (1) unrestricted use of the burdened chattel by subsequent purchasers threatens substantial harm to the person enjoying the benefit of the servitude, (2) subsequent purchasers can easily be put on notice of the servitude, and (3) it is not too difficult for subsequent purchasers to obtain release from the servitude where appropriate.

If the right of integrity can be rationalized as a reasonable exception to the general prohibition on servitudes in chattels, presumably it is because similar conditions are met. In particular, it must be true that the actions of current owners of works of art can seriously affect the interests of the artists who created those works or of other persons. Those interests are therefore worth examining with care.

## B. THE INTERESTS PROTECTED BY THE RIGHT OF INTEGRITY

It is frequently said that the interests protected by moral rights doctrine, and particularly by the right of integrity, are "personality" interests that are fundamentally different from the "economic" or "commercial" interests that are protected by the copyright, trademark, and right of publicity doctrines that, until recently, were the principal bodies of law governing the interests of artists in the United States. This characterization is reinforced by the language of the legislation in which moral rights are embodied, typified by the Berne Convention provision quoted above, which speaks of moral rights as being independent of "the author's economic rights." Although this characterization contains some truth, it also has its limitations. In particular, the interests protected by the right of integrity can have a distinctly commercial character, in the sense that the right can play an important role in protecting the market value of private property. Moreover, the right of integrity can serve to protect not just the pecuniary and nonpecuniary interests of the artist, but the interests – both pecuniary and nonpecuniary – of other persons as well.

### 1. Nonpecuniary interests of the artist

Physical alteration of an artist's work after the work has left the artist's hands, or prejudicial display of the work, can harm the artist in a variety of ways. The most direct is simply the subjective personal anguish the artist feels from seeing his work abused, quite apart from – and even in spite of – what anyone else might think about it. Thus, an artist may identify with his works as with his children: prize them for their present character and not want that character changed. . . .

For . . . these reasons, an artist may wish to maintain the integrity of his works after he has sold them, even if that reduces the value of the works to their current owners and to other prospective purchasers. The right of integrity permits an artist to do this. Moreover, at least where the right is waivable (an issue we discuss below), it encourages the artist to do so in a socially efficient manner. An artist who, for his own subjective reasons, casts his work in a form that is unpopular with potential purchasers, and retains his right of integrity to protect that form, will receive a lower initial sale price for the works as a consequence and thus will internalize the costs as well as the benefits of his choice.

All artisans, of course, presumably feel some attachment to their work and suffer when it is mutilated or mocked. Nevertheless, the law does not generally let them impose a servitude on their work preventing alteration or abuse. Why should the law treat artists more favorably? Perhaps because creators of those works we label "art," which are typically unique and highly individual works that require substantial skill and effort, commonly feel a peculiarly strong attachment of this sort.

Commentary on moral rights often, explicitly or implicitly, focuses on the potential for this type of subjective nonpecuniary harm as the principal justification for the right of integrity. And perhaps it is an adequate justification. We suspect, however, that much of the incentive for adopting moral rights legislation derives from other considerations, and particularly from the fact that those works we label "art" commonly involve important reputational externalities, thus giving both the artist and others an unusually strong interest in protecting the integrity of individual works.

## 2. Pecuniary interests of the artist

The language of the Berne Convention, and the similar language found in many nations' statutes, describes the right of integrity in terms of protection from actions that are "prejudicial to [the artist's] honor or reputation." This suggests that the right of integrity serves, in important part, to protect not just artists' personal feelings about their creations but rather (or in addition) their reputational interests. Those interests can, moreover, have a strongly pecuniary character.

In particular, alteration of works that an artist has already sold can, by damaging his reputation, lower the prices he can charge for other work that he sells subsequently. Buffet's refrigerator provides an example. The purchaser of the refrigerator evidently felt he could increase his total proceeds from resale of the work by subdividing it, so that he could sell the artist's name, as it were, six times. If much of the artist's work were cut up this way, however, his reputation as a whole could suffer. While the entire refrigerator of Buffet presumably had value as an artistic work in its own right, owning a mere panel of the refrigerator would probably have had value in large part just because the artist was known to have created other work of strong artistic value – which means, among other things, work that has a conceptual integrity, rather than just bits and pieces. Put differently, the seller of the refrigerator panels was, in an important sense, selling Buffet's other work. The same is true with the Calder mobile in the Pittsburgh airport. Given the fame of Calder's work as a whole, and given in particular the distinctive color schemes that have become familiar in Calder's work in general, the repainted mobile in the airport gains special notoriety. But, if all of Calder's work were altered and painted in such a fashion, that work – and hence Calder's name – would be less famous, and the prices Calder could charge for subsequent work would fall.

In effect, each of an artist's works is an advertisement for all of the others. The situation is analogous to a franchise. An individual franchisee has an incentive to skimp on quality, cutting his individual costs while still enjoying the reputation for high quality that is associated with the franchise in general. But, in doing so, he is free riding on the other franchisees and imposing a cost on them. For this reason, franchisors commonly impose strong quality standards on their individual franchisees. For the same reason, an artist has an interest in preventing the reputation of his work in general from being depreciated by the opportunistic adulteration of individual works. A franchisor, however, can protect his interests through his ongoing contractual relationship with his franchisee, whereas an artist does not have such a continuing contractual relationship with the purchasers of his work. Consequently, if the artist is to be given the same type of control, he must be given some device, such as the right of integrity, that goes beyond the tools generally available under the law of contracts.

Does it make sense for protection of this reputational interest to outlive the artist? Perhaps so, since his estate may well contain unsold works, and since the right of integrity may also serve to support the value of works by the artist, and of copyrights in his work, that are held by the artist's heirs.

## 3. Interests of other owners of the artist's work

Another way of describing the reputational interests just discussed is that, with a work of art such as a painting or a sculpture, there is other property – namely, the artist's other artistic creations – that constitutes a "dominant tenement" that benefits from the servitude imposed on the artist's work by the right of integrity. Damage to one of the artist's works, in effect, imposes external costs on the artist's other works.

Often a substantial portion of this other work will be in the hands, not of the artist himself, but of art collectors, galleries, and museums. By protecting the artist's reputation, the right of integrity therefore protects the interests of these other persons as well. Indeed, in the case of an artist whose productive career is finished and who has sold all of his works, it may be only these other persons whose pecuniary interests are protected by the right of integrity. Their interests, moreover, may last well past the artist's death and the expiration of the artist's copyrights.

. . .

## C. WHAT IS ART?

We have suggested here that an important function of the right of integrity is to protect the value of the artist's oeuvre as a whole – in effect, the artist's reputation – from opportunistic actions by the owners of individual works. With this in mind, we can discern two criteria for determining the type of work to which it is most appropriate to extend the right of integrity – that is, to determine for this purpose "What is art?" First, knowledge of the artist's name is considered informative or useful in assessing the work. Put in commercial terms, this means that the work of art sells for more if it can be attributed to the artist than if it is anonymous. Second, the reputation of the artist is, in turn, based on the entire body of work he has created.

Where the second element is missing, damage to one of an artist's works would not affect the value of the artist's other works. For example, where a person is famous for reasons unconnected to his art, it is possible that one of his paintings would sell for a large amount of money simply because of a reputation he acquired elsewhere – say, as a movie star or politician. In such a case, damage to one of the person's paintings might have no detrimental effect on his reputation in general and on the value of his other paintings in particular.

Clearly, at least in the twentieth century, much work that we term "art" meets the two criteria just suggested. This is reflected in the widespread concern for ascertaining the authenticity of works of art, in the sense of assuring that they are in fact the work of the individual to whom they are ascribed. There is much theorizing about why the identity of the artist has become so important in modern culture. For the present, we need not be concerned about the sources of the phenomenon but rather need only note its great contemporary importance in the field of art. Given this strong connection between the value of a work of art and the identity of the artist who created it, both the artist and the other owners of the artist's work have a special interest in protecting the "integrity" of the artist's work as a whole.

. . . .

In support of the view that reputational externalities are an important justification for the right of integrity, it is noteworthy that, in contrast to artists, inventors are generally not granted the right of integrity – even though inventors are highly creative and are otherwise given property rights in their inventions of a character similar to those given artists, and even though inventors are sometimes, like artists, granted the right of attribution. A plausible justification for this distinction between inventors and artists is that the marketability of an invention has little relationship to the personal identity of the inventor and, in particular, to the other items that the inventor has patented. That is, one of an individual's inventions generally does not gain higher value because he is known to have invented something else as well. It is important for Marconi that he invented the radio, hence the right of attribution; it is not important for the radio that Marconi invented it, hence no right of integrity.

## D. DESTRUCTION OF ART WORKS

A particularly interesting problem in defining the scope of the right of integrity, and one that illustrates nicely some of the conflicting interests affected by that right, involves the destruction of works of art. Although alteration or mutilation of works of visual art may be infringements of the right of integrity in the civil-law countries, complete destruction of a work of art generally is not. VARA's right of integrity also does not extend to complete destruction, except for works of "recognized stature."

Putting their financial interests aside, in general artists, whether they are successful or not, presumably would prefer not to have their work destroyed, even after they have sold the work. The public at large – that is, persons who do not personally own one of the artist's works – presumably are also best served in general by preservation of all of the work of an established artist and are unaffected one way or the other by destruction of the work of artists who will never have a substantial reputation.

From a pecuniary point of view, however, an artist's interests are more ambiguous, as are those of other owners of the artist's works. On the one hand, as we have noted, each of an artist's works serves as an advertisement for the others, and its merits also tend to be reflected positively, by association, in the value of the artist's other works. In this respect, then, destruction of one of an artist's works reduces the value of the others – including works not yet sold or even produced by the artist. On the other hand, destruction of one of an artist's works increases the scarcity value of the others, and in this respect tends to increase their market value. We cannot say with certainty, therefore, whether destruction of one of an artist's works will have, on net, a negative or positive effect on the financial welfare of the artist and of other owners of his work.

In addition to these sometimes conflicting interests, there are also the costs of preserving a work of art. Where, as is true in the vast majority of cases, the artist in question will never establish a reputation of any significance, and her work will never have a meaningful resale market, the costs of preserving her work could well exceed any modest reputational benefits that preservation would yield. It is presumably for this reason that VARA limits its right against destruction to works of "recognized stature." But, so limited, the fight against destruction may be largely empty, since rarely would the owner of a work of "recognized stature" have an incentive to destroy it. VARA may therefore, in practice, be little different from the right of integrity as commonly construed in the civil-law countries, where it provides no protection at all against complete destruction of a work of art.

If effect, the civil-law countries leave the owner of a work of art with a simple dichotomous choice. They can preserve the work unaltered, either keeping it for their personal enjoyment or selling it to someone who values it more, or they can destroy it. They have an incentive to follow the latter course only if the costs of preserving the work exceed the benefit of the work to any potential purchaser. Since the potential purchasers include the artist himself, this helps assure – though it does not guarantee – that works will be destroyed if and only if that is the efficient course.

## E. DOCTRINAL ALTERNATIVES TO THE RIGHT OF INTEGRITY

There are other doctrines that serve as potential alternatives to the right of integrity.

### 1. Copyright

By permitting authors and artists to reserve a continuing property right in expressive works they create, the law of copyright, like moral rights doctrine, establishes an exception to the general prohibition on servitudes in property other than real estate.

The conventional justification for the law of copyright is that it transforms what would otherwise be a public good – the ability to copy an author's work – into a private good, and in so doing creates stronger incentives for authors to create new works. But the law of copyright goes substantially further than this. By imposing appropriate restrictions on her transfers of copyright, the author of a literary work can not only establish a property right in all copies made of her work but also exercise substantial control over the quality of those copies. That is to say, modern copyright law permits an author to subdivide her copyright, retaining some aspects of it and transferring others. Only the particular rights transferred can be exercised by the transferee or, more important for the subject at hand, retransferred by the transferee to a third party. In particular, an author can decline to transfer the right to alter the work or to adapt it (for example, for a movie), insisting that it be reproduced only in its original form, and this restriction on the rights transferred will bind any subsequent third-party transferees of the copyright as well. Indeed, unless there is contrary language in the contract, when an author assigns the copyright in her work, the law assumes that she reserves the right to approve of any modifications in that work that are not clearly necessary and appropriate for the purpose for which the assignment was undertaken. Copyright therefore permits the author of a literary work to protect herself in very substantial degree against any harm she might suffer from alteration of her work.

Copyright law also permits an author to protect herself in some degree from injury that might result from prejudicial presentation of her work – that is, to control the context in which her work is published. For example, an author of short stories who does not wish her work to be published in anthologies where it might be associated or compared with works by certain other authors could transfer the copyright to publish the story in collections of the author's own stories, but not in anthologies.

The law of copyright could have been constructed narrowly to give an author a monopoly in her original creation without giving her control over the ways in which that monopoly is exploited once it has been transferred to other persons. That is, the law could have required that, if she transfers her copyright, she must transfer it in its entirety. One reason why modern copyright law permits an author to subdivide her copyright, retaining portions of it and transferring the rest, is evidently that this facilitates the assignment of different types of reproduction rights to different specialized publishers – say, hardcover book rights to a publisher and film rights to a movie production company. Another important reason, how-

ever, is presumably that this ability of an author to limit the authority she grants to transferees of her copyright permits her to protect herself against the harms she can suffer from
misuse of her work. Whether such protection was an intended purpose or simply a by-
product of the divisibility of copyright, the law of copyright as presently structured permits
authors of literary works to avoid the same types of harm to which the right of integrity is
addressed.

A separate right of integrity therefore offers only modest additional protection to authors of
literary works. That additional protection comes, where it exists at all, principally in one of
three forms. First, it permits broader control than does copyright over the contexts in which
work is presented to the public. For example, in Italy the right of integrity has been interpreted
to permit a composer and singer who was known for his environmentalism to prevent an
assignee of the copyright in his songs from selling cassettes containing those songs in conjunction with environmentally harmful detergent. In the United States, in contrast, copyright law
has been interpreted not to permit a songwriter to exert control over the products to which
purchasers of his recordings could tie those recordings when marketing them.

Second, even where a statutory right of integrity does not permit an author to retain rights
that he could not otherwise retain through conditions on his grants of copyright, it effectively inserts a default term in all assignments of copyright imposing such conditions unless
the author specifically waives or transfers them – hence reducing contracting costs and
avoiding inadvertent transfers of rights that most authors might wish to retain. Third, where
the right of integrity is inalienable, that right in effect imposes a term in the assignment of
copyright that is not merely a default term but a mandatory term.

Although painters, sculptors, and other visual artists can retain copyright in their works
even after they have sold the original, that copyright covers principally reproductions; it gives
the artist much less control over the uses made of his original painting or sculpture once that
object is sold by the artist. As a consequence, copyright is more useful to authors of literary
works than it is to visual artists as a means of controlling the way in which their work is
presented to the public. For example, while an author of a short story can license publication
rights to the story in collections of the author's own works while declining to permit
anthologizing of the work with stories by other authors, a painter cannot sell his painting
subject to the condition that it be displayed publicly only in shows confined to the artist's
own works. . . . [C]opyright for works of visual art might have been constructed more
flexibly, to incorporate display rights. As it is, however, so far as the law of copyright is
concerned, when an artist sells his original work of art he sells all rights concerning its
display to the current owner of the work and cannot impose servitudes on that right.

The situation is somewhat more ambiguous when it comes to alterations of the original
work of art itself. Serious alterations could be construed to involve the creation of an
"adaptation" or a "derivative work of art" as those terms are used in copyright law. Since the
right to create adaptations or derivative works is among the interests protected by copyright,
a visual artist who reserves all of his copyright in his work can prevent alterations of the
work that constitute an adaptation or derivative work, and this right is enforceable against all
subsequent purchasers of the artist's original work of art. The division of Buffet's refrigerator into six separate panels, for example, would arguably constitute the creation of derivative
work, as would the reconfiguration and repainting of Calder's mobile by the Pittsburgh
airport. A separate right of integrity, therefore, might be unnecessary to protect artists
against the kinds of abuse involved in these situations.

One reason why Calder was unsuccessful in obtaining a remedy against the Pittsburgh airport, presumably, was that he had not retained his copyright in the mobile and thus had given up his right to prevent creation of adaptations or derivative works based on it. . . .

## 2. Trademark law

Some of the interests protected by a right of integrity also receive protection in the United States under state and federal trademark law, and particularly under a catchall provision of the Lanham Act (the federal trademark statute) that outlaws false representations of goods or services. For example, the British comedy group Monty Python was able to invoke the latter provision to enjoin a U.S. television network from broadcasting a bowdlerized version of some of their television sketches, on the grounds that the broadcast could injure their reputation. Since reputational interests are arguably the most important of the interests protected by the right of integrity, there is substantial logic in this approach.

. . .

## H. INALIENABILITY

It appears that every jurisdiction that recognizes the right of integrity places restrictions on the artist's ability to alienate that right. Those restrictions typically take one of two forms. First, there are jurisdictions, such as France, that make the right of integrity completely inalienable. Second, there are jurisdictions, such as the United States and England, that make the right nontransferable but waivable.

We shall examine these two regimes here in reverse order. Although our discussion is confined to the right of integrity, much of the analysis applies as well to the other moral rights, which in any given country are typically covered by the same restrictions on alienability that apply to the right of integrity.

### 1. Rights that are nontransferable but waivable

Some countries grant artists a right of integrity that is nontransferable yet at the same time explicitly or implicitly permit artists to waive that right. Although this might at first seem contradictory, the resulting regime is quite coherent.

England offers a particularly clear example. By statute, English law specifically grants to artists moral rights, including the right of integrity, that are "not assignable." The statute also provides, however, that an artist can freely "waive" his moral rights, in whole or in part, so long as the waiver is in writing. Moreover, if this waiver is "made in favor of the owner or prospective owner of the copyright in the work or works to which it relates," it is transferable to the latter's licensees or successors in title.

The intent and effect of this English statute, it appears, is several. First, it permits an artist, if he wishes, to retain a right of integrity in his work whose burden runs with the work even after he has sold the work itself and the copyright to it. To the extent that these rights exceed those that could be reserved through retention of part or all of the artist's copyright, the right of integrity gives the artist powers to control uses of his work, through imposition of servitudes on it, that could not be constructed with the tools of contracting available in the common law.

Second, even to the extent that the right of integrity overlaps with rights that could be retained through limitations on the author's assignment of copyright, the separate statutory right of integrity creates a default rule under which, unless the right of integrity is specifically waived in whole or in part, it is presumed that the author retains the right to object to uses of his work that would violate that right even if he has assigned his copyright. If, as we have suggested, uses that would violate the right of integrity are generally inefficient uses of the work, then it can be assumed that artists in general would wish to prohibit such uses, and reading such a term into assignments of copyright will save contracting costs.

Third, by making the right "not assignable" but waivable, the statute is evidently seeking to bar the transfer of the right of integrity – that is, the right to object to mistreatment of the artist's work – to parties other than the current owner of the copyright to the work. The latter bar is not imposed, it seems, because there could never be good reason for a third party to have the power to enforce the right of integrity. As argued above, owners of other works by the artist, and also members of the public at large, can have an important interest in preventing alteration or other misuse of an artist's work. Rather, the bar is evidently posed to prevent a fragmentation of ownership rights in the work of art that, through high trans-action costs and holdouts, could frustrate valuable uses of the work.

Moreover, the latter bar seems unlikely to prevent arrangements that offer important efficiencies. For example, it would not seem to prevent a painter from transferring to a trustee both his copyright and his moral rights in paintings he has sold, to be exercised by the trustee for the combined benefit of both the artist (or his estate) and other owners of the artist's works. Consequently, it is not surprising that all legal regimes that recognize the right of integrity apparently make that right (and other moral rights they recognize) nonassignable to third parties who lack a copyright in the work.

## 2. Full inalienability

In some countries (France being the most extreme example), the right of integrity is made entirely inalienable. In effect, this does not mean that an artist cannot consent to acts that would violate his right of integrity, but rather that he cannot bind himself to such a waiver – that is, he cannot enter into an enforceable agreement not to change his mind in the future and seek a judicial remedy for the violation.

a. *Protecting the artist.* A popular explanation for making moral rights inalienable is that this protects the artist against exploitation by those to whom he sells his work, who may have greater "bargaining power." It is now a familiar point, however, that if individuals are well informed, one cannot make them better off by refusing to enforce contracts they might choose to enter into. Consequently, such an explanation for inalienability requires some further assumptions if it is to be persuasive. In particular, it is persuasive only if (*a*) artists commonly undervalue the benefits they derive from the right of integrity and, (*b*) for most artists, waiving the right of integrity would be inefficient (that is, the value of waiver to the owner of an artist's work would generally be less than the injury that the artist would suffer from waiver). Absent condition *a,* artists can safely be left to decide for themselves when to waive the right; absent condition *b,* the better solution to the informational problem described in *a* would be a regime with no right of integrity (for instance, forced waiver).

Whether condition *b* holds depends on the scope given the right of integrity – a question we shall return to below. What about condition *a?* While, lacking extensive empirical data, one cannot say anything definitive, it would seem surprising if it were true. At least if, as in the British system, waiver must be explicit and in writing, then it is hard to believe that the average artist could not make an intelligent judgment about the costs and benefits of granting a waiver.

. . .

b. *Protecting third parties.* The fact that third parties – other owners of an artist's work, and the public at large – may benefit from the artist's right of integrity arguably makes a stronger case for unwaivability than does the paternalistic argument just discussed. If the artist could waive his right of integrity, he might do so in situations where waiver would be worthwhile for him but not for third parties - for example, . . . toward the end of his productive career. Of course, the extent of protection granted third parties by inalienability is limited, since the artist generally has the sole right to enforce the right during his lifetime, and third parties have no power to compel him to enforce the right. Nevertheless, the artist's inability to grant a binding waiver is likely to inhibit many owners from acts that would clearly violate the integrity right.

Moreover, artists themselves may have an interest in being bound not to waive their right of integrity, since the consequence could be an increase in the prices they receive for their works in general. Purchasers of an artist's work might value some reassurance that the artist has committed himself never to compromise his reputation; consequently, they might be willing to pay more for the work of an artist who has done so. Such a commitment is difficult to make by ordinary contractual means, however: its benefit – that is, the ability to enforce the commitment – will not run to subsequent purchasers of the artist's work, and even the initial purchaser who personally obtains such a commitment from the artist will have no ability to nullify any subsequent waiver that the artist enters into contrary to his promise but rather will have recourse only to damages from the artist as a remedy for the latter's breach. By making the right of integrity unwaivable, in contrast, the law makes the commitment not to waive much more credible.

### 3. Degrees of waivability

Potential doctrinal approaches to waivability of the right of integrity span a broad spectrum. We have just considered one extreme, in which the right is entirely inalienable. . . . .

English law presents an intermediate point on the spectrum: moral rights are presumed to be retained by the artist unless specifically waived, but can be waived to any extent the artist desires. . . . .

### 4. How broadly to interpret the right of integrity?

As we have already suggested, it makes sense to make the right of integrity unwaivable only if waiver of the right would generally be inefficient. But the general inefficiency of waiver depends, in turn, on how broad the right is. If, on the one hand, we interpret the right of integrity to extend to any alteration whatsoever of a work of art, then making the fight unwaivable may well prevent many potentially efficient transactions. On the other hand, if the right of integrity is interpreted as extending only to "abusive" or "degrading" modifications or uses, or to "mutilation" of the work, then, almost by definition, waiver would be inefficient.

This suggests that it makes sense to turn the issue around: in regimes where the right of integrity is made unwaivable, it is appropriate to interpret the right narrowly to cover only uses or abuses of an artist's work that would clearly be inefficient. In effect, there is a choice here ... between a tort-type rule and a property-type rule. An unwaivable right that is narrowly formulated looks more like a tort-type rule, providing a cause of action for any unreasonable (inefficient) alteration of the work. Under a property-type rule, in contrast, a broad range of alterations can be made enjoinable, and it can be left to the artist, via waiver, to decide which particular alterations will be permitted.

Note that, even with a narrow tort-type right of integrity that is unwaivable, there is still potentially room for substantial contracting between an artist and the owners of his work concerning treatment of the artist's work. As we have observed above, an artist's copyright – in particular, the right to create adaptations or derivative works – gives artists the right to object to uses of his work that might not be sufficiently derogatory to constitute violations of the right of integrity. By deciding what, if any, types of adaptations or derivative works he will license, an individual artist can choose for himself how much protection he wishes to have beyond that afforded simply by the right of integrity.

. . . .

# VII. Conclusion

For observers sophisticated in economic analysis, the recent spread of moral rights doctrine from the civil-law systems to the common-law systems might at first seem regressive – a well-intentioned but ultimately misguided and counterproductive effort to protect artists and artworks by imposing paternalistic restrictions on contracts and property rights. Perhaps there is some truth to such a characterization. But there is an important sense in which moral rights doctrine *expands* freedom of contract in intellectual property, since it permits the creation of divided property rights – servitudes on chattels – that could not be formed under the conventional law of property and contract. Those servitudes can potentially serve a useful role in the field of fine arts, particularly in controlling reputational externalities.

In common-law countries such as the United States, the law of copyright alone, even without the addition of special moral rights doctrine, gives authors and artists sufficient flexibility to protect themselves from many of the harms to which moral rights are addressed. This is particularly true where manipulation of the work involves the creation of reproductions. The potential contribution of moral rights doctrine is therefore more conspicuous where copyright does not reach, such as the display of original works of painting and sculpture. At the same time, the overlap between moral rights and copyright emphasizes the extent to which copyright itself serves to give authors and artists continuing control over the way in which their work is exploited and, hence, over their reputation.

# Part IV

Contracts and Warranties

# 11

## A Theory of the Consumer Product Warranty

### George L. Priest

**EDITOR'S INTRODUCTION**

In most cases, warranties on automobile engines, computers, etc. are standard-form contracts where one side, typically the manufacturer, writes the contract, and the other side must accept if the item is purchased. There is no explicit bargaining back and forth. Does this resemble the bargaining for mutual gain described by Coase or does this resemble monopoly exploitation? In this article, George Priest compares the exploitation theory, signaling theory, and investment theory explanations of warranty terms. The exploitation theory argues that warranties are a way for monopolist suppliers of goods to extort wealth from consumers. The signaling theory suggests that strong warranties credibly tell the consumer that the product is reliable. What Priest calls the "investment" theory is a detailed application of Cooter's model of precaution to warranty contracts. Here investment or precaution by the consumer might mean more careful use or less use, while investment by the manufacturer might include more durable parts. Optimal warranties would suggest that scratches to the exterior paint surface would not be under warranty once a car left the showroom because the car owner would be best at preventing such damage (although the manufacturer could provide more scratch-resistant surfaces), while the cooling system would be warranted from leaks for a year or more because the manufacturer's input would be more important than the car owner's input, unless the consumer tried to open up the air conditioner, in which case, the warranty would be void. Priest shows that the investment theory explains warranties better than the signaling or exploitation theories. For example, he shows that monopolists would not exploit consumers through poor warranty terms, but rather through higher prices. With regard to empirical evidence, purchasers with market power (e.g., laundromats) often have less warranty protection than individual consumers and for good economic reasons (washing machines in laundries are much more likely to be used intensively).

Consumer product warranties are our most common of written contracts, but little is known about what determines their content or how they relate to the reliability and the durability of goods. Since the first appearance of standardized warranties early in this century, two theories have been proposed to explain their role in sales transactions. The first emphasizes the absence of bargaining over warranty provisions. It views warranties as devices of manufacturers to exploit consumers by unilaterally limiting legal obligations. The second and more recent theory focuses on the difficulty consumers face at the time of purchase in estimating the risk of product defects. This theory regards express warranties as messages signaling the mechanical attributes of goods. Both theories have influenced substantially judicial and legislative responses to product warranties. The view of the warranty as an exploitative device has provided crucial support to the policy of enterprise liability and the replacement of contract principles with tort principles in product defect cases. In addition, the exploitation theory is the intellectual basis for the modern judicial treatment of consumer warranty issues, in particular for the expansive interpretation of warranties implied by law, for the elimination of the requirement of privity of contract, and for the restriction of the manufacturer's authority to limit available remedies or to disclaim general obligations. More recently, the signal theory has informed the design of the federal Magnuson-Moss Warranty Act, which directly regulates both the form and content of consumer product warranties.

Neither the exploitation nor the signal theory, however, has contributed to the understanding of warranty practices. The exploitation theory derives from the presupposition of overwhelming manufacturer market power, but the connection remains vague between the extent of market power and the specific definition of warranty coverage. Similarly, the signal theory derives from the assumption of consumer misperception of product risks. However plausible this assumption as a general matter, consumer perceptions are very difficult to identify or to measure. As a consequence, hypotheses concerning the relationship between perceptions and specific warranty provisions are highly speculative and essentially nonfalsifiable.

This article proposes a new theory of the standardized warranty and of the determinants of the content of the warranties of individual products. The first Part reviews in more detail the exploitation and signal theories and their observable implications. Part II presents the theory itself. A warranty is viewed as a contract that optimizes the productive services of goods by allocating responsibility between a manufacturer and consumer for investments to prolong the useful life of a product and to insure against product losses. According to the theory, the terms of warranty contracts are determined solely by the relative costs to the parties of these investments. An insurance function of warranty coverage, of course, is well known. The novelty of the theory is its emphasis on the variety of allocative investments that consumers may make to extend productive capacity and its consideration of the difficulties of drafting warranty contracts to encourage such investments.

The third Part compares the investment theory of the article with the exploitation and signal theories in a review of the content of sixty-two consumer product warranties. Although more comprehensive and detailed data are needed for a confident judgment, the review demonstrates that the content of these various warranties is generally more consistent with the implications of the investment theory than of the exploitation or signal theory. . . .

## I. The Implications of the Exploitation and Signal Theories for Warranty Practices

During the last four decades, most approaches to consumer warranty issues by courts and legislatures have accepted the presuppositions of either the exploitation or signal theory. This Part defines the two theories and their implications and reviews the empirical evidence that has led to their acceptance.

## A. THE EXPLOITATION THEORY

Standardized product warranties were first introduced, apparently, in the last decades of the nineteenth century. Initially, these warranties were treated as normal contracts. The principles of nineteenth-century contract law derived from a view of the contract as an arms-length exchange between informed and competent parties. Because of its standardized character, no bargaining between the parties or adjustment of the terms of warranty contracts occurred. As a consequence, throughout the early decades of the twentieth century, courts vacillated between enforcing warranties strictly as normal contracts and enforcing them selectively according to other conceptions of the exchange.

Although common themes appear in early treatments, a coherent and persuasive theory of the standardized warranty first developed in the extensive literature and case law that followed Friedrich Kessler's celebrated manifesto, *Contracts of Adhesion – Some Thoughts about Freedom of Contract*. According to the theory, a standardized contract is unique principally because its terms are drafted unilaterally by the seller and only involuntarily "adhered to" by the consumer. The seller possesses "unfettered discretion" to incorporate terms that serve its interests because its bargaining position is superior to that of the consumer. In some industries, the manufacturer's superior position stems from the forces of natural monopoly. In others, firms gain power by unleashing corporate weapons such as patents or tying arrangements. Kessler, in fact, believed that standardized contracts themselves were "devices to build up and strengthen industrial empires," contributing to what he viewed as the "innate trend of competitive capitalism toward monopoly."

[According to Kessler,] even in industries with multiple sellers, . . . all warranties are alike or substantially similar so that the consumer "is not in a position to shop around for better terms." Some manufacturers directly collude in establishing warranty terms. Trade associations standardize warranty practices to achieve the same result. Thus, whether there is one seller or many, the consumer possesses no meaningful choice. In Kessler's words, the consumer's "contractual intention is but a subjection more or less voluntary to terms dictated by the stronger party."

The exploitation theory predicts, in general, that manufacturers will limit their legal obligations to consumers as much as possible. If collusion is widespread, then warranties within individual industries are likely to be similar. It also would be consistent with the assumptions of the theory, however, for the terms of coverage to be correlated with the degree of manufacturer market power. . . .

. . . More recent statements of the theory emphasize the marketing power gained from coordinating advertising that makes extravagant promises to consumers with warranties that disclaim responsibility for the promises. . . .

The exploitation theory found wide acceptance in part because it was the only coherent explanation of standardized warranties until the 1970s. The theory also seemed consistent with descriptions of warranty practices. . . .

The most convincing evidence to support the exploitation theory . . . arose from case histories of warranty practices. Courts were asked repeatedly to give effect to warranty provisions that they interpreted as exploitative. In the case of *Henningsen v. Bloomfield Motors, Inc. 32 N.J. 358* involving serious personal injury from an allegedly defective automobile, the terms of the warranty at issue disclaimed the implied warranty of merchantability, excluded consequential damages, and limited warranty remedies to repair or replacement of the defective part as long as the victim had prepaid transport charges for the part. The New Jersey Supreme Court remarked, "It is difficult to imagine . . . a less satisfactory remedy. . . . An instinctively felt sense of justice cries out against such a sharp bargain." In a decision that has been followed by virtually all other American jurisdictions, the court embraced the exploitation theory and refused to enforce the terms of the standardized warranty.

## B. THE SIGNAL THEORY

The signal theory of the consumer product warranty maintains that warranty terms provide information to consumers about the mechanical reliability of the product. The signal theory builds upon a growing economic literature that examines the "market for information" and views the warranty as a tool consumers can use to "process" information about products. According to the theory, a consumer finds it excessively costly to determine precisely product reliability at the time of purchase by direct inspection of the product. A consumer, however, may look to the warranty as a "signal" of product reliability because reliability is correlated negatively with the costs of warranty coverage; that is, the more reliable the product, the lower the costs of warranty coverage for the manufacturer, and the more extensive the coverage for the consumer. Thus, although a consumer has neither experience with nor knowledge of a product, he may infer its mechanical reliability by inspecting the terms of the warranty alone.

. . .

The signal theory has exerted substantial influence on consumer product warranty policy. The objective of the 1974 Magnuson-Moss Warranty Act is to make warranties more efficient signals. The Act requires manufacturers to redraft warranties in "simple and readily understood language," to disclose all important provisions "conspicuously," and to display warranties prominently so that they are available for consumer inspection prior to purchase of the product. The Act requires manufacturers to designate all express warranties as either "Full" (if they comply with certain minimum standards) or "Limited" (if they do not comply with those standards), in order to reduce the costs of comprehending warranty content. The drafters hoped that the pressures toward greater than average coverage would lead to universal compliance with Full warranty standards.

The Act's disclosure, availability, and designation requirements, however, affect only the central provisions of warranties. Subordinate provisions, which, according to the theory, consumers are less likely to comprehend, are subjected to direct regulation. The Act prohibits disclaimers of the implied warranties for all warranties, and expands consumer remedies and prohibits tying provisions for Full warranties.

## II. THE INVESTMENT THEORY OF WARRANTY

In this Part I develop a theory of the consumer product warranty based solely upon the relative costs to the consumer and manufacturer of investments to prolong productive capacity and to insure for product loses. I then define how warranty contracts are likely to be drafted in cases in which contract standardization reduces costs.

## A. THE BASIC THEORY DEFINED

. . .

In the common view, a warranty serves as both an insurance policy and a repair contract. As an insurance policy, a warranty provides that if, within a certain period, the product or some part of the product becomes defective, the manufacturer will compensate the buyer for the loss by repair, replacement, or refund of the purchase price. As a repair contract, a warranty fixes an obligation upon the manufacturer for some period of time to provide, without charge, services necessary to repair a defect in order to prolong the useful capacity of the product.

A warranty operates as an insurance policy to the extent that the occurrence of a product defect is probabilistic. To insure for a loss is to redistribute wealth from periods in which no losses are suffered to the period in which the loss occurs. A manufacturer can redistribute wealth in this manner by collecting a premium in the sale price from a broad set of consumers for whom the prospects of loss during any single period are unrelated. The market insurance premium reflects both the expected loss for the period and some share of the costs to the insurer of aggregating these unrelated contingencies, called loading costs. A consumer may prefer, however, some personal form of temporal wealth redistribution in the face of a loss. A consumer self-insures for product losses by accumulating savings for the replacement of defective products, by reserving future time for product repair, or, more simply, by expecting to tolerate a defect once it occurs. These methods of self-insurance, of course, also involve costs of transaction. As a general proposition, therefore, we may expect to observe market insurance in a warranty only where the sum of the expected loss and loading costs of market insurance is less than the sum of the expected loss and transaction costs of self-insurance.

As a repair contract, a warranty reflects the respective costs to the consumer and the manufacturer of repair services. Repair by the consumer and manufacturer are substitutes, and the consumer can be expected to purchase repair services as part of the warranty wherever the manufacturer's price is less than the consumer's cost of providing the repair himself. Obviously, a consumer can (and frequently does) provide many repair services more cheaply than a manufacturer. It is plausible, for example, that where shelves fall in a refrigerator, repair by the consumer is cheaper. . . . Thus, a warranty may be expected to allocate responsibility to the manufacturer for those types of repairs that most frequently are difficult or burdensome for consumers to provide themselves.

Although the above example, as well as most uses of the word "repair," refers to investments designed to return a product to a condition it enjoyed at some previous period of time, it is worthwhile to consider "repair service" to a product more broadly as any investment designed to optimize the performance of the product over time. Viewed in this light, for example, restraining young children from swinging on a refrigerator door represents an investment in a form of "repair" that may well be less costly than hiring a serviceman at a later date to install new hinges. Similarly, a manufacturer may anticipate future repair services by technological investments in the design of the product that make its operation less susceptible to interruption – designing brackets to hold refrigerator shelves more securely, for example – or by investments to control a consistent quality of production.

With respect to repair investments of this nature, however, a warranty serves a role beyond that of reducing transaction costs. The warranty promise establishes and enforces the obligation of the manufacturer to make investments in the design of the good or in quality control ... The warranty in this regard operates as a performance bond of the manufacturer. The value of the bond is equal to the costs to the manufacturer of defective product claims. As long as the manufacturer makes appropriate investments, the bond will not be forfeited. The decision to allocate repair investments of this nature between the manufacturer and consumer, however, is identical to the decision of who should bear typical repair costs. As before, we would expect the parties to allocate between themselves, according to relative costs, all investments in "repair," whether in the form of direct reconditioning services, of product design, or of a consumer's care for or maintenance of the product so as to extend its useful life.

It is evident that the various activities described as repair are substitutes for insurance. Repair, like insurance, is a means of reducing the magnitude of a loss from an unexpected event such as a defect. It is important now, however, to depart from the common view of the warranty and to distinguish more clearly between repair as a redistribution of wealth over time, like insurance, and repair as an allocative investment which alters the productive capacity of the good. The first example of repair – the reinstallation of the refrigerator shelves by the consumer – is a form of self-insurance for the loss. The owner bears the full cost of time and energy necessary to replace the shelves after the event occurs, which, in this case, appears to be cheaper than buying market insurance requiring the manufacturer to replace the shelves. But neither repair by the consumer nor by the manufacturer directly alters the probability of the loss occurring and, thus, is like insurance. The second example – restraining the child from swinging on the refrigerator door – is an allocative investment by a consumer that extends the useful life of the product by reducing the probability of a future loss. Certainly, the burdens of a parent increase as the discipline of children becomes more strict or specific. But, again, it may well be cheaper for a consumer to restrain his child than either to buy market insurance for repair of the door or to pay the manufacturer to design a refrigerator with hinges as sturdy as playground equipment.

Thus, in this terminology, a consumer's decision to accommodate himself to a scratch in the surface of an appliance is an example of self-insurance of the defect. The consumer's earlier efforts to reduce the likelihood of the scratch, for example, by increasing the level of his care or by isolating the appliance, is an allocative investment by the consumer. The manufacturer's promise in a warranty to repair the scratch after it occurs is market insurance. And the manufacturer's production decision to make the surface more resistant to abrasion is an example of an allocative investment by the manufacturer.

Self-insurance, market insurance, and allocative investments by consumers and manufacturers, therefore, are each substitute methods of reducing losses in order to optimize productive services. A consumer selects among these methods according to the relative prices and marginal productivities of each with respect to expected elements of product loss. As the price of market insurance rises, other things equal, the quantity of it demanded will decline, and the demand for self-insurance and for manufacturer or consumer allocative investments will increase. Similarly, as the cost of an allocative investment by the consumer rises – say, in our second example, by the addition of a child to the consumer's family, which makes it more difficult to reduce the probability of loss – the relative attractiveness of market insurance, self-insurance, or an allocative investment by the manufacturer is enhanced. These various ways of reducing product losses, however, may not be perfect substitutes. An individual is likely to select some combination of these four methods to optimize expected utility. For example, as the value of a consumer product or of the consumer's life increases – and, as a result, the potential risk from a defect increases – the consumer may increase consumption of each of the four.

A warranty in this view is the instrument that expresses consumer preferences for allocative or insurance investments. It is a contract that divides responsibility for allocative investments and insurance between the consumer and the manufacturer. The content of the contract is determined by the respective costs to the two parties of allocative investments or insurance. According to this approach, a manufacturer makes investments to prolong product life up to the point at which the marginal cost of such investments equals the marginal benefit. A manufacturer, then, offers market insurance for those losses or items of service for which market insurance is less costly than insurance or allocative investments by the consumer himself.

To the extent that a manufacturer disclaims liability or excludes or limits warranty coverage, however, it shifts to the consumer the obligation to make allocative investments to preserve the product or to self-insure for its loss. A disclaimer or an exclusion of coverage is the functional equivalent of provisions, common in other contracts, that explicitly require one of the parties to take certain actions to prevent breach or to insure for losses from uncertain events. The theory predicts that disclaimers of liability and exclusions of coverage will be observed in consumer product warranties for those specific allocative or insurance investments that the consumer can provide more cheaply than the manufacturer. In this view, disclaimers and exclusions can be said to be demanded by consumers because of the relative cheapness of consumer allocative investments or of self-insurance.

## III. An Empirical Examination of the Theories

This Part evaluates whether the exploitation, signal, or investment theory best explains the content of consumer product warranties . . .

. . .

### 1. The exploitation theory: Warranty coverage and manufacturer market power

According to the exploitation theory, manufacturers exercise their powerful market position by imposing one-sided warranty terms on weaker consumers.

A principal weakness of the exploitation theory is that it provides no theoretical link between market power and product warranty terms. Why would a firm with market power maximize its returns by offering one-sided warranty terms rather than by manufacturing shoddy goods or by charging a monopoly price? Generally, monopoly profits are maximized by selling a product identical in all respects (except price) to the product offered under competition. Thus, in theory, a monopolist (or a group of conspiring firms) will gain the greatest return by offering the consumer an optimal warranty, but at a price that exceeds marginal costs.

. . .

## 2. The commercial use exclusion

Product warranties commonly deny coverage altogether if the product is put to commercial, rather than to domestic use. Neither the exploitation nor the signal theory provides a plausible explanation of this exclusion. As a first approximation, the bargaining position of a commercial buyer is equivalent to that of a manufacturer, or at least is much less disparate than the bargaining position of a consumer. Yet it is the commercial buyer rather than the consumer who is excluded from coverage.

The exclusion of commercial use also seems inconsistent with the signal theory. The signal theory's fundamental implication . . . is that the relationship between warranty duration and service life expectancy is direct and positive and is a relationship upon which consumers can, with confidence, base their purchasing decisions.[1] If warranty terms signal the purely technological characteristics of a good at the time of purchase, then there is no reason to distinguish between domestic and commercial buyers. . . .

According to the investment theory, an exclusion from coverage reduces differences in risk between purchasers of a product. Commercial purchasers may subject a product both to a greater volume of use over a given period and to a greater intensity of use, especially where the product is rented to others, such as a washer or dryer at a laundromat. A person renting rather than owning a product is less likely to invest in "care" in order to optimize the productive life of the machine.

. . .

. . . The warranties of virtually all products terminate coverage if the consumer modifies or alters the product. Again, such a restriction has no apparent exploitative or signaling function. It is not implausible, however, that the consumer's decision to substitute his own design expertise for that of the manufacturer might lead to higher levels of product failure. . . .

. . .

## [3 .The investment theory]

I believe, that the investment theory explains warranty practices more comprehensively than either the exploitation or signal theory. The evidence tends to confirm that the allocation of responsibilities between manufacturers and different sets of consumers by standardized warranties is responsive to consumer preferences, and establishes coherent economic incentives for manufacturer and consumer investments to optimize productive services. Further research, of course, is required before a confident conclusion can be reached. . . .

## Conclusion

The superior predictive ability of the investment theory over the exploitation and signal theories could result from the greater empirical significance, at the margin, of the determinants of the investment theory. I do not believe, however, that sufficient evidence has been compiled to support such a conclusion. Rather, the superiority of the investment theory with respect to warranty content derives, in my view, from the nature of the determinants of the theories. The determinants of the investment theory are the costs of warranty coverage and differences in costs between consumers; the determinants of the exploitation theory, the relative bargaining position of manufacturers and consumers; and the determinants of the signal theory, the level of consumer information.

The determinants of the investment theory differ from the others in two important respects. First, the costs of warranty coverage are more easily defined and measured than either relative bargaining position or the quantum of consumer information. As a result, the investment theory's implications are likely to be both more precise and more readily verified or refuted. Market share and concentration measures, for example, are too crude to demonstrate any relationship between bargaining power and warranty content. Similarly, although it is admittedly costly for consumers to obtain information about product reliability, it is difficult to judge how costly it is and what alternative sources of information are available. The more specific implications of the signal theory thus have no verifiable basis. . . .

The second important advantage of the determinants of the investment theory over those of the alternative theories is that aspects of design, manufacture, and use of a product are more likely to be determined by costs than by relative bargaining position or consumer information. As a consequence, a theory based upon costs allows the immediate comparison of warranty practices to other production decisions and, thus, is more comprehensive than competing theories. It is the generality of costs as the determinant of warranty content that generates the rich and diverse implications of the investment theory.

## Note

1.  This statement has been moved from elsewhere in the article.

# 12

## Fixed-Price versus Spot-Price Contracts: A Study in Risk Allocation

### *A. Mitchell Polinsky*

#### EDITOR'S INTRODUCTION

Priest showed that contracts optimally allocate the prevention of damage between the two parties to the contract. Despite optimal precaution, bad outcomes may happen. Consequently, contracts may also allocate the risk of bad outcomes between the parties. Other things being equal, the less risk-averse side should bear the risk. Of course, the more risk-averse party must pay for being insured against risk. This is obvious when a homeowner purchases fire insurance – the risk-averse homeowner pays for risk-reduction.

Mitchell Polinsky considers a particular application of the allocation of risk – the choice between spot-price contracts and fixed-price contracts. In a spot-price contract, the price for future delivery of a good is based on the market price at the time of delivery. In a fixed-price contract, the price is set at the time of signing the contract. Polinsky shows that the relative riskiness of these contracts to the buyer and seller depends on whether the demand or supply curves are subject to risk. For example, if the supply curves of individual firms are shifting up and down in unison, a spot price (in comparison to a fixed price) is actually less risky for the suppliers as price goes up when their costs go up and goes down when their costs go down, so profits are relatively stable. At the same time, a fixed-price contract is less risky for the buyer. If instead, the individual demand curves were shifting up and down in unison and the supply curves for individual firms were constant, a fixed-price contract would be less risky for the seller and more risky for the buyer. Thus the choice between a spot-price and a fixed-price contract depends on which side is relatively risk-averse and whether demand or supply conditions are the source of uncertainty.

## 1. Introduction

When a seller and a buyer enter into a contract for the future delivery of some good, they can set the price to be paid in several ways. For example, they can specify the price in advance, which will be called a *fixed-price contract*. Or they can agree to the price prevailing in the spot market for the good on the date of delivery, which will be referred to as a *spot-price contract.* This article is concerned with the effects of these two contract forms on the allocation of risk between the parties when at least one of them is risk-averse. . . .

These and related contract forms are widely used in practice. For example, in a survey of members of the National Association of Purchasing Management, it was found that 90 percent used fixed-price contracts, 65 percent used "price at delivery" contracts (what I am calling spot-price contracts), and 50 percent used renegotiated price contracts (price adjustments only in unusual circumstances). Contracting practices in specific industries also illustrate the use of both fixed-price and spot-price contracts. In the natural gas industry, fixed-price contracts were common from 1930 through the 1950s, while contracts closely resembling spot-price contracts have been used frequently since then. In the uranium industry, fixed-price contracts were used occasionally until the early 1970s, while "market-price" contracts (spot-price contracts) have been used extensively since then.

. . . [T]o see how fixed-price and spot-price contracts differ in their allocation of risk, consider a simple example. . . . Suppose there are a large number of sellers with identical, but uncertain, production costs in an industry with a flat supply curve. Because of the firms' cost uncertainty, the supply curve also is uncertain. And because the supply curve is flat, the equilibrium price in the spot market equals the realized value of the firms' costs (regardless of the demand curve). Suppose further that there are many buyers (also firms) whose valuations are not uncertain.

In this example, a spot-price contract would insure a seller against risk for the following reason. If that seller's costs are high, so are all other sellers' costs, and so also is the supply curve and the spot price. The increase in revenue from the higher spot price exactly offsets the increase in production costs. Thus, in this example, a spot-price contract provides perfect insurance for the seller against production cost uncertainty. A fixed-price contract would leave all of the risk of production cost uncertainty on the seller.

However, a fixed-price contract would insure a buyer against risk in this example. This is because, assuming the value of the good to the buyer is fixed, a fixed-price contract would guarantee the buyer a certain level of profits. A spot-price contract would cause the buyer's profits to be uncertain.

Thus, in this example, a spot-price contract insures the seller and a fixed-price contract insures the buyer. A spot-price contract will be chosen over a fixed-price contract if and only if the seller is more risk-averse than the buyer.

The main contribution of this article is to derive and interpret the condition determining whether a spot-price contract or a fixed-price contract is superior in a model in which the following complications are added. First, it is assumed that the industry supply curve may be rising (rather than flat), and that the seller's uncertain production cost is positively, but imperfectly, correlated with shifts in the industry supply curve. Second, it is assumed that the buyer's valuation and the industry demand curve are uncertain and that the buyer's valuation is positively, but imperfectly, correlated with shifts in the industry demand curve. Note that if the supply curve is rising, the equilibrium spot price will depend on fluctuations of both the industry supply curve and the industry demand curve.

In this more general framework, a spot-price contract will still tend to insure the seller against production cost uncertainty. The reason is similar to that discussed in the previous example, although the upward slope of the industry supply curve and the less than perfect correlation between the seller's costs and shifts in the industry supply curve reduce the value of a spot-price contract as insurance against production cost uncertainty.

However, as noted, the spot price also will fluctuate because of shifts in the industry demand curve. A fixed-price contract would insure the seller against these demand-side uncertainties. Thus, in general, neither contract can protect the seller against both supply-side and demand-side risk.

The results regarding the buyer are the mirror image of those regarding the seller. A spot-price contract will tend to insure the buyer against valuation uncertainty, while a fixed-price contract will insure the buyer against supply-side uncertainties.

The preceding discussion shows that neither contract form is best in terms of risk allocation in all circumstances. Whether a spot-price or a fixed-price contract is preferred depends on: the parties' relative aversion to risk; the magnitudes of the supply-side and demand-side uncertainties; the degree of correlation between the seller's costs and shifts in the industry supply curve; the degree of correlation between the buyer's valuation and shifts in the industry demand curve; and the slopes of the supply and demand curves.

. . .

The analysis in the present article provides a possible explanation of why contracting practices in the uranium industry changed in the early 1970s. To apply the analysis, it is necessary to consider the risk preferences of the sellers and buyers of uranium and the nature of the risks that they faced. The sellers of uranium ore usually were private firms for whom the mining and sale of uranium was a major, if not principal, business. They included firms such as the Homestake Mining Company, the United Nuclear Corporation, and the Kerr-McGee Corporation. The buyers of uranium ore, on the other hand, primarily were public utilities who used the uranium to produce electricity and for whom the price of uranium constituted a small fraction (about 10 percent) of total costs. The utility-buyers also usually could pass input price changes through to consumers of electricity. It would seem reasonable, therefore, to assume that the sellers generally were more risk-averse than the buyers with respect to fluctuations in the price of uranium.

Assuming for simplicity that the buyers are risk-neutral and that the sellers are risk-averse, the contract form chosen by the parties will be the one that minimizes the risk borne by the seller. It was shown earlier in this article that sellers would prefer spot-price contracts with respect to production-cost uncertainty (unless such contracts overinsure them, which does not seem likely in this context) and fixed-price contracts with respect to demand uncertainty.

Before the early 1970s, there was relatively little uncertainty of either kind. Thus, in principle, the seller would be indifferent between the two contract forms. However, if the added transaction costs of using a spot-price contract are taken into account (for example, agreeing on the price index, resolving disputes), a fixed-price contract would be preferred.

But during the early 1970s, both production-cost uncertainties and demand-side uncertainties became significant. On the cost side, this was due in large part to changes in mine safety and environmental regulations that began in the late 1960s. Substantial cost-side uncertainty also existed because not much was known about the cost of developing the new reserves, mines, and mills that would be necessary if output were expanded beyond then prevailing levels. On the demand side, the reasons for uncertainty included changes in government enrichment policies, the effects of the environmental movement on the rate of growth of nuclear power, and the Arab oil embargo.

Without undertaking a major empirical study, it is impossible to say whether the production-cost uncertainties or the demand-side uncertainties were more important. But it is at least a plausible hypothesis that the cost uncertainties sufficiently dominated, in which case the analysis in this article would predict a switch from fixed-price contracts to market-price (spot-price) contracts at about the time the latter became more frequently used.

## [2.] Concluding Remarks

Although many simplifying assumptions have been made in this article, the principal observations seem quite general. A spot-price contract tends to insure a seller against production-cost uncertainty and a buyer against valuation uncertainty (although it may overinsure them). A fixed-price contract insures a seller against demand-side uncertainties and a buyer against supply-side uncertainties. Thus, which contract form will be preferred by the parties depends on their relative aversion to risk and the magnitudes of the supply-side and demand-side uncertainties.

. . . .

# 13

## The Theory of the Firm and the Structure of the Franchise Contract

*Paul H. Rubin*

### EDITOR'S INTRODUCTION

We have already considered two arguments for contract design – optimal allocation of precaution and optimal allocation of risk. We now consider a third reason – the minimization of opportunism. The potential for opportunism is high in any long-term relationship. For example, suppose that a seller agrees to produce a special item for a buyer at a certain price; once the specialized item is produced, the buyer could threaten not buy the item unless the price is cut in half.

Paul Rubin discusses the control of opportunism in the context of a franchise. Franchises are ubiquitous in the modern world. Most people know that McDonald's is a franchise, but few know that Visa is, as well. Franchises are two-headed beasts. Both the franchisor and the franchisee have control over different parts of the business. For example, McDonald's Corporation, the franchisor, provides training, advertising, and inspections in return for an upfront payment by the franchisee and continuing royalties. Why doesn't McDonald's corporation own all the hamburger stands outright? Why don't the franchisees become independent sellers of McDonald's burgers for a higher fee? Given that there is this franchise arrangement, how is opportunism by both the franchisor and the franchisee controlled? It is these questions that Paul Rubin answers.

## I. Introduction

A question of perennial interest to economists is the question of the nature of the firm.[1] In Coase's terms, we might ask why some decisions will be made within firms by fiat and others between firms by market transactions. But implicit within the entire literature is the idea that there is a reasonably sharp distinction between transactions within firms and transactions between firms; that is, there is an assumption that the border of the firm is sharp.

There are many types of transactions which profit-seeking individuals might find worthwhile in the marketplace; products and markets have sufficiently diverse characteristics so that a large number of arrangements might be profit-maximizing. Thus, it would be surprising if there were in fact a sharp distinction between interfirm and intrafirm transactions; rather, we would expect hybrid cases where markets allow various types of optimal blends. In fact, we do observe such mixed cases. One such intermediate case, much studied by economists, is sharecropping; another type of hybrid is franchising. In this paper, the nature of the franchise contract is examined, using the tools of the theory of the firm. . . . Section II discusses the institutional structure of the franchise. Section III considers and rejects the standard explanation of franchising in terms of capital markets. In Section IV an alternative explanation, consistent with economic theory, is proposed. Section V considers some additional aspects of franchising. . . . The last section is a summary.

## II. Institutional Structure

A franchise agreement is a contract between two (legal) firms, the franchisor and the franchisee. The franchisor is a parent company that has developed some product or service for sale; the franchisee is a firm that is set up to market this product or service in a particular location. The franchisee pays a certain sum of money for the right to market this product.

Franchise contracts have several more or less standard clauses. First, the franchisor may provide various sorts of managerial assistance to the franchisee. This assistance will usually include site selection; training programs, either on the job or institutional; provision of standard operating manuals; provision of ongoing advice; and miscellaneous assistance, such as design of physical layout of the plant and advertising. The extent of assistance varies from industry to industry; in some cases there is virtually none.

Second, the franchisee will agree to run the business in a manner stipulated by the franchisor. Control by the franchisor may extend over products sold, price, hours of operation, conditions of the plant, inventory, insurance, personnel, and accounting and auditing. (Some of these controls have been weakened or overturned by various antitrust rulings.)

Third, the franchisee will pay royalties, usually a percentage of sales, to the franchisor. In addition, the franchisee may be compelled to purchase inputs from the franchisor or from approved suppliers, though this requirement will vary from contract to contract.

Fourth, the contract will have a termination clause. Usually the franchisor will be able to terminate the agreement almost at will. Finally, there will be miscellaneous clauses, dealing with matters such as the right of the franchisee to sell the franchise, rights of heirs of the franchisee to inherit the business, and the right to open a competing business after ceasing to be a franchisee.

Although some of the ability of the franchisor to control the behavior of the franchisee has been limited by various antitrust rulings, we will consider contracts in the form which they took before such rulings, on the assumption that unrestricted contracts would have been profit-maximizing. Under such contracts, it is notable that the franchisor has almost complete control over the behavior of the franchisee – in fact, the relationship is almost that of a firm and an employee. This relationship is especially apparent when we consider the ease with which the franchise agreement can be terminated by the franchisor. In this sense, it appears that the definition of the franchisee as a separate firm, rather than as part of the franchisor, is a legal and not an economic distinction. In fact, part of the argument of this paper is that there exists no meaningful economic distinction – that is to say, the economic concept of "firm" does not have clear boundaries.

## III. Capital Market Explanations of Franchising

A common explanation for the franchising of independent firms, rather than reliance on expansion by wholly owned subsidiaries, is that franchising is a method used by the franchisor to raise capital. Thus, it is argued, the franchisor is able to expand his business more quickly than would otherwise be the case.

A consideration of this argument in the light of modern capital theory quickly indicates that it is fallacious. A franchisor will own outlets in many areas; a franchisee will in general own only one or a few outlets in the same area. Thus, the investment of the franchisee will be much riskier than the overall franchise chain. A risk-averse franchisee would clearly prefer to invest in a portfolio of shares in all franchise outlets, rather than confining his investment to a single store.

This means, essentially, that the franchisee will require a higher rate of return on his capital if he is required to invest in one outlet rather than in a portfolio. Conversely, the franchisor, by forcing a relatively large risk on the franchisee, will himself earn a lower rate of return. This argument thus appears to make sense only if we assume that franchisors are more risk-averse than franchisees. But since franchisees commonly invest a large share of their assets in acquiring the franchise, it is unlikely that this will be the case.

Let us make, arguendo, the strongest possible case for the capital market argument. Assume that franchisors are unable to use normal capital markets for expansion. Therefore also assume that they want to rely on their store managers for a source of capital. (Stating these conditions immediately indicates their implausibility.) Even in this case, the franchisor would do better to create a portfolio of shares of all outlets and sell these shares to his managers. This would diversify risk for the managers, with no (capital) effect on the franchisor. Thus, it is clear that capital market arguments do not explain franchising.

## IV. An Alternative Explanation

. . . Franchising is usually undertaken in situations where the franchisee is physically removed from the franchisor, and thus where monitoring of the performance and behavior of the franchisee would be difficult. In this situation, it pays to devise control mechanisms which give the franchisee an incentive to be efficient – to avoid shirking and excessive consumption of leisure. To the extent that such mechanisms can be devised, both the franchisee and the franchisor gain, for they have a larger amount to share in some way. In other words, the shirking that is avoided is shirking that both parties would find undesirable.

The simplest way to motivate the franchisee is to give him a share of the profits of the franchise. Then he will work as hard as is efficient; any leisure he consumes will clearly be worth the true cost. Thus, we would expect the franchise contract to be written in such a way as to give the franchisee much of the profits in the operation.

But presumably there is a well-defined market for people with the ability to be franchisees, and franchisors would not want to pay more for these people than this amount. There is, however, no assurance that the present value of these salaries would be equal to the present value of the profits of the franchise. Thus, the franchise fee is simply the difference between these two present values. The franchisee pays for the right to run the business and collect some of the profits from it for some period of time; presumably his payment is adjusted so that he will make a normal return on his time and on his investment in the business (that is, on the payment), with this return adjusted for risk.

Consider an example. Assume there exists some franchise which will pay $15,000 per year for ten years. If the interest rate is 6 percent, the present value of this stream is approximately $110,000. Assume the wage of a person competent to run this firm is $12,000. Then the present value of his earnings is approximately $88,000. Thus, the franchisee would pay $22,000 for the franchise and would earn a normal return on his time. (In fact, he would pay somewhat less than this, for he would also require a return on the investment.) This explanation of franchising, while rather obvious, has nonetheless not been pointed out in the literature, where the capital market explanation is universally held to apply.

The argument to this point would seem to imply that the franchisee would receive all of the profits of the enterprise. If he receives only a share of the profits, there will still be some residual shirking. We would expect the payment made by the franchisee, the franchise fee, to be equal to the expected present value of the stream of profits; there would then be no ongoing payment from the franchisee to the franchisor.

In fact, we do not observe this: rather the franchisor usually gets a share of the proceeds of the business. (Generally, the share is either a percentage of sales or a fee from selling goods and services to the franchisee.) It might appear that this method is used because of uncertainty: with a royalty payment, if the franchise should turn out to be more successful than predicted, the franchisor will obtain some of the excess profits; if it should turn out to be less successful than expected, the franchisee will not bear the full cost of this lack of success in his fee. However, due to the inefficiency of the reduction of the franchisee's property rights in the profits of the enterprise, we would expect that another method could be evolved for risk sharing. Another possibility may have to do with capital markets: franchisees are usually individuals with relatively small personal wealth, and it may be difficult for them to raise enough capital to pay the full expected value of the franchise profits. While we cannot reject this argument out of hand, reliance on imperfect capital markets as an explanation of behavior is generally not satisfactory. The most plausible explanation seems to be that the franchisee has some incentive to motivate the franchisor to be efficient – that is, just as the franchisor desires the franchisee to run the operation efficiently, so the franchisee desires to give the franchisor an incentive to be efficient in those aspects of the relationship which require an ongoing performance by the franchisor. One area of such behavior is the ongoing managerial advice which the franchisor is sometimes required to give the franchisee; another area is advertising by the franchisor.

It is unlikely that either of these aspects of control is important enough to justify the reduction in the franchisee's profits and the corresponding reduction in his incentives for efficiency. However, there is another area in which the franchisee would like to control the behavior of the franchisor. To understand this, we must consider what the franchisee is buying when he buys a franchise. The main item purchased is the trademark of the franchise. This is valuable because consumers have a good deal of information about price and quality sold by establishments with a given trademark. Consumers have this information precisely because the franchisor polices franchises and makes certain that quality standards are maintained. What is involved is a classic externality problem. If any one franchisee allows quality to deteriorate, he will generate revenue because consumers perceive him as being of the same quality as other stores with the same trademark. Thus, if one franchisee allows the quality of his establishment to deteriorate, he benefits by the full amount of the savings from reduced quality maintenance; he loses only part of the costs, for part is borne by other franchisees. All franchises would lose something as a result of this deterioration in one franchise: consumers would have less faith in the quality promised by the trademark.

There are several aspects to this policing. First, the franchisor must be careful to grant franchises to those who are likely to be competent in running them. Some screening of potential franchisees is important. Second, the franchisor must control the quality of products offered by the franchisees. We argued above that the franchisee could best run the day-to-day operations of the business; this is true in the sense that he can produce the desired good (including quality) at least cost. However, it is relatively inexpensive for the franchisor to monitor the quality of the good produced, as opposed to the method of production. This is the sort of monitoring which franchisors undertake. Third, errors will sometimes be made, and some franchises will not be profitable. Such businesses will operate in the short run if they are covering variable costs and will shut down in the long run, when capital has been sufficiently depreciated. But it is precisely this depreciation of capital that the franchisor wants to avoid. The franchisor wants to eliminate any operations not maintaining the quality of the franchise. Contracts calling for easy termination of franchises makes it possible to avoid the period of quality deterioration.

Because of the externality problem, all franchisees have an interest in having quality policed. Assume now that the franchisor sold the entire value of the profits to franchisees – that is, the franchisor obtained no royalty from current sales. If quality deteriorates, this would reduce his income because renewal fees would decrease, as would fees from sales of new franchises. In addition, profits of existing franchises would also be reduced, but this reduction would have no effect on the franchisor. He would bear only part of the cost of reduced quality, and thus would have an incentive to underinvest in resources used in policing franchisees.

Thus, giving the franchisee a large share of the profits of the operation creates an incentive for him to be efficient in that part of the operation he can most efficiently control; giving the franchisor a share of the profits of all franchises gives him an incentive to be efficient in those aspects of the enterprise under his control. Both parts of the contract can be understood as an attempt to give property rights to the parties to the transaction in those areas that they can efficiently control.

In virtually all franchise contracts, the receipts of the franchisor depend on the revenue (not profits) of the franchise. In some cases, there is a payment of a percentage of sales to the franchisor; in other cases, the franchisee is required to buy inputs from the franchisor at above market prices. Some [claim] that this type of contract is inefficient, in that it would be more efficient for the franchisor to share in profits rather than revenues. They claim that the reason sales, rather than profits, are used is because monitoring of sales is easier than monitoring of profits. But in fact, most contracts give the franchisor the right to order audits of the franchise, and it is not clear monitoring would be that difficult. Rather, it seems likely that the element of control of the franchisor – the policing of franchises – is more closely related to sales than to profits; thus, the contracts seem to be written in such a way as to give the franchisor the correct incentives.

The analysis to this point has some additional implications. First, there is some evidence ... that franchisors are buying back franchises in urban areas. If franchising is used because control of behavior of store managers is difficult, then we would expect the existence of several stores in an area to reduce this control problem; the franchisor could have an agent who would supervise several stores as a unit. (Of course, the problem of monitoring the monitor would remain; but this would be a reasonably straightforward employer-employee problem and would be less difficult than monitoring the behavior of a store manager.) If stores are geographically separated, on the other hand, this sort of supervision would be more expensive, for monitors would need to spend much time traveling from store to store. When a franchisor begins operations, he will not have many stores in any given area; after some time, if successful, he will have many outlets in large urban areas. At this point it becomes worthwhile to buy back the franchises. Thus, the existence of owned outlets in urban areas and franchised outlets elsewhere would be consistent with our hypothesis.

The argument also has some implications about types of contracts in different businesses. Businesses can vary in two relevant dimensions: the amount of discretion available to managers and the value to the business of the trademark. In those businesses where there is much managerial discretion, we would expect a higher percentage of the revenue of the franchisor to come from the initial fee and a relatively lower percentage to come from royalties; where there are relatively few managerial decisions to be made, we would expect more of the income of the franchisor to come from royalties. Second, where the trademark is more valuable, we would expect relatively more of the franchisor's revenue to come from royalties, for this would create an incentive for him to be efficient in policing and maintaining value. Thus, this theory has testable implications about the relationship between the nature of the industry and the franchise contract.

# V. Additional Issues

In this section, we discuss the behavior of the franchisee, the behavior of the franchisor, and some additional issues dealing with their interrelationship.

## A. FRANCHISEE BEHAVIOR

Perhaps the most important question to ask about the franchisee is why he would seek a franchise rather than operating an independent business. There appear to be four advantages from a franchise. First, the trademark of the franchise and the product sold appear to be valuable, and the franchisee is willing to pay something to sell these commodities. Second, the franchisor often gives managerial advice to the franchisee. This advantage would appear to be minimal, however, as the market is easily able to provide such training; indeed, many types of franchises involve no such training. Third, the franchisor often makes capital available to the franchisee in some form – either by cosigning for a bank loan or by actually buying the plant and leasing it to the franchisee. Presumably, franchisors are less risky borrowers than franchisees, and thus there can be a saving here. Finally, to the extent that franchisees are closer to being employees than entrepreneurs, they may simply lack the requisite human capital to open businesses without the substantial assistance of franchisors.

## B. Franchisor behavior

There are some aspects of franchisor behavior which we have not considered. First, franchisors often desire to closely control the behavior of franchisees. It appears that one major advantage of a franchise is the information it provides to consumers: when I take my family to a McDonald's I know what to expect, no matter where it is located. Thus, it would be worthwhile for McDonald's to spend a fair sum to maintain this situation and to curtail any local variation. . . .

. . .

## [VI.] Summary

In this paper we have used the modern theory of the firm – relying on an analysis of property rights, incentives, and monitoring – to explain the nature of the franchise contract. We have argued that the franchise relationship is intermediate between a single firm and a market transaction, and have shown that economic theory can explain the precise nature of the payments made by each party. In particular, the structure of the contract is such as to give each party property rights in those aspects of the operation under his control.

### Note

1.  See Ronald H. Coase, "The Nature of the Firm," 4 *Economica* 386 (1937), reprinted in *Readings in Price Theory* 331 (George J. Stigler and Kenneth E. Boulding eds. 1952 . . .

# 14

## Transaction Cost Determination of "Unfair" Contractual Arrangements

### *Benjamin Klein*

**EDITOR'S INTRODUCTION**

Certain contract provisions seem to be inherently unfair. Employees can be fired "at will" (that is, without need for justification by the employer) and franchisees can have their franchises terminated at the discretion of the franchisor with a significant loss to the franchisee. Some view these contract terms as a form of exploitation by the employer or franchisor made possible by unequal bargaining power. But the reply by the economist is that both sides voluntarily entered into the contract; so, the contract cannot exploit one side or the other. This itself is not a sufficient answer. Economic analysis of law should be able to provide an explanation for such provisions. It is this task, which Benjamin Klein undertakes. His argument proceeds as follows: Lawyers are expensive and the court may not be able to ascertain the truth regarding whether the parties have upheld their part of the contract. Therefore, the parties to a contract would like to find a less costly private alternative to enforcing contracts. Providing a greater than normal return to the franchisee if there is no cheating and a low-cost method of getting rid of the franchisee if there is cheating is a way to ensure no breach of contract by the franchisee. But what is to prevent the franchisor from cheating on the contract? Basically it is to make the cost of cheating by the franchisor less than the benefit. Reputation is very important in this regard. If the franchisor is known to terminate franchisees without cause, then it will be harder to get franchisees in the future. Also, if the benefit to the franchisor from unjustly terminating the franchisee is small (the costs to the franchisee are not readily fungible into benefits for the franchisor), then the inducement for franchisor cheating will be small.

Terms such as "unfair" are foreign to the economic model of voluntary exchange which implies anticipated gains to all transactors. However, much recent statutory, regulatory, and antitrust activity has run counter to this economic paradigm of the efficiency properties of "freedom of contract." ... This is done by declaring unenforceable or illegal particular contractual provisions that, although voluntarily agreed upon in the face of significant competition, appear to be one-sided or unfair. Presentation of the standard abstract economic analysis of the mutual gains from voluntary exchange is unlikely to be an effective counterweight to this recent legal movement without an explicit attempt to provide a positive rationale for the presence of the particular unfair contractual term. This paper considers some transaction costs that might explain the voluntary adoption of contractual provisions such as termination at will and long-term exclusive dealing clauses that have been under legal attack.

## I. The "Hold-up" Problem

In attempting to explain the complicated contractual details of actual market exchange, I start by noting that complete, fully contingent, costlessly enforceable contracts are not possible. This is a proposition obvious to even the most casual observer of economic phenomena. Rather than the impersonal marketplace of costlessly enforceable contracts represented in standard economic analysis, individuals in most real-world transactions are concerned with the possibility of breach and hence the identity and reputation of those with whom they deal. Further, even a cursory examination of actual contracts indicates that the relationship between transacting parties often cannot be fully described by a court-enforceable formal document that the parties have signed. . . . While the common law of contracts supplies a body of rules and principles which are read into each contract, in many cases explicit terms (which include these general unwritten terms) remain somewhat vague and incomplete.

Contracts are incomplete for two main reasons. First, uncertainty implies the existence of a large number of possible contingencies and it may be very costly to know and specify in advance responses to all of these possibilities. Second, particular contractual performance, such as the level of energy an employee devotes to a complex task, may be very costly to measure. Therefore contractual breach may often be difficult to prove to the satisfaction of a third-party enforcer such as a court.

Given the presence of incomplete contractual arrangements, wealth-maximizing transactors have the ability and often the incentive to renege on the transaction by holding up the other party, in the sense of taking advantage of unspecified or unenforceable elements of the contractual relationship. Such behavior is, by definition, unanticipated and not a long-run equilibrium phenomenon. Oliver Williamson has identified and discussed this phenomenon of "opportunistic behavior," and my . . . paper with Robert Crawford and Armen Alchian attempted to make operational some of the conditions under which this hold-up potential is likely to be large.[1] In addition to contract costs, and therefore the incompleteness of the explicit contract, we emphasized the presence of appropriable quasi rents due to highly firm-specific investments. After a firm invests in an asset with a low-salvage value and a quasi-rent stream highly dependent upon some other asset, the owner of the other asset has the potential to hold up by appropriating the quasi-rent stream. For example, one would not build a house on land rented for a short term. After the rental agreement expires, the landowner could raise the rental price to reflect the costs of moving the house to another lot.[2]

The solution we emphasized was vertical integration, that is, one party owning both assets (the house and the land). Because the market for land is competitive, the price paid for the land by the homebuilder does not reflect these potentially appropriable quasi rents. However, this solution will not necessarily be observed. The size of the hold-up potential is a multiplicative function of two factors: the presence of specific capital, that is, appropriable quasi rents, and the cost of contractually specifying and enforcing delivery of the service in question – the incentive for contract violation and the ease of contract violation. Even where there is a large amount of highly specific capital, the performance in question may be cheaply specifiable and measurable and a complete contract legally enforceable at low cost. Therefore, while a short-term rental contract is not feasible, a possible solution may be a long-term lease. In addition, since the cases we will be considering deal with human capital, vertical integration in the sense of outright ownership is not possible.

## II. Contractual Solutions

Since the magnitude of the potential holdup may be anticipated, the party to be cheated can merely decrease the initial price he will pay by the amount of the appropriable quasi rents. For example, if an employer knows that an employee will cheat a certain amount each period, it will be reflected in the employee's wage. Contracts can be usefully thought to refer to anticipated rather than stated performance. Therefore the employee's behavior should not even be considered "cheating." A secretary, for example, may miss work one day a week on average. If secretary time is highly substitutable, the employer can cut the secretary's weekly wage 20 percent, hire 20 percent more secretaries and be indifferent. The secretary, on the other hand, presumably values the leisure more than the additional income and therefore is better off. Rather than cheating, we have a voluntarily determined, utility-maximizing contractual relationship.

In many cases, however, letting the party cheat and discounting his wage will not be an economical solution because the gain to the cheater and therefore his acceptable compensating wage discount is less than the cost to the firm from the cheating behavior. For example, it is easy to imagine many cases where a shirking manager will impose costs on the firm much greater than his personal gains. Therefore the stockholders cannot be made indifferent to this behavior by cutting his salary and hiring more lazy managers. The general point is that there may not be perfect substitutability between quantity and quality of particular services. Hence, even if one knew that an unspecified element of quality would be reduced by a certain amount in attempting the holdup, an *ex ante* compensatory discount in the quoted price of the promised high-quality service to the cost of providing the anticipated lower-quality supply would not make the demander of the service indifferent. Individuals would be willing to expend real resources to set up contractual arrangements to prevent such opportunism and assure high-quality supply.

The question then becomes how much of the hold-up problem can be avoided by an explicit government-enforced contract, and how much remains to be handled by an implicit self-enforcing contract. This latter type of contract is one where opportunistic behavior is prevented by the threat of termination of the business relationship rather than by the threat of litigation. A transactor will not cheat if the expected present discounted value of quasi rents he is earning from a relationship is greater than the immediate hold-up wealth gain. The capital loss that can be imposed on the potential cheater by the withdrawal of expected future business is then sufficient to deter cheating.

In our . . . article, Keith Leffler and I develop this market-enforcement mechanism in detail.[3] It is demonstrated that one way in which the future-promised rewards necessary to prevent cheating can be arranged is by the payment of a sufficiently high-price "premium."

This premium stream can usefully be thought of as "protection money" paid to assure noncheating behavior. The magnitude of this price premium will be related to the potential holdup, that is, to the extent of contractual incompleteness and the degree of specific capital present. In equilibrium, the present discounted value of the price-premium stream will be exactly equal to the appropriable quasi rents, making the potential cheater indifferent between cheating and not. But the individual paying the premium will be in a preferable position as long as the differential consumer's surplus from high-quality (noncheating) supply is greater than the premium.

One method by which this equilibrium quasi-rent stream can be achieved without the existence of positive firm profits is by having the potential cheater put up a forfeitable-at-will collateral bond equal to the discounted value of the premium stream. Alternatively, the potential cheater may make a highly firm-specific productive investment which will have only a low-salvage value if he cheats and loses future business. The gap between price and salvageable capital costs is analytically equivalent to a premium stream with the nonsalvageable asset analytically equivalent to a forfeitable collateral bond.

## III. "Unfair" Contractual Terms

Most actual contractual arrangements consist of a combination of explicit- and implicit-enforcement mechanisms. Some elements of performance will be specified and enforced by third-party sanctions. The residual elements of performance will be enforced without invoking the power of some outside party to the transaction but merely by the threat of termination of the transactional relationship. The details of any particular contract will consist of forms of these general elements chosen to minimize transaction costs (for example, hiring lawyers to discover contingencies and draft explicit terms, paying quality-assurance premiums, and investing in nonsalvageable "brand name" assets) and may imply the existence of what appears to be unfair contract terms.

Consider, for example, the initial capital requirements and termination provisions common in most franchise contractual arrangements. These apparently one-sided terms may be crucial elements of minimum-cost quality-policing arrangements. Given the difficulty of explicitly specifying and enforcing contractually every element of quality to be supplied by a franchisee, there is an incentive for an individual opportunistic franchisee to cheat the franchisor by supplying a lower quality of product than contracted for. Because the franchisee uses a common trademark, this behavior depreciates the reputation and hence the future profit stream of the franchisor.

The franchisor knows, given his direct policing and monitoring expenditures, the expected profit that a franchisee can obtain by cheating. For example, given the number of inspectors hired, he knows the expected time to detect a cheater; given the costs of low-quality inputs he knows the expected extra short-run cheating profit that can be earned. Therefore the franchisor may require an initial lump sum payment from the franchisee equal to this estimated short-run gain from cheating. This is equivalent to a collateral bond forfeitable at the will of the franchisor. The franchisee will earn a normal rate of return on that bond if he does not cheat, but it will be forfeited if he does cheat and is terminated.

In many cases franchisee noncheating rewards may be increased and short-run cheating profits decreased (and therefore franchisor direct policing costs reduced) by the grant of an exclusive territory or the enforcement of minimum resale price restraints. Franchisors can also assure quality by requiring franchisee investments in specific (nonfully salvageable) production assets that upon termination imply a capital-cost penalty larger than any short-run wealth gain that can be obtained by the franchisee if he cheats. For example, the franchisor may require franchisees to rent from them short term (rather than own) the land upon which their outlet is located. This lease arrangement creates a situation where termination implies that the franchisor can require the franchisee to move and thereby impose a capital loss on him up to the amount of his initial nonsalvageable investment. Hence a form of collateral to deter franchisee cheating is created.

It is important to recognize that franchise termination, if it is to assure quality compliance on the part of franchisees, must be unfair in the sense that the capital cost imposed on the franchisee that will optimally prevent cheating must be larger than the gain to the franchisee from cheating. Given that less than infinite resources are spent by the franchisor to monitor quality, there is some probability that franchisee cheating will go undetected. Therefore termination must become equivalent to a criminal-type sanction. Rather than the usually analyzed case of costlessly detected and policed contract breach, where the remedy of making the breaching party pay the cost of the damages of his specific breach makes economic sense, the sanction here must be large enough to make the expected net gain from cheating equal to zero. The transacting parties contractually agree upon a penalty-type sanction for breach as a means of economizing on direct policing costs. Because contract enforcement costs (including litigation costs which generally are not collectable by the innocent party in the United States) are not zero, this analysis provides a rationale against the common-law prohibition of penalty clauses.

The obvious concern with such seemingly unfair contractual arrangements is the possibility that the franchisor may engage in opportunistic behavior by terminating a franchisee without cause, claiming the franchise fee and purchasing the initial franchisee investment at a distress price. Such behavior may be prevented by the depreciation of the franchisor's brand name and therefore decreased future demand by potential franchisees to join the arrangement. However, this protective mechanism is limited by the relative importance of new franchise sales compared to the continuing franchising operation, that is, by the "maturity" of the franchise chain.

More importantly, what limits reverse cheating by franchisors is the possible increased cost of operating the chain through an employee operation compared to a franchise operation when such cheating is communicated among franchisees. As long as the implicit collateral bond put up by the franchisee is less than the present discounted value of this cost difference, franchisor cheating will be deterred. Although explicit bonds and price premium payments cannot simultaneously be made by both the franchisee and the franchisor, the discounted value of the cost difference has the effect of a collateral bond put up by the franchisor to assure his noncheating behavior. This explains why the franchisor does not increase the initial franchise fee to an arbitrarily high level and correspondingly decrease its direct policing expenditures and the probability of detecting franchisee cheating. While such offsetting changes could continue to optimally deter franchisee cheating and save the real resource cost of direct policing, the profit from and hence the incentive for reverse franchisor cheating would become too great for the arrangement to be stable.

Franchisees voluntarily signing these agreements obviously understand the termination-at-will clause separate from the legal consequences of that term to mean nonopportunistic franchisor termination. But this does not imply that the court should judge each termination on these unwritten but understood contract terms and attempt to determine if franchisor cheating has occurred. Franchisees also must recognize that by signing these agreements they are relying on the implicit market-enforcement mechanism outlined above, and not the court to prevent franchisor cheating. It is costly to use the court to regulate these terminations because elements of performance are difficult to contractually specify and to measure. In addition, litigation is costly and time consuming, during which the brand name of the franchisor can be depreciated further. If these costs were not large and the court could cheaply and quickly determine when franchisor cheating had occurred, the competitive process regarding the establishment of contract terms would lead transactors to settle on explicit governmentally enforceable contracts rather than rely on this implicit market-enforcement mechanism.

The potential error here is, after recognizing the importance of transaction costs and the incomplete "relational" nature of most real-world contracts, to rely too strongly on the government as a regulator of unspecified terms. . . . While it is important for economic theory to handle significant contract costs and incomplete explicit contractual arrangements, such complexity does not imply a broad role for government. Rather, all that is implied is a role for brand names and the corresponding implicit market enforcement mechanism I have outlined.

## IV. Unequal Bargaining Power

An argument made against contract provisions such as termination-at-will clauses is that they appear to favor one party at the expense of another. Hence it is alleged that the terms of the agreement must have been reached under conditions of "unequal bargaining power" and therefore should be invalid. However, a further implication of the above analysis is that when both parties can cheat, explicit contractual restraints are often placed on the smaller, less well-established party (the franchisee), while an implicit brand name contract-enforcement mechanism is relied on to prevent cheating by the larger, more well-established party (the franchisor).

If information regarding quality of a product supplied by a large firm is communicated among many small buyers who do not all purchase simultaneously, the potential holdup relative to, say, annual sales is reduced substantially compared to the case where each buyer purchased from a separate independent small firm. There are likely to be economies of scale in the supply of a business brand name, because in effect the large firm's total brand name capital is put on the line with each individual sale. This implies a lower cost of using the implicit contract mechanism, that is, a lower-price premium necessary to assure non-breach, for a large firm compared to a small firm. Therefore one side of the contract will be relatively more incomplete.

For example, in a recent English case using the doctrine of inequality of bargaining power to bar contract enforcement, an individual songwriter signed a long-term (ten-year) exclusive service contract with a music publisher for an agreed royalty percentage.[4] Since it would be extremely costly to write a complete explicit contract for the supply of publishing services (including advertising and other promotion activities whose effects are felt over time and are difficult to measure), after a songwriter becomes established he has an incentive to take advantage of any initial investment made by a publishing firm and shift to another publisher. Rather than rely on the brand name of the songwriter or require him to make a specific investment which can serve as collateral, the exclusive services contract prevents this cheating from occurring.

The major cost of such explicit long-term contractual arrangements is the rigidity that is created by the necessity of setting a price or a price formula *ex ante*. In this song-publishing case, the royalty formula may turn out *ex post* to imply too low a price to the songwriter (if, say, his cooperative promotional input is greater than originally anticipated). If the publisher is concerned about his reputation, these royalty terms will be renegotiated, a common occurrence in continuing business relationships.

If an individual songwriter is a small part of a large publisher's total sales, and if the value of an individual songwriter's ability generally depreciates rapidly or does not persist at peak levels so that signing up new songwriters is an important element of a publisher's continuing business, then cheating an individual songwriter or even all songwriters currently under contract by refusing to renegotiate royalty rates will imply a large capital cost to the publisher. When this behavior is communicated to other actual or potential composers, the publisher's reputation will depreciate and future business will be lost. An individual songwriter, on the other hand, does not generally have large, diversified long-term business concerns and therefore cannot be penalized in that way. It is therefore obvious, independent of any appeal to disparity of bargaining power, why the smaller party would be willing to be bound by an explicit long-term contract while the larger party is bound only implicitly and renegotiates terms that turn out *ex post* to be truly divergent from *ex ante,* but unspecified, anticipations.

However, the possibility of reverse publisher cheating is real. If, for example, the songwriter unexpectedly becomes such a great success that current sales by this one customer represents a large share of the present discounted value of total publisher sales, the implicit contract enforcement mechanism may not work. Individuals knowingly trade off these costs of explicit- and implicit-enforcement mechanisms in settling upon transaction cost-minimizing contract terms. Although it would be too costly in a stochastic world to attempt to set up an arrangement where no cheating occurs, it is naive to think that courts can cheaply intervene to discover and "fix up" the few cases of opportunistic behavior that will occur. In any event, my analysis makes it clear that one cannot merely look at the agreed upon, seemingly "unfair" terms to determine if opportunism is occurring.

## V. Conclusion

Ronald Coase's fundamental insight defined the problem. With zero transaction costs, the equilibrium form of economic organization is indeterminate.[5] However, rather than distinguishing between the crude alternatives of vertical integration and market exchange, what we really have to explain are different types of market-determined contractual relationships. I have argued that a particular form of transaction cost based upon the existence of incomplete contracts (due to uncertainty and measurement costs) – a transaction cost I have called the hold-up problem – may be an important reason in many cases for termination-at-will and exclusive-dealing contractual arrangements.

The danger is that a discussion of hold-up-type transaction costs can lead to ad hoc theorizing. The discussion here was meant to be suggestive. If economists are to explain satisfactorily the form of particular complex contracts adopted in the marketplace, they must "get their hands dirty" by closely investigating the facts and state of the law to determine hold-up possibilities and contract enforcement difficulties in particular cases. The most useful legal input to obtain knowledge of the institutional constraints on the trading process, is not likely to come from professors of contract law. Rather, we should consider the knowledge accumulated by practicing attorneys familiar with the likely hold-up problems and the contractual solutions commonly adopted in particular industries. When all firms in a particular industry use similar contractual provisions, it is unlikely to be the result of duress or fraud and should not necessarily be considered (as some courts have) as evidence of collusion. Such uniformity suggests the existence of independent attempts within a competitive environment to solve an important common problem and signals the presence of a prime research prospect.

## Notes

1. [Oliver E. Williamson, *Markets and Hierarchies: Analysis and Antitrust Implications,* New York 1975. B. Klein, R. G. Crawford, and A. A. Alchian, "Vertical Integration, Appropriable Rents and the Competitive Contracting Process," *J. Law Econ.,* Oct. 1978, 21, 297–326.]
2. This problem is different from the standard monopoly or bilateral monopoly problem for two reasons. First, market power is created only after the house investment is made on a particular piece of land. Such postinvestment power can therefore exist in many situations that are purely competitive preinvestment. Second, the problem we are discussing deals with the difficulties of contract enforcement. Even if some preinvestment monopoly power exists (for example, a union supplier of labor services to harvest a crop), if one can write an enforceable contract preinvestment (i.e., before the planting), the present discounted value of the monopoly return may be significantly less than the one-time postinvestment hold-up potential (which may equal the entire value of a crop ready to be harvested).
3. B. Klein and K. Leffler, "Non-Governmental Enforcement of Contracts: The Role of Market Forces in Guaranteeing Quality," *J. Polit. Econ.*
4. See *Macaulay v. Schroeder Publishing Co., Ltd.* . . . .
5. R.J. Coase, "The Nature of the Firm," *Economica,* Nov. 1937, 4, 386–405.

# 15

## The Law and Economics Approach to Contract Theory

### *Alan Schwartz*

### EDITOR'S INTRODUCTION

Our attention is now turned to the role of the courts in contract law. In a nutshell, courts should promote efficient behavior between contracting parties, where efficiency takes into account the allocation of precaution and risk, the potential for opportunism, and court transaction costs. This is achieved in several ways.

First, the courts should generally treat the written contract as an optimal, albeit incomplete contract.[1] That is, the courts should not over-rule the written terms of the contract. As both Priest and Klein have argued, the parties to the agreement have incentives to write efficient contracts. Even though the contracts may have the appearance of being one-sided and exploitative, this is not the case.

Because it would be impossible to write in all of the contingencies in a contract, the second role of the court is to fill in gaps when unaccounted-for contingencies arise. Here, the courts try to figure out what the parties to the agreement would have written if they had explicitly considered the contingency. Once again the role of the courts is to promote efficiency, this time by undertaking an ex-post writing of the optimal contract. Suppose that the courts had a different objective from efficiency, say "fairness." It could not be achieved because, in the future, the parties to the contract would explicitly write the optimal solution to the contingency. That is, at the end of the day, contracts will be efficient; courts only increase the transaction costs of writing contracts when the courts have different objectives.

Alan Schwartz analyzes the law and economics contribution to our understanding of contract law and compares it to the more traditional approaches. He provides some simple cases to illustrate the advantages of the economic approach. In these cases, the traditional approaches lead to incorrect decisions by the court. He also discusses examples where the more traditional approaches yield similar recommendations to the economics approach. Here, the advantage of the economics approach is due to the deeper understanding of why the rules make sense.

## 1. Introduction

Contract theory asks two fundamental questions: (a) What promises, if any, should the state enforce? (b) What normative criteria should guide decision makers when filling gaps in enforceable but incomplete contracts? The traditional – that is, the noneconomic – answers to these questions are: Respecting question (a), the state should enforce promises on which the promisor wants the promisee to rely, and that are likely to induce reliance. Respecting question (b), the state should derive contract law rules from "basic principles of justice".

Law and economics scholars answer these basic questions differently. Respecting the first, the state should enforce promises in two cases: (1) when enforcement encourages parties to make investments whose value is highest in the particular relationship at issue; and (2) when enforcement permits parties to allocate the risk of changing economic circumstances. Respecting the second question, the state should supply parties with efficient rules to flesh out incomplete contracts. An efficient rule either maximizes the parties' joint gains under the contract or encourages the better informed party to reveal information that facilitates the maximization of joint gains. The state seldom should attempt to supply parties with fair rules.

This paper has [two] tasks. The first is to show how law and economics scholars came to give different answers to the central theoretical questions. The second is to argue that the law and economics approach is superior to noneconomic approaches for two related reasons: First, the law and economics theory rests on a sophisticated understanding of how commercial parties act. Respecting the second reason, on a deeper understanding, the law and economics approach and noneconomic approaches imply similar normative criteria for answering the question how the state should complete contracts. Then because of the first reason, the law and economics approach gives better answers. . . .

Part 2 discusses the grounds that justify the state in enforcing promises. Part 3 introduces the state function of completing incomplete contracts. Discussion there focuses on the law and economics analysis of contract remedies, where the approach began. . . . .

## 2. Enforcing Promises

In Anglo-American jurisdictions, promises supported by consideration are enforceable. A promise is supported by consideration if the promisor received either a return promise or a performance in exchange for the promise at issue. Noneconomic scholars argue that this definition is both over and under inclusive as a normative matter. The definition is over inclusive because promises that are unlikely to induce reliance should not be enforced; it is under inclusive because the law should enforce promises that do induce reliance whether they are supported by consideration or not. These scholars also argued that purely executory promises seldom are enforced and that promises not supported by consideration sometimes are enforced. In the law and economics view, reliance should have little to do with enforceability.

### 2.1 RISK ALLOCATION

Promises that allocate risks should be enforced whether there is reliance or not. To see why, consider this example. At $t^0$, S agrees with B that S will manufacture goods for B and deliver them at $t^1$. B plans to resell the goods at $t^2$. The goods are homogeneous, and S and B function in competitive markets. The competitive market assumption implies that the contract price at $t^1$ equals the market price. After the contract, S relies by purchasing materials necessary to performance. B refuses to take delivery at $t^1$. The market price of the goods at $t^1$, assume, is unchanged; hence, the later market price also equals the contract price.

S relied in this example but suffers no loss. After breach, it will sell the goods, receiving the later market price, which equals the contract price. Thus S's actual profit will equal its expected profit – the difference between the contract price and S's cost.

To understand the point of this example, assume that the market price was unlikely to change. Then the parties would not have contracted initially. Without a contract, S could sell the goods on the market at $t^1$ and earn the same profit as if a contract had been made; and B could purchase goods on the market at $t^1$ and earn the same profit as if it had contracted. Because to contract is costly and yields no gains, there would be no contract. And in fact, parties often do not make contracts prior to production. Rather, sellers produce goods to sell on the market.

A contract would be observed, in the circumstances of this example, only if the parties did expect market prices to vary with time. If there were no contract, and the market price had fallen between $t^0$ and $t^1$, then S would not earn the difference between the initial market price and its cost (as above), but rather the difference between the later market price and its cost, which is less. A contract would ensure that S earns the larger sum, the difference between the $t^0$ market price and S's cost. S thus would contract, if at all, in order to fix its revenue – that is, to allocate the risk of a price decline to the buyer.

A contract law that encouraged parties to allocate such risks would not focus on reliance. To see why, suppose that the buyer repudiated the contract, in the example, before S purchased materials. S would buy the materials and make the goods anyway because it is in business to do that. If the law would not enforce the contract because S had not relied before repudiation, however, it would put S in the position S contracted to avoid: that is, S would bear the risk of a price decline. A law that encourages parties to allocate risks contractually would not put S in that position.

Contract law enforces executory contracts that allocate risks. Enforcement is efficient because then parties can shift risks to those who can bear them best. Thus the law and economics claim, that the law should enforce contracts to encourage risk allocation, is both descriptively and normatively more compelling than the claim that courts enforce when and because there is reliance.

## 2.2 RELATION-SPECIFIC INVESTMENT

The law also should enforce promises to encourage relation-specific investment. To see what is meant, change the example above in this way: S can make two types of goods: those that are identical to the goods in the original example, in the sense that the goods can be sold to anyone; and specialized goods – those that only a particular buyer would want. The buyer, B, wants to purchase specialized goods because it can make a greater profit. The parties negotiate a price for specialized goods, and the seller then purchases materials and produces. Assume also that the parties' contract is not enforceable. On this assumption, the buyer would refuse delivery at $t^1$ and instead would offer the seller a fraction of the contract price. The goods are valuable only to the buyer, and so the seller cannot resell them on the market. The seller thus would have to take the contract buyer's later offer: for this buyer will pay a positive price while other buyers would pay zero.

It may be said, that the illustrative contract should be enforceable in order to protect sellers who rely, but that would be incorrect. There would be no need to protect such sellers in the absence of enforceability because no reliance would occur then. Rather, sellers such as S above would refuse requests to make specialized goods and make general-purpose goods instead; for these could readily be resold if buyers breach. A seller would pursue this strategy because the buyer's promise at $t^0$ to pay the full price for specialized goods after the goods are produced is not credible without enforceability; buyers have the incentive to make the exploitative offer following seller performance. Notice that buyers not sellers are harmed by nonenforcement. Sellers can protect themselves by making fungible goods, while buyers cannot otherwise realize the larger profit from purchasing specialized goods.

In the law and economics view, the law does not exist to protect particular parties but to increase efficiency. The contract thus should be enforced, in the example here, not because the seller relies or the buyer prefers, but rather because, on the facts assumed, the maximum economic gains flow from a contract for specialized goods. That contract would not be made without legal enforcement.

The law and economics theory of contract enforcement is descriptively and normatively superior to the traditional theory. The former explains more of the case law and offers better reasons for that law. Further, the theory is consistent with the rational behavior of economic actors, and shows just how enforcing promises facilitates the functioning of market economies.

# 3. The Function of Completing Contracts with State-Supplied Rules

Part 3 introduces the state's role of supplying parties with legal rules that complete contracts. ... The topic is presented through a discussion of the law and economics analysis of contract law remedies.

## 3.1 CONTRACT REMEDIES

### a. Efficient breach

Perhaps the first explanatory success of the law and economics theory was to show that protecting the promisee's expectation interest – the standard remedy – induces performance when that would be efficient and breach otherwise. To understand this result, consider a new example. At $t^0$ the parties contract whereby S will produce goods for B. When the contract is made, the seller does not know what its production cost will turn out to be, but knows the range of possible values. Suppose that production cost will be either "high" or "low". A high cost exceeds the value the buyer attaches to the goods; a low cost is below that value. The buyer knows its valuation when the contract is made, and that valuation, assume, never changes. The seller learns its true cost at $t^1$. It will either perform or breach at $t^2$ and the buyer either pays or sues at $t^3$.

In the efficiency story, the seller should perform if its cost turns out to be low and breach otherwise. When the seller has low cost, then the resources devoted to producing the goods are worth less than the gain the buyer would derive from them: production would generate a net surplus. In contrast, when the seller has high cost, the resources devoted to production would be worth more than the buyer would pay (for the buyer would not pay above its valuation); production thus would generate a social loss. An efficient contract damage remedy therefore would induce performance only when the seller turns out to have low cost.

The expectation interest remedy does this. To see why, consider the seller's decision after it learns its actual production cost, but before it begins production. If the seller goes on to perform, it receives the difference between the contract price and its cost; if it breaches, it must pay the buyer the difference between the buyer's valuation and the price as damages. The seller always will perform when the contract price exceeds its cost. To see why, realize that the seller would not agree to the contract unless the price exceeded its expected cost, the weighted average of the high and low costs. This implies that the price must exceed the low cost. The seller will want to breach when the cost is high because a high cost exceeds the price. This is so because the high cost is assumed to exceed the buyer's valuation, and the buyer would pay no more than its valuation. It follows that the damages the seller would pay when costs are high – the difference between the buyer's valuation and the price – are less than the loss the seller would incur from performance – the difference between the high production cost and the price. Thus when costs are high, the seller will breach and pay damages. This is the right result, from an efficiency point of view, because when costs are high the goods are not worth producing.

### b. Inefficient reliance

Protecting the expectation interest is efficient respecting the breach decision, but that is not the only decision the parties make. In one of the examples above, the seller purchased materials to make the goods. Lawyers call this behavior reliance while economists call it investment. The expectation interest remedy would be "globally efficient" if it induced both efficient breach and efficient investment decisions. The remedy, however, induces excessive reliance. To see how, return to the specialized goods example above, and assume that the buyer can make a costly reliance investment that increases the value of performance to it. The investment has the property of diminishing returns: each additional increment of reliance increases value by less. For example, the buyer may advertise that it has the goods for sale. More advertising produces more sales but, after a point, the additional advertising expense is not worth the increase in demand. Milan stores may advertise in Rome but not in Nome.

In the example, the seller will breach if its costs turn out to be high. The expectation interest remedy then would award the buyer the difference between the value of performance, which the buyer's reliance increases, and the price plus the reliance expense. The remedy thus has the property of making the buyer indifferent between performance and breach. It will either obtain the difference between value and cost by purchasing the goods from the seller, or it will obtain that difference as damages that the seller pays. Because the buyer's profit is assured, it will rely – here, advertise – until the marginal cost of further reliance equals the marginal gain in an increased value of performance.

From a social point of view, a buyer who maximizes private gain in this way relies too much; it "overinvests". To see why, recall that the seller breaches if production cost exceeds the buyer's valuation. The buyer's reliance is wasted when the seller breaches. For example, advertising expenses are wasted if the goods are not produced. To maximize the social surplus, the buyer thus should take into account the possibility that its reliance investment will be wasted; that is, the buyer should rely less than it would were performance certain. But because the expectation interest remedy awards the buyer its full profit if there is breach, performance is certain from the buyer's point of view; hence, the buyer overinvests.

A helpful explanatory analogy is to insurance. Assume that a party is fully insured against floods and can take precautions to reduce flood damage. From a social point of view, the party should take those precautions because then a flood would produce a minimum of harm. The party, however, is fully insured. Hence, the cost to it of taking precautions is positive but the gain is zero; and the precautions will not be taken. Similarly, the buyer, in the example here, should temper its reliance to take account of the possibility that reliance will be wasted if the seller faces high costs. However, the cost to the buyer of tempering reliance is positive – the buyer realizes a lower value from the deal when the seller performs – while the gain to the buyer is zero, for the damages on breach do not reward the buyer's restraint. In consequence, buyers rely too much.

The law of contract remedies should solve two problems. The first problem is to encourage parties to make relation-specific investments. The second problem is to prevent parties from overinvesting. The rule that awards the disappointed promisee its expectation interest solves the first problem but worsens the second. Indeed, no extant contract law remedy produces both efficient breach and efficient reliance.

The search for such a remedy has occupied contract theorists for over a decade. An instructive failure in this search holds that the law should award the buyer as damages the profit it would have earned on performance had the buyer made the socially optimal reliance investment. The buyer then would invest optimally because it could not recover as damages that part of its profit attributable to excessive investment. Therefore, the remedy of awarding the buyer the profit associated with the socially optimal investment would induce both efficient breach and efficient reliance.

This remedy is theoretically attractive but seldom could be applied. In order to determine the socially optimal level of investment, the court would have to know the probability that the seller's costs would turn out to exceed the buyer's valuation. The court also would have to know the buyer's "production function" – the incremental profit associated with each incremental reliance investment. Such data commonly is inaccessible to courts. . . . .

When a datum of information is too costly for parties to establish in a law suit, the datum is said to be "unverifiable". In the examples here, cost information is unverifiable. A legal rule should not "condition on" – that is, make relevant – unverifiable information because the rule could not sensibly be applied in cases.

. . .

## 3.2 DEFAULT RULES

### a. Default rules, the expectation interest remedy and public goods

To introduce the concept of default rules, note a crucial aspect of the investment example. The buyer's reliance is wasted there because, it is implicitly assumed, the buyer will not purchase from another seller when the contract seller breaches. The seller's performance, in that example, thus had a unique aspect. If the contract instead had called for fungible goods, the buyer would purchase on the market if the contract seller did not perform. Because performance then would be certain – the buyer will purchase either from the contract seller or on the market – reliance is never wasted; hence, to invest in reliance until marginal gain equals marginal cost is both privately and socially optimal. When fungible goods are involved, it was shown above, a contract would be made to allocate risks (rather than to encourage relation-specific investment).

Enforcing risk allocations is efficient, but the realization that it is raises the question why a legal rule is necessary. The parties can capture the gains from having an efficient rule by writing a term in their contract that awards the promisee the damages which the law now gives. Parties often do write such remedy terms (especially when they are members of trading exchanges) but more often do not. The standard explanation for party silence is that creating contract terms has a public goods aspect. Sometimes, the cost to particular parties of creating a term to resolve a potential problem will exceed the parties' gain from having a solution. At the same time, the rule creation cost may be less than the total social gain from having the problem resolved: for many sets of parties face the same problem and thus would benefit from the solution, were it to exist.

In liberal theory, the state exists partly to supply public goods. Thus the state should supply a legal rule – that is, a solution to a contracting problem – when the costs of rule creation for the typical set of private parties would exceed their gain, but those costs also are less than the total social gain. This conclusion implies the normative criterion that state-supplied rules should satisfy: the state should create efficient rules. A public good is something that people want but that private markets underprovide. Contract parties want efficient rules because these maximize the surplus that the parties can share. Therefore, the state should supply contract parties with welfare increasing terms.

. . . .

## 4. Information-Forcing Rules . . .

### 4.1 INFORMATION FORCING

. . . The rule that a disappointed promisee cannot recover unforeseeable damages is said to perform an information-forcing function. To see how, assume that a seller is facing a set of buyers who value the seller's performance differently. There is a risk that the seller will breach, but the seller can reduce the breach probability by investing in precautions. For example, the seller may be a common carrier who can instruct employees to take particular care when delivering expensive packages. The degree of care that such a seller should take depends on buyer valuations. Thus, a buyer would not want to compensate the seller for investing major resources to ensure the delivery of a cheap, easily replaceable item. The seller's problem is that buyer valuations often are private information; only the particular buyer may know the value it places on performance.

Now assume that the legal rule requires the breaching seller to pay as damages the lowest valuation that a buyer could have. For example, if the value of prompt delivery to a buyer in a certain industry can vary from $10 to $100, a seller who makes late delivery must pay only $10. When communication costs between parties are low, this rule induces every buyer with a valuation above $10 to disclose that valuation. A buyer with a high valuation would not want the seller to take few precautions against breach while a buyer with a low valuation would not want the seller to take many precautions; rather, buyers are willing to purchase the efficient amount of precaution, which they can only do if they disclose their valuations.

The legal rule in this example thus is an efficient default. Respecting the efficiency aspect, the rule induces buyers to reveal their valuations and thus enables sellers to take efficient precautions against breach. Respecting the default aspect, if there were no such rule, a seller would have an incentive to insert a clause in its contracts limiting its damages on breach to $10 or the valuation the buyer specifies. Thus the legal rule enacts the offer that the seller would otherwise make. Information-forcing defaults such as the one considered here function by punishing the informed party. Here the informed party is the buyer, who knows the valuation it places on performance, and it is punished for remaining silent by being undercompensated in the event of breach.

...

## 5. Noneconomic Approaches to the Task of Completing Contracts

Noneconomic approaches to the contract completion enterprise add little to the law and economics approach because these approaches turn out to ask the same questions as the law and economics approach, but to give inferior answers to these questions. To see why this is so, realize that the noneconomic view tells courts or the legislature to supply parties with rules that are commercially reasonable, consistent with business practice and fair. . . .

. . . [A] concern to make the law consistent with good business practice implies that the state should not create defaults that typical parties would reject as contract terms. Because commercial parties commonly prefer more to less, these parties would reject inefficient rules. The law and economics search for good defaults thus reflects a more rigorous way to answer a question that the noneconomic view also asks. Put another way, because a good default must be commercially reasonable and consistent with business practice, both the traditional and the law and economics analyst should search for efficient rules. The law and economics analyst then does better at this search because she has more tools; that is, she is accustomed to analyze commercial behavior with modern economic techniques.

In the noneconomic view, legal rules also should be fair. This view adds nothing significant to what has been discussed. To be sure, if several solutions to a particular contracting problem exist, each of which conditions on verifiable information, then perhaps the decision maker should choose the fairest solution. The actual task, however, almost never is to choose among good defaults, but rather to devise rules when because of asymmetric information no good default is apparent. A fair rule that conditioned on unverifiable information or that otherwise was inefficient would have no application beyond the case that created it. Future parties would not use the rule; they would "contract out of it" – for the reasons given. Hence, creating fair but inefficient contract law rules merely wastes transaction costs, the costs of contracting out of the rule. Noneconomic approaches thus again collapse into the law and economics approach: except in the so far purely theoretical case when more than one efficient rule exists and the efficient rules vary along a fairness dimension, the state can escape futility only by supplying efficient rules . . .

## 6. Conclusion

. . . The law and economics approach has been successful because it supplies a coherent and persuasive answer to the central theoretical question why the state should enforce promises; and it responds to the second central theoretical question how the state should complete incomplete contracts by developing more sophisticated default rules than any other approach has yielded.

  . . .

## Note

1.  Exceptions include certain types of mistakes (see Kronman) and those situations where third parties are involved (e.g., the courts will not enforce an agreement to kill a third party).

# Part V

## Corporations and Corporate Finance

# 16

## Limited Liability in the Theory of the Firm

### *Susan E. Woodward*

**EDITOR'S INTRODUCTION**

Most corporations have limited liability for their stockholders. That is, the owners of the shares are not liable for any loss beyond the value of their shares. For example, if the firm goes bankrupt, the other assets owned by the shareholders (e.g. their homes) cannot be used to pay off creditors. This means that other creditors such as bondholders are at greater risk since they cannot go after the stockholders' assets. Why do we have this form? Susan Woodward shows that limited liability reduces transaction costs and allows the corporation as we know it to exist. If stockholders were liable, then the riskiness of the stock or bond would depend on who was holding the stock. If some stockholders were very wealthy, then bondholders and other stockholders would face less risk. In order to know the amount of risk, all creditors would be constantly monitoring who owned the stock in order to know how much risk they were facing. Such monitoring would be extremely costly if the stockownership of the firm were widespread and would ultimately make the market less liquid. This transaction cost analysis yields numerous insights and answers questions such as the following: Why firms might be larger than production technology might indicate and why closely held firms are less likely to have limited liability of the major stockholders.

Limited liability is a standard feature of virtually every corporation with publicly traded shares. Creditors of limited liability firms acknowledge that debts will be paid only from the assets of the firm itself. The shareholders are not personally liable for more than they have invested in the firm.

When a firm limits liability, it does not eliminate risk, it merely reassigns it. The voluntary nature of the contracting (as opposed to tort) creditor's acknowledgement of limited liability implies that the creditor assesses the risk of lending to a limited liability organization, and charges accordingly for bearing that risk. All contracting risk-bearing parties are consequently, on average, fairly and competitively compensated. Why, then, do firms assign risk in this fashion by limiting liability? More generally, what explains the following stylized facts:

(a) All firms with publicly traded equity shares limit liability.
(b) Firms that are privately held, although they may have limited liability charters, frequently extend liability to shareholders/managers in the form of personal guarantees on loans to the firm.

Most of the explanations for the prevalence of limited liability appeal to risk-aversion. . . . . While I will agree that risk-aversion may motivate limited liability in small, closely held firms, I will argue that for the large, publicly traded firm, for which limited liability is universal, risk-aversion is neither necessary nor sufficient to explain the presence of limited liability. The explanation lies rather in the lower information and transaction costs associated with limited liability.

In particular, the most important feature of limited liability is that it accommodates transferable shares. Any extension of liability beyond the assets of the firm to the personal (extra-firm) assets of the shareholders must, in order to be enforceable, impair transferability of shares.

Little effort is necessary to motivate the desirability of transferable shares. When numerous investors cooperate in large, long-lived investment projects, transferability of the shares in these projects makes them much more desirable than they would otherwise be. Investors who wish to sell (or buy) shares to accommodate their inter-temporal consumption plans, to revise their portfolios, to achieve desired risk profiles, or to indulge changes in their beliefs about the enterprise, can do so without interfering with the management of the firm's physical assets so long as the shares are transferable. It is the transferability of the shares that allows for the separation of consumption/production decisions and consumption/investment decisions. . . .

The connection between transferability and liability assignment is easily seen by imagining a firm with unconditionally saleable shares which tries to extend liability to the shareholders (where the liable party is the holder of the share at the time request for resources is made). Were bankruptcy to threaten such a firm, any shareholders with assets worth the creditor's pursuit could simply sell their shares rather than pay up. The only willing buyers of the shares would be those whose wealth is too small for the creditors to bother pursuing. So whenever the creditors try to reach beyond the assets of the firm to the other assets of the shareholders, the shareholders found will be a group with no assets worth the cost of pursuit. If the shares are unconditionally saleable and liability extends only to the current holder of the share, extended liability simply cannot be enforced.

Thus, an easy answer to why firms limit liability is that freely transferable shares result in de facto limited liability. Making limited liability explicit simply saves transaction costs associated with the scramble of transfers when bankruptcy is imminent.

But between the extremes of perfectly transferable shares and perfectly inalienable shares (wherein shareholders could not escape specific liability) lies an array of restrictions on transfer that could make extended liability feasible. Thus, the task remains to explain why firms do not choose some interior combination of liability to shareholders and transferability of shares.

The explanation lies in understanding the costs imposed by extended liability. Any effective extension of liability makes the cash flows both to creditors and to shareholders depend on the personal wealth of each shareholder. This dependence creates incentives on the part of both creditors and shareholders to 1) invest in information about the shareholders, and also to 2) make side contracts in an attempt to control each others' behavior. Limited liability, by eliminating the dependence of firm credit on shareholder wealth, can lower the transaction and information costs for all parties connected with mutual investment projects, especially those with numerous shareholders.

Against the benefits of transferability conferred by limited liability we must consider the costs of limiting liability in order to understand the stylized facts. These costs are agency costs that arise when equity holders do not bear the full consequences of their decisions, as the equity holders of an indebted, limited liability firm do not. The nature of these costs will explain 1) why the small and closely held firms, where risk-aversion will motivate limited liability, frequently relinquish it, and 2) why the publicly traded firms (where I will argue risk-aversion cannot be the motivation for limited liability) all limit liability.

The rest of the analysis consists of first, an explanation of when and where risk-aversion is irrelevant to limited liability. Next, an analysis of the costs of extending liability, and an analysis of the costs of limiting liability. Finally, a brief discussion of the implications of this analysis for the tort creditors.

## 1. When is Risk-Aversion not the Issue?

Limited liability can be motivated solely by transaction and information costs in the case in which all firms are publicly traded. To see why risk aversion is not an issue, suppose

(1)  transaction and information costs are zero;
(2)  all firms and their creditors are firms with publicly traded shares;
(3)  shareholders all have the same beliefs and consequently hold market portfolios of risky securities.

If all firms have limited liability and one goes bankrupt, the liabilities not met by the firm's own assets will be borne as losses by its creditors (in which the shareholders of the bankrupt firm also own shares). Shares of the bankrupt firm will fall to a price of zero, and the prices of shares in the creditor firms will fall to reflect the change in anticipated receipts.

If the bankrupt firm had extended liability instead, ex ante of bankruptcy, the terms of credit will be "better" (reflect that more risk is borne by the firm itself and less by its creditors). Each firm will both pay less for the financing of its receivables and get less for financing its payables. Net risk borne across firms is unchanged. The net difference in income across firms is zero.

When one firm goes bankrupt, the price of its shares would still go to zero, but the price of creditor firm shares would remain unchanged. The amounts owed to the creditor would be met with funds provided by the shareholders (assuming they willingly pay, of course, an aspect of zero transaction costs). Thus, the effect of a bankruptcy on the shareholders' wealth is the same regardless of the liability rule. Whether a firm has limited liability or not does not affect the portfolio return distributions, nor the value of the firm, nor the allocation of resources. Risk-avoidance hence cannot be a motivation for limited liability here.

## 2. Costs of Extending Liability to Shareholders

Since we have already seen that the absence of information and transaction costs leads to the irrelevance of limited liability, we look to these costs to explain this institution.

The magnitude of the costs of extending liability to shareholders depends on the specific nature of the shareholder's responsibilities. The most common form of liability holds the shareholders jointly and severally liable for the debts of the firm. If the firm's assets are insufficient to meet its liabilities, each shareholder is initially responsible for a fraction of the debts proportionate to his/her shareholdings. If the other stockholders are unable to meet their obligations, each remaining shareholder can be held responsible for the obligations of the others. A milder form of extended liability holds shareholders responsible for only a fraction of firm debts proportionate to their shareholdings, leaving those debts unmet by individual shareholders as losses to the creditors, not the other shareholders. An even milder form (referred to in legal discussions as assessability), which prevailed on some U.S. bank shares even into the twentieth century, holds shareholders liable only for a specified amount per share.

All of these extended liability rules give rise to costly activity associated with enforcement and with anticipating enforcement. After a bankruptcy, shareholders owe creditors the difference between assets and liabilities. Other things equal, they would like to escape paying. But the creditors prefer to be paid, and will pursue the shareholders for what is due to them. The resources creditors will expend pursuing each shareholder will of course depend on what they anticipate they can recover. Under strong rules, such as joint and several liability, richer shareholders will be pursued more vigorously than they will be with weaker rules such as assessability. Shareholders themselves will have no motivation to pursue each other with a proportionate liability or assessability rule. With joint and several liability, however, the richer shareholders (who are most likely to be pursued by the creditors) will pursue poorer ones for their share.

But likely the greater costs of extending liability are not those associated with collections ex post of a bankruptcy, but with the dealings ex ante attempting to assure these collections can take place.

Prior to and in anticipation of a bankruptcy, creditors and shareholders alike are motivated to examine and assure the solvency of each shareholder, regardless of the form of the extended liability. The issue is not simply whether the shareholders will be able to pay their share in a bankruptcy, but also that even if no bankruptcy actually occurs, the mere likelihood of it implies that every stockholder's wealth influences the firm's credit, and consequently makes each shareholder care about who the other shareholders are and how they manage their other assets. Even if the liability rule is just assessability (liability only for a specified amount per share), the prospects of each shareholder to meet the assessment affect the firm's credit and as a result, the wealth of all other shareholders. Thus, the creditors (in order to assess the firm's credit) and each shareholder (in order to determine the firm's value) have incentives to invest real resources to secure information about the amount and composition of shareholder wealth – information unrelated to the firm's productive activities.

For example, if a wealthy shareholder sells to someone who has no appropriable wealth other than the shares, the inability of the new owner to meet the debts of an extended liability firm worsens the terms the firm receives from its creditors, and consequently lowers the wealth of the other shareholders. Thus, the other shareholders would be willing to spend some resources to inhibit this transaction. Likewise, a wealthy shareholder's extra-firm wealth may consist of Treasury Bills which he could trade for a highly infungible sailboat. This transaction also would impair the firm's credit and it is in the interest of the other shareholders to deter it.

The interest in shareholder wealth that accompanies extended liability also motivates shareholders and creditors to invest in making side contracts with one another to resolve the conflicts of interest that extended liability creates. One way to prevent a wealthy shareholder from selling to an impecunious one is to restrict the set of potential owners of the stock to those with at least some minimum wealth. This may improve the firm's credit, but it could also lower the demand price for the firm's shares and make the cost of capital higher. Another solution is to require any shareholder who could not bond wealth of a particular amount and composition to carry insurance. The investigation to determine the insurance premium and the enforcement of the purchase of insurance are themselves costly. Yet another suggestion is that the firm carry insurance on behalf of the shareholders.

Even this solution (insurance purchased by the firm) would not, however, resolve all conflicts of interest, as poor shareholders and rich shareholders would not agree on the level of insurance that ought to be carried. If the firm buys the insurance, the rich shareholders and poor shareholders bear equally (pro-rated by shareholdings) the cost of the insurance. But the rich shareholders have more assets to protect from extended liability than do the poor ones, and will likely desire a higher level of coverage. Even if the shareholders are unanimous on the probabilities of various states of the world, and consequently, how much should be invested in, say, finding oil, they will still not, because of their different personal situations, agree on the level of liability insurance to be carried.

The idea that limited liability prevails because of a failure of insurance markets . . . is wrong for two reasons. First, it takes as a premise that the motivation for limited liability is risk-aversion, which is incorrect. Second, it implies that insurance solves all of the problems which limited liability solves, which is also not true, because conflicts of interest among shareholders remain on just how much insurance should be carried, not because of differing degrees of risk-aversion, but because of the web of externalities among shareholders.

Another device to prevent shareholders from escaping liability on transferable shares is to hold liable those who owned the shares when the liability was created rather than those who own it when the bankruptcy occurs. Essentially this liability assignment makes inalienable the potential debts created during one's tenure of ownership. By assigning liability in this way, new shareholders, who control the firm, could appropriate wealth from former shareholders by managing old assets in a more risky way. This assignment of liability makes the new shareholders the owners of a "call" on the firm's assets, with the old shareholders the "writers" of the call. Increasing the riskiness of the underlying assets makes the call more valuable without compensating the call writers. The former shareholders would have even less opportunity than the creditors, who at least have continuing transactions with the firm, to influence how assets are managed. It would seem that the former shareholders would charge a price for this liability assignment that the new shareholders would never be willing to pay.

The lesson of this section is that the costs of extended liability rise with the number of shareholders. The costs seemingly would rise exponentially as shareholders are added until transfers become sufficiently frequent that a secondary market arises, at which point they become truly prohibitive. Thus, we have at least a partial explanation for the first of our stylized facts: publicly traded firms are more likely to limit liability because it is for these firms that extended liability is more costly.

## 3. Costs of Limiting Liability

Extended liability creates among shareholders conflicts of interest that are eliminated by limiting liability. But limiting liability exacerbates the conflicts of interest between the firm and its creditors.

When a firm operates partly with borrowed money, the equity holders have an incentive to manage the firm's assets in a more risky way than if the firm were financed purely with equity. With pure equity, all profits and all losses fall directly on the equity holders. With some debt financing, losses beyond the initial equity are born by the creditors (even with extended liability, as there is some chance shareholders cannot or will not pay the firm's debts). Creditors anticipate the incentives for the equity holders to take larger risks with borrowed money, and charge accordingly.

If the creditors could easily monitor the activities of the firm and influence the decisions about how assets are managed, they would make contracts to guarantee that the assets would be managed the same way regardless of the financing arrangements. But monitoring is costly. If creditors monitored to this limit, the terms on which they offered credit would reflect the monitoring costs, and by this amount reduce the value of the firm. More generally, creditors will monitor to the point where the marginal cost of monitoring equals the marginal benefit, and the value of the firm will be reduced (compared to pure equity) partly by the cost of monitoring and partly by the lower value of the set of projects chosen by levered equity interests.

Limiting liability increases the equity interests' motivation to manage assets in a more risky fashion, simply because creditors assume the burden of a larger share of the losses. We can thus expect the costs associated with conflicts of interest between creditors and stockholders to be higher with limited liability than with extended liability, and to rise with the firm's indebtedness.

Another cost of limited liability, unrelated to the monitoring problems of this arrangement, is that the party to whom the risk is transferred may be less well prepared to bear it than are the shareholders. This is especially true in the case of creditors who are other than traded firms – such as employees and customers. But the solution here is not to extend liability to shareholders, but for the firm to either have a larger capitalization, or to purchase insurance on behalf of these creditors. In fact, this is an important feature of corporate finance. ... [F]or U.S. firms, the total amount spent on insurance regularly exceeds the amount paid in dividends.

So far we have established 1) extended liability is costly in relation to the number of shareholders, and 2) limited liability is costly in relation to size of a firm's liabilities (clearly, a firm with no debt has no agency costs of dealing with its creditors). From this several prior questions demand consideration:

(1)   Why are some firms "big" and some firms "small" in total assets?
(2)   Why are some firms publicly traded and others not?
(3)   Why do firms use debt financing?

The classical notion of "economies of scale" serves as the usual explanation of firm size. But there is another dimension for "economics of scale" which should make us reconsider this explanation: the value of transferable shares traded in a secondary market. Other things being equal (issues of control, in particular) investors always prefer liquid (saleable) assets to illiquid ones, simply because they offer more flexibility. But there are big "economies of scale" in information production that prevent small companies from having publicly traded shares. The company must be large enough to overcome the fixed and variable costs of informing the market about itself before it can be publicly traded and must have a "critical mass" of value so that there is regular trading and a liquid market.

Thus, it is easy to understand why an oil refinery must be a large, publicly traded firm. Oil refineries cannot operate efficiently unless they are of such enormous scale that nobody can afford to own a whole one. Given the "classical" scale economy, the "market" scale economy affording transferable, liquid shares follows naturally.

But what about a firm like a car wash? Indeed, there is not much in the way of scale economies in a car wash (except that they dominate washing the car at home), but why do we not have national chains of car wash establishments, which are jointly owned and have publicly traded shares? The publicly traded shares would offer car wash investors much greater liquidity and diversifiability than the individual ownership system does.

Car washes do not survive as a national chain, jointly owned and publicly traded, because they will not be run efficiently unless the manager has the incentives provided by having full entitlement to the profits of the enterprise. Apparently the disadvantages of being less than fully diversified and holding an illiquid asset are overcome by the increased profits that result when the owner and manager are the same party. The car wash business is a very morally hazardous business: depending on whether a car wash is run by a hired manager or by an owner, the productive outcomes are very different. Firm size is not just a matter of classical economies of scale, but of organizational economies of scale.

There are likely some intermediate firms, where the assets would be operated more efficiently by a full owner than by a manager, but not enough so as to overcome the advantages of transferable liquid shares. So even if these enterprises have little in the way of classical economies of scale, they are grouped together and traded as a bundle on the stock exchange in order to exploit market economies of scale, and along the way some agency costs are borne.

Why do firms borrow? In the twentieth century the explanation seized with alacrity is of course taxes. Since interest is deductible for corporations, interest paid is a device for moving income outside the firm without paying corporate income taxes on it. But the corporate income tax is a creature of [modern times], and corporate debt, while more extensive now than in previous eras, arose along with the joint-stock company itself in the late sixteenth century.

For the large, publicly traded firm, risk-aversion cannot explain the presence of debt. The degree to which risks can be reshuffled and diversified in markets is hardly augmented by a firm's issuing debt. The "optimal" debt/equity ratio is found by trading off the moral hazard (monitoring, agency) costs of debt against the tax benefits of debt. Optimism could explain some debt on the part of even large firms, as optimists hold the equity and pessimists hold the debt. Although given the resources devoted to producing information about traded firms (plus the opportunities for short selling), it is difficult to believe that large information asymmetries remain.

For the privately held firm not only taxes and optimism explain debt. We have at least two other candidates: wealth constraints and risk-aversion. The sole owner may believe his operation could be profitably expanded, but either his wealth limits his ability to do it himself or he wishes to take no more risk himself. In either case, he will be willing to sell shares of equity to others if they will pay what he regards as the value of the equity. But if they are less optimistic than he, they won't. Consequently, he believes it cheaper to raise funds with debt than with equity.

Risk-aversion and optimism together will also explain why a privately held firm will debt finance and seek to limit liability. If the privately held firm's creditors are traded firms, they are better able to diversify the risk than can the non-traded firm itself, and hence are likely to be willing to bear the risk more cheaply than the equity holder. If the firm's creditor's are themselves also non-traded firms, limited liability still provides at least some diversification (and hence reduction) of the down-side risk as each firm takes a small piece of the (presumably non-perfectly correlated) down-side risks in many other firms by extending credit to them.

Yet it is precisely among non-traded firms that limited liability is most frequently offset contractually. The owner or a major shareholder in a closely held firm often guarantees a loan to the firm and agrees to be personally liable for the loan. Often the loan contract will explicitly impair the alienability of the owners' interest in the firm, treating that interest as the primary collateral for the loan.

And so here we have the explanation for our second stylized fact: The qualities which predispose a firm to be privately held – substantial monitoring costs and optimism – also imply the claims to its assets are already unlikely to be exchanged. Thus, extending liability will not be so costly for these firms, as other forces already preclude the volume of transactions and the dispersed ownership that make extended liability expensive. Where transferability has been inhibited by the nature of the investment project or the owners' beliefs, the transaction costs of extending liability are sufficiently small that it is feasible. And so despite the risk-avoidance afforded by limited liability, it is frequently relinquished by the owners of claims that are inherently not very liquid anyway.

## 4. Limited Liability and the Tort Creditors

For the tort creditors (the passer-by on whom a construction company inadvertently drops a brick, the pedestrian accidentally struck by a taxicab) limited liability can indeed mean failure of a corporation to compensate a creditor if the corporation's net assets are smaller than the damage done to the tort creditor. Unlike contracting creditors, the tort creditors have no opportunity to charge for the risks they bear through limited liability. Firms thus have an opportunity to impose uncompensated costs (externalities) on tort creditors by limiting liability. I would expect that firms with greater than average potential tort claims would make a greater than average effort to escape these claims. Perhaps this is why taxicabs are often incorporated separately and why construction companies often incorporate each project independently.

Insurance can extend the ability of a limited liability corporation to satisfy the claims of tort creditors. If correcting externalities is a proper role of government, it is appropriate to mandate that firms carry liability insurance. Then the issue becomes one of "adequate" insurance, not limited versus extended liability, and the problem of optimal insurance and incentives is fraught with all the difficulties of any problem involving externalities. Moreover, once firms and contracting creditors have settled upon the institution of perfectly transferable shares, the potential tort creditors gain no protection by the extension of liability to shareholders. If shareholders can escape their debts by mere sale, insurance is the only route for extending protection for potential tort creditors.

To a lesser degree the problem of the socially optimal amount of liability insurance remains with extended liability also. Even in the most insured of worlds, the possibility remains of an accident of such magnitude that the assets of the firm as well as its insurance company are exhausted. There is no such thing as unlimited liability.

## 5. Conclusion

Nature has endowed us with a number of productive opportunities whose large-scale and risky nature require amassing the resources of many individuals. The pre-eminent institutional form for exploiting such opportunities is the transferable share, limited liability corporation. The advantage of transferable shares is evident: differences in individual desires for consumption over time can be indulged, and changes in individual preferences, wealth, and beliefs about the future can be accommodated by revisions of individual portfolios that need not affect the productive decisions of the corporation itself.

The advantage of limited liability has been generally misconceived. The appeal of limited liability for the multi-shareholder firm lies not in its capacity to shift risk away from equity holders to creditors, but rather in accommodating the alienability of the firm's shares. Unlimited transferability of equity shares implies that creditors will recover at most the firm's total assets, as shareholders can escape liability simply by selling. To enforce extended liability, transferability must be restricted. Once such restrictions are imposed, creditors and shareholders alike want information about shareholders' personal financial situations, and conflicts of interest arise in managing the firm's assets and liabilities.

With limited liability, no shareholder or creditor need be concerned with the identity or characteristics of the other shareholders. Management can turn its attention to maximizing firm value, confident that any shareholder discontent with the selected risk profile or the timing of cash flows can simply sell to one who is not. It is the saleability of the shares in a firm, facilitated by limited liability, which endows the firm with a life of its own and allows the separation of consumption, risk-bearing, and production decisions so rightfully celebrated in economic theory.

# 17

# Theory of the Firm: Managerial Behavior, Agency Costs, and Ownership Structure

*Michael C. Jensen and William H. Meckling*

## EDITOR'S INTRODUCTION

Corporations are owned by stockholders (the principals), but they are run by managers (the agents). Stockholders want to maximize the return on their investments. Managers want to maximize their utility (e.g. keeping their jobs and obtaining perquisites). While monitoring, stock options and the like can help to align the interests of the managers with the stockholders, the alignment is never perfect and the methods to encourage alignment are themselves costly. Michael Jensen and William Meckling consider this agency problem (a type of transaction cost) and compare it to the transaction costs of raising capital via bonds. The risk to bondholders increases as the share of capital in the firm held by capital decreases because the stockholders are playing with other people's money. Therefore bondholders must also spend considerable resources monitoring the firm or writing complex contracts when the bond/equity ratio is high. This transaction cost theory explains the optimal mix between bonds and equity in a corporation. As Modigliani and Miller had shown in their Nobel prize-winning work, in the absence of transaction costs and tax advantages, there is no reason for choosing one form of capital over the other. Jensen and Meckling's article thus provides an explanation for the puzzle raised by Modigliani and Miller – what accounts for the debt/equity ratios in corporations. Jensen and Meckling also use transaction costs to explain the ratio of inside equity held by managers to outside equity held by parties otherwise unconnected to the firm.

In their article, Jensen and Meckling provide a deeper understanding of the internal organization of the firm than the isocost analysis typical of neoclassical economic theory. From their perspective, the firm is a nexus of contracts between various parties – stockholders, managers, bondholders, workers, suppliers, etc. The equilibrium of this nexus yields an outcome similar to, but more nuanced than, the neoclassical model of profit maximization. Once the firm is seen as a nexus of contracts most of the distinction between the theory of contracts and the theory of the firm is lost. Thus Rubin's article on franchises could be in this section and this article could have been placed under the contracts heading.

This paper integrates elements from the theory of agency, the theory of property rights, and the theory of finance to develop a theory of the ownership structure of the firm. We define the concept of agency costs, show its relationship to the "separation and control" issue, investigate the nature of the agency costs generated by the existence of debt and outside equity, demonstrate who bears these costs and why, and investigate the Pareto optimality of their existence. We also provide a new definition of the firm. . . .

> The directors of such [joint-stock] companies, however, being the managers rather of other people's money than of their own, it cannot well be expected, that they should watch over it with the same anxious vigilance with which the partners in a private copartnery frequently watch over their own. Like the stewards of a rich man, they are apt to consider attention to small matters as not for their master's honour, and very easily give themselves a dispensation from having it. Negligence and profusion, therefore, must always prevail, more or less, in the management of the affairs of such a company.
>
> Adam Smith, *The Wealth of Nations,* 1776, Cannan Edition (Modern Library, New York, 1937) p. 700.

# 1. Introduction and Summary

## 1.1. MOTIVATION OF THE PAPER

In this paper we draw on recent progress in the theory of (1) property rights, (2) agency, and (3) finance to develop a theory of ownership structure for the firm. In addition to tying together elements of the theory of each of these three areas, our analysis casts new light on and has implications for a variety of issues in the professional and popular literature such as the definition of the firm, the "separation of ownership and control," the "social responsibility" of business, the definition of a "corporate objective function," the determination of an optimal capital structure, the specification of the content of credit agreements, the theory of organizations, and the supply side of the completeness of markets problem.

Our theory helps explain:

(1)    why an entrepreneur or manager in a firm which has a mixed financial structure (containing both debt and outside equity claims) will choose a set of activities for the firm such that the total value of the firm is *less* than it would be if he were the sole owner and why this result is independent of whether the firm operates in monopolistic or competitive product or factor markets;

(2)    why his failure to maximize the value of the firm is perfectly consistent with efficiency;

(3)    why the sale of common stock is a viable source of capital even though managers do not literally maximize the value of the firm;

(4)    why debt was relied upon as a source of capital before debt financing offered any tax advantage relative to equity;

(5)    why preferred stock would be issued;

(6)    why accounting reports would be provided voluntarily to creditors and stockholders, and why independent auditors would be engaged by management to testify to the accuracy and correctness of such reports;

(7)    why lenders often place restrictions on the activities of firms to whom they lend, and why firms would themselves be led to suggest the imposition of such restrictions;

(8)    why some industries are characterized by owner-operated firms whose sole outside source of capital is borrowing;

(9)    why highly regulated industries such as public utilities or banks will have higher debt equity ratios for equivalent levels of risk than the average non-regulated firm;

(10)    why security analysis can be socially productive even if it does not increase portfolio returns to investors.

## 1.2. Theory of the firm: An empty box?

While the literature of economics is replete with references to the "theory of the firm," the material generally subsumed under that heading is not a theory of the firm but actually a theory of markets in which firms are important actors. The firm is a "black box" operated so as to meet the relevant marginal conditions with respect to inputs and outputs, thereby maximizing profits, or more accurately, present value. Except for a few recent and tentative steps, however, we have no theory which explains how the conflicting objectives of the individual participants are brought into equilibrium so as to yield this result.

   . . .

## 1.4. Agency costs

Many problems associated with the inadequacy of the current theory of the firm can also be viewed as special cases of the theory of agency relationships. . . .

   We define an agency relationship as a contract under which one or more persons (the principal(s)) engage another person (the agent) to perform some service on their behalf which involves delegating some decision-making authority to the agent. If both parties to the relationship are utility maximizers there is good reason to believe that the agent will not always act in the best interests of the principal. The *principal* can limit divergences from his interest by establishing appropriate incentives for the agent and by incurring monitoring costs designed to limit the aberrant activities of the agent. In addition, in some situations it will pay the *agent* to expend resources (bonding costs) to guarantee that he will not take certain actions which would harm the principal or to ensure that the principal will be compensated if he does take such actions. However, it is generally impossible for the principal or the agent at zero cost to ensure that the agent will make optimal decisions from the principal's viewpoint. In most agency relationships the principal and the agent will incur positive monitoring and bonding costs (non-pecuniary as well as pecuniary), and in addition there will be some divergence between the agent's decisions and those decisions which would maximize the welfare of the principal. The dollar equivalent of the reduction in welfare experienced by the principal due to this divergence is also a cost of the agency relationship, and we refer to this latter cost as the "residual loss". We define *agency costs* as the sum of:

(1)    the monitoring expenditures by the principal;
(2)    the bonding expenditures by the agent;
(3)    the residual loss.

Note . . . that agency costs arise in any situation involving cooperative effort (such as the co-authoring of this paper) by two or more people even though there is no clear-cut principal–agent relationship. . . .

   Since the relationship between the stockholders and manager of a corporation fit the definition of a pure agency relationship it should be no surprise to discover that the issues associated with the "separation of ownership and control" in the modern diffuse ownership corporation are intimately associated with the general problem of agency. We show below that an explanation of why and how the agency costs generated by the corporate form are born leads to a theory of the ownership (or capital) structure of the firm.

Before moving on, however, it is worthwhile to point out the generality of the agency problem. The problem of inducing an "agent" to behave as if he were maximizing the "principal's" welfare is quite general. It exists in all organizations and in all cooperative efforts – at every level of management in firms, in universities, in mutual companies, in cooperatives, in governmental authorities and bureaus, in unions, and in relationships normally classified as agency relationships such as are common in the performing arts and the market for real estate. . . . . We confine our attention in this paper to only a small part of this general problem – the analysis of agency costs generated by the contractual arrangements between the owners and top management of the corporation.

Our approach to the agency problem here differs fundamentally from most of the existing literature. That literature focuses almost exclusively on the normative aspects of the agency relationship; that is how to structure the contractual relation (including compensation incentives) between the principal and agent to provide appropriate incentives for the agent to make choices which will maximize the principal's welfare given that uncertainty and imperfect monitoring exist. We focus almost entirely on the positive aspects of the theory. That is, we assume individuals solve these normative problems and given that only stocks and bonds can be issued as claims, we investigate the incentives faced by each of the parties and the elements entering into the determination of the equilibrium contractual form characterizing the relationship between the manager (i.e., agent) of the firm and the outside equity and debt holders (i.e., principals).

## 1.5. SOME GENERAL COMMENTS ON THE DEFINITION OF THE FIRM

. . . .

It is important to recognize that most organizations are simply *legal fictions which serve as a nexus for a set of contracting relationships among individuals.* This includes firms, non-profit institutions such as universities, hospitals and foundations, mutual organizations such as mutual savings banks and insurance companies and cooperatives, some private clubs, and even governmental bodies such as cities, states and the federal government, government enterprises such as TVA, the Post Office, transit systems, etc.

The private corporation or firm is simply one form of *legal fiction which serves as a nexus for contracting relationships and which is also characterized by the existence of divisible residual claims on the assets and cash flows of the organization which can generally be sold without permission of the other contracting individuals.* While this definition of the firm has little substantive content, emphasizing the essential contractual nature of firms and other organizations focuses attention on a crucial set of questions – why particular sets of contractual relations arise for various types of organizations, what the consequences of these contractual relations are, and how they are affected by changes exogenous to the organization. Viewed this way, it makes little or no sense to try to distinguish those things which are "inside" the firm (or any other organization) from those things that are "outside" of it. There is in a very real sense only a multitude of complex relationships (i.e., contracts) between the legal fiction (the firm) and the owners of labor, material, and capital inputs and the consumers of output.

Viewing the firm as the nexus of a set of contracting relationships among individuals also serves to make it clear that the personalization of the firm implied by asking questions such as "what should be the objective function of the firm", or "does the firm have a social responsibility" is seriously misleading. *The firm is not an individual.* It is a legal fiction which serves as a focus for a complex process in which the conflicting objectives of individuals (some of whom may "represent" other organizations) are brought into equilibrium within a framework of contractual relations. In this sense the "behavior" of the firm is like the behavior of a market; i.e., the outcome of a complex equilibrium process. We seldom fall into the trap of characterizing the wheat or stock market as an individual, but we often make this error by thinking about organizations as if they were persons with motivations and intentions.

### 1.6. AN OVERVIEW OF THE PAPER

We develop the theory in stages. Sections 2 and 4 provide analyses of the agency costs of equity and debt, respectively. These form the major foundation of the theory. Section 3 poses some unanswered questions regarding the existence of the corporate form of organization and examines the role of limited liability. Section 5 provides a synthesis of the basic concepts derived in sections 2-4 into a theory of the corporate ownership structure which takes account of the tradeoffs available to the entrepreneur-manager between inside and outside equity and debt. . . . .

## 2. The Agency Costs of Outside Equity

### 2.1. OVERVIEW

In this section we analyze the effect of outside equity on agency costs by comparing the behavior of a manager when he owns 100 percent of the residual claims on a firm to his behavior when he sells off a portion of those claims to outsiders. If a wholly owned firm is managed by the owner, he will make operating decisions which maximize his utility. These decisions will involve not only the benefits he derives from pecuniary returns but also the utility generated by various non-pecuniary aspects of his entrepreneurial activities such as the physical appointments of the office, the attractiveness of the secretarial staff, the level of employee discipline, the kind and amount of charitable contributions, personal relations ("love," "respect," etc.) with employees, a larger than optimal computer to play with, purchase of production inputs from friends, etc. The optimum mix (in the absence of taxes) of the various pecuniary and non-pecuniary benefits is achieved when the marginal utility derived from an additional dollar of expenditure (measured net of any productive effects) is equal for each non-pecuniary item and equal to the marginal utility derived from an additional dollar of after-tax purchasing power (wealth).

If the owner-manager sells equity claims on the corporation which are identical to his (i.e., share proportionately in the profits of the firm and have limited liability), agency costs will be generated by the divergence between his interest and those of the outside shareholders, since he will then bear only a fraction of the costs of any non-pecuniary benefits he takes out in maximizing his own utility. If the manager owns only 95 percent of the stock, he will expend resources to the point where the marginal utility derived from a dollar's expenditure of the firm's resources on such items equals the marginal utility of an additional 95 cents in general purchasing power (i.e., *his* share of the wealth reduction) and not one dollar. Such activities, on his part, can be limited (but probably not eliminated) by the expenditure of resources on monitoring activities by the outside stockholders. But, as we show below, the owner will bear the entire wealth effects of these expected costs so long as the equity market anticipates these effects. Prospective minority shareholders will realize that the owner-manager's interests will diverge somewhat from theirs, hence the price which they will pay for shares will reflect the monitoring costs and the effect of the divergence between the manager's interest and theirs. Nevertheless, ignoring for the moment the possibility of borrowing against his wealth, the owner will find it desirable to bear these costs as long as the welfare increment he experiences from converting his claims on the firm into general purchasing power is large enough to offset them.

As the owner-manager's fraction of the equity falls, his fractional claim on the outcomes falls and this will tend to encourage him to appropriate larger amounts of the corporate resources in the form of perquisites. This also makes it desirable for the minority shareholders to expend more resources in monitoring his behavior. Thus, the wealth costs to the owner of obtaining additional cash in the equity markets rise as his fractional ownership falls.

We shall continue to characterize the agency conflict between the owner-manager and outside shareholders as deriving from the manager's tendency to appropriate perquisites out of the firm's resources for his own consumption. However, we do not mean to leave the impression that this is the only or even the most important source of conflict. Indeed, it is likely that the most important conflict arises from the fact that as the manager's ownership claim falls, his incentive to devote significant effort to creative activities such as searching out new profitable ventures falls. He may in fact avoid such ventures simply because it requires too much trouble or effort on his part to manage or to learn about new technologies. Avoidance of these personal costs and the anxieties that go with them also represent a source of on-the-job utility to him and it can result in the value of the firm being substantially lower than it otherwise could be.

. . .

## 2.4. THE ROLE OF MONITORING AND BONDING ACTIVITIES IN REDUCING AGENCY COSTS

. . . In practice, it is usually possible by expending resources to alter the opportunity the owner-manager has for capturing non-pecuniary benefits. These methods include auditing, formal control systems, budget restrictions, and the establishment of incentive compensation systems which serve to more closely identify the manager's interests with those of the outside equity holders, etc. . . .

. . . Suppose that the owner-manager could expend resources to guarantee to the outside equity holders that he would limit his activities which cost the firm *F*. We call these expenditures "bonding costs," and they would take such forms as contractual guarantees to have the financial accounts audited by a public account, explicit bonding against malfeasance on the part of the manager, and contractual limitations on the manager's decision-making power (which impose costs on the firm because they limit his ability to take full advantage of some profitable opportunities as well as limiting his ability to harm the stockholders while making himself better off).

. . . The manager finds it in his interest to incur these costs as long as the net increments in his wealth which they generate (by reducing the agency costs and therefore increasing the value of the firm) are more valuable than the perquisites given up. . . . In general, of course, it will pay the owner-manager to engage in bonding activities and to write contracts which allow monitoring as long as the marginal benefits of each are greater than their marginal cost.

## 2.5. PARETO OPTIMALITY AND AGENCY COSTS IN MANAGER-OPERATED FIRMS

In general we expect to observe both bonding and external monitoring activities, and the incentives are such that the levels of these activities will satisfy the conditions of efficiency. They will not, however, result in the firm being run in a manner so as to maximize its value. The difference between $V^*$, the efficient solution under zero monitoring and bonding costs (and therefore zero agency costs), and $V'''$, the value of the firm given positive monitoring costs, are the total gross agency costs defined earlier in the introduction. These are the costs of the "separation of ownership and control" which Adam Smith focused on in the passage quoted at the beginning of this paper and which Berle and Means (1932) popularized 157 years later. The solutions outlined above to our highly simplified problem imply that agency costs will be positive as long as monitoring costs are positive – which they certainly are.

The reduced value of the firm caused by the manager's consumption of perquisites outlined above is "non-optimal" or inefficient only in comparison to a world in which we could obtain compliance of the agent to the principal's wishes at zero cost or in comparison to a *hypothetical* world in which the agency costs were lower. But these costs (monitoring and bonding costs and "residual loss") are an unavoidable result of the agency relationship. Furthermore, since they are borne entirely by the decision maker (in this case the original owner) responsible for creating the relationship, he has the incentives to see that they are minimized (because he captures the benefits from their reduction). Furthermore, these agency costs will be incurred only if the benefits to the owner-manager from their creation are great enough to outweigh them. In our current example these benefits arise from the availability of profitable investments requiring capital investment in excess of the original owner's personal wealth.

In conclusion, finding that agency costs are non-zero (i.e., that there are costs associated with the separation of ownership and control in the corporation) and concluding therefrom that the agency relationship is non-optimal, wasteful, or inefficient is equivalent in every sense to comparing a world in which iron ore is a scarce commodity (and therefore costly) to a world in which it is freely available at zero resource cost, and concluding that the first world is "non-optimal" . . .

## 2.6. FACTORS AFFECTING THE SIZE OF THE DIVERGENCE FROM IDEAL MAXIMIZATION

The magnitude of the agency costs discussed above will vary from firm to firm. It will depend on the tastes of managers, the ease with which they can exercise their own preferences as opposed to value maximization in decision making, and the costs of monitoring and bonding activities. The agency costs will also depend upon the cost of measuring the manager's (agent's) performance and evaluating it, the cost of devising and applying an index for compensating the manager which correlates with the owner's (principal's) welfare, and the cost of devising and enforcing specific behavioral rules or policies. Where the manager has less than a controlling interest in the firm, it will also depend upon the market for managers. Competition from other potential managers limits the costs of obtaining managerial services (including the extent to which a given manager can diverge from the idealized solution which would obtain if all monitoring and bonding costs were zero). The size of the divergence (the agency costs) will be directly related to the cost of replacing the manager. If his responsibilities require very little knowledge specialized to the firm, if it is easy to evaluate his performance, and if replacement search costs are modest, the divergence from the ideal will be relatively small and vice versa.

The divergence will also be constrained by the market for the firm itself, i.e., by capital markets. Owners always have the option of selling their firm, either as a unit or piecemeal. Owners of manager-operated firms can and do sample the capital market from time to time. If they discover that the value of the future earnings stream to others is higher than the value of the firm to them given that it is to be manager-operated, they can exercise their right to sell. It is conceivable that other owners could be more efficient at monitoring or even that a single individual with appropriate managerial talents and with sufficiently large personal wealth would elect to buy the firm. In this latter case the purchase by such a single individual would completely eliminate the agency costs. If there were a number of such potential owner-manager purchasers (all with talents and tastes identical to the current manager) the owners would receive in the sale price of the firm the full value of the residual claimant rights including the capital value of the eliminated agency costs plus the value of the managerial rights.

### Monopoly, competition, and managerial behavior

It is frequently argued that the existence of competition in product (and factor) markets will constrain the behavior of managers to idealized value maximization, i.e., that monopoly in product (or monopsony in factor) markets will permit larger divergences from value maximization. Our analysis does not support this hypothesis. The owners of a firm with monopoly power have the same incentives to limit divergences of the manager from value maximization (i.e., the ability to increase their wealth) as do the owners of competitive firms. Furthermore, competition in the market for managers will generally make it unnecessary for the owners to share rents with the manager. The owners of a monopoly firm need only pay the supply price for a manager.

Since the owner of a monopoly has the same wealth incentives to minimize managerial costs as would the owner of a competitive firm, both will undertake that level of monitoring which equates the marginal cost of monitoring to the marginal wealth increment from reduced consumption of perquisites by the manager. Thus, the existence of monopoly will not increase agency costs.

Furthermore the existence of competition in product and factor markets will not eliminate the agency costs due to managerial control problems as has often been asserted. . . . If my competitors all incur agency costs equal to or greater than mine I will not be eliminated from the market by their competition.

The existence and size of the agency costs depend on the nature of the monitoring costs, the tastes of managers for non-pecuniary benefits, and the supply of potential managers who are capable of financing the entire venture out of their personal wealth. If monitoring costs are zero, agency costs will be zero or if there are enough 100 percent owner-managers available to own and run all the firms in an industry (competitive or not) then agency costs in that industry will also be zero.

# 3. Some Unanswered Questions Regarding the Existence of the Corporate Form

## 3.1. THE QUESTION

The analysis to this point has left us with a basic puzzle: Why, given the existence of positive costs of the agency relationship, do we find the usual corporate form of organization with widely diffuse ownership so widely prevalent? If one takes seriously much of the literature regarding the "discretionary" power held by managers of large corporations, it is difficult to understand the historical fact of enormous growth in equity in such organizations, not only in the United States, but throughout the world. . . . How does it happen that millions of individuals are willing to turn over a significant fraction of their wealth to organizations run by managers who have so little interest in their welfare? What is even more remarkable, why are they willing to make these commitments purely as residual claimants, i.e., on the anticipation that managers will operate the firm so that there will be earnings which accrue to the stockholders?

There is certainly no lack of alternative ways that individuals might invest, including entirely different forms of organizations. Even if consideration is limited to corporate organizations, there are clearly alternative ways capital might be raised, i.e., through fixed claims of various sorts, bonds, notes, mortgages, etc. . . . Those who assert that managers do not behave in the interest of stockholders have generally not addressed a very important question: Why, if non-manager-owned shares have such a serious deficiency, have they not long since been driven out by fixed claims?

## 3.2. SOME ALTERNATIVE EXPLANATIONS OF THE OWNERSHIP STRUCTURE OF THE FIRM

### The role of limited liability

Manne (1967) and Alchian and Demsetz (1972) argue that one of the attractive features of the corporate form vis-à-vis individual proprietorships or partnerships is the limited liability feature of equity claims in corporations. Without this provision each and every investor purchasing one or more shares of a corporation would be potentially liable to the full extent of his personal wealth for the debts of the corporation. Few individuals would find this a desirable risk to accept and the major benefits to be obtained from risk reduction through diversification would be to a large extent unobtainable. This argument, however, is incomplete since limited liability does not eliminate the basic risk, it merely shifts it. The argument must rest ultimately on transactions costs. If all stockholders of GM were liable for GM's debts, the maximum liability for an individual shareholder would be greater than it would be if his shares had limited liability. However, given that many other stockholders also existed and that each was liable for the unpaid claims in proportion to his ownership it is highly unlikely that the maximum payment each would have to make would be large in the event of GM's bankruptcy since the total wealth of those stockholders would also be large. However, the existence of unlimited liability would impose incentives for each shareholder to keep track of both the liabilities of GM and the wealth of the other GM owners. It is easily conceivable that the costs of so doing would, in the aggregate, be much higher than simply paying a premium in the form of higher interest rates to the creditors of GM in return for their acceptance of a contract which grants limited liability to the shareholders. The creditors would then bear the risk of any non-payment of debts in the event of GM's bankruptcy.

It is also not generally recognized that limited liability is merely a necessary condition for explaining the magnitude of the reliance on equities, not a sufficient condition. Ordinary debt also carries limited liability. If limited liability is all that is required, why don't we observe large corporations, individually owned, with a tiny fraction of the capital supplied by the entrepreneur, and the rest simply borrowed. At first this question seems silly to many people (as does the question regarding why firms would ever issue debt or preferred stock under conditions where there are no tax benefits obtained from the treatment of interest or preferred dividend payments). We have found that oftentimes this question is misinterpreted to be one regarding why firms obtain capital. The issue is not why they obtain capital, but why they obtain it through the particular forms we have observed for such long periods of time. The fact is that no well-articulated answer to this question currently exists in the literature of either finance or economics.

## The "irrelevance" of capital structure

In their pathbreaking article on the cost of capital, Modigliani and Miller (1958) demonstrated that in the absence of bankruptcy costs and tax subsidies on the payment of interest the value of the firm is independent of the financial structure. . . .

Modigliani and Miller are essentially left without a theory of the determination of the optimal capital structure, and Fama and Miller (1972, p. 173) commenting on the same issue reiterate this conclusion:

> And we must admit that at this point there is little in the way of convincing research, either theoretical or empirical, that explains the amounts of debt that firms do decide to have in their capital structure.

. . . .

# 4. The Agency Costs of Debt

In general if the agency costs engendered by the existence of outside owners are positive it will pay the absentee owner (i.e., shareholders) to sell out to an owner-manager who can avoid these costs. This could be accomplished in principle by having the manager become the sole equity holder by repurchasing all of the outside equity claims with funds obtained through the issuance of limited liability debt claims and the use of his own personal wealth. This single-owner corporation would not suffer the agency costs associated with outside equity. Therefore there must be some compelling reasons why we find the diffuse-owner corporate firm financed by equity claims so prevalent as an organizational form.

An ingenious entrepreneur eager to expand, has open to him the opportunity to design a whole hierarchy of fixed claims on assets and earnings, with premiums paid for different levels of risk. Why don't we observe large corporations individually owned with a tiny fraction of the capital supplied by the entrepreneur in return for 100 percent of the equity and the rest simply borrowed? We believe there are a number of reasons: (1) the incentive effects associated with highly leveraged firms; (2) the monitoring costs these incentive effects engender; and (3) bankruptcy costs. Furthermore, all of these costs are simply particular aspects of the agency costs associated with the existence of debt claims on the firm.

## 4.1. THE INCENTIVE EFFECTS ASSOCIATED WITH DEBT

We don't find many large firms financed almost entirely with debt-type claims (i.e., non-residual claims) because of the effect such a financial structure would have on the owner-manager's behavior. Potential creditors will not loan $100,000,000 to a firm in which the entrepreneur has an investment of $10,000. With that financial structure the owner-manager will have a strong incentive to engage in activities (investments) which promise very high payoffs if successful even if they have a very low probability of success. If they turn out well, he captures most of the gains, if they turn out badly, the creditors bear most of the costs.

. . .

## 4.2. THE ROLE OF MONITORING AND BONDING COSTS

In principle it would be possible for the bondholders, by the inclusion of various covenants in the indenture provisions, to limit the managerial behavior which results in reductions in the value of the bonds. Provisions which impose constraints on management's decisions regarding such things as dividends, future debt issues, and maintenance of working capital are not uncommon in bond issues. To completely protect the bondholders from the incentive effects, these provisions would have to be incredibly detailed and cover most operating aspects of the enterprise including limitations on the riskiness of the projects undertaken. The costs involved in writing such provisions, the costs of enforcing them, and the reduced profitability of the firm (induced because the covenants occasionally limit management's ability to take optimal actions on certain issues) would likely be non-trivial. In fact, since management is a continuous decision-making process it will be almost impossible to completely specify such conditions without having the bondholders actually perform the management function. All costs associated with such covenants are what we mean by monitoring costs.

The bondholders will have incentives to engage in the writing of such covenants and in monitoring the actions of the manager to the point where the "nominal" marginal cost to them of such activities is just equal to the marginal benefits they perceive from engaging in them. We use the word nominal here because debtholders will not in fact bear these costs. As long as they recognize their existence, they will take them into account in deciding the price they will pay for any given debt claim, and therefore the seller of the claim (the owner) will bear the costs just as in the equity case discussed in section 2.

In addition the manager has incentives to take into account the costs imposed on the firm by covenants in the debt agreement which directly affect the future cash flows of the firm since they reduce the market value of his claims. Because both the external and internal monitoring costs are imposed on the owner-manager it is in his interest to see that the monitoring is performed in the lowest cost way. Suppose, for example, that the bondholders (or outside equity holders) would find it worthwhile to produce detailed financial statements such as those contained in the usual published accounting reports as a means of monitoring the manager. If the manager himself can produce such information at lower costs than they (perhaps because he is already collecting much of the data they desire for his own internal decision-making purposes), it would pay him to agree in advance to incur the cost of providing such reports and to have their accuracy testified to by an independent outside auditor. This is an example of what we refer to as bonding costs.

## 4.3. BANKRUPTCY AND REORGANIZATION COSTS

We argue in section 5 that, as the debt in the capital structure increases beyond some point, the marginal agency costs of debt begin to dominate the marginal agency costs of outside equity and the result of this is the generally observed phenomenon of the simultaneous use of both debt and outside equity. Before considering these issues, however, we consider here the third major component of the agency costs of debt which helps to explain why debt doesn't completely dominate capital structures – the existence of bankruptcy and reorganization costs.

It is important to emphasize that bankruptcy and liquidation are very different events. The legal definition of bankruptcy is difficult to specify precisely. In general, it occurs when the firm cannot meet a current payment on a debt obligation, or one or more of the other indenture provisions providing for bankruptcy is violated by the firm. In this event the stockholders have lost all claims on the firm, and the remaining loss, the difference between the face value of the fixed claims and the market value of the firm, is borne by the debtholders. Liquidation of the firm's assets will occur only if the market value of the future cash flows generated by the firm is less than the opportunity cost of the assets, i.e., the sum of the values which could be realized if the assets were sold piecemeal.

If there were no costs associated with the event called bankruptcy the total market value of the firm would not be affected by increasing the probability of its incurrence. However, it is costly, if not impossible, to write contracts representing claims on a firm which clearly delineate the rights of holders for all possible contingencies. Thus even if there were no adverse incentive effects in expanding fixed claims relative to equity in a firm, the use of such fixed claims would be constrained by the costs inherent in defining and enforcing those claims. Firms incur obligations daily to suppliers, to employees, to different classes of investors, etc. So long as the firm is prospering, the adjudication of claims is seldom a problem.

When the firm has difficulty meeting some of its obligations, however, the issue of the priority of those claims can pose serious problems. This is most obvious in the extreme case where the firm is forced into bankruptcy. If bankruptcy were costless, the reorganization would be accompanied by an adjustment of the claims of various parties and the business could, if that proved to be in the interest of the claimants, simply go on (although perhaps under new management).

In practice, bankruptcy is not costless, but generally involves an adjudication process which itself consumes a fraction of the remaining value of the assets of the firm. Thus the cost of bankruptcy will be of concern to potential buyers of fixed claims in the firm since their existence will reduce the payoffs to them in the event of bankruptcy. These are examples of the agency costs of cooperative efforts among individuals (although in this case perhaps "non-cooperative" would be a better term). The price buyers will be willing to pay for fixed claims will thus be inversely related to the probability of the incurrence of these costs i.e., to the probability of bankruptcy. Using a variant of the argument employed above for monitoring costs, it can be shown that the total value of the firm will fall, and the owner-manager equity holder will bear the entire wealth effect of the bankruptcy costs as long as potential bondholders make unbiased estimates of their magnitude at the time they initially purchase bonds.

. . .

In general the revenues or the operating costs of the firm are not independent of the probability of bankruptcy and thus the capital structure of the firm. As the probability of bankruptcy increases, both the operating costs and the revenues of the firm are adversely affected. . . . For example, a firm with a high probability of bankruptcy will also find that it must pay higher salaries to induce executives to accept the higher risk of unemployment. Furthermore, in certain kinds of durable goods industries the demand function for the firm's product will not be independent of the probability of bankruptcy. The computer industry is a good example. There, the buyer's welfare is dependent to a significant extent on the ability to maintain the equipment, and on continuous hardware and software development. Furthermore, the owner of a large computer often receives benefits from the software developments of other users. Thus if the manufacturer leaves the business or loses his software support and development experts because of financial difficulties, the value of the equipment to his users will decline. The buyers of such services have a continuing interest in the manufacturer's viability not unlike that of a bondholder, except that their benefits come in the form of continuing services at lower cost rather than principle and interest payments. Service facilities and spare parts for automobiles and machinery are other examples.

In summary then the agency costs associated with debt consist of:

(1)  the opportunity wealth loss caused by the impact of debt on the investment decisions of the firm;
(2)  the monitoring and bonding expenditures by the bondholders and the owner-manager (i.e., the firm);
(3)  the bankruptcy and reorganization costs.

. . .

## 5. A Theory of the Corporate Ownership Structure

In the previous sections we discussed the nature of agency costs associated with outside claims on the firm – both debt and equity. Our purpose here is to integrate these concepts into the beginnings of a theory of the corporate ownership structure. We use the term "ownership structure" rather than "capital structure" to highlight the fact that the crucial variables to be determined are not just the relative amounts of debt and equity but also the fraction of the equity held by the manager. Thus, for a given size firm we want a theory to determine three variables:

$S_i$ : inside equity (held by the manager),
$S_o$ : outside equity (held by anyone outside of the firm),
$B$ : debt (held by anyone outside of the firm).

The total market value of the equity is $S = S_i + S_o$, and the total market value of the firm is $V = S + B$. . . .

### 5.1. DETERMINATION OF THE OPTIMAL RATIO OF OUTSIDE EQUITY TO DEBT

Consider . . . the determination of the optimal ratio of outside equity to debt, $S_o/B$. To do this let us hold the size of the firm constant. $V$, the actual value of the firm for a given size, will depend on the agency costs incurred, hence we use as our index of size $V^*$, the value of the firm at a given scale when agency costs are zero.

We argued above that: (1) as long as capital markets are efficient (i.e., characterized by rational expectations), the prices of assets such as debt and outside equity will reflect unbiased estimates of the monitoring costs and redistributions which the agency relationship will engender; and (2) the selling owner-manager will bear these agency costs. Thus from the owner-manager's standpoint the optimal proportion of outside funds to be obtained from equity (versus debt) *for a given level of internal equity* is that $E$ which results in minimum total agency costs.

    . . . .

### 6.2. THE CONTROL PROBLEM AND OUTSIDE OWNER'S AGENCY COSTS

The careful reader will notice that nowhere in the analysis thus far have we taken into account many of the details of the relationship between the part owner-manager and the outside stockholders and bondholders. In particular we have assumed that all outside equity is non-voting. If such equity does have voting rights then the manager will be concerned about the effects on his long-run welfare of reducing his fractional ownership below the point where he loses effective control of the corporation. That is, below the point where it becomes possible for the outside equity holders to fire him. A complete analysis of this issue will require a careful specification of the contractual rights involved on both sides, the role of the board of directors, and the coordination (agency) costs borne by the stockholders in implementing policy changes. This latter point involves consideration of the distribution of the outside ownership claims. Simply put, forces exist to determine an equilibrium distribution of outside ownership. If the costs of reducing the dispersion of ownership are lower than the benefits to be obtained from reducing the agency costs, it will pay some individual or group of individuals to buy shares in the market to reduce the dispersion of ownership. We occasionally witness these conflicts for control which involve outright market purchases, tender offers, and proxy fights. Further analysis of these issues is left to the future.

. . .

## 7. Conclusions

The publicly held business corporation is an awesome social invention. Millions of individuals voluntarily entrust billions of dollars, francs, pesos, etc., of personal wealth to the care of managers on the basis of a complex set of contracting relationships which delineate the rights of the parties involved. The growth in the use of the corporate form as well as the growth in market value of established corporations suggests that at least, up to the present, creditors and investors have by and large not been disappointed with the results, despite the agency costs inherent in the corporate form. Agency costs are as real as any other costs. The level of agency costs depends among other things on statutory and common law and human ingenuity in devising contracts. Both the law and the sophistication of contracts relevant to the modern corporation are the products of a historical process in which there were strong incentives for individuals to minimize agency costs. Moreover, there were alternative organizational forms available, and opportunities to invent new ones. Whatever its shortcomings, the corporation has thus far survived the market test against potential alternatives.

## References

Alchian, A.A. and H. Demsetz, 1972, Production, information costs, and economic organization, *American Economic Review* LXII, no. 5, 777–795.

Berle, A.A., Jr. and G.C. Means, 1932, *The Modern Corporation and Private Property* (Macmillan, New York).

Fama, E.F. and M. Miller, 1972, *The Theory of Finance* (Holt, Rinehart and Winston, New York).

Manne, H.G., 1967, Our two corporate systems: Law and economics, *Virginia Law Review* 53, March, 259–284.

Modigliani, F. and M. H. Miller, 1958, The costs of capital, corporation finance, and the theory of investment, *American Economic Review* 48, June, 261–297.

# 18

## State Law, Shareholder Protection, and the Theory of the Corporation

### *Ralph K. Winter*

### EDITOR'S INTRODUCTION

Corporate law (for example, rules regarding takeovers and fiduciary duties of the management) governs the relationships between management and the stockholders. In the United States, corporate law is the provenance of the states; there are few federal regulations. Some have argued that the competition between the states is a "race to the bottom." That is, states provide corporate laws that benefit managers at the expense of stockholders and that federal regulation would be better. Ralph Winter argues to the contrary – that there is a race to the top. His article shows the power of state competition in promoting economic welfare.

Winter also shows that many of the suggested federal regulations, such as increased number of outside directors, greater rights to minority shareholders, and, greater access to corporate information, even if they provide benefits (such as better supervision of the managers) come at a cost (monitoring is not free). Since the stockholders, including pension funds, are not clamoring for such regulation, this is a good indication that the suggestions are not very good. Thus "lax" controls may be profit maximizing.

Winter's argument for competition is much more vivid and encompassing than the diagrammatic exposition found in economics texts (where the horizontal demand curve of the perfect competitive firm leads to lower prices than the downward sloping demand curve of a monopolist firm). Here, competition involves more than just price competition and there are many more arenas for competition than just the simple market for the good.

## I. The Issues

.... It is almost universally the opinion of academic commentators that state corporation codes do not impose sufficiently stringent controls on corporate management and are lax in protecting shareholders. Only federal intervention, it is said, can correct this sorry situation. This article will test the intellectual underpinnings of the conventional wisdom and of the rather venerable proposals calling for the federal regulation of the governance of corporations against an economic theory of corporate function and control. It will conclude both that state corporate legal systems are protective of shareholders and that state regulation is generally preferable to federal.

Adoption of the proposals for federal intervention would drastically alter a number of elementary legal rules (or understandings about what the law is) which have accompanied the growth of the American economy for over a century. Elementary though they be, these rules bear repeating. First, most corporate charters are the creations of the laws of individual states. Second, incorporation laws are "general" rather than "special," which is to say only that the corporate form is readily available to all who would use it and not subject to the approval in each case of a bureaucrat or legislature. Third, the decision as to which state to incorporate in is in almost all cases a managerial decision, emanating from the (would-be) corporation itself, and not dictated by law or administrative decision. Fourth, state corporation law is almost exclusively concerned with the internal governance of the corporation and in particular with the relationship of the shareholders to management. Except for federal securities law, this relationship is largely subject only to state law. Fifth, most state corporation laws are "enabling" rather than regulatory. That is, they "enable" private parties to accomplish incorporation on terms which they freely choose. As a result, state laws do not impose extensive mandatory restrictions upon the discretion of corporate management, although such restrictions may be written into a corporate charter. Sixth, once incorporated in one state, a corporation may for the most part do business in any state and continue to be governed – whether because of constitutional command or judgments about comity between states – by the charter and corporation code of the state of incorporation.

Proposals for the federal regulation of the governance of corporations are generally of two distinct types. The first is federal "minimum standards" legislation which would subject the actions of corporate management to a variety of restrictions. The second category involves a requirement that certain corporations secure federal charters which embody mandatory provisions designed to reorder corporate structure and behavior so as to alter the shareholder-management relationship or the firms' relationship to the larger society. Because this article is concerned solely with the relationship of shareholders and the corporation, it will not discuss proposals designed to redirect corporate conduct in the name of social values.

Existing federal economic regulation is so pervasive that the absence of federal control over the governance of major economic units seems anomalous to some. But proposals for federal regulation do not, by that reason alone, command automatic acceptance. On the one hand, the Securities Acts are already a substantial exercise of federal responsibility in these areas. On the other, many vital functions of interstate commerce are governed essentially by state law. Virtually all mechanisms for the transfer of interest in property – whether by will, gift, sale, mortgage, or other secured transaction – are matters of state law. Reliance on state corporation codes for purposes of internal corporate governance may thus not be an anomaly. It is not enough to argue, as some have, that federal chartering or minimum standards legislation is necessary simply because interstate or international transactions are involved.

Where a private transaction imposes no substantial cost on society or third parties, the parties to it should be allowed to arrange their affairs in a way that satisfies them rather than some distant official; they should, in short, be given freedom to "make their own deal." Government intervention should be limited to enforcement of private bargains and, where feasible, to reducing the costs of bargaining (transaction costs), for example by providing a code of standard legal arrangements which reduce the complexity of bringing large numbers of participants together in an economic venture. "Enabling" corporation codes are such attempts at the reduction of transaction costs, and have been quite legitimately viewed as a species of the law of contracts rather than as a form of government economic regulation.

The academic literature on the federal role in the shareholder–corporation relationship makes two claims. (1) Because state corporation codes do not require strict judicial scrutiny of many acts of corporate management, they leave shareholders in a vulnerable position. (2) The cause of this "tilt" in state corporation law lies in the operation of competitive legal systems. Because corporate chartering can generate substantial revenue for state treasuries, states compete for charters. Since the decision as to where to incorporate is a management decision and management's interests are adverse to those of shareholders, competitive legal systems tend to permissiveness so far as management conduct is concerned and to inadequate protection for shareholders. The vast preponderance of academic opinion, and the conventional wisdom of those, such as Mr. Nader, who chronically favor further contraction of the private sector, is that the federal system works to benefit corporate management at a cost to shareholders and that federal regulation is necessary.[1]

This article is a critical examination of these two propositions of "common knowledge." It seeks to test these propositions against what economic theory tells us about the functions of, and constraints on, corporate management. It will attempt to elaborate an economic theory describing the various relationships which constitute the business corporation and to compare that theory with the legal doctrine which is the culmination of the competition between legal systems for corporate charters. It will conclude: (1) Contrary to the conventional wisdom, competitive legal systems should tend toward optimality so far as the shareholder's relationship to the corporation is concerned. (2) State corporation codes in fact seem quite consistent (optimality, of course, is not provable) with what economic theory suggests are optimal legal arrangements.

## II. Delaware's "Race for the Bottom" and the Capital Market

### A. Competitive Legal Systems and the Capital Market

No one denies that Delaware's open bidding for corporate charters has led to a steady lessening of the restrictiveness of state corporation law. Restrictions on the longevity of a corporation, the businesses in which it may engage, the issuance of stock, the classes of stock issued, dividend policy, discretion as to the holding of shareholder's meetings, charter amendments, means of electing directors, sales of assets, mortgaging, and the indemnification of officers, among others, have all been eliminated or diminished in a series of amendments to state corporation codes. It would further appear that the ability of a corporation to work fundamental changes, such as mergers or the elimination of minority shareholders, has been increased, as has management's power to work its will in a variety of matters, including some in which it may have a conflict of interest, e.g., management compensation.

The history of state corporation law is thus largely a history of drastic reduction of legal restrictions on management and of the legal rights of shareholders. This movement has not been at random but has rather occurred as corporations have sought charters in states with less restrictive codes. Other states have then adopted similar codes in response. As a result, the movement toward diminished restrictions has been national in scope and the Delaware Code is no longer significantly different from those of a number of other states.

An important mechanism generating change in American corporate law has thus been the competition among the states for charters. Both Delaware (40 percent of the largest industrial corporations are chartered there) and its competitors candidly admit that the purpose of corporate code revisions has been the attraction of charters to their state in order to produce significant tax revenues. Delaware has benefited in other ways. Not only is its corporation code an attraction to promoters and management but lawyers find it a hospitable jurisdiction in which to litigate issues of corporate law, with the result that the Wilmington Bar enjoys an unusually lucrative practice for a city of that size.

No one disputes these propositions. Rather, the controversy is over the effect on the governance of many of the nation's major economic units.

The most celebrated exposition of the conventional academic analysis, but avowedly not an original approach, is "Federalism and Corporate Law: Reflections Upon Delaware", by Professor William Cary[2] of the Columbia University Law School, a former Chairman of the Securities and Exchange Commission. Characterizing Delaware as leading a "movement toward the least common denominator" and a "race for the bottom," Professor Cary argues that Delaware's lessening of the restrictiveness of its corporation code has left shareholders an easy prey to self-dealing management. To this unhappy conclusion he adds an attack on the Delaware judiciary and argues that "Gresham's law applies" to its decisions, which "lean toward the status quo and adhere to minimal standards of director responsibility."

Having rejected full federal chartering as "politically unrealistic," Professor Cary calls for federal minimum standards legislation. This legislation, designed to "raise" the standards of management conduct, would, he claims, increase public confidence – and investment – in American corporations.

The claim, it is absolutely critical to note, is not that an overriding social goal is sacrificed by state law, but simply that Delaware is preventing *private* parties from optimizing their *private* arrangements. With all due respect both to Professor Cary and to the almost universal academic support for his position, it is implausible on its face. The plausible argument runs in the opposite direction: (1) If Delaware permits corporate management to profit at the expense of shareholders and other states do not, then earnings of Delaware corporations must be less than earnings of comparable corporations chartered in other states and shares in the Delaware corporations must trade at lower prices. (2) Corporations with lower earnings will be at a disadvantage in raising debt or equity capital. (3) Corporations at a disadvantage in the capital market will be at a disadvantage in the product market and their share price will decline, thereby creating a threat of a takeover which may replace management. To avoid this result, corporations must seek out legal systems more attractive to capital. (4) States seeking corporate charters will thus try to provide legal systems which optimize the shareholder–corporation relationship.

The conclusion that Delaware shares sell for less is implicit in Professor Cary's analysis, for if a "higher" legal standard for management conduct will increase investor confidence, investor confidence in Delaware stock must have been less than in stocks of other states for more than a generation. This lack of confidence would have long been reflected in the price of Delaware shares. Moreover, a reduction in the earnings of a corporation will affect its ability to raise debt capital, as well as equity, since the risk of a lender is thereby increased and a higher interest rate will be charged. Delaware corporations, therefore, not only face a lower share price but also must pay higher interest rates.

This analysis is not crucially dependent upon the consumer of securities or lenders understanding the intricacies of corporate law or knowing of the general permissiveness of the Delaware Code. That, indeed, must be what Professor Cary means when he argues that increased confidence will result from more protective legal systems. A simple comparison of earnings of various corporations, for example, will affect the price of Delaware stock. Moreover, institutional investors – not to mention investment counselors – cannot be unaware of such crucial facts and their role in the stock market is so critical that their knowledge alone will sharply affect share price. The claim that Delaware is leading a "race for the bottom" has been made so frequently and by so many that it can hardly be described as a carefully guarded secret. Recent work on the stock market strongly suggests that relatively obscure – even confidential – information is transmitted extremely swiftly and almost automatically affects share price. That the impact of a legal system on investors would be known only to law professors and Mr. Nader seems a rather tenuous proposition.

It is not in the interest of Delaware corporate management or the Delaware treasury for corporations chartered there to be at a disadvantage in raising debt or equity capital relative to corporations chartered in other states. Management must induce investors freely to choose their firm's stock instead of, among other things, stock in companies incorporated in other states or other countries, bonds, bank accounts, certificates of deposit, partnerships (general or limited), individual proprietorships, joint ventures, present consumption, etc. As discussed in detail later, a corporation's ability to compete effectively in product markets is related to its ability to raise capital, and management's tenure in office is related to the price of stock. If management is to secure initial capital and have continuous access to ready capital in the future, it must attract investors away from the almost infinite variety of competing opportunities. Moreover, to retain its position management has a powerful incentive to keep the price of stock high enough to prevent takeovers, a result obtained by making the corporation an attractive investment.

The Cary analysis thus seems implausible at an *a priori* level, because, when analyzed, it appears as little more than a claim that Delaware can facilitate the monopolization of the capital market, just as it can grant exclusive franchises for taxicabs in Wilmington. But the market for capital is international in scope and involves an undifferentiated product with no transportation costs. Delaware cannot create barriers which prevent it from flowing to the most attractive investments; any attempt at monopolization will only drive capital from that state.

The fact that other states have found it necessary to change their law in response to Delaware, therefore, strongly suggests that investors do not share Professor Cary's view and in fact believe that they do better under Delaware law than under the laws of the other states.

## B. Laxity or efficiency: The costs and benefits of restricting management discretion

The implausibility of the "race for the bottom" argument is obscured because the literature calling for stricter regulation stresses only expected benefits while ignoring costs and is in a real sense the victim of its own rhetoric. To say a legal system is marked by "laxity" implies a cost-benefit judgment about more stringent regulation but such rhetoric in the shareholder protection area is rarely accompanied by the analysis such judgments call for. In truth, a "lax" legal system is neither intuitively nor empirically inferior to a stringent one.

All regulation imposes costs in the way of consumed resources, such as the efforts of accountants or lawyers, which might be put to other uses. Where regulation is imposed on private transactions, such as the purchase of a car or investment in a corporation, those transactions are made more costly for all involved. For example, it has been argued that whatever reduction in securities fraud is caused by S.E.C. requirements is offset by the higher costs imposed on securities transactions.

Another way in which regulation imposes costs is in restricting the ability of private parties to arrange their affairs in the way they find most suitable. Often these costs result from well-meaning attempts to protect those parties. For example, assume that the quality of widgets can be determined only by extended use rather than consumer examination. Most consumers purchase widgets on the basis of a company brand name or on the advice of a local merchant, both of whom find it in their economic interest to maintain a good business reputation. Other consumers, however, purchase low-quality widgets (at the high-quality price) from manufacturers hoping to make a quick profit even at the cost of a bad reputation in the long run. Regulation designed to protect such consumers may operate by general rules applicable to all transactions, not just those the government seeks to prevent. For example, government testing of widgets would apply to all widgets, not just those of low quality, and would thus impose costs on (and thereby reduce in number) the beneficial transactions in high-quality widgets. Regulation may deter blameless conduct as well as that which is conceded to have no social value, and those who call for regulation make an incomplete argument when they take account only of anticipated benefits.

Intervention in private transactions which impose no social cost can be justified only as a means of reducing the costs to the private parties. Thus, a prime function of state corporation codes is to supply standard terms which reduce the transaction costs, and thereby increase the benefits, of investing by eliminating costly bargaining which might otherwise accompany many routine corporate dealings. But substituting a mandatory legal rule for bargaining also may impose a cost in the form of the elimination of alternatives which the parties might prefer.

Much of the legal literature calling for further federal regulation either assumes that no costs will fall upon shareholders or merely undertakes a cursory " eyeballing" of the potential costs. To be sure, self-dealing and fraud exist in corporate affairs and their elimination is desirable. But at some point the exercise of control by general rules of law may impose costs on investors which damage them in both quantity and quality quite as much as self-dealing or fraud. A paradox thus results: maximizing the yield to investors generally may, indeed almost surely will, result in a number of cases of fraud or self-dealing; and eliminating all fraud or self-dealing may decrease the yield to shareholders generally.

For example, numerous proposals have been made to increase the power of shareholders over the corporate destiny by enabling them to initiate proposals to be submitted to shareholders, by requiring cumulative voting, by compelling management to make extensive information available to any requesting shareholder, by requiring shareholder votes on certain matters, and so on. There is, however, no established or even apparent connection between increasing shareholder power and increasing the yield to investors. To be sure, the lack of shareholder control may have led to some self-dealing, but the elimination of self-dealing by increasing that control involves a trade-off with corporate efficiency and may well reduce the return to shareholders generally. Whether the amount saved in eliminating isolated instances of self-dealing through increased shareholder control is greater than a general loss in corporate efficiency is the issue, and it is neither intuitively nor empirically self-evident that the Delaware Code is not a satisfactory resolution.

Similarly, Professor Cary has criticized the Delaware courts for too easily ratifying management conduct and for not applying a standard of "fairness" to its actions. Even assuming his description of Delaware law is accurate and that is not without some considerable doubt – his analysis provides no solution.

No one is against "fairness" in the treatment of shareholders. The issue to be addressed is the criteria by which the fairness or unfairness of acts are to be determined. Except perhaps for the implication that whatever the Delaware Supreme Court does is unfair, Professor Cary sets out no relevant criteria. One case that Professor Cary attacks, *Sinclair Oil Corp. v. Levien*,[3] for instance, involved a parent corporation which held 97 percent of the stock of a subsidiary and which decided to contract the subsidiary's activities by paying out dividends far in excess of earnings. Although other firms held by the parent were at the time expanding, no corporate opportunities were lost to the subsidiary in question, and the dividends were on a *pro rata* basis.

Professor Cary would create a rule, based on "traditional concepts of fairness," prohibiting a parent from contracting the operations of a subsidiary during a period of expansion when there are minority stockholders. Consider how deeply such a rule intrudes on a corporation's power to make business decisions. Among the matters which become irrelevant are estimates of the subsidiary's likely success in expansion and the value of competing investment opportunities. No weight whatsoever is given to the much greater risk in those respects taken by a 97 percent holder than by a 3 percent holder. Nor is there any way of preventing the 3 percent holder from blackmailing the 97 percent with the threat of preventing the latter from pursuing the more valuable opportunities. In effect, Professor Cary would give the 3 percent holder a veto on these matters, a rule which cannot plausibly be in the interests of shareholders generally.

Another example involves the standard of care required of directors. Here the Delaware decision attacked by Professor Cary held that directors might rely on summaries, reports, and corporate records as evidence that no antitrust violations were being committed by the company, even though 19 years earlier the Federal Trade Commission had issued a cease and desist order against price fixing. Professor Cary's suggestion is that an internal control system to prevent repeated antitrust violations would have prevented the fines and treble damages paid by the company. The issue, however, is not whether damages might be avoided but whether, even employing a simple negligence calculus, the expected value of damages (probability times likely amount) is greater than the cost of avoiding them. Requiring perfect fail-safe systems in every corporation can be far more costly than any potential loss to shareholders, and Professor Cary presents an incomplete analysis in concluding that loss could have been avoided. He is on more solid ground in suggesting that the need for preventive measures was greater in the particular case in light of past conduct since that is relevant to the likelihood of loss.

The point is not that Professor Cary's position is the "wrong" rule. Rather, it is that interventionist legal rules may reduce the yield to shareholders generally and this cost must be weighed against the benefits to be gained by the reduction of self-dealing or mismanagement. Only by ignoring the cost side of the cost-benefit judgment can one assume that "laxity" always injures shareholders and thus sustain the conclusion that the competition among states for chartering has worked to their detriment.

What rules of law optimally protect shareholders is not self-evident except at ends of the spectrum. For example, proposals to increase shareholder "power" which aid only tiny groups of shareholders or forces outside the corporation to influence corporate behavior through obstruction will not protect shareholders generally. And proposals for extensive judicial scrutiny of business decisions on behalf of 3 percent shareholders would probably entail rigid rules restricting management's ability to make business judgments. Between these extremes, however, lie a vast number of cases in which the cost-benefit judgment seems inconclusive and the proper role of law unclear. That role can be determined only after an excursion into the question of the extent to which economic considerations discipline the behavior of corporate management.

## III. The Theory of the Corporation: Product Competition, the Market for Management Control and Management Discretion

### A. DO CORPORATIONS LIVE BY LAW ALONE?

With a few exceptions, the legal literature is single-mindedly concerned with the discretion corporate management can exercise as a result of the "separation of ownership and control" popularized by Berle and Means.[4] This phrase is no more than a description of the fact that the legal controls on management behavior, e.g., shareholder voting, derivative suits, election of directors, etc., seem unsatisfactory methods of exerting control over corporate affairs.

And so they are, but the structure of a legal system does not necessarily reflect the realities of the institutions it governs. A literal student of the Constitution might well be appalled that voters in presidential elections are not even told the names of the people they are voting for (the electors). He might then conclude that there is a "separation of voting and control" in presidential elections and call for a strengthening of the Electoral College. We all know, of course, that a party system unsanctioned by the Constitution transformed the Electoral College into an institution with no functional resemblance to the legal system which surrounds it. So too, an obsession with the formal legal system surrounding corporations can obscure the actual functional relationships involved.

For example, the "separation of ownership and control" is a problem only if one views corporation law as a comprehensive functional description of corporate governance. Viewed in another perspective, however, the "separation" is no more than a perfectly sensible division of labor. As Richard Posner has written,

> . . . The [management] group consists of people who are experienced in the business and involved in it on a full-time, day-to-day basis. In contrast, the typical shareholder . . . is not knowledgeable about the business of the firm, does not derive an important part of his livelihood from it, and neither expects nor has an incentive to participate in the management of the firm. He is a passive investor and, because of the liquidity of his interest, has only a casual, and frequently quite brief, relationship with the firm. His interest, like that of a creditor, is a financial rather than managerial interest. . . .
>
> It is no more anomalous that shareholders do not manage or control 'their' corporation than that bondholders do not manage or control the corporations whose bonds they hold, or trust beneficiaries the trustee. All three groups have an investment interest.[5]

Similarly, many have criticized the role played by institutional investors in controlling corporate behavior. For the most part, such investors have not attempted to influence management behavior by invoking their rights as shareholders but find their remedy in the stock market. The criticism, a striking demonstration of the depths of misunderstanding corporate critics are prone to, is directed at a nonproblem. If a pension fund, for example, were to exert direct control over the firms in which it owned stock, it would have to hire a sufficient number of managerial personnel to keep informed about the activities of each firm. This would impose enormous additional salary costs upon the fund and would compel it to reduce its diversification, since the marginal cost of buying stocks in firms not then in the portfolio would be increased by the need for additional personnel to keep informed about the new firm's activities. And for all this, what would be gained? The fund's managerial personnel are unlikely to be better qualified than those in the corporations and their additional "control" is unlikely to add much in the way of financial return to the pension fund while surely adding very substantial costs and decreasing diversification.

The fact that shareholders generally, and major institutional investors in particular, find little need for "control" strongly suggests that forces other than formal legal structure profoundly shape corporate performance and provide substantial protection for shareholders. If the law of corporate governance is to make sense, it must take into account the constraints these forces impose on the parties to corporate transactions. These constraints arise largely from competition in two markets which interact with each other and with the capital market: (1) the market for products and services and (2) the market for management control.

## B. THE MARKET FOR PRODUCTS AND SERVICES

The market for products and services in which a corporation competes has three dimensions. The first is defined by the range of goods or services which are by their nature reasonably substitutable for those offered by the corporation. The second is geographic and defined by the area in which the goods and services offered by the corporation reasonably compete with those offered by others. The third is temporal and defined by the time it will take reasonably substitutable products to enter after a given price change.

This market is an obvious constraint on corporate management. Virtually all of the criticism of state corporation codes assumes success in the product market, for it is that success which creates the alleged opportunity for corporate management to profit at the expense of shareholders. This constraint exists, moreover, whether or not management profit maximizes on behalf of itself. The management which chooses inefficient growth or extravagant expenses in the name of corporate social responsibility will only reduce the share it might have appropriated directly for itself. As demonstrated in the next section, a drop in share price will endanger management. Since shareholders will not distinguish between reductions in yield to them because of larceny, high management compensation, inefficient growth for prestige purposes, or socially responsible expenditures, success in the product market is a precondition to management's enriching itself or indulging in nonprofit activities. Whether management maximizes the return to it or adopts other goals does not, in short, affect the share available to shareholders. Management discretion in either case depends upon success in the product market.

## C. The market for management control

. . . . Share price and the capital market exert discipline on the behavior of corporate management. . . .

Corporate management's attention to the price of the firm's stock is perfectly understandable. . . The lower the share price, the easier it will be for others to take over the corporation and hire new management. Thus, if a firm is mismanaged, robbed, or overly attentive to nonprofit goals, the price of its shares will drop and others will perceive an opportunity to take over the corporation and install new and more efficient management to raise the share price. The takeover may be by way of a proxy fight, purchase of control, or merger. Those who take over the corporation will profit by the compensation received as successful managers and/or by capital gains generated by the increase in share price through greater earnings. Trading in corporate shares, therefore, involves not only the market for capital but also the market for management control. This latter market, because it is related to the behavior of the former, constitutes a substantial constraint on management conduct.

The implications of this for the debate over corporate governance are profound. Product market competition alone is a pressure on corporate management to profit maximize on behalf of the corporation because pursuit of nonprofit goals will be reflected in the company's earnings and in the price of its stock. Management thus has substantial incentive to maximize the profits of the corporation, and this incentive is directly related to investor behavior.

. . . .

# IV. The Proper Role of Law in Corporate Governance

## A. General propositions

We return now to the costs and benefits of legal intervention and to a consideration of what are proper legal rules. The discussion will be by way of general approach and illustration.

The corporation is a device which performs both the functions of raising substantial amounts of capital and of efficiently mixing this capital with other inputs. These inputs are directed and monitored by a management which increases its own return and maintains its security in office by keeping share price high, that is, by profit maximizing on behalf of the corporation. These functions can now be seen to be largely independent of all but a few basic rules and do not correspond to the apparent legal structure of "ownership" in the shareholders and "unaccountable" discretion in the management. If anything, management "owns" control, subject to divesting by the owners of common stock.

While a variety of markets constrain management and create incentives for it to benefit shareholders, the corporate relationship also creates substantial opportunities for fraud, self-dealing, and "one-shot" raids on corporate assets. The job of law is to reduce these opportunities in a way which benefits shareholders.

A wholly accurate weighing of the costs and benefits of every legal intrusion is, of course, not possible, and in a spectrum of alternatives, several may arguably be correct. An out-of-hand rejection of a corporation code because it is less restrictive of management than codes of other states, however, is wholly uncalled for. Minimal restriction on management's discretion may maximize the yield to shareholders. It may not also, but this uncertainty reflects only our ignorance about the impact of law rather than the inherent worthiness of restrictions on management.

The Delaware Code is thus not open to the kind of attack Professor Cary and others have leveled at it. While it lacks many restrictive provisions of older laws, not all limits on management have been removed. Basic protection for shareholders is written into the code and a fiduciary duty is imposed on management. Moreover, unlike many states, Delaware procedure is geared to *facilitating* suits by shareholders since the situs of shares of a Delaware corporation is deemed to be Delaware. Stockholder plaintiffs are thus afforded means to obtain quasi-in-rem jurisdiction over nonresident directors. Delaware also does not require the posting of security for expenses and has eliminated other obstacles to shareholder litigation.

Neither Delaware's nor any code, nor the case law interpreting it, is perfect. Cases are often wrongly decided and statutes poorly drafted. A good legal system is always in evolution and expectations of unvarying correctness are unrealistic. But in the case of corporation codes there is a mechanism which, over time, reasonably guarantees to shareholders and management alike a proper legal system to govern their relationship in the capital market. That process is the very one reviled by proponents of federal intervention: *competition among the states for corporate charters.*

A state which rigs its corporation code so as to reduce the yield to shareholders will spawn corporations which are less attractive as investment opportunities than comparable corporations chartered in other states or countries, as well as bonds, savings accounts, land, etc. Investors must be attracted before they can be cheated, and except for those seeking a "one shot," "take the money and run," opportunity to raid a corporation, management has no reason to seek out such a code. Just as shareholder yield and management discretion rise together, so too they may descend in tandem. Low yields to shareholders mean low stock prices which mean low costs of takeover which . . . reduce the parameters of management discretion. The chartering decision, therefore, so far as the capital market is concerned, will favor those states which offer the optimal yield to both shareholders and management.

It is in neither management's nor the shareholders' interest to see the ability of a corporation to raise capital impaired. . . . Even a relatively small need for capital from stock issues can impose discipline on a firm. Moreover, raising capital through equity or debt are closely related since investors and lenders both are making similar judgments about the long-run earning potential of the firm, and management's power to drain off assets obviously affects either judgment. In short, the lower the stock price the higher the interest rate.

. . . .

So far as the capital market is concerned, it is not in the interest of management to seek out a corporate legal system which fails to protect investors, and the competition between states for charters is generally a competition as to which legal system provides an optimal return to both interests. Only when that competition between legal systems exists can we perceive which legal rules are most appropriate for the capital market. Once a single legal system governs that market, we can no longer compare investor reaction. Ironically, in view of the conventional wisdom, the greater danger is not that states will compete for charters but that they will not.

We turn now to particular legal issues.

## B. MORE POWER TO SHAREHOLDERS?

The idea that more in the way of operational control of corporate affairs should be placed in the hands of shareholders – e.g., the power to initiate proposals, cumulative voting, required votes on some issues, etc. – seemingly will not die, no matter how often it is dispatched by rational discussion.

Corporate efficiency calls for decisional and operational processes wholly inconsistent with periodic, much less constant, intrusion by shareholders. Such intrusion not only reduces efficiency but carries with it other costs, such as legal fees and increased personnel needs, which the shareholders themselves must ultimately bear. That this is so is amply demonstrated by the notorious fact that the vast, vast majority of shareholders in large corporations do not want the power to interfere in corporate affairs, would not use it if they had it, and do not regard themselves as corporate overseers. Instead, they quite sensibly view themselves solely as investors whose "control" is in the stock market.

. . . .

It has even been argued that shareholders are simply more optimistic and less risk-averse investors than bondholders and need not be accorded any vote, their principal protection being in laws against fraud and the like. So far as the capital market is concerned, this view may well be correct and is confirmed by the existence of warrants and convertible preferred stocks which smell a good deal like nonvoting shares of equity. The operation of the market for management control, however, depends upon voting shares which have the power to replace an inefficient management and offer the opportunity for capital gains.

Many of the calls for "reform" seem not to be based firmly on any theory of economic function or constraint, except perhaps proposals for stockholder voting on "fundamental changes." These do not, however, seem highly prized by their supposed beneficiaries. State law does not prohibit corporations from adopting the reforms suggested, and the demand by shareholders for their inclusion in corporate charters seems either satisfied or nonexistent. In the case of closely held corporations, surely the potential shareholders themselves are the best judges of what is appropriate to their needs, and they have the power to write whatever kind of charter they want. In the case of widely held corporations, it can be assumed that if institutional investors believed in the worthiness of such measures in any significant degree, corporations would respond accordingly. Most of the proposals, after all, have been tried and if they benefited shareholders generally, the investment community would make that fact known to the corporate world. The lack of any such reaction is strong evidence that the trend of state law away from shareholder "power" is in the shareholder interest.

## C. CONFLICT OF INTEREST PROBLEMS

A single-minded focus on legal structure accompanied by an indifference to economic function has generated considerable unease among legal commentators over the present law governing transactions between directors and the corporations they serve. Because directors are said to be fiduciaries and, like trustees, owe a duty of loyalty to the shareholders, transactions with the corporation from which directors may profit are said to be tainted by a conflict of interest. Nineteenth-century law made all contracts in which a director was interested voidable at the instance of the corporation or shareholders no matter whether it was objectively fair. Today, the law is dramatically different. Generally, no such contract is voidable if, after disclosure, it is adopted by a majority of disinterested directors, ratified by the shareholders or unless a court finds it unfair to the corporation, a standard far below that imposed on fiduciaries such as trustees. This dramatic movement in corporate law is regarded by many critics as wholly unjustified and a source of considerable financial injury to shareholders.

For all the criticism, however, the shareholder losses are not visible to the naked eye. The movement from the legal rules which prevailed earlier (at a time labeled by these same critics as the Era of the Robber Barons) to those which prevail now has not been accompanied so far as one can tell by a corresponding decline in yield to shareholders or a movement by investors away from this alleged legalized robbery. . . . .

. . . .

## E. OF OUTSIDE DIRECTORS

Concern over the power of corporate officers and "inside" directors has generated over time a number of proposals for legal structures to provide checks to that power. Thus, some have called for greater supervision of management by institutional investors which hold large blocs of stock. Others – and more frequently today – call for a requirement that corporate boards have a majority of outside directors.

It should be said straight out that "outside" directors – and the term includes those designated by large institutional shareholders – can perform important functions. They are, for example, an element of protection against a "one-shot," "take the money and run" management. They are a check on self-dealing, fraud, or excessive compensation. They can insist on proper auditing procedures and review corporate decisions of a magnitude sufficient to entail such risks. Outside directors thus perform important functions in the area of the greatest vulnerability of shareholders. Additionally, "outside" directors can provide a perspective different from those who are immersed in the corporation's affairs and provide helpful analysis in the decision-making process. They can ask tough questions about a proposal which even a fully conscientious management may not face directly because of an unconscious pride of authorship.

Beyond these important but limited functions, however, what can realistically be expected of "outside" directors is a matter of some doubt. Management's knowledge and experience in the corporation's affairs must always be superior to those who play a part-time role and receive part-time compensation. The resources available to management in terms of staff and other useful perquisites are also so superior to those available to "outsiders" that the latter must inevitably give great weight to management proposals.

Corporate critics really don't challenge this analysis so much as avoid it by calling for a variety of measures to strengthen the hand of "outside" directors. Give them more pay, provide them with a staff, require them to spend more time on corporate business and so on. Such measures, however, do not provide an independent check on management discretion so much as duplicate and relocate the very same discretion. An "outside" director, after all, will never be on an equal footing with management until he spends a comparable amount of time, receives comparable compensation, and has comparable resources at his disposal. Then, however, he is in every sense an "inside" director.

The issue evaded by the critics is the definition of functions to be performed by "outside" directors. One cannot catalog the necessary resources until the job description is completed. This requires a differentiation, rather than duplication, of functions and "outside" directors must be assigned functions other than a wholesale second-guessing of management, if for no other reason than the relative (so long as they do not become "insiders") inferiority of their information and knowledge. And it would surely stand matters on their head to locate operating authority in the least knowledgeable directors.

The first question is thus "What should they do?", not "What do they do it with?" The remedies offered by the corporate critics assume that the function of "outside" directors is essentially the same as "inside" directors and seek only to provide them with comparable responsibilities and comparable resources. This does not solve the problem of the "unaccountability" of management power. . . . Until our present band of corporate critics answers the first question and defines functions for "outsiders" going beyond those listed above, the remedies they cry for must necessarily be beside the point. If "outside" directors are to oversee auditing functions, for example, then the resources necessary to the independent performance of this function should be provided. But that tailors the resources to a discrete responsibility.

Federal regulation, moreover, seems inappropriate since a realistic appraisal of the function of "outside" directors must be made on a case-by-case basis. Corporations troubled by fraud may need a substantial majority of outsiders. Corporations in industries in which scarce technological or other elaborate and complex knowledge is important may be unable to afford a substantial number of outside directors. Variations abound between industries, markets, and firms (a point academics are usually insensitive to, until government does to universities what it has routinely been doing to business), and any attempt to impose a general rule through federal legislation will not likely benefit shareholders generally. This does not, of course, preclude state corporation codes or private bodies such as stock exchanges from imposing such a requirement.

. . . .

## Summary and Conclusion

The almost universal belief that the competition between states for corporate charters works to the disadvantage of shareholders is on its face implausible. Corporations must attract capital from a vast range of competing opportunities and the state which "rigs" its code to benefit management will drive debt and equity capital away. Much of the criticism of the Delaware Code, moreover, rests on the assumption that greater regulation of corporate transactions will not impose costs as well as benefits on shareholders.

. . . .

An expanded federal role in corporate governance would almost surely be counterproductive. At the federal level, there is no mechanism by which optimal legal rules governing the shareholder–corporation relationship can be determined. One must thus turn to the proposals put forth by the advocates for further intervention. These, however, are at best academic guesswork, e.g., more power to shareholders, in which investors themselves are palpably disinterested, or at worst, generalized calls for more regulation which do not spell out content in any detail. There is, moreover, more than a little evidence that shareholder protection is to advocates of federal regulation a catchphrase behind which parade a variety of measures designed principally to increase the role of the public sector at the expense of the private. The most striking thing about this movement is that it exists, if at all, only in extremely isolated pockets in the investment community. Rather, it finds its principal support among academics and self-designated "consumer advocates" whose attachment to the private sector is suspect. How else explain the fact that proposals for more rigorous control of management in the name of shareholder protection are routinely coupled with proposals which are wholly antithetical to the interests of shareholders? Thus, Professor Cary, after excoriating Delaware for injuring shareholders, suggests, "We might go even farther and ask what representation the modern constituency of the corporation – employees, consumers, and the public, as well as shareholders – should have in the governance of the corporation." . . . . And Mr. Nader, whose previous relationship with the investment community has resembled a holy war, joins his "shareholder protection" proposals to the usual potpourri of anti-business measures. One ought to be skeptical about such reformers accomplishing much in the way of benefits to investors.

. . .

The American corporation has proven to be a remarkable device for the raising of large amounts of capital and for mixing that capital with a complex of other factor inputs. Because the productivity of other inputs such as labor are correspondingly increased and economies of scale reduce costs to consumers, all groups have benefited. These events have been largely independent of legal regulation. In fact, they took place after the corporate form was made generally available and ceased to be a privilege specially granted, and granted then often only as a means of franchising a monopoly. It was the movement from "special" incorporation as a state-granted privilege to "enabling" corporation codes as a species of contract law that permitted private parties to seek out the most efficient means of doing business and competing freely. Regulation was important to this very beneficial turn of events only in its disappearance. Critical to the process was the competition between states for corporate charters because investors and management were enabled to seek out the best available legal systems. And the legal systems themselves were thereby induced to evolve in a way consistent with the underlying economic functions of the resulting business units. The call for federal intervention is a call to move away from this view of corporate charters as a species of contract and to move toward the older and well-rejected view of charters as a species of government privilege. The fact that the movement finds it necessary to parade under the banner of shareholder protection only serves to demonstrate how thoroughly discredited it is.

## Notes

1. Ralph Nader, Mark Green, and E. Joel Seligman, *Constitutionalizing the Corporation: The Case for the Federal Chartering of Giant Corporations* (1976).
2. William L. Cary, "Federalism and Corporate Law: Reflections Upon Delaware," 83 *Yale L. J.* 663 (1974).
3. Del. Sup. 280 A.2d 717 (1971).
4. Adolf A. Berle and Gardiner C. Means, *The Modern Corporation and Private Property* (rev. ed. 1968).
5. Richard A. Posner, *Economic Analysis of Law* (2d ed. 1977) at 301.

# 19

## The Proper Role of a Target's Management in Responding to a Tender Offer

### *Frank H. Easterbrook and Daniel R. Fischel*

**EDITOR'S INTRODUCTION**

Tender offers present shareholders with the opportunity to sell some or all of their stock at a premium above market price. The people acquiring the stock hope to gain a majority of the stock and take a controlling interest in the company, thereby overcoming the problem of diffuse ownership (which is inadequate monitoring of the managers). Under existing federal and state law, a corporation's managers can resist and often defeat a premium tender offer without liability to either the corporation's shareholders or the unsuccessful tender offeror. Methods of resistance include staggering of the board of directors and "poison pills." Frank Easterbrook and Daniel Fischel argue that resistance by a corporation's managers to premium tender offers, even if it triggers a bidding contest, ultimately decreases shareholder welfare. This is because the threat of a takeover is a major method of aligning the interests of the managers with the interests of the stockholders. Any artificial reduction in the threat of a takeover, therefore, increases agency costs and reduces the value of the stock.

In making their argument, Easterbrook and Fischel also provide a nice explanation of the efficient market hypothesis.

A cash tender offer typically presents shareholders of the "target" corporation with the opportunity to sell many if not all of their shares quickly and at a premium over the market price. Notwithstanding the apparent benefit both to shareholders of the target and to the acquirer when such offers succeed, the target's management may oppose the offer, arguing that the premium is insufficient or that the corporation would be harmed by its new owners. To defeat the offer, management may file suits against the offeror, sell new shares to dilute the offeror's holdings, manufacture an antitrust problem by acquiring one of the offeror's competitors, or engage in a wide variety of other defensive tactics. Sometimes the resistance leads to the target being acquired at a price above the initial bid, either by the original bidder or by a "white knight," and sometimes the resistance defeats the takeover attempt altogether.

The ability of management to engage in defensive tactics in response to a cash tender offer is a relatively recent development in contests for corporate control. Prior to the enactment of the Williams Act in 1968, offerors were free to structure offers in a manner designed to force shareholders to decide quickly whether to sell all or part of their shares at a premium. The target's management consequently had little time to mobilize a defensive strategy to impede the offer. The Williams Act, however, has deprived the offeror of this advantage of speed by regulating the conditions under which the offer can be made. More than half the states have enacted tender offer statutes that go beyond the Williams Act in placing restrictions on the ability of an offeror to wage a tender offer. The effect of state and federal regulation of tender offers has been to give the target's management the time to undertake a defensive strategy.

The reaction of shareholders to managerial resistance depends on the outcome. Few protest when resistance leads to a takeover at a higher price. When resistance thwarts the takeover attempt altogether, however, litigation usually follows. Although defeat of the takeover attempt may deprive the target's shareholders of a substantial premium, shareholders' suits against management to recover this loss are almost always unsuccessful. Relying on the business judgment rule, courts typically have held that the target's management has the right, and even the duty, to oppose a tender offer it determines to be contrary to the firm's best interests. Commentators generally have applauded the results of these cases.

We argue in this Article that current legal rules allowing the target's management to engage in defensive tactics in response to a tender offer decrease shareholders' welfare. The detriment to shareholders is fairly clear where defensive tactics result in a defeat of a takeover, causing shareholders to lose the tender premium. Even where resistance leads to a higher price paid for the firm's shares, however, shareholders as a whole do not necessarily benefit. The value of any stock can be understood as the sum of two components: the price that will prevail in the market if there is no successful offer (multiplied by the likelihood that there will be none) and the price that will be paid in a future tender offer (multiplied by the likelihood that some offer will succeed). A shareholder's welfare is maximized by a legal rule that enables the sum of these two components to reach its highest value. Any approach that looks only at the way in which managers can augment the tender offeror's bid, given that a tender offer has already been made, but disregards the effect of a defensive strategy on the number of offers that will be made in the future and the way in which the number of offers affects the efficiency with which corporations are managed, ignores much that is relevant to shareholders' welfare.

We attempt in Part I to furnish what the existing legal literature and case law lacks: a framework for understanding how defensive tactics affect the number of tender offers, the price if an offer is made, and the price of stock in the event no offer is made. Our investigation leads to the conclusion that shareholders' welfare is maximized by an externally imposed legal rule severely limiting the ability of managers to resist a tender offer even if the purpose of resistance is to trigger a bidding contest. In Part II we consider and reject a number of the arguments which have been raised against our analysis of the proper role of a target's management in response to a tender offer. . . .

## I. Defensive Tactics and Shareholder Welfare

A cash tender offer at a premium over the market price gives each shareholder the opportunity to obtain, with certainty, a return exceeding the current market value of the target's stock. It would be possible, if overly simple, to stop at this point and conclude that tender offers are beneficial to the target's shareholders. Simple ideas do not always survive scrutiny, and this one has been subject to challenge on the ground that the market price of shares does not reflect their real worth. Instead, it is argued, the price of shares must be too low at the time of the offer, for how else could the prospective acquirer offer to pay a premium? We address these concerns in Section A below. In subsection 1 we examine how the price of shares comes to reflect their value. In subsection 2 we discuss why bidders might offer more than the market price. We then use the principles explained in Section A to show in Section B how shareholders would be best off if managers did not resist tender offers.

## A. TENDER OFFERS AND THE MARKETS FOR STOCK AND MANAGERS

### 1. Efficient capital market theory and the price of tender offers

It is very unlikely that price and "value" will diverge in large markets for shares. If there were such divergences, investors could reap substantial gains by identifying and buying under-priced shares and selling overpriced shares. Since there are many sophisticated investors with ample capital, the arbitrage process would proceed quite quickly, and it would become impossible to make systematic gains by finding undervalued shares. As investors bought and sold on the basis of what they knew, their very activity would drive the price toward the correct one. The change in the price would reduce the gains available from identifying mispriced shares. Indeed, once information about a firm reached the market, prices would adjust quickly whether or not anyone traded, because no trader with rational expectations would sell for less than the price he expected the shares to reach once the news became widespread.

The process of estimation and trading leads to prices that embody all of the available information about the value of the shares. Commonly referred to as the "efficient capital market hypothesis," the proposition that it is not possible to make abnormal gains by identifying and trading in mispriced stocks has been widely accepted. It means that the price of shares reflects the collective wisdom of all traders about the value of the stock, and it also means that there is no reliable way to determine the direction, amount, or even existence of any difference between today's and tomorrow's price. If capital markets are efficient, as the evidence shows them to be, then any statement that a given stock is really worth more than its price is not believable; if a guess better than the market's guess could be devised, the cost of making the improvement (including the payments to researchers and analysts) would exceed the gains from the knowledge.

It may be helpful to think of stock prices as reflecting estimates of the probabilities of future states of the world. To a great extent, price movements depend on the state of the economy, the rate of interest, demand for the firm's product, the skill (or luck) of the firm's managers, and so on. The price of the stock on any given day will be a composite of the prices the stock would assume under different assumptions about the future. Suppose that the fortunes of one firm depend on the success of some innovative process. If the process works, the future earnings of that firm will be worth $100 per share; if it flops, the earnings will be worth only $20. If failure is three times as likely as success, then the shares will trade for $40. The price of the shares will rise or fall as new information sheds light on either the probability of success (an increase to one chance in two will lead to a price of $60) or the profits if the venture succeeds. Changes in the interest rate would affect the way in which these earnings streams are discounted to present value, thus affecting the price of shares. Other influences work in a similar way.

This illustrates why the constant, sometimes violent, movement of share prices is consistent with the proposition that markets are efficient. When price changes, the change does not show that the old price was wrong; it shows only that new information has been incorporated into the price of the stock.

We can conclude from this, with some confidence, that a tender offer at a price higher than the prevailing one also exceeds the value of the stock. True, the target's managers may know something about the firm's prospects not yet incorporated into the price of the shares. But the disparity between price and worth could not last long. If a bidder tried to steal the target by capitalizing on its special information, the target's managers could defeat the offer by disclosing the information to the public. The price would adjust to reflect the new information, and the offer would succeed only if it were higher than the new price. Tender offers at a premium thus must benefit the target's shareholders.

## 2. Agency costs and takeovers

Although the efficiency of capital markets implies that shareholders gain from tender offers, it also seems to imply that bidders are irrational. Why can a bidder identify underpriced stocks if market professionals cannot? The bidder's knowledge would be shared by the target's management in most cases, and management could release the information, causing a price adjustment. The simple fact that the bidder has made an offer might cause the information to leak to the market. Unless stock markets are substantially inefficient, the bidder will not be able to acquire a company for less than its value under current conditions.

Commentators have proposed a bewildering number of explanations for mergers and takeovers. They include gains from increasing the ability of firms to employ information that would leak if conveyed between independent entities, "synergy" gains as the combined firms obtain the value of some savings in joint operations, and tax benefits. None of these explanations is implausible, and none is inconsistent with a belief that tender offers improve shareholders' welfare. But the savings and benefits attributable to each could be achieved by friendly merger as well as by hostile tender offer. Since a tender offer is by far the more costly device, one must consider whether some source of benefit both accounts for large cash premiums and explains why a friendly merger did not occur.

The most probable explanation for unfriendly takeovers emphasizes their role in monitoring the performance of corporate managers. The tender bidding process polices managers whether or not a tender offer occurs, and disciplines or replaces them if they stray too far from the service of the shareholders. We offer the following explanation both to show what we mean by agency costs and to illustrate how the tender bidding process influences these costs.

Corporate managers (which include both officers and members of the board), like all other people, work harder if they can enjoy all of the benefits of their efforts. In a corporation, however, much of the benefit of each manager's performance inures to someone else, whether it be shareholders, bondholders, or other managers. The investors must be given a substantial share of the gains to induce them to put up their money. Because no single manager receives the full benefit of his work, he may find that, at the margin, developing new ventures and supervising old ones takes too much effort to be worthwhile; each manager may reason that someone else is apt to do the work if he does not or to take the rewards even if he does well. No manager will be completely vigilant. So some managers will find it advantageous to shirk responsibilities, consume perquisites, or otherwise take more than the corporation promised to give them. One especially important way in which managers' performance falls short of the ideal is in choosing the firm's other agents. Because no manager can obtain all of the benefits available to the firm from making good decisions, none takes all cost-justified steps to recruit and train those employees best suited for their jobs. As a result, many firms will have some employees less than completely dedicated to their jobs and other employees who, although fully dedicated, ought not to be in the positions they hold. These agency costs of less than optimal management cause the firm's shares to trade for less than the price they would achieve if agency costs were zero.

Shareholders might be able to reap substantial gains from improving the performance of managers as their agents. But this improvement is difficult to achieve, and the difficulty is the reason why outsiders (tender bidders) play an important role. The agency costs typically will go undetected by individual shareholders. Most shareholders are passive investors seeking liquid holdings. They have little interest in managing the firm and less incentive to learn the details of management. No one shareholder can collect all or even a little of the gains available from monitoring the firm's managers. The benefits would be dispersed among all stockholders according to their investments, not according to their monitoring efforts. Because other shareholders take a free ride on any one shareholder's monitoring, each shareholder finds it in his self-interest to be passive. He simply sells his shares if he is dissatisfied.

The free-riding problems that inhibit monitoring by shareholders are aggravated by the difficulty any shareholder would face in doing anything about the firm's managers once he discovered the existence of excessive agency costs. The shareholder who makes the discovery has no authority to compel the firm to change its ways. He must either persuade the managers or induce his fellow shareholders to oust the managers and install new ones. Yet persuasion is lost on misbehaving managers who need not listen. The cry of "turn the rascals out" also is not of much use, because other shareholders still find it in their self-interest to be passive. The shareholder who has made the discovery must persuade his fellow shareholders to invest a significant amount of time in studying the corporation's affairs. These shareholders would be willing to do so only if their attention and study could yield a benefit. But here, too, free riding makes things difficult. Each shareholder will recognize that his votes will not affect the outcome of any dispute unless he has a large bloc of shares. As a result, each shareholder's self-interest leads him to ignore the controversy; it is costly to become informed, and the cost produces little prospect of benefit. If each shareholder reasons in the same way, as he should, the managers of the firm will prevail in any contest about their operation of the company. And that is the pattern in the market. Shareholders routinely vote for managers or pay no attention to elections. Successful campaigns against managers are rare, and they seldom succeed even if one dissident shareholder holds a large bloc of stock that he can vote in his own favor.

Corporate managers recognize that they can improve the performance of the firm by reducing agency costs. Managers monitor each other's performance and reward achievements; bonuses and salary adjustments could be a form of "ex post settling up" that substantially alleviates incentive problems ... [I]f managers enjoy especially favorable salaries or other terms of employment, they may be disciplined by the prospect of being fired. Pensions and retirement bonuses also help to coax good performance from managers.

These devices, although more useful than monitoring by shareholders, still are imperfect. They depend on the ability of the firm to discriminate good performance from inferior performance by each employee. But because managers typically work in teams, it is hard to determine the contribution of each person. The output of one group of managers depends on the quality of information and options supplied by another group, and so on. The attempt to determine the marginal contribution of each manager is bound to be difficult and costly. Worse, the attempt to meter the contributions of each manager, and to dispense rewards accordingly, encounters the free-rider problem we have discussed. Because no manager can obtain all of the benefits of monitoring his colleagues, each one will be less than fully dedicated to the task. Even the most dedicated manager will find it difficult to fire or discipline an old friend when the benefits of ruthlessness accrue to distant and unknown shareholders.

The methods of metering and monitoring within a firm are thus unlikely to work well unless the management team as a whole is subject to supervision and, if necessary, discharge. The prospect that the team's work will be judged as a whole gives senior managers a powerful incentive to create and use intra-management control devices. Yet, as we have explained, shareholder monitoring cannot supply the necessary supervision.

Tender offers are a method of monitoring the work of management teams. Prospective bidders monitor the performance of managerial teams by comparing a corporation's potential value with its value (as reflected by share prices) under current management. When the difference between the market price of a firm's shares and the price those shares might have under different circumstances becomes too great, an outsider can profit by buying the firm and improving its management. The outsider reduces the free-riding problem because it owns a majority of the shares. The source of the premium is the reduction in agency costs, which makes the firm's assets worth more in the hands of the acquirer than they were worth in the hands of the firm's managers.

All parties benefit in this process. The target's shareholders gain because they receive a premium over the market price. The bidder obtains the difference between the new value of the firm and the payment to the old shareholders. Nontendering shareholders receive part of the appreciation in the price of the shares.

More significantly for our purposes, shareholders benefit even if their corporation never is the subject of a tender offer. The process of monitoring by outsiders poses a continuous threat of takeover if performance lags. Managers will attempt to reduce agency costs in order to reduce the chance of takeover, and the process of reducing agency costs leads to higher prices for shares. We now explore how different responses to takeover bids influence the size of the benefit derived from monitoring by outsiders in advance of any offer.

## B. THE CONSEQUENCES OF MANAGEMENT'S DEFENSIVE TACTICS

### 1. Resistance and agency costs

The argument presented above establishes that takeovers are beneficial to both shareholders and society. It follows that any strategy designed to prevent tender offers reduces welfare. If the company adopts a policy of intransigent resistance and succeeds in maintaining its independence, the shareholders lose whatever premium over market value the bidder offered or would have offered but for the resistance or the prospect of resistance. This lost premium reflects a foregone social gain from the superior employment of the firm's assets.

The target's managers, however, have a substantial interest in preserving their company's independence and thus preserving their salaries and status; the less effective they have been as managers, the greater their interest in preventing a takeover. They may disguise a policy of resistance to all offers as a policy of searching for a better offer than any made so far. Extensive manuals describe both the stratagems of resistance and the methods of disguise. There is no signal that separates intransigent resistance from honest efforts to conduct an auction for the shareholders' benefit. The fact that the first tender offer or any subsequent offer is defeated supplies little information, because any auctioneer understands that determined efforts to collect the highest possible price may lead to no sale at all in the short run.

    . . .

### 2. The acquiescence paradigm as an implicit shareholder agreement

Our argument implies that resistance is costly to shareholders and that logically they should seek to avoid those costs by instructing managers to acquiesce in tender offers. Theoretically, shareholders could assure acquiescence by insisting on appropriate provisions in the articles of incorporation or bylaws. Such provisions would facilitate monitoring of managerial performance, and consequently the price of shares of corporations with antiresistance provisions should rise relative to other firms. Moreover, corporations must compete in the capital markets for funds, and they could obtain these funds at lower cost if their articles constrained the defensive maneuvers of management.

Yet articles of incorporation rarely if ever contain antiresistance provisions. To the contrary, they sometimes contain provisions to make acquisition difficult. Classified boards, cumulative voting, supermajority consent rules, and similar provisions may frustrate the tender offeror's attempts to take control after it has purchased a majority of the common stock. These provisions raise the effective price of an acquisition and increase the offeror's risk. Managers sometimes recommend to shareholders that such provisions be added to the articles of incorporation, and shareholders routinely follow these recommendations.

But these facts hardly suggest that shareholders approve of management resistance. The great majority of public corporations have *not* adopted "porcupine" provisions making acquisitions more difficult, and general principles of fiduciary duty restrict managers' options to do so. . . .

## II. The Arguments Supporting the Right of Target Management to Adopt a Defensive Strategy

Our analysis cuts against the grain of many cases and a substantial amount of commentary. The rationales offered to support the right of target management to resist tender offers can be grouped in four categories: (1) tender offers do not increase welfare; (2) the target's shareholders benefit from price increases when tender offers are defeated; (3) the target's management has obligations to noninvestor groups that may be adversely affected by a tender offer; and (4) the target's management is obligated to prevent unlawful conduct. In the sections that follow, we consider and reject each of these rationales as a basis for resistance.

## A. THE ARGUMENTS THAT TENDER OFFERS DO NOT INCREASE WELFARE

Our argument relies on the premise that tender offers increase social welfare by moving productive assets to higher-valued uses and to the hands of better managers. Numerous commentators, however, have reached a contrary conclusion. It has been observed, for instance, that many target companies are "well run," have substantial amounts of cash from successful operations, and that the offeror retains the target's management after acquiring control. These observations are invoked to support an assertion that the acquired firms were not doing poorly; consequently, the argument concludes, tender offers do not move assets to better managers.

This is unpersuasive. It amounts to second-guessing the market. Unless the acquirer is giving away its money, the premium price paid for the shares indicates a real gain in the productivity of the assets. If General Motors is willing to bid $100 for a ton of steel owned by General Electric, and GE sells, we would count this as a value-increasing transaction despite the fact that GE otherwise would have put the steel to "good use" (perhaps $90 worth). The highly subjective observation that acquired firms are well run does not exclude the possibility that, in new hands, the firms would be better run. Only proof that markets are not efficient in pricing shares could support the argument that tender offers do not improve the use of resources.

That acquired firms often are cash rich, perhaps implying successful past operations, also does not demonstrate that takeovers are undesirable. To the contrary, that a firm holds a substantial cash position indicates agency costs. Cash can be invested. The acquirer usually invests the cash it obtains in the takeover, thus putting idle resources to work. The retention of the target's management after a takeover also is not significant. Although the management may keep their old titles, they often lose effective control to officers of the acquirer. Retention in office may be a form of bribe, paid to secure acquiescence in the takeover, rather than a signal of satisfactory performance.

. . . .

Tender offers have also been characterized as "raids" in which the offeror pays a premium for a working majority of the shares in order to loot the firm to the detriment of the minority shareholders. It is unlikely, however, that any tender offer for a substantial percentage of a company's shares will be motivated by a desire to loot the acquired corporation. A looter generates no new value, and thus cannot afford to pay a premium price for all shares. Even if a bidder seeks less than all shares, it cannot pay a significant premium for those it obtains. If, for example, the offeror acquires for $15 per share 70 percent of a firm whose shares had been trading for $10, it cannot hope to make a profit by looting. Also, looting from minority shareholders violates established rules, and a bidder would not be likely to escape detection if it violated these rules.

Another argument against tender offers portrays them as reducing the welfare of the shareholders of the acquirers by more than the premium paid to the target's shareholders. In this view, tender offers represent self-aggrandizing empire building by acquiring managers who err in deciding what firms to acquire or what price to pay. The difficulty with this view is its implicit assumption that product and labor market constraints (and the tender offer process itself) do not discipline managers. A corporation headed by an empire-building management team that did not maximize profits would fare poorly in the product market and would have lower share prices; its managers would fare poorly in the employment market. The corporation itself would become a takeover candidate.

. . .

## B. The argument that share price increases justify resistance from target's management

Several commentators have noted that even if a tender bid fails, the share price of the target often rises, sometimes to more than the tender offer price. If shareholders so benefit, the argument goes, then management is justified in resisting tender offers. . . .

The most plausible reason for a price increase following the tender offer's defeat is that the market sees the defeat as simply one round in an extended auction. The market anticipates that in the future another offeror – one not saddled with the first offeror's higher costs of information – will acquire the target. Many management-induced withdrawals are followed by higher offers, and share prices increase as the eventual acquisition becomes more likely.

. . .

Regardless of the cause of the price increase, shareholders in general have little cause for rejoicing. The price rise comes about because someone is taking a free ride on information generated by the first offeror. Free riding of this sort reduces the incentive to make the first offer, and, for the reasons we have developed earlier, decreases the amount of monitoring, decreases the number of offers, and harms shareholders in the long run.

. . .

# 20

## The Regulation of Insider Trading

### Dennis W. Carlton and Daniel R. Fischel

#### EDITOR'S INTRODUCTION

At present there are federal regulations against "insider trading." Here insider trading refers to limitations on the buying and selling of stock in a publicly held corporation by its directors and officers. For example, corporate officers are not allowed to sell short (that is, promise to sell stock which they do not presently own at some time in the future), nor are they allowed to both buy and sell stock within a six-month period even if the transactions were not a result of insider information. The main arguments for such regulations are that it creates "a level playing field" and that it prevents the managers from "throwing a monkey wrench into the works" in order to make good on their bets that the stock price will go down when they sell short.

Dennis Carlton and Daniel Fischel argue against this commonly held view. They argue that banning insider trading does not create a level playing field only a more costly one as then outsiders such as stock brokers may have an informational advantage (obtained in a more costly way than the information obtained by insiders). They also cast doubt on the monkey wrench problem. Most important, they show that the market for corporate control (the state competition for chartering corporations) and the common law, more generally, have not found this type of insider trading a problem.

Rather than viewing insider trading as a problem, Carlton and Fischel view it as a means of conveying the value of the firm's stock continuously and reliably. In a nutshell, the allocation of this "intellectual" property right to the managers is optimal.

This paper is interesting, not only because of the subject matter, but also because it provides a thoughtful example of comparative advantage (between governments and firms) and insight into the relationship between information and stock prices.

Imagine two firms, A and B, which are identical in all respects except that, in its charter, firm A prohibits the trading of its shares based on inside (nonpublic) information. The firm requires insiders (employees) to report their trades, which a special committee or an independent accounting firm then checks to ensure compliance with the charter provision. Firm B, by contrast, neither prohibits insider trading nor requires reporting. Insiders openly trade shares of firm B and regularly earn positive abnormal returns. In competitive capital markets, which charter provision will survive?

Despite the deceptive simplicity of this question, it has no obvious answer. The consensus, to the extent that any exists, appears to be that firm A's charter will survive because it eliminates various perceived harmful effects of insider trading. Thus, investors would pay less for shares in B. The managers of B, in order to maximize the value of B shares, would have to adopt a similar charter provision.

As for these harmful effects, many believe that insider trading is "unfair" and undermines public confidence in capital markets. Other critics have argued that insider trading . . . encourages managers to invest in risky projects, impedes corporate decision making, and tempts managers to delay public disclosure of valuable information. . . . Still others have claimed that insider trading allows insiders to divert part of the firm's earnings that would otherwise go to shareholders and therefore raises the firm's cost of capital. Under this "insider trading is harmful to investors" hypothesis, competitive capital markets would force firm B to prohibit insider trading.

The difficulty with this hypothesis is that it appears to be contradicted by the actions of firms. Although no one has conducted rigorous empirical research in this area, it is generally believed that firms have made little, if any, attempt to prohibit insider trading, at least until very recently and then perhaps only as a response to regulation. Today the area is federally regulated, but the federal insider trading prohibitions are limited, have rarely been enforced, and have had little observable effect on insider trading. . . . Critics of insider trading have offered no explanation for why firms have made so little attempt to prohibit insider trading.
. . .

Also puzzling is the common law which, in the main, permitted insider trading. Because capital is highly mobile, firms, in order to attract investors, have strong incentives to incorporate in states that have efficient corporation laws. Because incorporations are profitable to the state, the states in turn have strong incentives to provide a set of legal rules that maximize shareholders' welfare. If eliminating insider trading produced gains, states that prohibit insider trading would have a comparative advantage over other states, and firms that incorporated in such states would have a comparative advantage over other firms. Yet no evidence suggests that this has occurred.

Similarly, insider trading in the capital markets of many other countries historically has been subject either to regulations that have not been enforced or to no regulation at all. This phenomenon, like the absence of domestic private and state prohibitions, suggests that the question of the desirability of insider trading is far more complex than commonly assumed.

Finally, insider trading in this country, despite the widespread perception to the contrary, is generally permitted. A fundamental difference exists between the legal and economic definitions of insider trading. Insider trading in an economic sense is trading by parties who are better informed than their trading partners. Thus, insider trading in an economic sense includes all trades where information is asymmetric. This definition includes all trades, whether or not in securities, where one of the parties has superior information. By contrast, federal law has focused on purchases or sales by certain insiders within a six-month period or on trading on the basis of "material" information by a broader, more amorphous group of insiders or their tippees. Insider trading in an economic sense need not be illegal. The law never has attempted to prohibit all trading by knowledgeable insiders.

. . . In assessing the arguments for and against insider trading . . . we will focus on trading

by managers or other employees in securities of their own firms based on superior knowledge regardless of whether the trade is illegal. We emphasize, however, that the arguments
for and against insider trading may apply equally to trading by others.

We attempt in this article to analyze critically the arguments in favor of prohibiting insider
trading and to suggest why allowing the practice may be an efficient way to compensate
corporate managers. Part I demonstrates that the insider trading debate is really a debate
about whether the firm, as a matter of contract, should be able to allocate property rights in
valuable information to managers or to investors. We argue that the parties' self-interest will
lead them to reach by private agreement the optimal allocation of what is simply one element
of a compensation arrangement. We discuss in Part II several incentive and information
effects which suggest that there may be gains from allocating property rights in valuable
information to managers as opposed to investors. These gains may explain the lack of
pervasive private, common law, and foreign and domestic restraints on insider trading. Part
III analyzes some of the numerous objections to insider trading. The various legal rules
regulating insider trading are critically analyzed in Part IV. Part V is a conclusion.

## I. Insider Trading and the Coase Theorem

Critics of insider trading draw a sharp distinction between the proper legal response to
insider trading and to other forms of managerial compensation. Salaries, bonuses, stock
options, office size, vacation leave, secretarial support, and other terms of employment are
all, it is generally assumed, properly left to private negotiation. Nobody would argue seriously
that these terms and conditions of employment should be set by government regulation –
that a federal agency, for example, should monitor the amount of leisure time taken by
corporate managers. Most would agree that these decisions are better made through negotiations between firms and managers, given the constraints of capital, product, and labor
markets as well as the market for corporate control. Although the negotiation and enforcement of these employment agreements are costly, these costs are presumptively lower than
would be the case if negotiation and enforcement were handled by government regulators
who are undisciplined by markets.

Precisely the opposite presumptions have been applied with respect to insider trading.
Most believe that existing government regulation is necessary and should be extended;
virtually no one has considered the possibility, let alone has argued, that private negotiations
between a firm and its employees can most efficiently determine whether insiders should be
allowed to profit by trading on inside information.

Does whatever difference that exists between profits from trading in shares and other
forms of compensation warrant such different legal responses? It is no answer to argue that
insider trading is unfair, constitutes theft, destroys investors' confidence, or compensates
inefficiently. These characterizations just as aptly describe a hypothetical compensation scheme
whereby managers pay themselves huge salaries and consume unlimited perquisites, regardless of their productivity. Government need not prohibit this type of compensation agreement because, given competitive markets, firms will have strong incentives to avoid such a
scheme. The identical argument applies to insider trading: If it is bad, firms that allow insider
trading will be at a competitive disadvantage compared with firms that curtail insider trading.

Coase's famous insight is quite relevant in this regard. Whether insider trading is beneficial depends on whether the property right in information is more valuable to the firm's managers or to the firm's investors. In either case, the parties can engage in a value-maximizing exchange by allocating the property right in information to its highest-valuing user. If the critics of insider trading are correct, therefore, both the firm's investors and the firm's insiders could profit by banning insider trading, thereby allocating the property right in information to the firm's investors.

It is important to recognize that this mutual incentive to allocate the property right in information to its highest-valuing user does not depend on actual negotiations between insiders and investors. As long as investors understand the possibility of insider trading, both share price and managers' compensation will be higher if the efficient allocation is reached than if it is not.

. . .

The notion that the dispute concerning insider trading is really a dispute about which party more highly values a property right and that whatever bargain is reached can be enforced (albeit imperfectly) by the parties themselves undermines the case for regulatory prohibition of insider trading. Such a prohibition could be justified only if it were clear that the parties themselves had attempted to deter insider trading by contract and that the government had a comparative advantage in enforcing such contracts. But the comparative advantage in enforcement is irrelevant without a showing that firms generally have attempted to limit insider trading by contract. Without such a showing, a regulatory prohibition will likely displace efficient private arrangements with inefficient regulatory solutions, much in the same way that regulation of salaries, bonuses, office size, leisure time, and all other terms of employment would be inefficient.

Our conclusion that a regulatory prohibition of insider trading (which would involve a substantial extension of existing regulations) is unwarranted has relied heavily on the apparent lack of widespread attempts by firms to prohibit insider trading. Insider trading in an economic sense continues to be widespread. (Curiously, the proponents of regulation have failed to cite any evidence of private prohibitions to support their contention that firms desire to ban insider trading.) Of course, the allocation of the property right in valuable information to managers might not be optimal in all circumstances for every firm. But even if some firms would attempt to ban insider trading in the absence of regulation, other firms should nonetheless be able to opt out of the regulations if they so desire. No justification exists for precluding firms from contracting around a regulatory prohibition of insider trading.

## II. Why Firms Might Want to Allocate the Property Rights in Valuable Information to Managers as Opposed to Shareholders

Thus far, we have argued that firms and managers are able to allocate property rights in valuable information by private negotiation. In this section, we explain why the parties might choose to allocate these property rights to managers and thus allow insider trading. Because unambiguous welfare statements can be very difficult to make even in simple economic models involving uncertainty, to expect any analysis to prove that insider trading is solely harmful or solely beneficial is unrealistic. The desirability of insider trading is ultimately an empirical question. Nevertheless, analyzing how insider trading affects information transmission and shapes incentives will enable us to understand better the consequences of different allocations of the property rights in valuable information.

## A. INFORMATION EFFECTS

The social gains from efficient capital markets are well known. The more accurately prices reflect information, the better prices guide capital investment in the economy. From the perspective of an individual firm, however, efficient capital markets are a public good, unless private, as opposed to social, gains accrue to the firm when the prices of its own securities convey accurate information. Why, then, does a firm disclose information about itself?

One reason is that disclosure can reduce wasteful expenditures on search and reduce investor uncertainty about the firm. This may make the firm more valuable to investors. Investors expend resources to identify overvalued or undervalued securities until the next dollar they spend on information no longer produces an additional dollar of return. If the firm can produce information about itself at the lowest cost, disclosure of information by the firm will save resources by reducing the amount of expenditures on search and will lead to less investor uncertainty about the firm.

A second reason is that disclosure of information by the firm also may enable the firm's current investors to sell their shares to outsiders at a higher price, on average. If the firm discloses no information, outsiders may assume the worst and discount the price they are willing to pay for shares by a factor that reflects their uncertainty. Because every firm has an incentive to distinguish itself from those firms about which the worst is true, so that outsiders will pay a higher price for its shares, information will be produced.

Finally, accurately priced securities will enable firms to observe more accurately when corporate managers are successful. Thus, markets for managerial services and for corporate control will function more effectively. Also, the better managers will signal their quality by their willingness to tie a higher proportion of their compensation to stock performance. Accurate prices then enable these managers to receive the rewards for their superior performance. For these reasons, shareholders would want managers to disclose information about the value of the firm.

Complete disclosure, however, would not be optimal. Disclosure is costly, and at some point the costs will outweigh the benefits of increased disclosure. Moreover, in some cases, disclosure might destroy the information's value. It would not be in the investors' interest to disclose, for example, that a confidential study revealed the presence of valuable mineral ore deposits on land the firm intends to purchase.

Since the firm's shareholders value the ability to control information that flows to the stock market, they may also value insider trading because it gives the firm an additional method of communicating and controlling information. If insiders trade, the share price will move closer to what it would have been had the information been disclosed. How close will depend on the amount of "noise" surrounding the trade. The greater the ability of market participants to identify insider trading, the more information such trading will convey. At the extreme, trading by insiders is as fully revealing as complete disclosure. But since insiders will limit the size of their positions because of risk aversion and will camouflage their trading to some degree, they convey less information by trading than that conveyed by (credible) full disclosure.

Several reasons explain why communicating information through insider trading may be of value to the firm. Through insider trading, a firm can convey information it could not feasibly announce publicly because an announcement would destroy the value of the information, would be too expensive, not believable, or – owing to the uncertainty of the information – would subject the firm to massive damage liability if it turned out ex post to be incorrect. ... In other words, announcement of information need not be continuous, while trading on inside information can be. Thus, insider trading gives firms a tool either to increase or to decrease the amount of information that is contained in share prices.[1]

## III. The Arguments against Insider Trading

Critics have marshaled a wide array of arguments against insider trading. We do not attempt to analyze all of these arguments in detail, but rather focus on the major claims made by critics of insider trading. Nor is our purpose to demonstrate that none of the arguments against insider trading has any merit. But to show that insider trading would not be optimal in a world of perfect information is not a compelling argument for prohibiting insider trading in a world of costly monitoring and imperfect information. Whether the costs of insider trading outweigh the benefits is an empirical question. The apparent absence of widespread prohibitions of insider trading in employment contracts and corporate charters and the existence of common law rules permitting insider trading create a strong presumption that the practice may be beneficial in some circumstances. We argue in this section that the opponents of insider trading have not overcome this strong presumption.

### A. THE PROBLEMS OF MORAL HAZARD . . .

Many commentators have argued that insider trading is harmful because it creates a moral hazard by allowing insiders to profit on bad news. At the extreme, they claim that allowing insiders to profit on bad information makes managers indifferent between working to make the firm prosperous and working to make it bankrupt. . . .

Prohibiting insider trading may be an overly blunt weapon to combat the problem of moral hazard . . . . [This problem is] most acute if short selling is permitted and therefore would be substantially eliminated if short selling, but not other forms of insider trading, were forbidden. Even limited to short selling, however, the argument is far from persuasive. . . . . Managers often work in teams and thus must first persuade one another that the firm should undertake a particular strategy. If a manager uncovers a good opportunity, his efforts will be magnified by the efforts of other managers and employees who themselves will profit by increasing the value of the firm because their own compensation is thereby increased. The same is not true for poor opportunities. Because each manager will be concerned with his own compensation, which will be tied to the performance of the firm, as well as his long-run interest in his human capital, he will be unlikely to go along with a strategy that decreases the value of the firm. Thus, the ability of any one manager to pursue bad opportunities will be constrained because other managers and employees will attempt to maximize the firm's value. Collusion to decrease the value of the firm among managers in pursuit of trading profits is unlikely to succeed because, as in all cartels, each rational member will cheat insofar as the gains to a lone cheater from exposing others will exceed his gains from collusion.

Moreover, the moral hazard and unbundling problems are potentially present in a wide variety of situations where existing insider trading rules do not apply, and casual empiricism suggests that the resulting costs are insignificant. For example, with respect to insider trading, the actions of a key executive of a firm do not differ in principle from those of a key supplier to the firm. If short selling creates a serious moral hazard for a key executive, it must also do so for a key supplier. An executive of the supplier could sell the firm's shares short with little fear of penalty from insider trading laws and then, as long as damages for breach (including those to the supplier's reputation) were less than trading gains, profit from failing to deliver urgently needed materials to the firm. But this possibility is not perceived as a problem, presumably because of the incentives of the supply executive and the supplier itself to develop a reputation as reliable and trustworthy for future commercial dealings. Precisely the same is true for key executives of the firm, who have analogous reputational interests that provide incentives for them to maximize the value of their services.

Similarly, instead of selling their own firm short, key executives, by taking a long position in the securities of competitors whose income streams are highly correlated with the income stream of their own firm, can profit by taking actions unfavorable to their own firm. No evidence suggests, however, that the availability of this practice seriously distorts the incentives of insiders to maximize the value of their firms.

In short, the perverse incentive effects that some attribute to insider trading would, for the same reasons, lurk in many practices that are currently unregulated. Given the lack of problems that short selling seems to have engendered (we are not aware of any empirical documentation in the economic literature pointing out the seriousness of these problems), it seems likely that the critics of insider trading have exaggerated the magnitude of the perverse incentives associated with short selling.

. . .

## F. THE LIQUIDITY OF THE STOCK MARKET

Insider trading allows individuals to profit by trading on superior information. If transactions occur between uninformed and informed traders who are otherwise identical and if the uninformed know this, then the uninformed should realize that they could be better off not trading. In order to induce trade, something must prevent the uninformed from holding the "market" and not trading. Otherwise, markets for stock would become less liquid, and consequently, the people who have to trade for exogenous reasons (e.g., to pay for a child's tuition or to reallocate portfolios because of new inheritances) perforce would provide the profits for insider trading. Insider trading could be detrimental to the extent it reduces liquidity.

This problem raises the more general question of why the uninformed ever trade in individual stocks, a question to which theory provides no convincing answer. Suffice it to say that no obvious logic indicates that insider trading has any substantial effect on liquidity. If insiders could not trade, the gains to noninsiders from discovering nonpublic information would be higher and investors would have an incentive to expend resources to uncover such information. In fact, the only effect a ban on insider trading might have is that those with better access to information, such as brokers, would reap some of the gains from inside information. While this may be inefficient because brokers can become informed only at a higher cost, the informed-uninformed trader problem remains. Smart brokers, in other words, cause the same problem as smart insiders. Uninformed traders who know they are uninformed should not trade in either situation. That trade occurs suggests that traders either do not believe they are uninformed or realize that enough informed trading occurs for the prevailing prices to reflect most material information.

## G. Fairness arguments

We have left for last the most common argument against insider trading – that it is unfair or immoral. The prevalence of this intuition is so powerful that many commentators have argued that insider trading should be prohibited even if it is efficient. What is commonly left unsaid is how and why insider trading is unfair.

Kenneth Scott has pointed out that if the existence of insider trading is known, as it surely is, outsiders will not be disadvantaged because the price they pay will reflect the risk of insider trading.[2] This is a useful insight and in some sense is a complete response to the claim that investors are exploited by insider trading. But the argument does not address the desirability of insider trading. If traders knew that a firm burned half of its assets, the price would fall and subsequent investors in the firm would have the same expected returns as any other asset of comparable risk. But the fact that investors would not be fooled does not mean that burning assets is a beneficial practice. On the contrary, firms that followed this strategy to a substantial degree, like firms that adopted inefficient compensation schemes, could not survive over time.

A more powerful response to the argument that insiders profit at the expense of outsiders is that if insider trading is a desirable compensation scheme, it benefits insiders and outsiders alike. Nobody would argue seriously that salaries, options, bonuses, and other compensation devices allow insiders to profit at the expense of outsiders because these sums otherwise would have gone to shareholders. Compensating managers in this fashion increases the size of the pie, and thus outsiders as well as insiders profit from the incentives managers are given to increase the value of the firm. Insider trading does not come "at the expense of" outsiders for precisely the same reason.

Contrary to popular sentiment with respect to insider trading, therefore, there is no tension between considerations of fairness and of efficiency. To say that insider trading is a desirable method of compensating corporate managers is to say that shareholders would voluntarily enter into contractual arrangements with insiders giving them property rights in valuable information. If insider trading is efficient, no independent notions of fairness suggest that it should be prohibited.

## IV. Legal Rules Restricting Insider Trading

In this section, we analyze the common law and various state and federal rules governing insider trading. At the outset, we should note the fundamental difference between state and federal rules governing internal corporate relationships. States' ability to enact rules that reduce investors' welfare is limited by competition between states. If one state adopts inefficient rules, it is a simple matter for a firm to avoid them by reincorporating in another state. Therefore, state statutory and common law rules that survive over time, like private contractual arrangements, are presumptively welfare increasing. Not surprisingly, enabling statutes such as Delaware's, which allow private parties to structure their affairs with relative freedom, have demonstrated the greatest survival qualities.

Analysis of federal rules yields exactly the opposite conclusion. Federal rules – whether pertaining to the amount of information produced, the types of issues on which shareholders are entitled to vote, or whether firms can structure compensation packages that include a property right in information – displace private arrangements and the competition between states. Although firms can avoid these rules by not incorporating or by "going private," they obviously would find these alternatives more costly than simply changing the state of incorporation. Federal rules governing insider trading or any other aspect of intracorporate activity, therefore, are not entitled to the same presumption of efficiency as are long-standing state rules.

## A. COMMON LAW RULES

The general common law rule is that insider trading in publicly traded corporations is permitted. Failure by an insider to disclose information before trading is not actionable. Neither the corporation nor an investor trading on the opposite side of a transaction to the insider has any legal remedies against the insider. This general common law rule has some exceptions. Some jurisdictions allowed suits against insiders for trading if the plaintiff could prove "special facts" – that his trade was induced by express or implied misrepresentations concerning the value of the securities or the identity of the purchaser. Corporations also have been allowed to bring actions under the corporate opportunity doctrine against insiders who take advantage of their knowledge in ways that harm the firms' business. For example, an employee who, upon learning of an impending land purchase or corporate repurchase plan, rushes out and purchases the land or shares in order to resell to the firm at a high price would be held to have usurped a corporate opportunity.

This general common law rule is consistent with our analysis. Because trading by insiders appears to be consistent with their contract with the firm, no action lies for the firm or for a shareholder on the firm's behalf. If the insider (or someone acting on his behalf) makes misrepresentations about the value of the firm or his identity in convincing an uninformed outsider to sell, however, the informational effect of the trade that we have discussed above is lost. Indeed the trade, like other types of fraud, will move prices away from, rather than towards, the "correct" price, particularly if the trade is a face-to-face transaction as opposed to an impersonal one. Moreover, the incentive effect created by allowing such trades would be to distort information as opposed to producing new information. The "special facts" rule, therefore, is a recognition that trading by insiders need not be protected when such trading is not efficient.

The rationale for applying the corporate opportunity doctrine to insider trading also seems clear. If actions based on insider information harm the firm, those actions will be prohibited. In the land case, the firm instead of buying land in a competitive market must now negotiate with the employee. Transaction costs have risen. Firms would prefer to ban such behavior and pay the employee through increased salary. Similarly, the purchase of a target's shares in advance of a takeover probably would be considered a usurpation of a corporate opportunity. The action bids up the price of the target firm's shares and thereby makes the corporate action more expensive. This reduces the value of the takeover to the firm. Thus, fiduciary duties under common law ban nonconsensual use of inside information, whether through trading in shares or otherwise, where the precipitating event is so rare as not to justify an explicit contractual prohibition.

. . .

# V. Summary and Conclusion

The most important points to understand in order to assess the desirability of insider trading laws are as follows:

1.  Both the common law and state law place few, if any, restraints on insider trading. Section 16 of the Securities Exchange Act of 1934 restricts the trading of a select few insiders. . . . The existing law places no restrictions on transactions involving shares of competitors or trading based on "nonmaterial" information. . . . The existing laws make an artificial distinction between insiders and outsiders even where the outsiders have dealings with the firm, and these laws fail to constrain the trading activities of "outsiders." Therefore, existing federal regulations ban only a small percentage of trades by individuals with superior information.
2.  No evidence suggests that firms generally have attempted to prohibit insider trading or, after 1934, attempted to plug the large gaps in the federal bans against insider trading.
3.  The recent articles in the economic literature as well as the older general criticisms that illustrate some possible inefficiencies associated with trading by insiders do not justify the current federal regulations, but rather would justify far broader restrictions on insider trading. Such broader restrictions seem inconsistent with the desires of firms as revealed through their own choices of contractual terms and corporate charter provisions and with the development of state and common law rules.
4.  Firms have strong incentives to allocate property rights in valuable information to the highest-valuing user. The absence of widespread prohibitions on insider trading in employment agreements and corporate charters indicates that firms may, in some situations, want to allocate this property right to managers or other employees. We have suggested several information and efficiency effects of insider trading to explain why this might be the case.
5.  Even if the property right in information is allocated to the firm, federal regulation of insider trading would be justifiable only if the federal regulations could enforce contracts against insider trading at a lower cost than private firms or states. The evidence does not conclusively support (or refute) this conclusion.
6.  Even if federal regulation is justified on the basis of low enforcement costs, firms should have the opportunity to opt out of the regulation in the absence of any showing of third-party effects. Firms are the best judges of how to structure the terms of their employment contracts.

. . .

Based on the available evidence (which admittedly is scanty in some places), it appears that the allocation of the valuable property right in information would be better left to private negotiations and common law development.

## Notes

1.  An alternative to insider trading to communicate information is for the firm itself to convey information by the purchase and sale of shares. The difficulty with this alternative is that there is little incentive for an employee to reveal information to the firm's trader.
2.  Scott, "Insider trading: Rule 10b-5, Disclosure and Corporate Privacy," 9 *J. Legal Stud.* 801 (1980) at 807–09.

# 21

# Corporate Reorganizations and the Treatment of Diverse Ownership Interests: A Comment on Adequate Protection of Secured Creditors in Bankruptcy

*Douglas G. Baird and Thomas H. Jackson*

## EDITOR'S INTRODUCTION

When a firm goes bankrupt, many parties are affected. Employees may lose their jobs and the people who service the employees may, in turn, lose their jobs. More directly, the holders of the firm's assets, including secured lenders, bondholders, and stockholders are at risk of losing their assets. While some have argued that bankruptcy courts should consider the effect of the firm's bankruptcy on the community, Douglas Baird and Thomas Jackson argue that the role of bankruptcy law is to maximize the value of the assets of the firm. From their point of view, bankruptcy law is a way of facilitating Coasean bargains to create a unity of interest. It is unity of interest and consistency with the nonbankruptcy state that allows for efficient outcomes. When a firm faces bankruptcy, holders of secured debt want their collateral right away while owners of stock are willing to risk losing other people's secured assets if the gamble might result in a large payoff for the stockholders. Baird and Jackson suggest a way of converting secured debt into stock so that there is a unity of interest instead of one group of asset holders trying to shift the cost onto another group. In this way, those decisions that are made in bankruptcy will maximize the return on all of the assets. Furthermore, by keeping the rules of asset division the same for bankruptcy and nonbankruptcy states, an owner of a particular set of assets will not choose bankruptcy in order to get a larger slice of the pie.

. . .

The filing of a bankruptcy petition automatically stays creditors from repossessing property of the debtor in which they have a security interest. These creditors, however, can demand that the stay be lifted unless their interests in the debtor's property are "adequately protected." As a matter of statutory illustration, adequate protection is the granting of relief that "will result in the realization by [the holder of the interest] of the indubitable equivalent of such entity's interest in such property." In the context of secured credit, the need for adequate protection, according to the legislative history of the Bankruptcy Code, rests "as much on policy grounds as on constitutional grounds. Secured creditors should not be deprived of the benefit of their bargain."

. . .

In this article, we suggest that bankruptcy law at its core should be designed to keep individual actions against assets, taken to preserve the position of one investor or another, from interfering with the use of those assets favored by the investors as a group. . . . Bankruptcy law should change a substantive nonbankruptcy rule only when doing so preserves the value of assets for the group of investors holding rights in them. For this reason, bankruptcy law necessarily overrides the remedies of individual investors outside of bankruptcy, for those "grab" rules undermine the very advantages sought in a collective proceeding. Changes in substantive rules unrelated to preserving assets for the collective good of the investor group, however, run counter to the goals of bankruptcy. Such rule changes in bankruptcy can induce an individual investor to seek bankruptcy merely to gain access to rule changes that offer him benefits, regardless of whether there are any benefits – or indeed costs – to the investor group as a whole.

Based upon this view of bankruptcy law, we examine the protection afforded to secured creditors in bankruptcy, asking, first, what exactly the secured creditors' nonbankruptcy rights are and, second, whether any modification of those rights is necessary in order to preserve or enhance the firm's assets for the general benefit of the investor group. What these nonbankruptcy rights should be is a question that is unrelated to whether they should be followed in bankruptcy. We show that protecting the value of a secured creditor's nonbankruptcy rights – whatever they might be – actually reinforces the bankruptcy policy of putting the firm's assets to their best use by placing the costs of trying to keep the assets of a firm together on those who stand to benefit from such an effort. If these parties do not bear these costs, they will have an incentive to place a firm in bankruptcy and to draw out the proceeding, even though doing so does not work to the advantage of those with rights to the firm's assets when their interests are considered as a group.

## I. The Problem of Diverse Ownership Interests

Those who have argued that secured creditors should not be given the full value of their rights under state law in bankruptcy often also argue that a bankruptcy proceeding must respond to the greater social problems that attend a business failure. The failure of a firm affects many who do not, under current law, have cognizable ownership interests in the firm outside of bankruptcy. The economy of an entire town can be disrupted when a large factory closes. Many employees may be put out of work. The failure of one firm may lead to the failure of those who supplied it with raw materials and those who acquired its finished products. Some believe that preventing such consequences is worth the costs of trying to keep the firm running and justifies placing burdens on a firm's secured creditors.

We think that this view is, as a matter of bankruptcy policy, fundamentally wrong. Fashioning remedies for all the harm a failing business may bring is difficult and beyond the competence of a bankruptcy court. The wider effects of the failure of a particular enterprise are not easy to assess. A principal characteristic of a market economy is, after all, that some firms fail, and postponing the inevitable or keeping marginal firms alive may do more harm than good. Forcing investors to keep assets in a relatively unproductive enterprise may limit the freedom of the same or different investors to use those assets in a different and more productive one. Keeping a firm in one town from closing may have the indirect effect of keeping a new one in a different town from opening. Moreover, limiting the ability of investors to reclaim their assets may reduce their incentive to invest (rather than consume) in the first instance. Instead of weighing these effects equally, a bankruptcy judge is likely to focus on the demonstrable harms of those who are before him.

But there is a more important reason for denying a bankruptcy judge broad license to protect people in the wake of economic misfortune. The problems brought by business failures are not bankruptcy problems. A bankruptcy proceeding should not be the place to implement a policy that society does not enforce outside of bankruptcy and that is unrelated to the preservation of assets for the firm's investor group. Most businesses fail without a bankruptcy petition ever being filed. If it is a bad policy to protect secured creditors in full while workers remain unpaid, it should not matter whether a bankruptcy petition has been filed. So, too, if a secured creditor should properly share with everyone else in the economic misfortunes of a debtor, he should be required to carry his share of the loss in every instance, not just in the minority of cases in which a bankruptcy petition is filed.

Nonbankruptcy concerns, we believe, should not be addressed by changing bankruptcy policy. Our view derives from two related observations: first, that bankruptcy law is, and should be, concerned with the interests of those (from bondholders to unpaid workers to tort victims to shareholders) who, outside of bankruptcy, have property rights in the assets of the firm filing a petition, and, second, that in analyzing the interests of these parties with property rights, our baseline should be applicable nonbankruptcy law. A collective insolvency proceeding is directed toward reducing the costs associated with diverse ownership interests and encouraging those with interests in a firm's assets to put those assets to the use the group as a whole would favor.

. . .

Just as the filing of a petition in bankruptcy provides little justification for altering the relative rights of owners and non-owners of the firm, so should it have little effect on the rights of owners inter se. Changes in nonbankruptcy rights should be made only if they benefit all those with interests in the firm as a group. A rule change unrelated to the goals of bankruptcy creates incentives for particular holders of rights in assets to resort to bankruptcy in order to gain, for themselves, the advantages of that rule change, even though a bankruptcy proceeding was not in the collective interest of the investor group. Moreover, as we develop below, once a bankruptcy proceeding begins, the change in nonbankruptcy rights impedes collective decision making by the investor group about the deployment of the firm's assets.

When a firm files a petition in bankruptcy, two questions arise. First, one must decide what to do with the firm's assets, and, second, because of the presence of diverse owners, one must decide who gets them. Our principal proposition is that the answer to the second question should not, ideally, alter the answer to the first. Consider the case where only one person has all the rights to the firm's assets. Such a person, the sole owner of the assets, would have no creditors, consensual or otherwise; no one but he would have a right to use those assets. Irrespective of any thought of bankruptcy, this sole owner would continually reevaluate his use of the assets. He might decide to sell the assets piece by piece. Alternatively, he might decide to keep the assets together (along with the firm's accumulated good will and expertise). In the latter event, he would still need to decide whether to keep running the business himself or to sell it as a unit to a third party. He would be utterly indifferent to bankruptcy policy because, unless his firm's use of it benefited him (by permitting his firm, for example, to escape a nonbankruptcy charge), he would have no occasion to use the bankruptcy process. If a charge were placed upon assets only in bankruptcy law (such as that a firm could not go out of business without first protecting employees), this owner would remain free to ignore it by going out of business outside of bankruptcy. He could only be obligated to take account of such a charge if it were imposed by nonbankruptcy law. Because a sole owner has no distributional decision to make, his only concern is the best deployment of the assets.

The unique function of a bankruptcy system comes into sharp focus when the situation of the sole owner, who does not need bankruptcy and can ignore its policies, is compared to that of diverse owners. Bankruptcy law is fundamentally a collective proceeding and as such, is needed only when there is no such sole owner of the firm's assets. When the "rights" to the assets are spread among more than one person, as they almost always are, someone must decide not only how best to deploy the assets, but also how to split up the returns from those assets. The answer to this second question, however, should not affect the determination of how to deploy the assets. As a group, these diverse owners – bondholders, tort victims, trade creditors, shareholders, and others – would want to follow the same course as a sole owner. The owners as a group, in other words, would want to keep the distributional question from spilling over into the deployment question.

When ownership of a firm is diverse and the individual owners have different packages of rights, however, all have an incentive to take actions that will increase their own share of the assets of an ailing firm, even if in so doing they deploy the assets in a way that a sole owner would not. Bankruptcy law, at bottom, is designed to require these investors to act collectively rather than to take individual actions that are not in the interests of the investors as a group. Individual diverse owners have a particular incentive to act against the collective interest in cases where, under nonbankruptcy law, some owners are entitled to be paid before others and where the available assets are insufficient to satisfy all those with rights to them. A fully secured creditor, for example, has the right to be paid before more junior creditors receive anything. Like any other person assured of full payment if the business were to stop, he will tend to favor an immediate liquidation, even in circumstances in which a sole owner would keep the assets together. As a senior debtholder he has nothing to gain from waiting and attempting to keep the firm intact, but he can do worse if the firm continues and its fortunes decline – a possibility that always exists, in an uncertain world, whether the firm is solvent or insolvent, in or out of bankruptcy.

By contrast, junior parties, who, under current law, are typically general creditors and shareholders, often have interests that pull them in the opposite direction. Members of any group of investors that would be eliminated by a present liquidation or sale of assets have nothing to lose by seeking a solution that avoids a final distribution today.[1] A group that would get nothing if the business ceases will resist an immediate liquidation, even if liquidation is best for the owners as a group. If there is any chance, however remote, of an upswing that will bring them value, they will want to take that chance. Waiting for the upswing, however, and trying to preserve the firm's good will and expertise in the meantime, involves a gamble for the owners as a group.[2] Like all gambles, sometimes it is worth taking and other times it is not.

No single group, then, if unconstrained, will necessarily make a decision that is in the best interests of the owners considered together. As a first approximation, therefore, the law governing bankruptcy in general, and corporate reorganizations in particular, should ensure that the disposition of the firm's assets is in the interest of the owners as a group. How a firm's assets are deployed should not turn on whether one, ten, or 10,000 people have rights in them. Bankruptcy law, accordingly, should aim to keep the asset-deployment question separate from the distributional question, and to have the deployment question answered as a single owner would answer it.

The best way to approach this goal is to ensure that the parties who decide how to deploy the assets enjoy all the benefits and incur all the costs of their decisions. Bankruptcy rules that enable classes of investors to gain from any upswing in the firm's fortunes, while avoiding the full costs of an attempt to keep the assets together, create an incentive for those investors to make such an attempt, even if it is not worth making for the investors as a group. That is, they will attempt to reorganize even when an individual who had complete ownership of the assets would liquidate them immediately. Imposing on junior parties the risks of keeping a firm intact removes this incentive, They become like a sole owner in the sense that they suffer the consequences of making the wrong decision and enjoy the benefits of making the right one. Unless the law imposes these burdens on them, junior parties will systematically make decisions that ignore the real costs of keeping a firm together.

## II. The Secured Creditor's State-Law Rights

. . .

We can focus our analysis of the rights of secured creditors in bankruptcy . . . by posing two questions suggested by the view of bankruptcy law set forth in Part I. First, what are the existing nonbankruptcy rights of secured creditors, and second, is any modification of those rights necessary to ensure that the assets of the firm are deployed in a way that is in the interests of the owners of the firm as a group? We address the first of these questions in this Part of the article, turning to the second in Parts III and IV.

### A. THE NATURE OF SECURITY: A FORM OF OWNERSHIP PRIORITY

Many analyses of secured credit assume that its characteristic feature is the ability of the secured creditor to seize property of the debtor should the debtor default on a primary obligation. This right, however, is relatively unimportant in distinguishing between secured and unsecured creditors. Virtually all extensions of credit give a creditor a contingent right to take possession of a debtor's property if the debtor should fail to pay his debts when due. . . . While the secured creditor has the right, not enjoyed by the unsecured creditor, to take property without the post-default consent of the debtor and without going to court, this right is insubstantial in practice, for a debtor's active objection will require the secured creditor to go to court as well.

The essence of a secured creditor's rights, therefore, is not captured by focusing on the debtor–creditor relationship. Rather, secured credit is concerned with ensuring that the secured creditor receives priority rights in certain assets over the rights of other owners with claims against the assets of a debtor. The property right, in other words, is principally a means to an end – priority as against third parties with regard to repayment. As one would expect, however, secured creditors must pay a price for the package of rights that assures their priority and, hence, their lower degree of risk. Because a secured creditor bears less risk of his debtor's insolvency than does an unsecured creditor, he enjoys a lower interest rate than the unsecured creditor. In this respect, however, the secured creditor's right is no different from that of an unsecured creditor to get paid ahead of the shareholders, and it is a mistake to treat it as somehow different in kind. Secured creditors, unsecured creditors, and shareholders all ultimately have some rights against the assets. That the rights are hierarchically arranged merely reflects the different bargain each interest holder has struck in acquiring those rights.

. . .

## III. Bankruptcy and the Secured Creditor

Under existing nonbankruptcy rules, a sole owner of assets may freely decide whether to continue an unsuccessful business venture or to do something else with the assets, depending upon what he thinks is in his interest. A bankruptcy proceeding helps to ensure a comparable freedom where ownership of the ailing firm is diverse. In the absence of a coercive and collective proceeding, the dispersed owners' individual interests will prevent them from acting as a single owner would. In this Part of the article, we ask whether recognizing the rights of a secured creditor to repossess collateral interferes with that goal.

In a world without friction, it would not. If the secured party's collateral is, in fact, worth more to the firm than to a third party, that collateral should end up back in the hands of the firm notwithstanding its repossession by the secured creditor in the interim. As a practical matter, however, to permit a secured creditor the full exercise of his rights may hinder efforts to preserve the going-concern value of the business. It may be in the interests of the owners as a group to stay the repossession rights of the secured creditor and to substitute a requirement that the secured creditor instead accept the asset's liquidation value. Because of the costs repossession and subsequent repurchase may bring, it is consistent with the purposes of bankruptcy to substitute for a secured creditor's actual substantive *rights* under nonbankruptcy law a requirement that the secured creditor accept the equivalent value of those rights.

We then must ask if there is anything in the goals of the bankruptcy process that suggests that respecting the value of a secured creditor's rights in full also interferes with the goals of bankruptcy. The relevant bankruptcy goal, as we have seen, is not that a firm stay in business, but rather that its assets are deployed in a way that, consistent with applicable nonbankruptcy restrictions, advances the interests of those who have rights in them. When there is no "going-concern surplus," a reorganization would seem inappropriate because the firm's assets are worth more (and hence the owners recover more of what they advanced the debtor) if the assets are sold and used by third-party purchasers than they are if kept together. Conversely, when a firm's assets are worth more as a going concern, the owners, as a group, are probably better off if the assets are kept together, even though the firm may have defaulted on some of its obligations or may be insolvent.

The crucial question we have to face is whether giving the secured creditor the benefit of his bargain is inconsistent with the policy of ensuring that the firm's assets are deployed in a way that brings the most benefits to the owners as a group. The rights of a creditor who has a security interest in a drill press are fixed by seeing how much the drill press would bring if it were sold to some third party on the open market. If the firm is in fact worth more as a going concern than sold piecemeal, then there must necessarily be enough to pay a secured creditor the full liquidation value of the machine. One follows from the other. To say that a firm has a going-concern surplus is simply to say that the sum of the liquidation values of its assets if sold one by one is less than the going-concern value of those assets kept together.

. . .

In principle, any firm that is worth more as a going concern than chopped up will be able, then, to give the secured creditor the value of his state-law rights. To be sure, giving the secured creditor the benefit of his bargain does mean that other investors, such as general creditors or shareholders, receive less or perhaps nothing of what is owed to them, but how rights to the assets are divided among the investors is, we have seen, a question distinct from that of how the assets are deployed. It is the difference between the size of the slices and the size of the pie. Only the latter is a bankruptcy question. Giving the secured creditor the benefit of his bargain should not prevent a firm from staying together when a sole owner would keep it together. Indeed, a failure to recognize the secured creditor's rights in full will *undercut* the bankruptcy goal of ensuring that the assets are used to advance the interests of everyone. If those who stand to benefit from delay do not bear its cost (including the costs that secured creditors face), they will have an incentive to keep firms together even when a sole owner would not.

## IV. The Secured Creditor and the Costs of Uncertainty in Corporate Reorganizations

Reorganizations take time. In the world as we actually find it, valuations are hard to come by. It may not be clear whether a firm is worth keeping intact. One may need time to decide whether liquidation piece by piece is the only course that is available. Whether the firm's assets have value if kept together may turn on whether there is an as-yet undiscovered third party that needs such assets in their present form (perhaps for no other reason than the tax loss they bring with them). It may depend upon whether the market for the firm's goods or services changes or whether the economy as a whole turns around. Determining the optimal capital structure of a reorganized firm, moreover, takes time. But it does not follow that protecting the value of the secured creditor's state-law rights promotes liquidations when the appropriate course is patience. Again, the appropriate focus is one that takes benefits and costs into account.

. . .

Let us . . . [consider the following] example. To keep it simple, we shall discount all values to current dollars. The firm . . . consists of assets that can be sold piecemeal for $10,000 today. Assume, however, that this firm has an 80 percent chance of being worth (discounted to current dollars) $12,000 in one year's time if an effort is made to keep the business running. There is, however, a 20 percent chance that the effort will fail and the assets will have to be sold on the open market at the end of the year. Such a sale will realize only $8,000 in current dollars. (The $2,000 difference between liquidation today and liquidation in a year's time arises from the time value of money and perhaps also from the depreciation that the assets will suffer in the intervening year.) In this case, the attempt to keep the business running ought to be made. If the assets are kept together for another year, the best guess of their worth in present dollars is $11,200,[3] while they are only worth $10,000 if sold today piece by piece. A third party would pay $11,200 today for the assets as a unit, while various third parties would pay only $10,000 for the assets on a piecemeal basis. A sole owner, therefore, would keep the assets together, either in his own hands or sold to a third party.

Giving the secured creditor the value of his state-law rights in the face of uncertainty does not impair the effort to keep the assets together. If the assets are kept together and sold for $11,200 to a third party, the secured creditor can receive his $10,000 from the proceeds, If the firm is reorganized (in effect a sale to the existing investors who pay for the assets by relinquishing their claims against the assets), nothing changes except the nature of the compensation. The secured creditor can be given a share in the reorganized company – approximately 89.3 percent of it[4] – worth $10,000 today, and the next class of investors, be they general creditors or shareholders, can divide among themselves a 10.7 percent share in the reorganized company worth $1,200.

If an effort is made to reorganize, there is, of course, a 20 percent chance that the reorganized firm will fail and be sold piecemeal for $8,000 (in present dollars) in a year's time, in which event a secured creditor who did not resell his shares would eventually receive less than full payment (approximately $7,140),[5] and the other investors would receive something (approximately $860) for their new 10.7 percent share. But if the secured creditor is compensated for the risk of failure, he is not being injured. In other words, he is fully compensated if he is given enough stock so that, in the event of success, his share in the reorganized company will be worth, in today's dollars, approximately $10,715.[6] The extra $715 of present value in the event of success compensates the secured creditor for the one chance in five that he will suffer a $2,860 loss in the event of failure.

Unlike a sole owner, dispersed investors, because their relative rights differ, have an incentive to make the wrong decision if unchecked. The secured creditors will rush to liquidate, while the general creditors and shareholders (who often have more to gain than to lose from delay) will be too optimistic and push for a reorganization. Bankruptcy law makes a grave mistake if it assumes that a junior class (or another class) will make the correct decision about the deployment of the assets without a legal rule that forces it to take account of the investors as a group. In the world as we find it, chances of success or failure over time can never be calculated with certainty. But to say that they cannot be calculated with certainty is not to say that they cannot be calculated at all. Everyone in his day-to-day life weighs the benefits of certain sums in the present against the benefits of uncertain sums in the future. Wrong decisions are surely made, but the best way of ensuring the correct decision – by which we mean the decision that is not distorted by the self-interest of individuals at the expense of the interests of the group – is to create a legal rule that imposes upon the person who makes the decision all the benefits if he decides correctly and all the costs if he guesses wrong. A rule that forces general creditors and shareholders to give secured creditors the full value of their claims (including compensation for the time value of money) puts the cost of a decision to reorganize the firm entirely on the junior classes, who already stand to benefit if the firm succeeds. As a consequence, they have incentives that approximate those of a sole owner, and their decision about how to deploy the firm's assets will not be distorted by self-interest.

## V. Bankruptcy Policy and the Bankruptcy Code

To this point, our argument has been both abstract and normative. We have not looked at the Bankruptcy Code as it is actually implemented in bankruptcy practice. The record of bankruptcy courts has been mixed at best. ... Most Chapter 11 petitions are filed by the managers of a corporation, who sometimes enter Chapter 11 not because it seems the best possible forum in which rights to the firm's assets can be adjudicated while simultaneously being preserved, but rather because it seems to be a way for them to preserve their jobs, at least for a time. Delay may also save something for the shareholders they represent, who are otherwise doomed. Petitions in bankruptcy are typically filed only moments before a secured creditor repossesses the firm's assets or the IRS levies on them. The managers are often literally only one step ahead of the sheriff. A Chapter 11 proceeding typically buys time for the managers, the shareholders, and other junior owners at the expense of the more senior ones. It is often only a way-station in a journey toward liquidation either under Chapter 7 or under state law. Indeed, even when the assets of the firm should be kept together, Chapter 11 provides a vehicle for delay, and advantage-taking, that could be avoided by a going-concern sale of the assets. The costs most often are imposed on the secured creditors and perhaps the general creditors; the benefits almost always accrue to the shareholders and their managers.

Bankruptcy judges sometimes seem inclined to do little to remedy this state of affairs. A few seem to show either an inability or an unwillingness to comprehend the possibility that secured credit may be something more than a perverse and unfair creature of state law that should be thwarted at every turn. Even more remarkable is their wonderful capacity for hope, their unshakable faith that, given time, the firm's ship will come in. Often, bankruptcy judges seem to think that markets systematically undervalue firms that have filed petitions in bankruptcy. ...

... Congress explicitly came to grips with the tendency of bankruptcy judges to undercompensate the secured creditor and overestimate a firm's chances of surviving as a going concern. The Bankruptcy Code provides that during the reorganization process the secured creditor cannot be forced to accept the promise of a first claim upon the firm's unsecured assets at the conclusion of the bankruptcy proceeding in exchange for his matured state-law right to repossess the firm's property. The bankruptcy judge must give the secured creditor who insists upon it a right in the here and now (such as a lien on specific assets, cash, or its "indubitable equivalent"), not pie in the sky.

The effect of this requirement is that a firm must either reach a deal by consent or provide specific protection. A firm without unencumbered assets, a ready source of cash, or anything else beyond a vision of a brighter future must persuade either the secured creditor or a third-party lender that the firm has value as a going concern. It may, of course, be difficult to make the case for keeping the assets intact, but it should not be more difficult in principle to persuade one out of many potential third-party lenders than it is to persuade any other *neutral* third party, judicial or otherwise. An inability to persuade anyone – other than a bankruptcy judge – that the firm should stay alive seems good evidence that it should not.

Overvaluations by bankruptcy judges cause undercompensation of secured creditors. But the degree of undercompensation depends on the relative priority of the compensation received. Section 361, accordingly, requires that relatively senior forms of compensation be used before a secured creditor can be kept in the picture involuntarily . . .

# Conclusion

Junior classes, be they equity holders or unsecured creditors, resort to reorganization in bankruptcy because they want the opportunity to sort things out for their benefit and to capture any upside potential in giving their firm a future, however uncertain. The precise nature of that uncertainty is irrelevant, but if the choice between liquidation and reorganization of the firm is not to be skewed, the residual classes must pay for the opportunity they seek. Such a requirement does not violate any well-conceived notion of fairness or equity. After all, someone must bear the risk that the reorganized firm will fail. To insist that the residual class bear the burden by way of a rule that provides secured creditors with the value of their rights under state law does not prevent desirable reorganizations. To the contrary, it encourages junior owners to put the firm's assets to the use that the owners as a group would prefer.

We have not addressed in this article the wisdom of allowing secured creditors to be paid ahead of anyone else, because this question is not one peculiar to bankruptcy law. Although we would defend, and in fact have defended, the institution of secured credit as a general matter, the question is a difficult and complex one and we do not pretend to have the last word. Nothing in our argument, however, depends in the slightest on showing that secured credit is a good thing, for the argument would apply with equal force to any group given favored treatment under nonbankruptcy law. The desirability of secured credit − or other nonbankruptcy property rights − is ultimately not a bankruptcy question and attempting to transform it into one creates incentives that are perverse and counterproductive.

# Notes

1. If the firm were propelled into a bankruptcy proceeding because of cash-flow problem, it is conceivable that the firm's assets would exceed its liabilities. In such a case, the shareholders, in addition to the general creditors, have valuable rights in the debtor's assets. Shareholders share in the debtor's assets as of right only if the general creditors have been satisfied in full.
2. This group would also resist a sale of the assets as a going concern to a third party. Such a sale would "cash out" their upside potential, yielding them nothing. Their interests have value only so long as the firm's assets are not converted into cash.
3. This is the case because $0.8(\$12,000) + .02(\$8,000) = \$11,200$.
4. The expected value of the company today is $11,200. If the secured creditor is given a little less than 89.3 percent of the stock in the company, assuming no other form of ownership claim is used, his stock will have a present value of $10,000.
5. Again, to lay things out explicitly, $0.893(\$8,000)$ equals approximately $7,140.
6. If the firm succeeds and in one year's time is worth $12,000, discounted to present dollars, then the secured creditor's share of slightly less than 89.3 percent will be worth $10,715 in today's dollars.

# Part VI

Family Law

# 22

## The Economics of the Baby Shortage

### *Elisabeth M. Landes and Richard A. Posner*

### EDITOR'S INTRODUCTION

In most advanced industrial nations babies cannot be sold to another family for adoption. Instead, the baby must be given to an adoption agency, put into foster care, or sometimes given to a private third-party who finds someone wanting to adopt a child. Because the supply price of healthy babies is restricted below the market equilibrium price, there are too many abortions and too few babies available for adoption; and those who want to adopt either pay an artificially high price to the adoption agency or facilitator (who skim for themselves the social surplus ordinarily going to the adoptive parents) or are forced to wait interminably long. Elisabeth Landes and Richard Posner suggest that a legal market for babies would get rid of the artificially induced shortage. Unlike most transactions, the welfare of the thing being bought, in this case the baby, must be taken into account. Landes and Posner deal with this and other concerns about legalizing the sale of babies.

## Introduction

Sometimes natural parents do not want to raise their child; the typical case is where the birth is illegitimate. And in some cases where the natural parents do raise the child initially, their custody is later terminated for one reason or another – death or other incapacity, abuse, or extreme indigence. In either case – the unwanted infant or the abused, neglected, or abandoned child – there are potential gains from trade from transferring the custody of the child to a new set of parents. Where the new parents assume full parental rights and obligations over the child, one speaks of adoption; where they obtain simply a temporary custody (usually being partially compensated for their custodial services by the state), one speaks of foster care. An alternative to foster care in a home is foster care in an institution.

Ordinarily, potential gains from trade are realized by a process of voluntary transacting – by a sale, in other words. Adoptions could in principle be handled through the market and in practice, as we shall see, there is a considerable amount of baby selling. But because public policy is opposed to the sale of babies, such sales as do occur constitute a "black market."

Part I of this paper develops a model of the supply and demand for babies for adoption under the existing pattern of regulation and shows (1) how that regulation has created a baby shortage (and, as a result, a black market) by preventing a free market from equilibrating the demand for and supply of babies for adoption, and (2) how it has contributed to a glut of unadopted children maintained in foster homes at public expense. Part II explores the objections to allowing the price system to equilibrate the adoption market and argues that the objections do not justify the existing regulations though they might justify a more limited regulation of the baby market. . . . We also discuss, though much more briefly, the problem of foster care.

# I. Disequilibrium in the Adoption Market

## A. The baby shortage and the baby glut

Students of adoption agree on two things. The first is that there is a shortage of white babies for adoption; the second is that there is a glut of black babies, and of children who are no longer babies (particularly if they are physically or mentally handicapped), for adoption. . . .

Contrary to popular impression, . . . the increased availability of contraception and abortion has not perceptibly diminished the number of illegitimate births. A partial explanation may be that the availability of contraception and abortion, by reducing the risk of producing an unwanted child (but not to zero), has reduced the expected cost and hence increased the incidence of sexual intercourse outside of marriage. However, while the illegitimate birth rate remains high, the availability of babies for adoption has declined, apparently because a larger proportion of parents of illegitimate children are keeping them. . . .

Students of adoption cite factors such as the declining proportion of illegitimate children being put up for adoption as the "causes" of the baby shortage. But such factors do not create a shortage, any more than the scarcity of truffles creates a shortage; they merely affect the number of children available for adoption at any price. At a higher price for babies, the incidence of abortion, the reluctance to part with an illegitimate child, and even the incentive to use contraceptives would diminish because the costs of unwanted pregnancy would be lower while the (opportunity) costs to the natural mother of retaining her illegitimate child would rise.

The principal suppliers of babies for adoption are adoption agencies. Restrictive regulations governing nonagency adoption have given agencies a monopoly (though not a complete one) of the supply of children for adoption. However, while agencies charge fees for adoption, usually based on the income of the adoptive parents, they do not charge a market-clearing (let alone a monopoly-profit-maximizing) price. This is shown by the fact that prospective adoptive parents applying to an agency face waiting periods of three to seven years. And the (visible) queue understates the shortage, since by tightening their criteria of eligibility to adopt a child the agencies can shorten the apparent queue without increasing the supply of babies. Thus some demanders in this market must wait for years to obtain a baby, others never obtain one, and still others are discouraged by knowledge of the queue from even trying. Obtaining a second or third baby is increasingly difficult.

The picture is complicated, however, by the availability of independent adoptions. An independent adoption is one that does not go through an agency. Most independent adoptions are by a relative, for example a stepfather, but some involve placement with strangers and here, it would seem, is an opportunity for a true baby market to develop. However, the operation of this market is severely curtailed by a network of restrictions, varying from state to state (a few states forbid independent adoption by a nonrelative) but never so loose as to permit outright sale of a baby for adoption.

Just as a buyer's queue is a symptom of a shortage, a seller's queue is a symptom of a glut. The thousands of children in foster care . . . are comparable to an unsold inventory stored in a warehouse. Child welfare specialists attribute this "oversupply" to such factors as the growing incidence of child abuse, which forces the state to remove children from the custody of their natural parents, and the relatively small number of prospective adoptive parents willing to adopt children of another race, children who are no longer infants, or children who have a physical or mental handicap. No doubt these factors are important. However, some children are placed in foster care as infants and remain there until they are no longer appealing to prospective adoptive parents. We believe that the large number of children in foster care is, in part, a manifestation of a regulatory pattern that (1) combines restrictions on the sale of babies with the effective monopolization of the adoption market by adoptive agencies, and (2) fails to provide effectively for the termination of the natural parents' rights.

## B. A MODEL OF THE ADOPTION MARKET

Here we present a simple analytical model of the adoption market as it exists today in the United States. Queues for some children (mainly white infants) in the legal market, over-stocks of others (older, nonwhite, or physically or mentally handicapped children), and black-market activity in infants are all shown to be the result of the peculiar market structure in adoption that has been brought about by public regulation.

. . . While agencies are generally not limited in the fees they may charge prospective adoptive parents, they are constrained to other inefficient restrictions. . . . The most significant restriction is the regulation of the price at which the agencies may transact with the natural parents. Adoption agencies that are also general child-welfare agencies must accept all children offered to them at a regulated price (but may place them in foster care rather than for adoption); and they may offer no additional compensation to suppliers (the natural parents) in order to increase the supply of babies. The regulated price is generally limited to the direct medical costs of pregnant women plus (some) maintenance expenses during the latter part of the pregnancy. To be sure, agencies have some flexibility in the kinds of services they may offer the natural parents, such as job counseling, but they cannot thereby transfer to the natural parents anything approaching the free-market value of the child.

. . .

The constraints on the baby market may also be responsible in part for the glut of children in foster care – and this quite apart from the possible incentives of adoption agencies to place children in foster care rather than for adoption. Since the natural parents have no financial incentive to place a child for adoption, often they will decide to place it in foster care instead. This is proper so long as they seriously intend to reacquire custody of the child at some later date. But when they do not, the consequence of their decision to place the child in foster care may be to render the child unadoptable, for by the time the parents relinquish their parental rights the child may be too old to be placed for adoption. This would happen less often if parents had a financial incentive to relinquish their rights at a time when the child was still young enough to be adoptable.

The total effect of the baby-market constraints on the number of foster children is, to be sure, a complicated question. In particular, the limited supply of desirable babies for adoption may lead some prospective adoptive parents to substitute children who would otherwise be placed in foster care. we suspect that this substitution effect is small, but in any event it is partly controlled by the agencies; they can manipulate the relative "prices" of infants and children residing in foster care by modifying the criteria for eligibility that must be satisfied by prospective adoptive parents.

## II. Objections to a Free Baby Market

The foregoing analysis suggests that the baby shortage and black market are the result of legal restrictions that prevent the market from operating freely in the sale of babies as of other goods. This suggests as a possible reform simply eliminating these restrictions. However, many people believe that a free market in babies would be undesirable. Representative of this point of view is the conclusion of a recent law-review note on baby selling:

> The black market in adoptions is a thriving business. Destructive of the best interests of parents, children, and society, such dealings in human flesh should be thwarted by strong, strictly enforced state laws and equally stringent barriers to interstate trade. . . . If state and federal governments show a determination to discover and punish black-market activities, this taint on civilized society can be removed.[1]
>   The objections to baby selling must be considered carefully before any conclusion with regard to the desirability of changing the law can be reached.

. . .

   . . . Rationing of the supply of babies to would-be adoptive parents by price [is] not calculated to promote the best interests of the children, the objective of the adoption process. This criticism cannot be dismissed as foolish. The ordinary presumption of free-enterprise economics is no stronger than that free exchange will maximize the satisfaction of the people trading, who in this case are the natural and adoptive parents. There is no presumption that the satisfactions of the thing traded, in most instances a meaningless concept, are also maximized. If we treat the child as a member of the community whose aggregate welfare we are interested in maximizing, there is no justification for ignoring how the child's satisfactions may be affected by alternative methods of adoption.

   Very simply, the question is whether the price system would do as good a job as, or a better job than, adoption agencies in finding homes for children that would maximize their satisfactions in life. While there is no direct evidence on this point, some weak indirect evidence is provided in a followup study of independent adoptions which suggest that children adopted privately do as well as natural children.

   . . . .

   One valuable function agencies may perform is screening out people whose interest in having children is improper in an uncontroversial sense – people who wish to have children in order to abuse or make slaves of them. The criminal statutes punishing child abuse and neglect would remain applicable to babies adopted in a free market, but the extreme difficulty of detecting such crimes makes it unlikely, at least given current levels of punishment, that the criminal statutes alone are adequate. This may make some prescreening a more effective method of prevention than after-the-fact punishment. But the logical approach, then, is to require every prospective baby buyer to undergo some minimal background investigation. This approach would be analogous to licensing automobile drivers and seems as superior to the agency monopoly as licensing is to allocating automobiles on a nonprice basis.

Moreover, concern with child abuse should not be allowed to obscure the fact that abuse is not the normal motive for adopting a child. And once we put abuse aside, willingness to pay money for a baby would seem on the whole a reassuring factor from the standpoint of child welfare. Few people buy a car or a television set in order to smash it.

. . .

A further point is that today some fetuses are probably aborted because the cost to the mother of carrying them to term and placing them for adoption exceeds the permissible return. In a free adoption market, some of the . . . fetuses aborted . . . would have been born and placed for adoption. If the welfare of these (potential) children is included in the calculation of the welfare of adopted children, both actual and potential, the heavy costs imposed on the market by adoption regulation may actually decrease child welfare.

. . .

Other objections to legalizing the market in babies are more symbolic than pragmatic. For example, to accord a property right in the newborn child to the natural parents seems to some observers to smack of slavery. But allowing a market in adoptions does not entail giving property rights to natural parents for all purposes. Laws forbidding child abuse and neglect would continue to be fully applicable to adoptive parents even if baby sales were permitted. Further, we are speaking only of sales of newborn infants, and do not suggest that parents should have a right to sell older children. The creation of such a right would require identification of the point at which the child is sufficiently mature to be entitled to a voice in his placement. However, the question is largely academic given the lack of any significant market for adopting older children.

Moreover, it is incorrect to equate the possession of property rights with the abuse of the property, even if the property is a human being. For example, a serious problem with foster care is the foster parents' lack of any property rights in the foster child. The better the job the foster parents do in raising the child, the more likely are the natural parents to reclaim the child and thereby prevent the foster parents from reaping the full fruits of their (emotional as well as financial) investment. This possibility in turn reduces the incentive of foster parents to invest in foster children, to the detriment of those children's welfare.

. . .

The emphasis placed by critics on the social costs of a free market in babies blurs what would probably be the greatest long-run effect of legalizing the baby market: inducing women who have unintentionally become pregnant to put up the child for adoption rather than raise it themselves or have an abortion. . . . . What social purposes are served by encouraging these alternatives to baby sale?

The symbolic objections to baby sale must also be compared with the substantial costs that the present system imposes on childless couples, aborted fetuses (if they can be said to incur costs), and children who end up in foster care. In particular, many childless couples undergo extensive, costly, and often futile methods of fertility treatment in order to increase their chances of bearing a child. Some people produce unhealthy offspring (due to various genetic disorders) because of their strong desire to have children. And no doubt many people settle for childlessness because of the difficulties of obtaining an adopted child.

# Note

1.   Note, "Black-Market Adoptions," 22 *Catholic Lawyer* 48 (1976) at 69.

# 23

## A Market for Babies

### J. Robert S. Prichard

#### EDITOR'S INTRODUCTION

The work by Elisabeth Landes and Richard Posner on adoptions sparked considerable controversy. Robert Prichard considers the arguments and counter-arguments that have been made in the wake of the Landes and Posner article. Although Prichard claims that he wants to focus on the limits of economic analysis, indeed stating that he does not agree with the market approach to adoption, he shows how markets overcome many of the objections that people have against them. He also considers some of the standard concerns with markets – there may be externalities that undermine the efficiency results of market transactions, there may be bad distributional effects, and it is fundamentally wrong to put a price on a life. In each case, he shows how the concerns may be misguided. For example, some have argued that putting a price on babies will have bad distributional effects because only the rich would be able to afford babies. Prichard argues to the contrary – that, if anything, the distributional effects are likely to be positive. First, the price of babies put up for adoption would be low (factoring in the cost of pregnancy) since the market would be competitive with few barriers to entry. Second, the market price would be lower than the implicit price paid under the bureaucratic system of allocating babies as time and resources used to manipulate the system would be reduced. Third, mothers putting up the baby for adoption would be paid for their services rather than the relatively wealthier third-parties such as lawyers and bureaucrats who get paid under the present bureaucratic system.

The analysis made here applies to other controversial areas such as the supply of body parts, surrogate motherhood, and the market for medical care.

## Introduction

The market is perhaps the most commonly used mechanism for allocating scarce resources. As an allocative mechanism it has many attractive features which permit it to predominate over other systems such as bureaucracies, regulatory agencies, lotteries, juries, queues, and the like. But despite its predominance, the market is far from universal in its use. As a result, an important aspect of economic analysis is to examine the characteristics of situations in which the market is not used as the primary allocative device in order to illuminate the limits and implications of the market as an allocative mechanism.

This essay addresses that task in the context of family law. In particular, I examine the reasons why we are reluctant to use a market mechanism in place of existing bureaucratic procedures for the adoption of newborn babies. The purpose of the essay is to understand the limits of the market rather than to promote its use. However, I pursue the topic by first detailing the affirmative case for a market in babies and then examining its deficiencies. My intention is to use the specific case as a vehicle for a more general understanding of the limits of market mechanisms and concepts in family law and related areas, thus contributing perspective to . . . the economic analysis of family law.

In proceeding in this way I run the risk of being misunderstood as advocating a market mechanism for allocating newborn babies. The opposite is true. My primary motivation is writing this essay has been a desire to reconcile my intuitive opposition to such a system (opposition which I assume is widely, if not universally, shared) with the analytical methods of economic analysis of law. Indeed, the purpose runs deeper, extending to the vitality of economic analysis of law. For if economic analysis is to remain a vital and creative role within legal scholarship, its limits must be explored as vigorously as its strengths.

. . .

The remainder of the essay consists of four parts. First, a brief review of the current adoption system and the resulting baby shortage is presented. Second, an alternative, market-based mechanism is sketched and its likely effects are suggested. Third, in the most substantial part of the paper, the, primary objections that might be made to such a mechanism are listed, categorized, and evaluated. Finally, in the fourth and concluding part, this assessment of a possible market for babies is related back to the central purpose of the paper: an enhanced understanding of the limits of markets.

## The Present Situation

The results of the existing regulatory system governing the allocation and adoption of newborn children are in many respects tragic. At present in Canada and the United States many people unable to have children naturally want to adopt, but there are far too few newborn children to meet the demand, leaving many couples deprived of the privileges and joys of child rearing. In addition, the existing regulatory procedures allocating these scarce newborns subject childless couples to very substantial costs.

. . .

The consequences of this very substantial undersupply of adoptable babies are varied. The primary effect is that many couples who desire children are left childless. . . . Given the existing short supply of babies, the magnitude of the social tragedy from the perspective of childless couples is readily apparent. The other consequences are somewhat less obvious. Childless couples are tempted to use fertility drugs and other fertility-increasing treatments which necessarily increase the risk of children being born with various kinds of infirmities. Couples are also tempted to have children naturally even in circumstances where genetic counseling indicates they should not, since the alternative of adoption is so unavailable. On the supply side, there is no incentive for mothers to give up their newborns since at present those who do so are not remunerated in any way for their children. As a result the decision that the child is unwanted is often delayed for a year or two until the opportunities for and desirability of adoption are substantially decreased. Furthermore, the pregnant woman who plans to give up her child is under no economic incentive to care for her child while it is in utero since no reward is paid for producing a well cared for child. Thus, injury-reducing abstinence such as forgoing smoking and drinking is not economically encouraged by the present system.

In Ontario the present scheme of regulation is created by the Child Welfare Act. This statute creates a virtual monopoly in the adoption business for certain licensed agencies, although it does permit individually licensed adoptions under restrictive conditions. Under the statute, the Children's Aid Societies, which are the primary agencies charged with adoption regulation, must screen and approve prospective adopting couples. Once a couple is approved, they join a queue formed at a central registry in each geographic district in the province. As a general rule, there is an attempt to match the educational backgrounds and economic circumstances of the couples and the natural mother. In addition, subject to the best interests of the child, an attempt is made to respect the desires of the natural mother as to the type of home environment she wishes for her child.

One's ability to qualify or even be screened by a Children's Aid Society is determined by the geographic location of one's residence. Thus, in order to qualify for Metropolitan Toronto's Children's Aid Society, a couple must maintain a residence in Metropolitan Toronto. Since some districts in Ontario have considerably shorter waiting lists than others, an incentive is created to maintain a second residence in a district with a shorter list merely to qualify for an adoption. . . . .

In addition to creating this regulatory scheme, . . . the Child Welfare Act provides that "no person, whether before or after the birth of a child, shall make, give or receive or agree to make, give or receive a payment or reward for . . . an adoption or a proposed adoption". As a result, market transactions in babies are strictly prohibited.

Similar administrative and regulatory schemes are in place across Canada. Their details vary substantially but their essential characteristic – administrative allocation – remains constant. A clear alternative would be a market-oriented system in which babies would be allocated to couples based on the prices the couples were prepared to pay. In the section which follows, the possible advantages of such a mechanism are set out.

## The Market Mechanism

At first blush the market mechanism might seem to be considerably more attractive than the existing regulatory scheme in that it appears to be able to make most people better off. The reasons are numerous.

First, one would anticipate an increase in the quantity of babies supplied in order to meet the demand, thus eliminating the present queue and satisfying the desires of virtually all the childless couples left unsatisfied by the present system and shortage. Women would engage in the production of children for adoption, responding to the financial incentives of the market-place.

Second, one would anticipate that the market would lead to the realization of comparative productive advantages in that the supply of newborns would be undertaken by those best able to produce, satisfying the needs of those unable to have children and providing a realistic alternative for those for whom childbirth is possible but genetically unwise. Furthermore, one might anticipate some substitution of producers with relatively low opportunity costs for those with high opportunity costs. . . .

Third, one would anticipate that the market would generate information about the pedigrees of newborns which would permit the matching of couples' desires and the newborns' attributes. One would anticipate that there would be an incentive to disclose the quality of the newborns and that information certification procedures and agencies would develop to enhance the information market.

Fourth, one would expect the newborns to be of a higher quality than the existing newborns available for adoption. The promise of remuneration for prospective mothers would lead to an incentive for the appropriate care of children in utero since a warranty of such behaviour would attract a positive reward in the market-place. In addition, one would anticipate that prospective mothers would exercise greater care in the selection of their sexual mates since the quality of the mate would also influence the price to be obtained upon birth.

Fifth, one would expect an extremely competitive market structure. There would be extremely low entry barriers, a very large number of producers, both actual and potential, slight economies of scale, and enormous difficulties in cartelization. While there might be some brand name identification over time, one would not anticipate that this would lead to significant barriers to entry.

Sixth, the market process would provide an incentive for parents to correct errors in judgment and shortcomings in contraceptive devices since they would be in a position to sell the child for a positive reward rather than simply give it away. This should reduce the number of foster-children since the market for newborns would create an incentive to make the disposal at the time of birth. At the same time, however, reducing the cost of errors in judgment and inadequate contraceptive techniques and devices might lead to a corresponding decrease in the care exercised by sexually active friends and couples.

Seventh, one would expect the market to produce the children at a relatively low cost and certainly a cost much below the existing black market prices. The market would be free from the costs of hiding transactions from law enforcement officials, from substantial legal penalties, and from fraudulent practices and the like which at present permeate the black market. Furthermore, one would anticipate that the suppliers of the children would get a substantial portion of the economic return and that lawyers and physicians would be in a less strong position to take advantage of their clients and patients. With respect to price, one would anticipate that it would approximate the opportunity cost of a woman's time during pregnancy. It should be stressed that this need not by any means equal the amount of compensation that a person would earn in other market activities for the full nine months since pregnancy is far from totally disabling. . . . .

Eighth, the market could develop various efficiency-enhancing mechanisms. In particular, one might anticipate that a futures market would develop in which children in utero could be traded, permitting the reallocation of the risks inherent in childbirth so as to better reflect the various tastes for risks of different participants in the market. Furthermore, one might imagine that market intermediaries might form so as to hold portfolios of children in utero, thus diversifying and reducing the non-systematic risk.

Ninth, on the distributive side, the market would be likely to display qualities considerably more attractive than the existing system. One would expect that the producers would be persons with relatively low opportunity costs who at present have very limited opportunities for income-earning activities. This would present a new source of productive activity at a reasonable level of reward. Furthermore, one could anticipate that this would result in some shift of wealth away from the purchasers of babies to the producers, who would presumably be from less advantaged circumstances. In addition, the distributive effects of devoting some of the economic returns to the mothers and taking it away from those at present able to exploit the illegality of the black market would surely be attractive.

## The Objections

In sum, quite a robust case for the market can be made. It would appear to work well. It would satisfy a lot of unsatisfied people, have attractive distributive results, and increase the degree of individual freedom and choice in the adoption process as the monopolistic regulatory powers at present enjoyed by the Children's Aid Societies would be eliminated.

Despite these attractions, and despite the inadequacies of the present system, most would find the prospect of a market for babies to be grotesque. Indeed, the mere description has a ring of parody to it as the incongruity of market notions and babies jars the reader. Somewhere within most of us there is at least an intuitive reaction that there is something indecent about the prospect of a market for babies. The prospect of prices, contracts, advertising, credit, discounts, specials, and all the other attributes of consumer transactions seems disquieting. But when asked for an explanation for this reaction, can one do better than simply assert its unacceptability? In what follows, I consider a number of possible objections.

There are three categories of objections to relying on a market mechanism. The first might be termed market failure concerns. Here the argument meets the proposal on its own terms, not objecting to the market in principle but stressing that the market would not work well in this particular context. The second category of objections concedes that the market would work essentially as I have suggested, but that, as a market mechanism, it would possess one or more objectionable characteristics which cause us to reject the mechanism as a whole. The third category of objections attacks the entire proposal, not just its market aspects, arguing that it fails in its essential conception.

### MARKET FAILURE OBJECTIONS

The first line of reaction to the proposal for a baby market is to meet it on its own terms. That is, a critic might ask whether or not this is a situation in which the market would in fact produce optimal results even if the other categories of objections canvassed below are found unpersuasive. A number of doubts might be raised.

First, there is the problem that "good" babies may drive out the "bad." At present, given the shortage of babies, childless couples are prepared to adopt children who are available although, in the eyes of the adopting parents, less than perfect. If the market proposal were adopted, the supply of children with highly desired characteristics would increase and the demand for other children would diminish. This would presumably increase the number of unadopted children suffering from retardation, birth defects, and other undesired characteristics who would subsequently become foster-children. This would presumably reduce the level of welfare of both these children and society in general and must be counted as a substantial negative effect of the market proposal.

. . . .

A [second] concern with the market solution may be that it would generate a higher total population since one would anticipate there would be some increase in the supply of newborns. It might be argued that this population increase is an externality which the individual market decisions would fail to recognize, leading to what in social terms may be an oversupply of babies. While it is certainly true that the population should increase with the adoption of this proposal, it is enormously difficult to make any judgment as to whether this is a good or bad thing, and even if it is a bad thing whether or not that is cause to reject the proposal. If there is a concern with the total level of baby production, there is a wide range of existing social policies which create financial incentives and disincentives for the production of children. It would seem more appropriate to control the overall level of population through these mechanisms rather than through depriving some small segment of the community of the ability to experience the joys of raising a family. If society must bear a burden with respect to the control of population, it would seem only just that this burden be spread relatively equally across the population.

The [third] concern relates to the possibility that this scheme might permit or indeed encourage genetic breeding in that people would be able to "order" the baby they desire as opposed to merely relying on the genetic lottery that natural parents face. While hypothetically plausible, it does not seem probable in reality that there would be serious breeding effects. While some couples may favour blue-eyed, blond-haired boys and others dark-haired girls, no one set of tastes is likely to dominate, for the same reason that no particular colour or make of car seems to capture universal approval. One would anticipate a full range of tastes with respect to children's characteristics as with other commodities, and so while there should be a better matching of couples' preferences with the children they actually receive through the market, the total distribution of children by type should remain relatively unchanged.

A [fourth] concern expressed by some critics is that permitting a market in newborns might also encourage a market in "used" children as people be tempted to "trade in" unsatisfactory children and "trade up" by purchasing a newborn. If the state did not regulate parental obligations with regard to child support, this concern would no doubt be realized. However, under the market for babies proposal, once a couple has purchased a child they could be required to assume the same obligations, liabilities, and responsibilities that accrue to couples who now adopt children or have children naturally. To the extent there is a trade-in phenomenon at present, it would be continued, but it seems unlikely that it would be substantially increased. Indeed, one might deny entry to the market to any couple who traded in their child if this were thought to be a serious social problem so as to eliminate that couple's access to the market for a second purchase.

## OBJECTIONS IN PRINCIPLE

### Distributive concerns

A common critique of market-oriented solutions relates to their distributive consequences. That is, the typical critic will concede that the market, would be efficient, but then stress that its impact on the distribution of wealth would be so unacceptable that the efficiency advantages should fade into insignificance. In essence, the distributive consequences are said to be so strong as to dominate any possible efficiency gains. Is that concern well founded with respect to a proposal for a market for babies? Some might argue that the effect of such a market would be that some people would be so impoverished by having paid for their baby that they would be unable to provide sufficiently high-quality care for the child. This seems implausible. It would appear to assume an extremely high price for children, an assumption which would ignore the realities of the low opportunity cost of likely mothers. Furthermore, it ignores the costs incurred by persons attempting to manipulate the existing regulatory system, whether by maintaining a second residence or by spending money to impress social workers as to their ability to provide a comfortable home environment for the child. In addition, it ignores the cost of childbirth which all natural parents go through. The opportunity costs incurred by most natural parents would not be substantially less than the market price I would anticipate for a child under the market system. In sum, this concern built around the cost of the child seems unpersuasive.

An alternative formulation of the distributive concern is that the rich would get all the "good" babies. In response it should first be noticed that the objection seems to assume that this does not happen already, thus ignoring the reality that one's income and wealth are generally thought by adoption agencies to be important variables in determining one's suitability for parenthood. The objection also seems to ignore the prospect of an increased supply of "good" babies, which one would anticipate under the market system. That is, if supply were held fixed, the concern might be persuasive in that the rich would presumably be better able to pay in order to satisfy their desires for children with characteristics found most desirable by adopting parents. However, under the market system the supply of such children would presumably be dramatically increased, leaving the rich with what they want but also leaving many others fully satisfied. Again, the objection seems unpersuasive.

Any arguments as to distributive effects of the proposal must also be counterbalanced by the distributive effect identified earlier of a shift in rents to the suppliers of children, that is, mothers, who would be drawn from a generally poorer class and away from the . . . lawyers, . . . physicians, and others who at present trade on the tragedy of the existing regulatory failure and the fears of pregnant women.

One way of testing whether the issue of the distributive impact of the market proposal goes to the core of one's objection to it is to ask whether one would feel better about the proposal if the market were made wealth neutral as opposed to wealth sensitive. If not, then distributive arguments are probably not the central source of one's intuitive opposition to the proposal.

## Cost of costing

Another principled objection to the market focuses on one of its inevitable aspects: the creation of prices. The concern is that a market for babies would generate negative secondary consequences as a result of the fact that a market mechanism by definition generates explicit prices. In particular, the pricing of babies might violate two principles, each of which we hold dear. The first is that life is infinitely valuable – "a pearl beyond price." With prices of $3000 per baby, the reality of the limited price of life (at least at the point of creation) and the ideal of the infinitely valuable would contrast starkly. The second principle is that all lives are equally valuable. With higher prices for white than non-white children, and higher prices for healthy than sick children, and other similar forms of price differentials, the reality and the ideal would again clash.

The concern here is real but difficult to evaluate. It is but one example of a much more general problem of public policy. Whenever life is at stake the difficulties of pricing and of costing must be faced. Thus, whether it is the standard of care in tort law, the design of a Pinto, highway design, or medical research one cannot avoid implicitly or explicitly dealing with the price of life. Perhaps it is the degree of explicitness that would be inherent in this scheme that gives rise to the vigour of the opposition. It may also be that the differences in prices would correspond with differences which we strive particularly hard to overcome by means of other social policies. That is, to the extent that differences in price fell along racial grounds, to adopt a policy of a market for babies would be directly contradictory to the wide range of social policies designed to minimize discrimination on racial grounds.

. . .

### *The absence of a relationship between willingness to pay and quality of parent*

Another line of attack on the proposal would be to point out that while willingness to pay for a commodity may be the best measure of desire, some people may desire children for the wrong reasons. That is, someone may wish to acquire a child for the purpose of beating or otherwise abusing it, rather than loving it or caring for it. This is no doubt true, but again does it go to the heart of the problem? Presumably the same perverted desires motivate people to give birth naturally. We do not . . . require an ex ante check on the reasons for having natural children, and thus one must question why ex ante review of suitability for parenting should be required under the market scheme. However, even if some ex ante scheme is desired (as it is under the existing regulatory mechanism), it is, of course, not inconsistent with having a market scheme of allocation. That is, it would be quite simple to require anyone wishing to make a bid in the baby market first to obtain a parenting certificate from some regulatory agency. This license would be granted or denied on the basis of whether or not one met the minimum necessary qualifications for parenting. There would be no limit on the number of certificates granted. If this step were adopted, it is difficult to see how the divergences of willingness to pay and quality of parent would be any more extreme under the market for babies proposal than under the existing regulatory mechanism.

## MISCONCEPTION OBJECTIONS

The first category of objections focused on market failure and the second on principled objections to the use of the market in the context. The third category, while related to the second, attacks the proposal as being wrong in its very conception of the problem. This objection can be stated in [various] ways.

### *The improper objective*

The market for babies proposal would meet what is at present the unmet demand of childless couples who wish to adopt a child and are unable to do so as a result of the insufficient supply of children. A critic might suggest that the proposal is directed towards a social end which is misconceived from the start. That is, it can be argued that the purpose of the existing process is not to meet the desires of childless couples for children, but rather to take care of a limited number of unwanted newborns, with the merely incidental side effect of bringing great joy and happiness to childless couples. Under the latter formulation the number of couples satisfied or left dissatisfied is largely irrelevant to our judgment about the allocative mechanism, since it is assumed that the function of the system is to distribute those babies which are produced as a by-product of the existing sexual and marital activities and rules. The success of the mechanism should therefore be judged in terms of the welfare of the unwanted newborns, not that of childless couples. Furthermore, any system which would increase the supply of such children requiring adoption would be directly counter-productive in terms of the objective of designing a system whose sole function is the distribution of unwanted babies.

This line of argument is compelling if it is accepted that no weight should be given to the preferences of childless couples. How such a judgment could be taken, though, is somewhat more problematic, since it is not at all clear what value is being preserved or promoted by means of denying this fundamental happiness to the large number of couples left childless under the existing scheme. If it were possible to identify that value, perhaps all the other concerns about the market solution might be derived from it.

### *The second best argument*

Another response to the market for babies proposal is to acknowledge that it would be better than the existing situation but to argue that that does not make it the best possible mechanism. That is, alternatives such as banning abortion or prohibiting contraceptive devices might be better responses in that they would increase the supply of babies. Or it may be argued that leaving the supply fixed and instituting a pure lottery might be better than the existing distribution mechanism. Or indeed, it might be argued that an alternative source of supply – foreign babies from third world countries with excess newborns – might represent a better and distributively more attractive source of babies. All these possibilities have merit. However, none of them seem to go to the heart of the matter, which is why the market itself is seen to be so objectionable. That is, most people's reaction to the market for babies proposal is that it is bad per se, not bad relative to alternative mechanisms. The interesting question remains why the market is seen to be bad per se.

. . .

## Conclusion

I end where I started, focusing on the limits of markets by asking whether these objections to a market for babies are persuasive. To the extent that they are, they may help define the limits of markets in other situations requiring an allocative device.

The need for a coherent appreciation of the limits of market-based allocative mechanisms is enhanced at a time when we are being inundated by signs of the increased commercialization of activities closely related to a market for babies. Campus newspaper advertisements seek sperm donors . . . News reports tell of surrogate mothers who charge a fee for carrying a child for a couple who are not otherwise able to produce their own child but who desire the injection of at least the husband's genes: . . . Speculation is common that the near-future holds promise of commercial banks for sperm, body parts, and other life-creating products.

In many of these situations, a market mechanism may offer the promise of increased supply. For example, kidneys, livers, hearts, and other body parts would no doubt be far more available – at a price – if financial rewards could be paid to the donors. But despite this promise of supply, the predominant reaction is to resist and to look to alternatives. This common pattern of resistance surely reflects concerns of the kind identified in this essay. At the same time, I believe that these concerns should be understood as to some extent contingent upon cultural and social values that themselves change over time. Transitions in these values can and do occur, responding to a complex shifting social consensus.

We may well be in just such a period of transition to a society in which the objections to the baby market will lose much of their force. Such a transition was experienced in the late nineteenth century with respect to life insurance, which was thought for a time to represent a form of trafficking in and valuing of lives. Whether or not the same transition is about to occur with respect to the market for babies, semen, surrogate mothers, body parts, and the like may well depend in part on the strength, coherence, and nature of the objections to the market for babies proposal and the extent to which we can identify them and commit ourselves to the preservation of the values which inform them.

# 24

## Marriage, Divorce, and Quasi Rents; Or, "I Gave Him the Best Years of My Life"

### *Lloyd Cohen*

#### EDITOR'S INTRODUCTION

Whenever people make specific investments in a relationship, there is a potential for opportunism by the other side. Marriage involves a number of specific investments, particularly children.

Either side may behave opportunistically, but Lloyd Cohen believes that the potential for opportunism tends to be greater for men since women invest relatively more than men in the early stages of the marriage (the reverse happens later in the marriage). Cohen argues that because women have a greater decrease in fertility as they age and there is a much greater supply of older women than older men, women are at disadvantage in the remarriage market. Men may opportunistically take advantage of these circumstances by trying to get a more desirable mate when they are older or extracting more in the marriage by threatening to do so. Cohen views marriage as a contract. The remedies for breach of contract (here breach means divorce) help to reduce opportunism. He considers various imperfect legal and social solutions to minimize such opportunism.

## 1. Introduction

All marriages are entered into with the promise, and most with the intention, that the relationship will last a lifetime. This basic promise represents and implies a vast set of other promises as to how the marriage shall be conducted. All too frequently these promises are broken, and the parties seek to dissolve their agreement; that is, to divorce. Precisely because marriage is a species of contract, many of the problems inherent in fashioning an efficient and equitable law of divorce, alimony, and property division are variations and special cases of the difficulties that surface in the enforcement of commercial contracts.

In marrying, men and women exchange promises to deliver a lifetime stream of spousal services. These services are peculiar in that their value is crucially dependent on the attitude with which they are delivered and received. In reliance on the promise of these services, each party invests in assets specific to this marriage and forgoes other opportunities both for marriage and for other activities.

Over time, the utility functions, information, and opportunities of both marriage partners change. Frequently, one or the other party will, during the course of the marriage, have an incentive to breach the contract. A party who breaches destroys much of the life-cycle value of the marriage for his or her spouse. When a marriage ends in divorce, both parties usually return to the marriage market, the conceptual place in which the original marriage partner was secured and the marriage agreement concluded. The loss that each party suffers is at least the cost of finding a spouse of equivalent "value" the second time around. Often, however, the losses will be much higher, for that equivalent match may simply be unavailable after divorce. The problem here is not symmetrical; women as a class, lose systematically far more than do men. Women are generally less highly valued in the marriage market following a divorce than they were prior to their first marriage.

Although the problem of divorce may be most visible at its occurrence, the prospect of divorce will influence the type of contractual structure that the parties adopt at the formation of marriage. Adaptation to the problem of divorce by changing the structure of marriage is not a perfect solution. These structures are not costless to adopt, and even where the best of them is chosen, substantial difficulties remain. The various possible legal structures . . . each have significant shortcomings as attempts to achieve an efficient solution to the problem of enforcing the marriage contract. Nor are market alternatives to legal institutions, such as prenuptial contracts, an effective means of protecting spouses from inefficient breaches of the marriage contract. There is no single ideal contract solution to the myriad problems attendant to this area of the law. . . .

The plan is as follows. Section II of this paper addresses the problem that people are attempting to solve through marriage. Section III then describes the special features of the marriage contract, and Section IV gives a brief overview of the law of divorce. Section V advances empirical evidence to support the proposition that in general the value of a woman in marriage declines with time more rapidly than does the value of a man. Section VI shows how the relative decline in the value of women on the marriage market exposes a woman to the risk of the expropriation of her greater investment in the marriage – her quasi rents – by the opportunistic behavior of her breaching husband. Section VII then examines informal schemes that could be used to control the difficulties of the long-term marriage contract. Section VIII discusses the shortcomings of various kinds of prenuptial agreements and the different regimes for divorce and property separation that might be adopted by the state. Section IX concludes the paper.

# II. Why Marry?

Romantic relationships between men and women are almost always initially undertaken without any long-term commitment. Considering the profound restriction on personal free-dom entailed and the obvious difficulty of predicting the continuation of one's ardor, it is less than obvious why the long-term contract like commitment of marriage is so popular. In most commercial contracts, the gains of contracting are purely instrumental. The contract is not valued for itself but rather for what it provides. It is the substance of the contract that is important, not the fact that it was formed. Marriages, by contrast, are not purely instru-mental, for there are also two significant direct gains. First, the entrance into a consecrated state entailing a spiritual joining of two souls into one strikes a religious/psychological chord deep in our consciousness and is seen by the contracting parties as valuable in itself. Second, the willingness of another to offer one a lifetime commitment indicates a deep and abiding love and is evidence that one is worthy of such love.

But the instrumental gains from marriage cannot be ignored either. First, and most important, marriage allows for investment in assets of peculiar value to this relationship. Husbands and wives may be viewed as unique capital inputs in the production of a new capital asset, namely, "the family." The analogy to the contract between a factory owner and a prospective tenant, while not perfect, captures some of the flavor of the dilemma faced by a couple seeking to form a family. Neither the landlord nor the tenant would be likely to desire a long-term contract if no investment by either were to be undertaken that would be of peculiar value to the use of this factory by this tenant. Each would prefer to be free to take advantage of as-yet-unknown opportunities to employ their resources more profitably. If either party expects to make specific investments in this factory, however, a long-term contract would be desired in order to protect the value of that investment to the party undertaking it. If both parties are making such an investment, then each would want a long-term contract.

In the romantic relationship between a man and a woman, the most significant investment in a specific asset is the bearing and raising of children. The existence and presence of children are, in general, valued particularly and peculiarly by their natural parents. Both the cost and return from children span a long time period; hence, if a conjugal relationship between a man and a woman ends, two kinds of losses are created by the presence of children. First, each parent, as a parent, may still have significant costs to bear in a situation in which the associational value of the children will be diminished. Second, the presence of children will impose costs without commensurate benefits on a new romantic partner of either parent. That new partner will therefore be more difficult to acquire and to keep either in marriage or outside it. Thus a fundamental reason to marry is to allow for optimal investment in assets peculiar to the relationship – primarily, but not exclusively, children.

Another gain from marriage is its inherent provision of insurance. The vow to fulfill one's duty "for rich or for poor, in sickness and in health" is not idly spoken. Instead it captures the insurance aspect of marriage. At the present, one may be attractive, so the company of highly valued companions may be available; nonetheless, the future may prove to be less rosy. Therefore, risk aversion may induce one to give up the opportunity to find a new companion in the event that one's own prospects have improved, or that one's current companion has declined in value, in exchange for the other party making a sacrifice of symmetrical opportunities. If the gains from the long-term commitment of marriage, both direct and instrumental, outweigh the losses due to the forgone opportunity to separate from this partner at some unknown future point, then it will be in the ex ante interest of each party to marry.

. . . .

## III. Marriage as Contract

Although it is undoubtedly far more than a contract when viewed from religious, social, cultural, psychological, and philosophical perspectives, the marriage agreement is also a contract. Nothing that follows is intended to diminish the significance of these other perspectives of marriage, but the current discussion will be limited to the contractual analysis of marriage.

Marriage is a peculiar contract. It cannot be dissolved solely by the parties but only with the concurrence of a court; none of the personal rights or obligations of a marriage may be assigned or delegated; and, most important, some of the rights and obligations of the parties are defined by law and cannot be waived by mutual consent. Nonetheless, from the legal and, more important, the economic perspective, it is a species of contract.

The failure of the parties to specify and articulate the terms of the agreement may make marriage seem less like a contract. While the parties undertake what seems to be a substantial commitment to one another, usually they make no agreement specifying the duties and rights of each party. This lack of explicit detail, in light of the importance of the agreement, makes it difficult to identify a contract. In this respect, however, a marriage contract is similar to, and an extension of, an employment contract. It is precisely the complexity, the subtlety, and the exigent quality of the almost infinite set of duties of each party that make it inefficient if not impossible to specify them with any precision.

The essence of the marital contract can be found in the marriage vows. Even seemingly vague and poetic marriage vows imply, yet conceal, a set of rights and obligations that are generally understood by the parties. The man promises to the woman that he will be a husband and the woman that she will be a wife. Each promises that he or she will carry out his or her duties in a spirit of "loving," "honoring," and "cherishing" his or her spouse. In reliance on the assurances of the other, each spouse sacrifices current actual and future potential love interests and invests in this particular marriage, The specific acts that will be required of each party cannot be anticipated and specified because they are contingent on the exigencies of life. Nonetheless, each spouse promises that whatever changes are wrought by the winds of time, whether for ill or good, the parties will continue to perform their duties in the proper spirit for the remainder of their joint lives.

The meaning of husband and wife and the specific rights and duties that will attach to each role following marriage is dependent on the subculture and social class in which the parties have been born and raised and, most important, on their prenuptial relationship. Each party contracts for this future stream of services. The provision of these services is the standard by which substantial performance is judged, and the value of the withdrawn services is a first approximation of damages in the event of breach.

The significant loss to the innocent party from a breach resulting in divorce is a lifetime stream of spousal services. The value of this loss is the cost of finding a replacement spouse of equivalent value. This consists of a number of distinct components. First, there are [high] transactions costs [which are] a result of the lack of fungibility of potential candidates and the variety of dimensions on which they can be judged. The uniqueness of spouses . . . increases the costs of advertisement and search.

Second, there are stochastic changes in one's value on the market that each party initially had sought to insure against through marriage. For example, the handsome athletic man with much promise who has become crippled through injury or disease will, all else constant, not be able to do as well on the marriage market the second time around.

Third, predictable changes often result from an investment in assets specific to this marriage. The divorced woman with custody of two children will have more difficulty on the marriage market than she would without the children. These children will represent a net cost to most potential future husbands.

Fourth, and finally, predictable changes may occur because one spouse will lose value in the marriage market relative to the other solely as a function of time. As will be argued more extensively in Section V, women in general lose value in the marriage market relative to men over time. The stream of services offered by women on the marriage market are more front-end loaded. Consequently, a woman's capital asset value as a wife is consumed more quickly than is a man's capital asset value as a husband.

## IV. The Law of Divorce

While making passing references to marriage as a contract, courts and legislatures have had difficulty in treating marriage as a contract with substantive duties to perform. The problems of determining breach and of enforcing specific performance or measuring money damages makes the task of the courts difficult if not impossible. Divorce is the legal dissolution of marriage, but it does not by itself unscramble the complex arrangement that preceded it. In the last three decades there has been a radical transformation of the legal treatment of divorce. As recently as thirty years ago, divorce was only available on a fault basis in most states, requiring strict proof of substantial breach. Under the older, more restrictive laws, divorce, if granted to a party following a showing of breach (for example, desertion or infidelity), released the party suing for divorce from their obligations. The spouse found at fault was more likely to pay alimony (if a man) or not to receive alimony (if a woman).

Divorce is now generally available on a no-fault basis. In most jurisdictions, either party may petition for divorce on the grounds of marital breakdown. As a consequence, the divorce rate has skyrocketed. The modern liberal divorce laws have an obvious appeal. Just as it is often efficient for contracts to be dissolved, so too both parties to a marriage may gain as a result of a divorce. . . .

. . .

## V. Sex, Age, and the Marriage Market

. . . .

Being a husband or a wife is not coextensive with being a man or woman. It is useful to conceive of husbands and wives as a capital asset. In the same way that a man can sell his services on the labor market, so too can he offer his services as a husband on the marriage market. Some of the characteristics that add to one's value on the marriage market can be deliberately acquired, such as wealth and status. Other desirable characteristics are inherent in the person and do not change over time, such as race and ethnicity. Still others wax and wane with the passage of years, such as fertility and beauty. In addition, age itself is a factor in one's value on the marriage market.

Since the capital asset of a wife is different from that of a husband, there is no reason a priori why they should be characterized by the same time profile of growth and depreciation. I will argue that women in general are of relatively higher value as wives at younger ages and depreciate much more rapidly than do men. . . . .

. . .

Marriage in this country is monogamous. Therefore, the number of wives and husbands are identically equal. But the number of men and women are not usually equal to one another. While the number of live births are slightly more male than female, a slightly higher mortality rate for men at all ages results in approximate equal numbers of men and women at age twenty. The higher male mortality rates create an ever-widening gap between the number of men and women of the same age as age increases

The gap between the number of men and women is only part of the story. The percentage of men who are married rises steadily as a function of age up to age sixty-five. Therefore, the ratio of unmarried women to unmarried men rises at a faster rate than does the overall sex ratio. The sex ratio of unmarried females to unmarried males rises from less than one for twenty-year-olds to over two for fifty-five-year-olds. . . . Because people generally marry those near their own ages and husbands are generally older than their wives, older women have a great deal more competition for potential spouses and have a much smaller possibility of finding a suitable spouse than do older men and, more important, than those same women had when they entered the marriage market for the first time.

. . .

Children are frequently a product of marriage. At the time of divorce, women receive custody of the children in the large majority of cases. This imposes two significant costs on women in the marriage market. First, making oneself visible and available to prospective husbands is an important factor in the search for a mate. Children are a significant restriction in this regard. Second, and undoubtedly of even greater significance, children are frequently considered a liability by prospective husbands, ceteris paribus. Men usually prefer to marry childless women, among other reasons because such a woman is better able to care for the couple's future offspring.

. . . .

This loss in value by women is in part explainable by factors that have analogs on commercial markets: Typically during marriage a man develops some kind of skill or career which, if he is successful, will provide him with higher and higher earnings as time goes on. On the other hand, the increase in homemaking skills gained by the traditional wife are of little market value. This market valuation of some of the tasks performed by each spouse reflects and symbolizes a deeper cause for the fall in the value of women on the marriage market, that is, that wives and husbands are reciprocal, not symmetrical, roles performed by spouses. Since what a man wants in a wife is different from what a woman wants in a husband, there is no obvious reason why the ability to satisfy these requirements should vary with age at the same rate for wives as for husbands. The demands that men and women place on prospective spouses are significantly if not primarily psychological in nature. It is beyond the scope of this paper to explore in detail the root cause and nature of the desirable characteristics of wives and husbands; nonetheless, it is possible to make some observations on what those characteristics are, their sources, and how they vary with age.

Among other things, men, in general, look to fertility, beauty, and femininity in prospective wives. Similarly, the qualities that women seek in husbands include the ability to sire children as well as more generalized masculine qualities. The ability to bear children is an inverse function of age. The prime childbearing years of women are from eighteen to thirty-five, declining sharply thereafter. The ability to sire children is also inversely related to age; however, it does not decline nearly as precipitously as does female fertility. Men in their fifties, sixties, or older are still quite capable of impregnating women. . . . .

The loss in value of women on the marriage market as a function of age is in large part a function of the reciprocal rather than the symmetrical nature of wives and husbands. . . .

## VI. Quasi Rents, Marriage, and Divorce

The shift in relative values between men and women over time has an important role to play in the formation of the marriage contract. At the time of formation, the marriage contract promises gains to both the parties who enter into it. Yet the period of time over which these gains are realized is not symmetrical. As a rule, men tend to obtain gains early in the relationship when their own contributions to the marriage are relatively low and that of their wives relatively great. Similarly, later on in marriage women tend as a general rule to obtain more from the contract than do men. The creation of this long-term imbalance provides the opportunity for strategic behavior whereby one of the parties, generally the man, might find it in his interest to breach the contract unless otherwise constrained.

This problem is well understood in long-term commercial contracts in the context of appropriable quasi rents. A quasi rent is a return to one party to a contract above what the party could receive if the contract could be dissolved at will at that moment. For example, assume that Amos, a tenant, contracts with Benjamin to rent Benjamin's factory for a rent of $1,000 per month for one year. This rent in part reflects a promise by Benjamin to modify his factory in a way that is useful only to Amos. Before Benjamin began his renovations, he contracted for a return equal to his opportunity cost. However, after he has completed the renovations, the rental fee represents in part a return on investments that have already been made, that is, a quasi rent.

Amos can hold him up. Amos can demand that Benjamin accept a lower rent – one that is equal to Benjamin's present opportunity cost of leasing the premises – under threat that Amos will walk away from the contract. Amos himself may suffer certain losses if he abandons these premises, so his strategy may not be entirely successful. But he could force Benjamin to absorb part of the costs of modifying the factory. Similarly, he can impose certain bargaining costs on Benjamin while being forced to bear similar costs himself. Much of the law of contract is an effort to design rules and institutions that prevent this kind of strategic behavior, the control of which is in the mutual interest of both Amos and Benjamin at the time of contract formation.

The problem of quasi rents and their appropriation is important in the marriage market as well. When people court and marry, they are in effect purchasing spouses on a market. The market for spouses is monopolistically competitive. All men are potential husbands; all women are potential wives. Although some men are close substitutes for one another, most others are very imperfect substitutes. Nonetheless, there is substantial choice and competition in this market. Therefore, it is reasonable to treat each party to a marriage as having forgone an alternative spouse of nearly equivalent value to the one they have actually married.

Quasi rents can be generated in a marriage in a variety of ways. The sources of quasi rents are intimately related both to the reasons people marry and to the kinds of damages they will suffer from breach. First, both parties may earn a quasi rent as a result of the mere existence of the marriage relationship. The participation in a holy union has a value to many people and therefore generates a flow of rents. Second, both parties are likely to earn rents from the investment in assets specific to this marriage. The production of children and a unique family life are quintessential examples of this sort of investment. Third, that party who has either experienced a stochastic fall in value during the marriage or whose spouse has experienced a stochastic increase in value will earn quasi rents as a result of the insurance aspect of marriage. Finally, one party (probably the wife) will earn quasi rents because of predictable changes in the relative values of men and women on the marriage market as a function of age. Since women tend to fall in value relative to men as they age, they earn quasi rents later in the marriage.

In many instances, the emotional and psychological investments in marriage will be so great, and the union so successful, that neither party will choose to breach the contract even if no damages had to be paid. Even today, not all marriages end in divorce. On the other hand, if only one party is earning quasi rents, the breach of the contract by the other will cause either the appropriation or the destruction of these quasi rents.

In a commercial contract the uncompensated breach by one party will result in the breaching party capturing the other's rents. However, in marriage, because the rents are usually not received in marketable form, the rents are only partially captured and are also partially destroyed. The distinction between appropriating or capturing rents and destroying rents in a breached marriage contract can be illustrated by example. If a man of thirty-four divorces his thirty-four-year-old wife after twelve years of marriage to marry a younger woman, her quasi rents, to be earned in the later stages of marriage, are best viewed as being captured by him. She gave him her years of greatest attractiveness (at a time when his earning power and so on did not make him as attractive) in exchange for a promised reverse transfer at a later stage of their marriage. After receiving the benefit of the early years of the bargain, he is able to terminate without completing the exchange. He has thus captured the quasi rents she has lost in the breach of the contract. On the other hand, if the couple are married for only one year and in that time have had a child, the loss in quasi rents that she will experience as a result of having to return to the market as a single mother is not likely to result in a transfer to him. The quasi rents she expected to earn as a result of investment in this marriage by having a child are simply lost and destroyed rather than captured by her former spouse.

## VII. Informal Methods of Protecting Quasi Rents

The possibility for substantial breaches of the marriage contract has always existed. Until recent times, though, there were greater costs associated with such breaches. The religious nature of marriage and the religious consciousness of the people who participated and sanctioned the institution placed substantial internal psychological and external social costs on the parties in the event of breach. Rather than the formal legal constraints that prove to be tenuous and imperfect, it was the informal social and psychological constraints that by and large protected marriages. The decline in religious consciousness, its causes and consequences, can be analyzed from a variety of perspectives including, but not limited to, the sociological, sociobiological, religious, psychological, and ontological. As interesting as that might be, it is beyond the scope and focus of this paper. My purpose in raising the issue of the change in consciousness is twofold: first, to show that the shortcomings of a legal system – which perhaps inherently lacks the capacity to perform the role required for efficient allocation of resources in marriage – can be masked by other societal institutions and that, when those institutions decline, the inadequacies of the legal structures, whether inherent or correctable, come to the fore and, second, to point out that the prior enforcement mechanism of the marriage contract was not legal but, rather, sociopsychological, which sets the stage for a discussion of other informal enforcement mechanisms.

## A. . . . TAKING HOSTAGES

. . . .

One . . . possible way of preventing the destruction or appropriation of quasi rents to be earned on a contract is by taking hostages. Hostage taking in the context of marriage would require that the wife could take something of value from the husband to be held until she is assured of his performance of the contract. This hostage would serve as a guarantee of the contract and perhaps be retained as a form of liquidated damages in the event of his breach of the contract.

There are problems with applying this technique to marriage. First, discussion of breach, damages, hostages, and so on would be considered indelicate during courtship and might do much to destroy the romantic attachment between parties. Second . . . bridegrooms in our economy are generally far more well endowed with human capital than with physical or money capital. Since they cannot transfer their human capital to their wife, they frequently have very little to give as a hostage. Fourth, married couples have lifetime consumption patterns in which they are likely to spend in the early years of their marriage; therefore, the holding of the substantial amount of property by the wife as a hostage will constrain a consumption of the family. Even with all these constraints and drawbacks, there still exists some possibility for the application of hostage taking.

. . .

## [B.] REDUCED INVESTMENT IN MARRIAGE

The failure of the legal system or any other institution or strategy to answer adequately the problem of the destruction and appropriation of quasi rents by breach of the marriage contract has resulted in one response by market participants that may be seen as a solution by default. If you cannot protect the quasi rents that you believe you will receive from investing in assets specific to marriage, then invest less in this marriage or in being married.

The tendency of middle-class families to have fewer children and for women to acquire more marketable skills are of course consistent with and explainable by one another as well as by a variety of other variables of our changing culture. Nonetheless, both phenomena are also consistent with women investing fewer resources in being wives in general and in being one man's wife in particular out of fear of uncompensated breach. Considering the enormous magnitude of the consequence of breach on the value of the specific assets of marriage, it is inconceivable that the greater likelihood of breach has not significantly affected the level of those investments.

## VIII. Legal Methods for the Protection of Quasi Rents

The use of informal and legal methods to protect women from the appropriation of quasi rents is complementary. If, as has been argued, the informal social mechanisms are today insufficient to protect marriage partners (especially women) from the appropriation of quasi rents, then legal methods of protection will increase in importance. It is at this point that marriage is best understood as a legal contract, albeit one with very special incidents.

As a general proposition, whenever contracts are not fully enforceable, an inefficient allocation of resources will follow. Marriage contracts are no exception from this general rule. If the legal remedies for breach of marriage promises are inadequate, then prospective spouses will adapt to this contracting peril in the same two ways that they respond to a breakdown in the social sanctions supporting marriage. First, fewer parties will enter into formal marriages. Second, those parties who do marry will commit fewer resources to the formation of specific marriage assets than they would if optimal contractual protection were available.

Viewed in this light, the legal remedies provided by the state in the event of divorce influence both the decision to marry and the way in which the marriage partners behave toward each other. The wrong set of divorce rules may lead to too many divorces or to too few. Or they may induce divorce when parties might prefer to remain married or prevent divorce when it would be in their mutual interest. The question is: Which forms of legal arrangements best prevent the destruction and appropriation of the quasi rents in marriage? Here it is possible to consider both voluntary prenuptial agreements and the standard-form marriage contract that is provided by the state, in large measure through its divorce laws.

. . .

The use of prenuptial marriage contracts has increased in recent years. These contracts take a variety of forms and are motivated by a variety of forces. . . . The parties could try to incorporate a liquidated-damage clause as part of the marriage contract. But these clauses are hardly workable. Any such marriage contract must specify a variety of damage amounts, each reflecting the stage in the marriage when the breach occurs, the circumstances of the parties at the time of marriage, and the circumstances at the time of breach. The imperfect knowledge of the future cannot be overcome. . . . . Yet it does not follow that the ideal solution is simply to leave the question of property division to the discretion of judge and jury, as much of the modern legal rules tend to do. . . . [T]he problems of specifying and enforcing marital obligations are inherent in the nature of the relationship. These problems cannot be solved in any final and authoritative sense by either prenuptial agreements or legislative codes.

. . . .

## IX. Conclusion

In this paper I have sought to apply the general theory of long-term contracts to a special contract that falls within the general class, that is, the contract of marriage. The application of that theory does not yield any obvious or optimistic conclusions as to the proper way to structure the marriage arrangement. The nature of the underlying duties assumed by the marriage partners is not capable of precise definition, much less effective legal enforcement. Yet the success of the marriage often requires the two partners to invest heavily in the relationship even though they may be able to salvage little of their original investment should the marriage turn bad. To make matters more difficult, the roles of men and women, even today, are not symmetrical. As a general matter, a wife places more human capital in the marriage in the early years than does her husband. In technical terms, it follows that her quasi rents from the marriage are more susceptible to appropriation than are those of her husband. In ordinary English, it follows that she typically has more to lose by divorce. The question then arises, What, if anything, can be done to insure the integrity of the long-term marriage arrangement, which redounds ex ante to the benefit of both marriage partners? Various legal regimes of divorce and property settlement may be adopted. . . . It is quite clear that each of these devices has substantial drawbacks. Nor do antenuptial marriage contracts offer much hope for the general population. It is difficult, therefore, to suggest with any conviction a definitive solution to the marriage problem. There is much to be said for the older view that relies on informal and social sanctions and the good moral sense of the parties for the greatest protection of the marriage relationship.

# Part VII

---

## Crime and Criminal Law

# 25

## Crime and Punishment: An Economic Approach

### *Gary S. Becker*

### EDITOR'S INTRODUCTION

In this Nobel prize-winning work, Gary Becker argues that criminals are rational and re-spond to incentives, just like non-criminals do. In particular the supply of criminal activity decreases as the probability and severity of punishment increases. Society can increase the probability of punishment ($p$) by hiring more police and spending more on prosecutors; and society can increase the severity of punishment ($f$) by imprisoning criminals for more years. Either method is costly. As a consequence, society must take into account these costs of prevention as well as the direct harm from the crime itself in determining the optimal amounts of $p$ and $f$. From the opposite perspective, society chooses the optimal amount of crime. In this regard, the analysis is quite similar to the analysis of torts and accidents. Society reduces the amount of crime until the marginal benefit of reduced crime equals the marginal cost of reducing the crime. Because imprisonment, unlike a fine, involves a social cost instead of being a mere transfer, Becker shows that the elasticity of criminal response must be taken into account when the punishment is imprisonment. Variables that affect the elasticity, such as intent, must then be considered.

This paper demonstrates the power of economics in analyzing "non-economic" behavior. It not only provides substance to such statements as "the punishment should fit the crime," but also provides insight into why criminals might be deterred more by a doubling of the probability of punishment rather than a doubling of the punishment, itself.

## I. Introduction

Since the turn of the century, legislation in Western countries has expanded rapidly to reverse the brief dominance of laissez faire during the nineteenth century. The state no longer merely protects against violations of person and property through murder, rape, or burglary but also restricts "discrimination" against certain minorities, collusive business ar-rangements, "jaywalking," travel, the materials used in construction, and thousands of other activities. The activities restricted not only are numerous but also range widely, affecting persons in very different pursuits and of diverse social backgrounds, education levels, ages, races, etc. Moreover, the likelihood that an offender will be discovered and convicted and the nature and extent of punishments differ greatly from person to person and activity to activity. Yet, in spite of such diversity, some common properties are shared by practically all legislation, and these properties form the subject matter of this essay.

In the first place, obedience to law is not taken for granted, and public and private resources are generally spent in order both to prevent offenses and to apprehend offenders. In the second place, conviction is not generally considered sufficient punishment in itself; additional and sometimes severe punishments are meted out to those convicted. What determines the amount and type of resources and punishments used to enforce a piece of legislation? In particular, why does enforcement differ so greatly among different kinds of legislation?

The main purpose of this essay is to answer normative versions of these questions, namely, how many resources and how much punishment *should* be used to enforce different kinds of legislation? Put equivalently, although more strangely, how many offenses *should* be permitted and how many offenders should go unpunished? . . .

The optimal amount of enforcement is shown to depend on, among other things, the cost of catching and convicting offenders, the nature of punishments – for example, whether they are fines or prison terms – and the responses of offenders to changes in enforcement. The discussion, therefore, inevitably enters into issues in penology and theories of criminal behavior. A second, although because of lack of space subsidiary, aim of this essay is to see what insights into these questions are provided by our "economic" approach. It is suggested, for example, that a useful theory of criminal behavior can dispense with special theories of anomie, psychological inadequacies, or inheritance of special traits and simply extend the economist's usual analysis of choice.

## II. Basic Analysis

### A. THE COST OF CRIME

Although the word "crime" is used in the title to minimize terminological innovations, the analysis is intended to be sufficiently general to cover all violations, not just felonies – like murder, robbery, and assault, which receive so much newspaper coverage – but also tax evasion, the so-called white-collar crimes, and traffic and other violations. Looked at this broadly, "crime" is an economically important activity or "industry," notwithstanding the almost total neglect by economists. . . . [The costs of crime include] [p]ublic expenditures . . . on police, criminal courts and counsel, and "corrections"; . . . private outlays on burglar alarms, guards, counsel, and . . . other forms of protection; . . . a myriad of private precautions against crime, ranging from suburban living to taxis. . . .; the value of crimes against property, including fraud, vandalism, and theft; [and] the loss of earnings due to homicide, assault, or other crimes. . . .

### B. THE MODEL

It is useful in determining how to combat crime in an optimal fashion to develop a model to incorporate the behavioral relations behind the costs. . . . These can be divided into five categories: the relations between (1) the number of crimes, called "offenses" in this essay, and the cost of offenses, (2) the number of offenses and the punishments meted out, (3) the number of offenses, arrests, and convictions and the public expenditures on police and courts, (4) the number of convictions and the costs of imprisonments or other kinds of punishments, and (5) the number of offenses and the private expenditures on protection and apprehension. The first four are discussed in turn. . . .

## 1. Damages

Usually a belief that other members of society are harmed is the motivation behind outlawing or otherwise restricting an activity. The amount of harm would tend to increase with the activity level. . . . The concept of harm and the function relating its amount to the activity level are familiar to economists from their many discussions of activities causing external diseconomies. From this perspective, criminal activities are an important subset of the class of activities that cause diseconomies, with the level of criminal activities measured by the number of offenses.

The social value of the gain to offenders presumably also tends to increase with the number of offenses. . . . The net cost or damage to society is simply the difference between the harm and gain. . . .

[It] seems plausible [that] offenders usually eventually receive diminishing marginal gains and cause increasing marginal harm from additional offenses . . . [This means that the *net* damage is eventually positive.]

. . .

## 2. The cost of apprehension and conviction

The more that is spent on policemen, court personnel, and specialized equipment, the easier it is to discover offenses and convict offenders. . . .

## 3. The supply of offenses

Theories about the determinants of the number of offenses differ greatly, from emphasis on skull types and biological inheritance to family upbringing and disenchantment with society. Practically all the diverse theories agree, however, that when other variables are held constant, an increase in a person's probability of conviction or punishment if convicted would generally decrease, perhaps substantially, perhaps negligibly, the number of offenses he commits. In addition, a common generalization by persons with judicial experience is that a change in the probability has a greater effect on the number of offenses than a change in the punishment, although, as far as I can tell, none of the prominent theories shed any light on this relation.

The approach taken here follows the economists' usual analysis of choice and assumes that a person commits an offense if the expected utility to him exceeds the utility he could get by using his time and other resources at other activities. Some persons become "criminals," therefore, not because their basic motivation differs from that of other persons, but because their benefits and costs differ. I cannot pause to discuss the many general implications of this approach, except to remark that criminal behavior becomes part of a much more general theory and does not require ad hoc concepts of differential association, anomie, and the like, nor does it assume perfect knowledge, lightning-fast calculation, or any of the other caricatures of economic theory.

This approach implies that there is a function relating the number of offenses by any person to his probability of conviction, to his punishment if convicted, and to other variables, such as the income available to him in legal and other illegal activities, the frequency of nuisance arrests, and his willingness to commit an illegal act. . . .

. . .

. . . An increase in either [*the probability of punishment*] or [*an increase in the severity of punishment*] would reduce the utility expected from an offense and thus would tend to reduce the number of offenses because either the probability of "paying" the higher "price" or the "price" itself would increase. . . . The effect of changes in some components of [utility] could also be anticipated. For example, a rise in the income available in legal activities or an increase in law-abidingness due, say, to "education" would reduce the incentive to enter illegal activities and thus would reduce the number of offenses. Or a shift in the form of the punishment, say, from a fine to imprisonment, would tend to reduce the number of offenses, at least temporarily, because they cannot be committed while in prison.

This approach also has an interesting interpretation of the presumed greater response to a change in the probability than in the punishment. An increase in [*the probability of conviction*] "compensated" by an equal percentage reduction in [*the severity of punishment*] would not change the expected income from an offense but could change the expected utility, because the amount of risk would change. It is easily shown that an increase in [*the probability of conviction*] would reduce the expected utility, and thus the number of offenses, more than an equal percentage increase in [*the severity of punishment*] if [the person] has preference for risk; the increase in [*the severity of the punishment*] would have the greater effect if he has aversion to risk; and they would have the same effect if he is risk neutral. The widespread generalization that offenders are more deterred by the probability of conviction than by the punishment when convicted turns out to imply in the expected-utility approach that offenders are risk preferrers, at least in the relevant region of punishments.

. . . .

A well-known result states that, in equilibrium, the real incomes of persons in risky activities are, at the margin, relatively high or low as persons are generally risk avoiders or preferrers. If offenders were risk preferrers, this implies that the real income of offenders would be lower, at the margin, than the incomes they could receive in less risky legal activities, and conversely if they were risk avoiders. Whether "crime pays" is then an implication of the attitudes offenders have toward risk and is not directly related to the efficiency of the police or the amount spent on combating crime. . . .

## 4. Punishments

Mankind has invented a variety of ingenious punishments to inflict on convicted offenders: death, torture, branding, fines, imprisonment, banishment, restrictions on movement and occupation, and loss of citizenship are just the more common ones. In the United States, less serious offenses are punished primarily by fines, supplemented occasionally by probation, petty restrictions like temporary suspension of one's driver's license, and imprisonment. The more serious offenses are punished by a combination of probation, imprisonment, parole, fines, and various restrictions on choice of occupation. . . .

The cost of different punishments to an offender can be made comparable by converting them into their monetary equivalent or worth, which, of course, is directly measured only for fines. For example, the cost of an imprisonment is the discounted sum of the earnings foregone and the value placed on the restrictions in consumption and freedom. Since the earnings foregone and the value placed on prison restrictions vary from person to person, the cost even of a prison sentence of given duration is not a unique quantity but is generally greater, for example, to offenders who could earn more outside of prison. The cost to each offender would be greater the longer the prison sentence, since both foregone earnings and foregone consumption are positively related to the length of sentences.

Punishments affect not only offenders but also other members of society. Aside from collection costs, fines paid by offenders are received as revenue by others. Most punishments, however, hurt other members as well as offenders: for example, imprisonment requires expenditures on guards, supervisory personnel, buildings, food, etc. . . .

The total social cost of punishments is the cost to offenders plus the cost or minus the gain to others. Fines produce a gain to the latter that equals the cost to offenders, aside from collection costs, and so the social cost of fines is about zero, as befits a transfer payment. The social cost of probation, imprisonment, and other punishments, however, generally exceeds that to offenders, because others are also hurt. . . . .

## III. Optimality Conditions

The relevant parameters and behavioral functions have been introduced, and the stage is set for a discussion of social policy. If the aim simply were deterrence, the probability of conviction, $p$, could be raised close to 1, and punishments, $f$, could be made to exceed the gain: in this way the number of offenses, $O$, could be reduced almost at will. However, an increase in $p$ increases the social cost of offenses through its effect on the cost of combating offenses, $C$, . . . . as does an increase in $f$ [the social cost of punishment when prison is used instead of a fine]. At relatively modest values of $p$ and $f$, these effects might outweigh the social gain from increased deterrence. Similarly, if the aim simply were to make "the punishment fit the crime," $p$ could be set close to 1, and $f$ could be equated to the harm imposed on the rest of society. Again, however, such a policy ignores the social cost of increases in $p$ and $f$.

What is needed is a criterion that goes beyond catchy phrases and gives due weight to the damages from offenses, the costs of apprehending and convicting offenders, and the social cost of punishments. The social-welfare function of modern welfare economics is such a criterion, and one might assume that society has a function that measures the social loss from offenses. . . . The aim would be to select values of $f$, and [$p$] that minimize the social loss. . . .

. . .

## IV. Shifts in the Behavioral Relations

This section analyzes the effects of shifts in the basic behavioral relations – the damage, cost, and supply-of-offenses functions – on the optimal values of $p$ and $f$. . . . [Here o]nly intuitive proofs are given. The results are used to explain, among other things, why more damaging offenses are punished more severely and more impulsive offenders less severely.

An increase in the marginal damages from a given number of offenses . . . increases the marginal cost of changing offenses by a change in either $p$ or $f$. . . . The optimal number of offenses would necessarily decrease, because the optimal values of both $p$ and $f$ would increase. . . . [T]he optimal values of $p$ and $f$ move in the same, rather than in opposite, directions.

An interesting application of these conclusions is to different kinds of offenses. Although there are few objective measures of the damages done by most offenses, it does not take much imagination to conclude that offenses like murder or rape generally do more damage than petty larceny or auto theft. If the other components of the loss in income were the same, the optimal probability of apprehension and conviction and the punishment when convicted would be greater for the more serious offenses.

. . .

Sometimes it is possible to separate persons committing the same offense into groups that have different responses to punishments. For example, unpremeditated murderers or robbers are supposed to act impulsively and, therefore, to be relatively unresponsive to the size of punishments; likewise, the insane or the young are probably less affected than other offenders by future consequences and, therefore, probably less deterred by increases in the probability of conviction or in the punishment when convicted. The trend during the twentieth century toward relatively smaller prison terms and greater use of probation and therapy for such groups and, more generally, the trend away from the doctrine of "a given punishment for a given crime" is apparently at least broadly consistent with the implications of the optimality analysis.

. . .

## V. Fines

### A. Welfare Theorems and Transferable Pricing

The usual optimality conditions in welfare economics depend only on the levels and not on the slopes of marginal cost and average revenue functions, as in the well-known condition that marginal costs equal prices. The social loss from offenses was explicitly introduced as an application of the approach used in welfare economics, and yet slopes as incorporated into elasticities of supply do significantly affect the optimality conditions. Why this difference? The primary explanation would appear to be that it is almost always implicitly assumed that prices paid by consumers are fully transferred to firms and governments, so that there is no social loss from payment.

If there were no social loss from punishments, as with fines, the elasticity of supply would drop out of the optimality condition . . . If [there were a social loss from punishments], as with imprisonment, some of the payment "by" offenders would not be received by the rest of society, and a net social loss would result. The elasticity of the supply of offenses then becomes an important determinant of the optimality conditions, because it determines the change in social costs caused by a change in punishments.

Although transferable monetary pricing is the most common kind today, the other is not unimportant, especially in underdeveloped and Communist countries. Examples in addition to imprisonment and many other punishments are the draft, payments in kind, and queues and other waiting-time forms of rationing that result from legal restrictions on pricing . . . and from random variations in demand and supply conditions. It is interesting, and deserves further exploration, that the optimality conditions are so significantly affected by a change in the assumptions about the transferability of pricing.

## B. Optimality conditions

If [the social cost of punishment were zero], say, because punishment was by fine, and if the cost of apprehending and convicting offenders were also zero, the [optimality condition would be to set the number of offenses such that the marginal net harm were 0].

Economists generally conclude that activities causing "external" harm, such as factories that pollute the air or lumber operations that strip the land, should be taxed or otherwise restricted in level until the marginal external harm equaled the marginal private gain, that is, until marginal net damages equaled zero. . . . [I]f the costs of apprehending, convicting, and punishing offenders were nil and if each offense caused more external harm than private gain, the social loss from offenses would be minimized by setting punishments high enough to eliminate all offenses. Minimizing the social loss would become identical with the criterion of minimizing crime by setting penalties sufficiently high.

. . .

If the cost of apprehension and conviction were not zero, the optimality condition would have to incorporate marginal costs as well as marginal damages and . . . offenders [would] have to compensate for the cost of catching them as well as for the harm they directly do, which is a natural generalization of the usual externality analysis.

. . .

## C. The case for fines

Just as the probability of conviction and the severity of punishment are subject to control by society, so too is the form of punishment: legislation usually specifies whether an offense is punishable by fines, probation, institutionalization, or some combination. Is it merely an accident, or have optimality considerations determined that today, in most countries, fines are the predominant form of punishment, with institutionalization reserved for the more serious offenses? This section presents several arguments which imply that social welfare is increased if fines are used *whenever feasible*.

In the first place, probation and institutionalization use up social resources, and fines do not, since the latter are basically just transfer payments, while the former use resources in the form of guards, supervisory personnel, probation officers, and the offenders' own time . . .

Moreover, the determination of the optimal number of offenses and severity of punishments is somewhat simplified by the use of fines. A wise use of fines requires knowledge of marginal gains and harm and of marginal apprehension and conviction costs; admittedly, such knowledge is not easily acquired. A wise use of imprisonment and other punishments must know this too, however, and, in addition, must know about the elasticities of response of offenses to changes in punishments. As the bitter controversies over the abolition of capital punishment suggest, it has been difficult to learn about these elasticities.

I suggested earlier that premeditation, sanity, and age can enter into the determination of punishments as proxies for the elasticities of response. These characteristics may not have to be considered in levying fines, because the optimal fines. . . do not depend on elasticities. Perhaps this partly explains why economists discussing externalities almost never mention motivation or intent, while sociologists and lawyers discussing criminal behavior invariably do. The former assume that punishment is by a monetary tax or fine, while the latter assume that non-monetary punishments are used.

Fines provide compensation to victims, and optimal fines at the margin fully compensate victims and restore the status quo ante, so that they are no worse off than if offenses were not committed. Not only do other punishments fail to compensate, but they also require "victims" to spend additional resources in carrying out the punishment. It is not surprising, therefore, that the anger and fear felt toward ex-convicts who in fact have *not* "paid their debt to society" have resulted in additional punishments, including legal restrictions on their political and economic opportunities and informal restrictions on their social acceptance. . . .

One argument made against fines is that they are immoral because, in effect, they permit offenses to be bought for a price in the same way that bread or other goods are bought for a price. A fine *can* be considered the price of an offense, but so too can any other form of punishment; for example, the "price" of stealing a car might be six months in jail. The only difference is in the units of measurement: fines are prices measured in monetary units, imprisonments are prices measured in time units, etc. If anything, monetary units are to be preferred here as they are generally preferred in pricing and accounting.

Optimal fines . . . depend only on the marginal harm and cost and not at all on the economic positions of offenders. This has been criticized as unfair, and fines proportional to the incomes of offenders have been suggested. If the goal is to minimize the social loss in income from offenses, and not to take vengeance or to inflict harm on offenders, then fines should depend on the total harm done by offenders, and not directly on their income, race, sex, etc. In the same way, the monetary value of optimal prison sentences and other punishments depends on the harm, costs, and elasticities of response, but not directly on an offender's income. Indeed, if the monetary value of the punishment by, say, imprisonment were independent of income, the length of the sentence would be *inversely* related to income, because the value placed on a given sentence is positively related to income.

We might detour briefly to point out some interesting implications for the probability of conviction of the fact that the monetary value of a given fine is obviously the same for all offenders, while the monetary equivalent or "value" of a given prison sentence or probation period is generally positively related to an offender's income. . . . [A]ctual probabilities of conviction are not fixed to all offenders but usually vary with their age, sex, race, and, in particular, income. Offenders with higher earnings have an incentive to spend more on planning their offenses, on good lawyers, on legal appeals, and even on bribery to reduce the probability of apprehension and conviction for offenses punishable by, say, a given prison term, because the cost to them of conviction is relatively large compared to the cost of these expenditures. Similarly, however, poorer offenders have an incentive to use more of their time in planning their offenses, in court appearances, and the like to reduce the probability of conviction for offenses punishable by a given fine, because the cost to them of conviction is relatively large compared to the value of their time. The implication is that the probability of conviction would be systematically related to the earnings of offenders: negatively for offenses punishable by imprisonment and positively for those punishable by fines. Although a negative relation for felonies and other offenses punishable by imprisonment has been frequently observed and deplored . . . , I do not know of any studies of the relation for fines or of any recognition that the observed negative relation may be more a consequence of the nature of the punishment than of the influence of wealth.

Another argument made against fines is that certain crimes, like murder or rape, are so heinous that no amount of money could compensate for the harm inflicted. This argument has obvious merit and is a special case of the more general principle that fines cannot be relied on exclusively whenever the harm exceeds the resources of offenders. For then victims could not be fully compensated by offenders, and fines would have to be supplemented with prison terms or other punishments in order to discourage offenses optimally. This explains why imprisonments, probation, and parole are major punishments for the more serious felonies; considerable harm is inflicted, and felonious offenders lack sufficient resources to compensate. Since fines are preferable, it also suggests the need for a flexible system of installment fines to enable offenders to pay fines more readily and thus avoid other punishments.

This analysis implies that if some offenders could pay the fine for a given offense and others could not, the former should be punished solely by fine and the latter partly by other methods. In essence, therefore, these methods become a vehicle for punishing "debtors" to society. Before the cry is raised that the system is unfair, especially to poor offenders, consider the following.

Those punished would be debtors in "transactions" that were never agreed to by their "creditors," not in voluntary transactions, such as loans, for which suitable precautions could be taken in advance by creditors. Moreover, punishment in any economic system based on voluntary market transactions inevitably must distinguish between such "debtors" and others. If a rich man purchases a car and a poor man steals one, the former is congratulated, while the latter is often sent to prison when apprehended. Yet the rich man's purchase is equivalent to a "theft" subsequently compensated by a "fine" equal to the price of the car, while the poor man, in effect, goes to prison because he cannot pay this "fine."

Whether a punishment like imprisonment in lieu of a full fine for offenders lacking sufficient resources is "fair" depends, of course, on the length of the prison term compared to the fine. For example, a prison term of one week in lieu of a $10,000 fine would, if anything, be "unfair" to wealthy offenders paying the fine. Since imprisonment is a more costly punishment to society than fines, the loss from offenses would be reduced by a policy of leniency toward persons who are imprisoned because they cannot pay fines. Consequently, optimal prison terms for "debtors" would not be "unfair" to them in the sense that the monetary equivalent to them of the prison terms would be less than the value of optimal fines, which in turn would equal the harm caused or the "debt."

It appears, however, that "debtors" are often imprisoned at rates of exchange with fines that place a low value on time in prison. Although I have not seen systematic evidence on the different punishments actually offered convicted offenders, and the choices they made, many statutes in the United States do permit fines and imprisonment that place a low value on time in prison. For example, in New York State, Class A Misdemeanors can be punished by a prison term as long as one year or a fine no larger than $1,000 and Class B Misdemeanors, by a term as long as three months or a fine no larger than $500 *(Laws of New York,* 1965, chap. 1030, Arts. 70 and 80). According to my analysis, these statutes permit excessive prison sentences relative to the fines, which may explain why imprisonment in lieu of fines is considered unfair to poor offenders, who often must "choose" the prison alternative.

. . .

## VIII. Summary and Concluding Remarks

This essay uses economic analysis to develop optimal public and private policies to combat illegal behavior. The public's decision variables are its expenditures on police, courts, etc., which help determine the probability *(p)* that an offense is discovered and the offender apprehended and convicted, the size of the punishment for those convicted *(f),* and the form of the punishment: imprisonment, probation, fine, etc. Optimal values of these variables can be chosen. . . .

"Optimal" decisions are interpreted to mean decisions that minimize the social loss in income from offenses. This loss is the sum of damages, costs of apprehension and conviction, and costs of carrying out the punishments imposed, and can be minimized simultaneously with respect to $p$, $f$, and the form of $f$ unless one or more of these variables is constrained by "outside" considerations. The optimality conditions derived from the minimization have numerous interesting implications that can be illustrated by a few examples.

If carrying out the punishment were costly, as it is with probation, imprisonment, or parole, the elasticity of response of offenses with respect to a change in $p$ would generally, in equilibrium, have to exceed its response to a change in $f$. This implies, if entry into illegal activities can be explained by the same model of choice that economists use to explain entry into legal activities, that offenders are (at the margin) "risk preferrers." Consequently, illegal activities "would not pay" (at the margin) in the sense that the real income received would be less than what could be received in less risky legal activities. The conclusion that "crime would not pay" is an optimality condition and not an implication about the efficiency of the police or courts; indeed, it holds for any level of efficiency, as long as optimal values of $p$ and $f$ appropriate to each level are chosen.

If costs were the same, the optimal values of both $p$ and $f$ would be greater, the greater the damage caused by an offense. Therefore, offenses like murder and rape should be solved more frequently and punished more severely than milder offenses like auto theft and petty larceny. Evidence on actual probabilities and punishments in the United States is strongly consistent with this implication of the optimality analysis.

Fines have several advantages over other punishments: for example, they conserve resources, compensate society as well as punish offenders, and simplify the determination of optimal $p$'s and $f$'s. Not surprisingly, fines are the most common punishment and have grown in importance over time. Offenders who cannot pay fines have to be punished in other ways, but the optimality analysis implies that the monetary value to them of these punishments should generally be less than the fines.

Vengeance, deterrence, safety, rehabilitation, and compensation are perhaps the most important of the many desiderata proposed throughout history. Next to these, minimizing the social loss in income may seem narrow, bland, and even quaint. Unquestionably, the income criterion can be usefully generalized in several directions, and a few have already been suggested in the essay. Yet one should not lose sight of the fact that it is more general and powerful than it may seem and actually includes more dramatic desiderata as special cases. For example, if punishment were by an optimal fine, minimizing the loss in income would be equivalent to compensating "victims" fully . . . ; or it would be equivalent to deterring all offenses causing great damage if the cost of apprehending, convicting, and punishing these offenders were relatively small. Since the same could also be demonstrated for vengeance or rehabilitation, the moral should be clear: minimizing the loss in income is actually very general and thus is more *useful* than these catchy and dramatic but inflexible desiderata.

This essay concentrates almost entirely on determining optimal policies to combat illegal behavior and pays little attention to actual policies. The small amount of evidence on actual policies that I have examined certainly suggests a positive correspondence with optimal policies. For example, it is found for seven major felonies in the United States that more damaging ones are penalized more severely, that the elasticity of response of offenses to changes in $p$ exceeds the response to $f$, and that both are usually less than unity, all as predicted by the optimality analysis. There are, however, some discrepancies too: for example, the actual tradeoff between imprisonment and fines in different statutes is frequently less, rather than the predicted more, favorable to those imprisoned. Although many more studies of actual policies are needed, they are seriously hampered on the empirical side by grave limitations in the quantity and quality of data on offenses, convictions, costs, etc., and on the analytical side by the absence of a reliable theory of political decision making.

Reasonable men will often differ on the amount of damages or benefits caused by different activities. To some, any wage rates set by competitive labor markets are permissible, while to others, rates below a certain minimum are violations of basic rights; to some, gambling, prostitution, and even abortion should be freely available to anyone willing to pay the market price, while to others, gambling is sinful and abortion is murder. These differences are basic to the development and implementation of public policy but have been excluded from my inquiry. I assume consensus on damages and benefits and simply try to work out rules for an optimal implementation of this consensus.

The main contribution of this essay, as I see it, is to demonstrate that optimal policies to combat illegal behavior are part of an optimal allocation of resources. Since economics has been developed to handle resource allocation, an "economic" framework becomes applicable to, and helps enrich, the analysis of illegal behavior. At the same time, certain unique aspects of the latter enrich economic analysis: some punishments, such as imprisonments, are necessarily non-monetary and are a cost to society as well as to offenders; the degree of uncertainty is a decision variable that enters both the revenue and cost functions; etc.

Lest the reader be repelled by the apparent novelty of an "economic" framework for illegal behavior, let him recall that two important contributors to criminology during the eighteenth and nineteenth centuries, Beccaria and Bentham, explicitly applied an economic calculus. Unfortunately, such an approach has lost favor during the last hundred years, and my efforts can be viewed as a resurrection, modernization, and thereby I hope improvement on these much earlier pioneering studies.

# 26

# Blackmail, Privacy, and Freedom of Contact

## *Richard A. Posner*

### EDITOR'S INTRODUCTION

Blackmail presents a puzzle for economists. In general, economists are in favor of voluntary contracts. So how can there be a good economic argument for outlawing a voluntary agreement between the blackmailer and the party being blackmailed? After all, it is perfectly legal for the blackmailer to sell the information to a third party. Furthermore, many negotiations involve an implicit or explicit threat. For example, if the seller does not offer a good price, the buyer can threaten to take his business elsewhere; and one person can threaten a second person that he will take the person to court unless the second person settles on terms satisfactory to the first person. Richard Posner provides an economic analysis of blackmail that gets us out of this apparent conundrum.

## Introduction

Blackmail is an exotic crime, and quite possibly . . . a rare one. But it exerts considerable fascination at both the popular and the theoretical level, and it has evoked a substantial literature to which this article seeks to contribute. . . . . I argue that blackmail is, and should be, forbidden because, although ostensibly a voluntary transaction between consenting adults, it is likely to be, on average, wealth-reducing rather than wealth-maximizing.

The economic cast of my analysis is no accident. Economists and economically minded lawyers have found the prohibition of blackmail more problematic than have other students of the legal system. Economists tend to be great believers in voluntary transactions. Blackmail is, in the usual case, a voluntary transaction between competent adults. The blackmailer possesses information about his prospective victim that the latter would prefer not be made public. The victim values the blackmailer's silence more than the blackmailer values the right to publicize the information. Accordingly, the blackmailer sells the victim the right to the information. Since blackmail is a crime, the actual transactions do not much resemble those of ordinary commercial intercourse, but that is an artifact of their illegality. If blackmail were legal, blackmailers and their customers (today called "victims") would enter into legally enforceable contracts whereby the blackmailer would agree for a price never to disclose the information in question; the information would become the legally protected trade secret of the customer.

Economists are troubled by prohibitions against voluntary transactions unless the transactions impose involuntary costs on third parties. Who might the third parties be in the case of blackmail? We can, at least for the moment, elide that question by taking a slightly different approach to freedom of contract, one that asks whether prohibiting a particular class of contracts would raise or lower the net social product. This is the easiest approach to contracts made under duress, a class of contracts with which blackmail is often grouped. If an assailant points a gun at you, saying, "Your money or your life," you will doubtless be very eager to accept the first branch of this offer by tendering your money. There are third-party effects, but the essential objection to the transaction is that the victim would prefer a regime in which such transactions were outlawed, because it would reduce the probability of his receiving such unwanted offers (a qualification is discussed later). In this case a restriction on freedom of contract protects a contracting party ex ante.

Similarly, people desperately eager to pay blackmail would prefer not to be blackmailed and would therefore prefer a regime in which blackmail is forbidden. That cannot be decisive against legalizing blackmail, because others might benefit. But it shows that blackmail cannot be approved on economic grounds just because it is a voluntary transaction between consenting adults; not all such transactions are wealth-maximizing. One alternative to economic analysis in both the duress and the blackmail cases is to play with the meaning of "voluntary," for example by confining "voluntary" acts to those in which severe constraints are absent; but this just adds a layer of uncertainty.

Another way of bringing out the commonality between duress and blackmail is to note that both involve threats. Threats have the interesting property that both parties involved – the threatener and the person threatened – are made worse off if the threat is actually carried out. This fact does not by itself condemn a threat as inefficient, since the deterrence theory of punishment is constructed on the premise that threatening is a good way of getting people to behave. But extortionate threats, whether to beat or kill or lie – or tell the truth – that is, threats designed to induce the person threatened to pay the threatener, are not intended to regulate behavior. They are intended to transfer wealth from the person threatened to the threatener. Such a transfer does not, on its face, increase social wealth; indirectly, it diminishes social wealth by the sum of the resources employed by the threatener to make his threat credible and of the victim to resist the threat. So, prima facie at least, it is a sterile redistributive activity, like (simple) theft.

Of course, this seemingly sterile redistributive activity might confer a social benefit; that is the argument for blackmail. But if there is no good reason to suppose it does, then, on purely economic grounds, blackmail should be forbidden.

# I. A Taxonomy and a New Economic Theory of Blackmail

The best way to anatomize blackmail is to distinguish among the seven categories of acts or conditions that a blackmailer might threaten to reveal:

1. Criminal acts for which the blackmailer's victim has been duly punished.
2. Criminal acts that were not detected, hence not punished.
3. Acts that are wrongful but not criminal, such as acts that the common law classifies as torts.
4. Acts, whether civilly or criminally wrongful, of which the blackmailer (or his principal) was the victim.

5. Disreputable, immoral, or otherwise censurable acts that do not, however, violate any law, or at least any commonly enforced law.
6. Involuntary acts or conditions that are a source of potential shame, ridicule, or humiliation.
7. Any of the above, except that the blackmailer's victim did not in fact commit the act for which he is being blackmailed.

## A. CATEGORY 1: CRIMINAL ACTS FOR WHICH THE BLACKMAILER'S VICTIM HAS BEEN DULY PUNISHED

Here, allowing blackmail would interfere with the penalties prescribed by law, and by doing so might reduce the social product. Or it might not. . . . .

Suppose the blackmailer's victim is a person who had been convicted of a crime, served his time, incurred all collateral penalties such as loss of civil rights, and eventually been pardoned. Years later the blackmailer appears on the scene and threatens to expose the victim's criminal past. If the blackmailer is allowed to collect money from the victim in exchange for silence, then to the victim's prescribed penalties will be added the amount of the blackmail, an amount equal to the lower of (1) the cost to the victim of the stigma of being exposed as an ex-convict and (2) his financial resources. Of course, the blackmailer may be legally entitled to divulge the information, depending on how broadly the tort of invasion of privacy is defined. But if deterred from engaging in blackmail, he will lack – though not completely, as we shall see – an incentive to expend the resources necessary to obtain the information in the first place. So in all likelihood the information about the victim's past will not be divulged. This may seem a shame, since the information might have some, even considerable, value to people who transact with the victim. But that is irrelevant. If blackmail were permitted, the information would not be divulged either. Blackmail is payment for secrecy. The only effect of blackmail would be to increase the victim's punishment by the amount of the blackmail paid. If the original punishment was optimal, that punishment plus the blackmail would be excessive and the transaction costs of the blackmail would be an additional social waste.

That "if" is a big one, because punishment is rarely optimal in any strong sense. But we must consider the situation as it would appear to a legislature mulling over the question whether to forbid blackmail. If dissatisfied with the combination of probability and severity of punishment for crimes, the legislature could alter the combination directly. If satisfied, it will want to forbid the blackmail in Category 1 of my taxonomy. Granted, this assumes that the legislature has decided to use a system of public punishments. An alternative would be a system of private punishments, of which blackmail would be (as we shall see) a natural component. But legislative preference for public punishments is a fact, and may be (again, as we shall see) efficient.

Granted, too, blackmail is not the only private conduct that adds to public punishments. An employer who refuses to hire a person with a criminal record adds a market sanction to the person's official punishment. The difference is that the employer benefits from imposing this additional sanction; presumably it is a cost-minimizing policy. A blackmail transaction does not confer an equivalent social benefit, once its deterrent effect is discounted because of concern with overdeterrence. It merely transfers wealth to the blackmailer. The reason is that blackmail does not actually increase the stock of information in a socially useful sense. This is a paradox. Legalizing blackmail would increase the resources devoted to acquiring information about people's criminal acts and other behavior or dispositions to which opprobrium attaches, and how could an increase in the resources devoted to gathering information *not* increase the amount of information? The amount gathered has to increase, all right, but the amount disseminated need not; for the information gathered by the blackmailer may be suppressed.

He will suppress it, it is true, only if suppression is worth more to the blackmail victim (and hence to the blackmailer) than it is to third parties. Otherwise he will disseminate it to them, and if he does, his activity will have brought about a net increase in the usable stock of information after all. The blackmailer is not interested in secrecy per se, but in money. If someone will pay more for the dirt he has gathered than the blackmail victim will pay, the blackmailer will sell to that third party rather than rebury the information he has unearthed. But these cases will be rare even if the information is socially valuable. Often the benefits of the information will be highly diffuse, being spread across a variety of actual and potential transactors with the blackmail victim, some of whom may not even be identifiable. Blackmailing a person who is trying to conceal from his future sexual partners that he is a carrier of the AIDS virus would be an example. It may be difficult to transform these diffuse benefits into a commensurate gain appropriable by the blackmailer. Also, it is difficult to sell a secret without revealing it before the sale. If the blackmailer tells the victim's wife that he has some information about the victim that she would value highly, how does she know how much to pay? If he reveals the information to her before she signs a contract, she will not pay anything unless she wants proof, say, for use in a divorce action. Solutions to analogous problems in the area of legitimate intellectual property such as inventions and entertainment exist, but they are not simple. The more costly a transaction, the less likely it is to be made. For both reasons it seems a fair guess that allowing blackmail would not increase the usable stock of information significantly. Indeed, we shall soon consider the possibility that it might actually reduce that stock.

This conclusion is important. If blackmail is unlikely to increase the stock of usable information, one possible third-party benefit from allowing the practice is eliminated from consideration. Another possible benefit is to make criminal punishments more severe, but this may well be an additional cost rather than a benefit. Therefore, the case for carving an exception to the crime of extortion for blackmail in our first category has not been made.

## B. CATEGORY 2: CRIMINAL ACTS THAT WERE NOT DETECTED, HENCE NOT PUNISHED

Here the blackmailer is in effect a supplementary law enforcer. His efforts increase the probability that offenders will be caught but by doing so interfere with a criminal justice system. . . .

Private enforcement can be disruptive in another way as well. Suppose police obtain valuable information by paying informers. The price they pay will be lower if blackmail is forbidden, since competition between police and blackmailers for information concerning guilt would drive up the price of the information. So blackmail might actually reduce the usable stock of information. We cannot be certain. Blackmail increases the incentive to gather information, so more is gathered, and some of it is disseminated rather than reburied, either because the blackmailer and his victim fail to come to terms or because someone offers the blackmailer a higher price than the victim is willing and able to pay. But blackmail also enables some information to be concealed that would otherwise be divulged.

. . . .

The basic argument in this section is thus a simple one: blackmail is a form of private law enforcement, so in areas where private law enforcement is banned (and we have seen that there are economic reasons why one might want to ban it in some areas), blackmail should be banned. The implication is that in areas where private law enforcement is permitted, blackmail-like activities, though not called by that pejorative name, will be permitted; and we shall see shortly that they are.

The argument is not conclusive, however, for banning blackmail. To begin with, private enforcers might have so much lower costs of operation than public enforcers as to make private enforcement more efficient on balance than public enforcement. Private enterprises generally have lower costs than public ones for the same quality and quantity of output. A blackmailer, moreover, will frequently come upon incriminating information by accident. His blackmail victim might be his spouse, coworker, employer, companion in crime, client or patient, student or teacher, or social acquaintance. Of course if blackmail were legal there would be an incentive to expend more resources on obtaining incriminating information about people; there would be a blackmail industry, though maybe not a very large one, at least if we confine our attention to the blackmailing of people who have committed crimes. One reason for distinctive criminal penalties, such as imprisonment, is that criminals rarely have financial resources commensurate with the injury they do. Such people will not be able to pay huge blackmail either, and this will limit the scale of the industry. But by how much? Far more people commit crimes than are caught and prosecuted, so the aggregate gains from lawful blackmail might be huge.

One might try to defend the blackmailing of criminals (whether or not they have been caught and formally punished) differently, as a way of generating a more discriminating scale of punishments. The people most susceptible to blackmail on account of their past crimes are, first, those with the largest incomes and, second, those who occupy jobs or other situations in which the expected cost of a repetition of their crime would be highest. Examples are the convicted embezzler who is once again working in a bank and the wife-slayer who has remarried. Allowing blackmail would enable a greater use of monetary sanctions because a fine, payable out of current assets, plus blackmail payable out of future income would together constitute a heavier such sanction than a fine by itself would. Thus, blackmail might actually promote Becker's program of optimal sanctions,[1] and it would optimize the preventive effect of criminal punishment by steering criminals away from the activities in which the expected costs of their recidivism would be highest. But employers may, as we have seen, be able to protect themselves. And sentencing courts have the power to impose conditions on a criminal's subsequent activities, such as that he keep out of a particular profession (this is a common sanction in securities cases); this may be a simpler solution than blackmail.

But there is more to be said on behalf of blackmail as an ancillary method of law enforcement. The threat of blackmail would not only deter criminal activity directly; it would raise the costs of that activity by inducing criminals to take steps to reduce the likelihood of being blackmailed by each other. Also, some people (especially criminals) may be more willing to engage in blackmail than to report incriminating information to the police, even if there is a reward; for the information may have been obtained illegally, or in circumstances that reveal the informer's own illegalities. So here is a class of cases where allowing blackmail would yield socially productive information even though the information was not disseminated to the authorities: it would be socially productive because it would make the criminal pay for his crime.

The discussion in this section may seem inconclusive. Certainly no confident conclusion that allowing the blackmailing of undetected criminals would undermine the enforcement of the criminal laws is possible. . . .

## C. CATEGORY 3: ACTS THAT ARE WRONGFUL BUT NOT CRIMINAL SUCH AS ACTS THAT THE COMMON LAW CLASSIFIES AS TORTS

With respect to this category of acts, the law has given the exclusive right of enforcement to the victim, and although overenforcement is not a problem (because for most private wrongs the probability of detection is close to one, and therefore the optimal sanction approximates the social cost of the wrong), the law's decision to give the victim a property right in rectifying the wrong would be undermined by allowing a third party to blackmail the injurer-defendant. Blackmail would deplete the wrongdoer's resources and thus make it more difficult for the victim of the wrong to enforce his right to damages.

## D. CATEGORY 4: ACTS, WHETHER CIVILLY OR CRIMINALLY WRONGFUL, OF WHICH THE BLACKMAILER (OR HIS PRINCIPAL) WAS THE VICTIM

The difference between Categories 2 and 3 is that when the victim of wrongdoing, rather than the state, is the authorized enforcer, practices superficially indistinguishable from blackmail often (though not always, hence the need for the fourth category) are permitted. It is broadly true that "[n]o one seems to object to a person's collecting information about his or her spouse's adulterous activities, and threatening to disclose that information in a divorce proceeding or other forum, in order to extract maximum compensation for the offending spouse's breach of the marital obligations." . . . There is a division of legal opinion on "whether it is or should be illegal to threaten to disclose damaging information to the press in order to settle a contract or tort claim." A threat merely to litigate a civil suit, however, and not to trumpet the defendant's conduct to the press or other media, is much less likely to be classified as blackmail than a threat to lodge a criminal complaint. This is so even though many civil suits are in fact settled because the defendant does not want the details of his misconduct to become known, as they would be if the case went to trial: trials are public. Settlement agreements often contain confidentiality clauses, and these agreements are not classified as blackmail.

This analysis implies that if private enforcement were permitted generally – if the criminal laws, for example, were privately enforced – then blackmailers would merely be private enforcers who had compromised their enforcement proceedings, much as public law enforcers compromise their enforcement proceedings through plea bargaining. If this were the case, it would be hard to object to blackmail.

## E. CATEGORY 5: DISREPUTABLE, IMMORAL, OR OTHERWISE CENSURABLE ACTS THAT DO NOT, HOWEVER, VIOLATE ANY LAW, OR AT LEAST ANY COMMONLY ENFORCED LAW, AND CATEGORY 6: INVOLUNTARY ACTS OR CONDITIONS THAT ARE A SOURCE OF POTENTIAL SHAME, RIDICULE, OR HUMILIATION

. . . .

To begin with, the qualification in the definition of Category 5 ("or at least any commonly enforced law") is important. Some "immoral" conduct, such as fornication, adultery, and homosexual intercourse, is nominally criminal in many states but so rarely punished as to call into question the existence of any social commitment to extirpate the conduct. When a blackmailer threatens to reveal the victim's immoral conduct, this rarely will be interpreted as a threat of criminal prosecution, though sometimes as a threat to stir up a divorce proceeding. Still, the very overinclusiveness of the criminal law is a possible reason against legalizing the blackmail in Category 2 (criminal acts committed but not punished). Allowing such blackmail would bring into existence an industry devoted to enforcing criminal laws that remain on the books because of legislative inertia or because of their symbolic importance to influential interest groups but that society as a whole has decided not to enforce. That decision might be undermined by allowing blackmail. One can only say "might" and not "would" because the decision may have been based on considerations peculiar to criminal law and not engaged by informal methods of "law enforcement," including blackmail. . . .

It will help in getting a handle on these questions to approach Category 5 through Category 6 (involuntary acts or conditions that are a source of potential shame, ridicule, or humiliation). Indeed, the original motivation for this paper came from my research into the law and economics of sex, a field rich in cases in this category. Suppose a man is a homosexual in the sense of having a strong, and basically lifelong, preference for sex with other males. This condition is almost certainly involuntary. Of course, having a homosexual preference and acting on it are different things; the preference may be involuntary but the homosexual acts themselves are not. So, to begin, let me assume that the blackmailer's victim is a homosexual and confides this to a friend but refrains from homosexual acts, and in fact is married. The "friend" threatens to tell the victim's wife about his homosexuality unless the victim will pay him to keep silent. This is a classic blackmail threat, yet it is difficult to see what the benefits would be of allowing it to be made. In fact the net social product would probably be diminished if this class of contracts were permitted.

To see this, consider the effects of such permission. One would be to raise the cost of having a homosexual preference – of being a homosexual. Another would be to increase the resources expended on discovering homosexual preference and on negotiating contracts to prevent the discovery from being revealed. A third would be to increase the resources devoted to concealing homosexuality and to other defensive measures against the threat of blackmail.

The second effect cannot be dismissed with the argument that the resources that would be devoted to blackmailing, if it were a lawful activity, would be slight because most blackmailers concerned with intimate acts probably obtain their information as a byproduct of their transactions with the victim (the spurned lover, etc.) rather than through elaborate investigation; even so, a fair amount of sexual blackmail involves entrapment of the victim. To repeat an earlier point, the illegality of blackmail reduces the amount expended on investigation and entrapment, making that amount a poor predictor of what the costs of blackmail would be if blackmail were legal. . . . .

If raising the cost of being a homosexual has no allocative effect because homosexuality is an involuntary and unalterable condition, then legalizing blackmail would channel real – and, I have just argued, considerable – resources into bringing about a pure redistribution of wealth from the homosexual to the blackmailer. There would be no net social gain but instead a net social loss equal (at a minimum, as we shall see) to the resources expended in the blackmailing. Here is where the involuntary character of being a homosexual is important, which is what caused me to specify a separate Category 6 for cases of involuntary, unalterable conditions. If a condition cannot be changed by incentives, taxing it is unlikely to have any allocative effect. No gain, much cost.

I am oversimplifying. There would be some allocative effects. Some homosexuals would be less likely to marry, to enter traditionally heterosexual or homophobic occupations (notice the parallel to the occupational effects of allowing blackmail with respect to past criminal convictions), or in short to try to "pass" as heterosexual, since a known homosexual cannot be blackmailed. Others, however, would try all the harder to pass, in an effort to reduce the risk of blackmail by raising potential blackmailers' costs of information. Both classes of response would be defensive measures akin to the purchase of a security system by a householder fearful of burglary. If we anticipated a social gain from homosexuals making either greater or fewer efforts to pass as heterosexuals, and if we knew which effect would be more likely on balance if blackmail were permitted, then we could evaluate a suggestion that allowing homosexuals to be blackmailed would generate social benefits. But there is no basis in existing knowledge for either judgment. For example, while it could be argued that a male homosexual who marries a woman to whom he does not disclose his sexual preference commits a fraud upon her and therefore that such marriages should be discouraged, we do not know whether allowing blackmail would reduce the number of such marriages by increasing the cost of the marriage to the homosexual or would increase the number of such marriages by increasing the benefits of marriage to homosexuals through its camouflage effect (married men are presumed heterosexual). In the face of this uncertainty, the safest guess is that allowing the blackmailing of homosexuals would yield a net social loss equal to the resources expended in blackmailing and in defending against blackmailing. Additional resources would be squandered on efforts to entrap people in compromising situations.

The analysis is more complicated if the focus is switched from the *condition* of being homosexual (in the sense of having a homosexual orientation) to homosexual *acts*. One way a homosexual can reduce the probability of detection is by reducing the number of homosexual acts he engages in, and in particular the number of different homosexual partners he has. Indeed, if he simply screens his partners more carefully, this will raise his sexual search costs and so indirectly reduce the number of his sexual partners. If, perhaps because of the AIDS epidemic, we thought it a good idea to create incentives for homosexuals to reduce the number of their homosexual acts or homosexual sex partners, allowing blackmail might generate a net social benefit. This seems unlikely, though. The expected cost of AIDS to homosexuals who do not practice safe sex is very high and must swamp the expected cost of blackmail (more precisely, the higher expected cost of blackmail if blackmail were legal). Put differently, a person willing to risk AIDS is probably willing to risk being blackmailed. This conclusion requires qualification, however, because the blackmail risk would soar if blackmail were decriminalized. Nevertheless, the blackmail "tax" would probably remain a minor factor in most homosexuals' decision calculus. What is more, the danger of infection with AIDS is greatly reduced by the use of condoms, and blackmail would do nothing to induce such use.

Here is an even clearer example of a case in Category 6: A man is impotent, and is obtaining treatment from a sexual therapist. Suspecting the victim's condition, a blackmailer follows him to the therapist's office, discovers (without breaking any law) what the problem is, and blackmails him. What would be the consequences if such blackmail were permitted? Not less impotence, surely, but more. An impotent man would hesitate to seek professional assistance for fear of increasing the probability that blackmailers would discover his problem. The increase in impotence would generate (after subtracting the reduction in the use of therapists' services) a net social cost, to be added to the cost of the resources expended by the blackmailer. This is another example of defensive and offensive expenditures on wealth redistribution that yield no social gain.

Thus far I have been assuming that the victim's secret is worth more to his potential transacting partners than it is to himself. As such, the objection to blackmail is that, when successful, it bottles up socially valuable information. In many cases, however, the secret may be worth more to the victim than unmasking it would be worth to others. Impotence is a good example. The condition will be known to the man's sexual partners; and of what interest would it be, except as a source of mild titillation, to anyone else? The embarrassment to the victim if his condition becomes known to the public may greatly outweigh the benefits of the information to the public.

To summarize, Category 6 involves the levying of a private tax on an activity that either is unlikely to be discouraged by the tax or that society has no interest in discouraging. . . . .

Category 5, consisting of disreputable but not unlawful acts, is difficult to analyze because there is no enforcement scheme to be disrupted and there are potential allocative gains from taxing disreputable conduct (as with a pollution tax). . . . .

Society has an informal and very cheap system of deterring the lesser forms of wrongdoing: gossip. Its efficacy would be undermined by blackmail because the gossip would sell his information to the blackmailer and thence to the wrongdoer and thereafter his lips would be sealed. This scenario both underscores the analogy between trade secrecy and lawful blackmail and illustrates how blackmail can reduce rather than increase the usable stock of information. It is true that, at the same time the efficacy of this informal system of regulation was reduced by allowing blackmail, so would be the need for it, because the tax effect of blackmail would reduce the incidence of wrongdoing. But it cannot be assumed that, overall, the amount of wrongdoing would be less. If it were not less, then the costs of blackmail would be a deadweight loss.

This argument against Category 5 blackmail is hardly conclusive. The possibility that blackmail would be an efficient intermediate method of discouraging relatively minor forms of wrongdoing between the criminal law (effective but too costly) and gossip (cheap but perhaps not very effective) cannot be excluded. . . . .

An intimate is likely to come across incriminating information by accident, that is, without an expenditure of resources. So the basic economic objection to blackmail –

that it is, on balance anyway, a sterile expenditure of resources – is weakened. But it would be wrong to conclude that blackmail by intimates is a socially costless activity. It raises the cost of intimacy, much as would a rule requiring a person to testify to admissions made by his or her spouse. Of course, intimacy can be used for bad as well as for good purposes . . .

. . . .

## Note

1. Gary S. Becker, "Crime and Punishment. An Economic Approach," 76 *J. Pol. Econ.* 169, 180–85 (1968).

# Part VIII

## Norms

# 27

## Approximate Optimality of Aboriginal Property Rights

### *Martin J. Bailey*

#### EDITOR'S INTRODUCTION

It has been argued that the concept of property rights is intimately connected with capitalism and modern industrial societies. Martin Bailey argues to the contrary – that if there are benefits to private property, they should be observable in aboriginal societies that live on the edge of existence. They cannot afford the luxury of inefficiency, including the inefficiency that might arise when property rights are optimal, but missing. In reviewing anthropological studies of 50 aboriginal societies, Bailey discovers certain patterns. In general, property rights in land are more likely when individual inputs improve the productivity of the land (e.g., clearing the land or providing some sort of fertilizer). In contrast, communal rights are more likely when the group are hunter-gatherers. Game, which is large and migratory, is more likely to be shared communally because the food cannot be stored, there are benefits to group hunting, and it is hard to identify ownership of the animal before it is slain. Finally, articles of clothing are almost always considered private property.

In contrast to the relatively rich literature, enlightened by many cases, on property rights in modern societies, the corresponding literature by economists on aboriginal societies is peremptory and uninformed by interdisciplinary studies. This relatively brief literature is enlightened by only a few case studies and concrete examples. Both the analysis and its credibility can be improved by more use of relevant data, covering a wider variety of cases. This article undertakes such an endeavor, using the observations of anthropologists of the diverse set of rights, customs, and practices of over 50 aboriginal peoples. The cases considered here include peoples who used their group territories for hunting and fishing; for gathering wild roots, fruit, vegetables, and invertebrates; and (sometimes) for primitive horticulture. Among the studied groups, one observes almost all conceivable structures of rights.

The study of aboriginals can make especially clear the advantages of one type of property right over another because, in most cases, these people lived at the margin of subsistence. In more developed societies, departures from optimality mean lower living standards and lower growth rates – luxuries these societies can afford. By contrast, in societies near the margin of subsistence, with populations under Malthusian control, such departures had harsher effects, which one would expect to see reflected in the surviving societies. Unsound rights structures generally implied lower population size and, perhaps, the disappearance of the society. (Where the balance of advantage and disadvantage between alternative institutions was reasonably close, however, more than one could be found.) One therefore expects the data on aboriginals to provide relatively direct evidence on the structure of an optimal system of property rights under various circumstances. These circumstances generally include a small population when compared to a modern nation state, so that the enforcement of various behavioral norms through social pressure was much easier. For this and other technological reasons, optimal rights structures in aboriginal societies could include more common property and group enterprises and fewer disjoint individual rights than are workable in developed societies.

. . .

# I. Premises and Principal Considerations

*def*  I take as well established the Malthusian view of population, which implies that land tends to be scarce and valuable when viewed on a large-scale basis. If accessible land exists that can support more people than live there, then, given their customs and technology, the population grows and fills out the usable area until there is no longer surplus land available. Therefore, the conventional arguments for the superiority of exclusive control over absolutely common property apply to land on the relevant, large scale. Social institutions reflect this elementary circumstance in accordance with the survival pressures mentioned above. Almost everywhere, each group lived on territory on which it had exclusive rights to hunt, fish, gather, or garden. Neighboring groups either accepted these territorial boundaries peaceably or fought. In either case, the boundaries were usually reasonably well defined at any given time, even if they were impermanent. . . .

. . . Groups of primitive peoples differed . . . in the rights of households and individuals versus those of the tribe, district, village, or band. Either the people held and used the territory in common, or households and single persons held separate parcels, or, most often, some combination of the two existed. A similar state of affairs existed (and was observed) with respect to other types of property, such as food, shelter, and clothing.

Single parcels of land for households made sense if a parcel had a sufficiently reliable supply of food to provide a significant part of the household's subsistence in a season of scarcity and if there were no economies of scale to larger parcels used in common for food. Common property for the group made sense if either of these criteria failed to hold. In this connection, one can view a tribe's subsistence activity as an enterprise analogous to a firm. Under some circumstances, the minimum efficient size of the enterprise was the household, under other circumstances, it was a band of families or the tribe; there were economies of scale to the enterprise up to that size.

Moreover, the minimum efficient size of the enterprise could vary according to the specific hunting or gathering activity, and the allocation of rights could, and usually did, vary accordingly. For some activities, the households had their own parcels, whereas for other activities they acted communally over the group territory and disregarded the boundaries of individual parcels. There were also variations among groups in the type or degree of private property in the food itself once taken (within the group it might vary by the time of year or type of food resource). . . .

## II. The Efficient-Sized Enterprise

A single household could subsist on a fixed parcel if the relevant food resources were distributed in a relatively fixed, predictable manner over the tribal territory. In some cases, small game, fish, and so forth were distributed in fixed ways among the parcels so that one household's takings did not appreciably affect the resources available to other households. Further, there was no advantage to common or shared rights to the yields of different parcels because the variability of yield either was offsetting among the different resources within a parcel or, if not, was correlated among different parcels. Where these attributes held approximately true, the well-known incentive advantages of private property dominated, and one would expect to see separate household parcels. This conclusion applies with special force to horticulture. For garden plots, the advantages of a private property system seem especially clear.

By contrast, in many instances, either food resources could not be allocated efficiently through ownership of separate household parcels or their efficient taking required a group size larger than the household. These instances usually involved larger prey animals, such as large antelope or buffalo, but might also involve smaller prey or even seemingly nonmobile plant foods. Regarding either land or prey, the following attributes of the resource or technology favored common property over private property rights: (1) the low predictability of prey or plant location within the tribal territory; (2) the public-good aspect of information about the location of this kind of unpredictable food resource; (3) the high variance of the individual's success because of 1, 2, or other circumstances beyond the individual's control; (4) the superior productivity of group hunting techniques, such as driving prey into ambush or over a cliff; (5) the safety from large predators, especially when bringing home the product of a successful trip out. These attributes occurred in various combinations in the different groups. The first, second, and fourth were pertinent to the balance of advantage between common property and private property in land in different groups. The second, third, fourth, and fifth were pertinent to the corresponding balance in already taken food.

The first attribute – low predictability of location – was important for major food sources such as buffalo or other migratory animals. As a general rule, such animals appeared only in one season and were not the group's sole source of food. When they migrated into a tribe's territory, they were plentiful for a time but did not stay in or around any one location. Hunters could take them freely, subject to the limits of their technology and ability, until the animals left the territory. As Demsetz points out, "The value of establishing boundaries to private hunting territories is thus reduced by the relatively high cost of preventing the animals from moving to adjacent parcels." Indeed, sometimes there was arguably no value at all in establishing such boundaries. In some cases, because of a group's primitive hunting technologies and their dependence on other food sources in winter (which limited expansion of their population), there was no appreciable depletion of the herds of migratory animals; that is, there was no appreciable negative externality of hunting. (The buffalo on the great plains is an obvious example.) Moreover, these circumstances in no way affected the balance between the incentive to hunt effectively or to shirk. This balance depended, instead, on property rights in the animals *after* a successful hunt, that is, on the response of custom to the balance of the other listed factors.

The second attribute – the public-good aspect of information – existed in those cases where the group could not easily locate a herd of migratory game or another food source. Coordinated searching and sharing the information gained would then produce better total results for the group than would an individual's solitary tracking or information. Where this attribute was not present, the balance of considerations often favored private ownership and nonsharing of the food. But sharing information and coordinating searches meant that all participants had a joint marginal product not solely attributable to the successful hunter. Accordingly, some method of sharing the food would provide incentives to more effective effort and tactics. Sharing would also promote individual specialization by comparative advantage: that is, the best trackers might not be those most skilled at closing for the kill. One would therefore expect a tendency to find effort-inducing sharing rules for these cases, taking due account of other circumstances.

The third attribute – the high variance of hunting or gathering success – sometimes implied a high risk of starvation. It also meant that the successful hunter or gatherer sometimes had more food than one household could consume before the food spoiled due to the lack of a technology for preserving it. Where the success of different households was random and uncorrelated, sharing would reduce appreciably the variance for the group: that is, common ownership or a practice of equivalent effect would reduce it.

The fourth attribute – the superior productivity of group hunting techniques – is logically similar to the second. As in that case, one would expect the results of the hunt to be shared. Whereas the second attribute would apply only to migratory animals or to plant foods that had to be searched out each year, group hunting was also productive for game such as rabbits, which were widely distributed and could be reliably found on each household's private land, if private land existed in the group. In that case, a group that otherwise respected separate household plots for other purposes might join in a group hunt and share the results.

The fifth attribute – safety from predators – was particularly relevant in Africa. Game taken in a successful hunt had to be carried back to the household or group camping place, a dangerous enterprise better performed by a group. As in the case of tracking information, a consideration of the incentives indicates the appropriateness of sharing the results of the hunt with those who cooperate in bringing it home.

## III. Some Examples

The most striking examples of aboriginal property rights are the cases of those tribes that have separate household parcels of land (private real estate) in winter but not in summer. The best-known cases are the Bushmen of the Kalahari desert in Africa and the Penobscot, Montagnais, Naskapi, and other nearby tribes living in the northeastern U.S. woodlands, Quebec, and western Labrador. In both these cases, food was relatively scarce in winter, and the best chances of survival were gained by solitary or familial hunting and gathering. Family property boundaries were well defined.

The Bushmen adjusted the family properties, which were not heritable, from year to year. They had no horticulture at any time of the year. Food location and scarcity in winter favored private property. In the winter, game was relatively small, territorial rather than migratory, and distributed fairly evenly. They knew the distribution of plant foods at the beginning of winter, and they delimited the family parcels in such a way as to give every family a good chance of making it through the winter. As a matter of custom, households scrupulously respected each others' boundaries and rights to game.

In summer, food was generally more plentiful, and the Bushmen could efficiently indulge their preference for bringing their families together in bands. Larger, migratory game and any available water favored group cooperation. Sharing game-tracking information (and information about plants), coordinating hunting plans, and occasional group hunting, all involved a large minimum-efficient group size. There was a public-good aspect to maintaining waterholes and locating those that had recently received rain. If a single hunter took a large game animal, the tribe had no technology to preserve the meat; therefore, it would spoil unless shared. As noted above, bringing meat safely back to camp was a group enterprise. Although the successful hunter "owned" the meat, he was obligated to share it according to a set of customary rules that rewarded those who contributed. By contrast, plants gathered by each family belonged to that family alone.

The native tribes in northeastern North America shared this seasonal pattern of land use. The family parcels of land were comparatively permanent and generally heritable. Their concept of private property (including personal property such as food, canoes, and implements), however, was a more circumscribed case than with the Bushmen. In the value structure of these tribes, the problem of variable food supplies outweighed incentive effects, *to be productive* so sharing and rent-free lending were generally practiced. . . . .

Examining the aboriginal peoples studied in this article, there is a rule for the hunters and gatherers that appears to be universally applicable: wherever the advantages of group searching and hunting were appreciable, they dominated every other consideration. In these cases, a lineage group, band, or village held common access, and the private property rights of "nuclear" families were irrelevant until the game was taken. Almost all American Indian tribes practiced group hunting over the entire tribal territory even if private property in land existed for other food sources. Also, in those areas where game still existed at the time the African peoples were studied, most practiced some form of group hunting. Sometimes the right to hunt on specific land was held by large lineage groups and at other times by the king or chief for the entire tribe or district.

## IV. Horticulture and Property Rights

As there was for hunting and gathering, there is a rule for horticulture and agriculture that appears to be universally applicable: wherever either appeared, each household or narrow kinship group had private property in the crop, which also meant, at least temporarily, in the land. This, in conjunction with the opposite tendency in the case of hunting rights, offers the clearest systematic confirmation . . . that the structure of rights tends to respond to economic incentives.

In most observed cases of horticulture prior to European contact, the aboriginals did not maintain or improve soil fertility. . . . Because they lacked such techniques, these groups moved periodically or used lengthy periods of fallowing land to enrich the soil for further cultivation. In any case, with no way for the individual household to improve the land's fertility, a right to inherit or keep the land for long periods would have no economic consequence. By contrast, in those cases where an aboriginal people discovered fertilization the right to inherit would provide a positive incentive to maintain the soil's fertility, so that heritability would serve the best interests of the tribe.

In all cases, the right to use a given plot for a full crop cycle, to own its produce, and to keep it for several cycles (if the family expended the labor to clear it) held obvious economic advantages. A family with exclusive rights to the crop (usufruct rights) will be more likely to effectively perform the efforts of clearing, preparing the ground, planting, harvesting, and guarding the plot (against birds, rodents, and other creatures that might damage it).

. . .

Several North American tribes domesticated food crops and also possessed some variant of either temporary or long-term property rights in land.[1] . . . The Ojibwa in eastern sub-Arctic Canada did not domesticate the wild rice they harvested, but they did possess private plots in the wild rice beds, where they invested in temporary improvements to increase their yields.

In two exceptional North American cases – the Penobscot of the northeast and the Natchez of the southeast – the tribes practiced horticulture but had little or no private rights to the crops. The Penobscot worked individual garden plots but had to share food on demand with anyone who "needed" it. The Natchez managed the entire crop cycle as a communal effort and shared the produce.

In Africa, private property was also generally the rule for horticultural land, although there existed a rich variety in the details and scope of the rights . . .

Private property in land was found much less frequently among people without horticulture. Two notable instances – the Hupa of California and the northwest coast tribes – strongly emphasized private property and were relatively prosperous, as one would expect. They had family property rights in the superior fishing, hunting, and gathering sites and in personal property, which included slaves. The emphasis on family property, ostentation, and social standing probably reduced population pressure: food and artifacts were plentiful.

A great diversity of household rights within group territories has been observed in aboriginal humans. It is similar to what is observed among birds and many other animals. It reflects the similar pressures that sometimes favor a separate territory for each mating pair and in other cases favor group territories. Another parallelism is that some of the variations in observed practices have no obvious relation to survival pressures; in apparently similar circumstances, different species sometimes resolve the issue differently.

# V. Conclusion

This article broadly confirms the conjectures . . . that the structure of property rights will usually reflect economic advantage in those cases where the balance of advantage is clear. A nuanced and detailed picture emerges from the data, one that could scarcely be foreseen when reflecting on just one or two cases. Within each culture, not only do property rights vary among kinds of property, but, in the case of land, they vary according to the use, resources, or circumstances involved. . . . I do not find that private property rights for individual families would always be advantageous were it not for the costs of creating and enforcing them. Instead, I find that economic advantage sometimes rested clearly and positively with group exploitation of its entire territory. It was not unusual for families to have private property in land with recognized boundaries for one food resource but not another.

Indeed, almost all aboriginal peoples engaged in group hunting, fishing, or gathering in their common territory without regard to any individual household's property rights in the land for other purposes. This practice and the exclusiveness of group territories were the most widespread features of aboriginal property rights.

Private property in food and other personal property was the norm. There were occasional exceptions, usually where sharing provided social insurance against localized famine, that is, as a means of reducing variance to people who were understandably risk averse. In these and other cases, the risk of famine tipped the balance in favor of common property in land. Survival pressure, however, sometimes led families to separate and subsist on individual parcels of land, whether or not they viewed them as strictly private property.

Finally, the most important finding is that those people who engaged in horticulture or agriculture generally tended to have private property rights (either temporary or long term) in the use of land for a crop. These rights were, in some cases, heritable, and this attribute prevailed most reliably in those few groups that knew how to maintain and improve soil fertility. These findings provide food for thought about the probable interactions among the various influences in neolithic times that led to the emergence of property rights in our own and other societies.

## Note

1. These included, among others, the Pueblos, the Mohave of the southwest, the Hidatsa and Mandan of the Great Plains, the eastern woodland tribes such as the Iroquois, and the Creek of the southeast.

## Bibliography

Demsetz, Harold. "Toward a Theory of Property Rights." *American Economic Review Papers and Proceedings* 57 (1967): 347–73.

. . .

# 28

## Property in Land

### *Robert C. Ellickson*

### EDITOR'S INTRODUCTION

Perhaps the most fundamental issue regarding property rights is whether land should be owned privately or communally. This issue has been central to the competing ideologies of the 20th century – capitalism and communism. Not only is physical productivity affected by this choice, but also community and privacy. Robert Ellickson explores this issue, both theoretically and historically. Private ownership of land reduces the costs of collective decision making and monitoring. Collective ownership is viable in the long run only when interests are homogeneous and/or there is a clear hierarchy of control. This paper shows how the reality of self-interest determines the nature of the basic institutions of society. It provides a very deep explanation for why there is private property in land and how it affects other social institutions.

There is nothing which so generally strikes the imagination, and engages the affections of mankind, as the right of property; or that sole and despotic dominion which one man claims and exercises over the external things of the world, in total exclusion of the right of any other individual in the universe. . . . William Blackstone, *Commentaries* (1766)

The proletariat will use its political supremacy to wrest, by degrees, all capital from the bourgeoisie, to centralize all instruments of production in the hands of the State, i.e., of the proletariat organized as the ruling class. . . .

[I]n the most advanced countries, the following [measures] will be pretty generally applicable
1. Abolition of property in land. . . .
3. Abolition of all right of inheritance. . . .

Karl Marx and Friedrich Engels, *The Communist Manifesto* (1848)

## Introduction

Because human beings are fated to live mostly on the surface of the earth, the pattern of entitlements to use land is a central issue in social organization. As the epigraphs suggest, this issue has been the subject of fierce ideological controversy. Blackstone's paean to private property comports with the mainstream Anglo-American exaltation of decentralized ownership of land. This vision underlies the Homestead Acts, the Jeffersonian wish for a polity of

yeoman farmers, and the American dream of homeownership. Defenders of private ownership of land argue that it promotes individual liberty, political stability, and economic pros-
perity. . . .

To commentators such as Marx and Engels, by contrast, the creation of private property
in land is a fount of evils, particularly inequality in wealth and the splintering of more organic
communities into atomized, untrusting social environments of individual competition. The
vision of collective living on shared land has had a broad and enduring appeal. It has
inspired, among others, the Protestant sectarians, secular kibbutzniks, and counterculture
experimentalists who have founded intentional communities. During the past century, skeptics
of private property in land have come into power in a number of nation-states. In Israel,
where the prevailing philosophy holds that land should belong collectively to the Jewish
nation, 93% of the land area is state owned; the Israeli Basic Law of Lands prohibits the
government from transferring any of it except under special circumstances. Hewing to the
program of Marx and Engels, Stalin collectivized Russian agriculture from 1929 to 1933 at
the price of some nine million lives. Drawing on the same inspiration, Mao began China's
Great Leap Forward in 1957, precipitating a famine that killed some 20 million. . . . Beyond
dispute, botched land policies have been the chief domestic source of human woe during the
past century.

This Article has four aims. First, and most conventionally, it aspires to identify and
explore fundamental issues of land ownership – the rules that establish the foundation of
virtually all human activity. . . . By staying with basics, the Article strives to demonstrate that
customary land rules are not a shapeless jumble, but instead form an unauthored strategy
that cleverly allocates a prized resource with confoundingly complex attributes.

Second, the Article brings to bear on this policy terrain a particular theoretical perspective,
namely the rational-actor model that many social scientists employ. . . . . .

Third, to keep the theory grounded, the Article amasses historical evidence on the evolution of land institutions. . . .

Fourth, and finally, from both theory and evidence, the Article derives and advances a
number of positive and normative propositions about the evolution of land regimes. The
most general of the positive propositions, *the efficiency thesis*, asserts that *land rules within a close-
knit group evolve so as to minimize its members' costs.* This upbeat proposition envisions that people
on the ground recognize that property in land is a positive-sum game and play it cooperatively. For example, this thesis asserts, contrary to Garrett Hardin's analysis in the *Tragedy of
the Commons*, that a traditional village's grazing commons is unlikely to be tragic.

In a seminal article on the economics of property rights, Harold Demsetz propounded a
related hypothesis that should be distinguished at the outset from the efficiency thesis
advanced in this Article. Demsetz theorized that "property arrangements in all societies
evolve efficiently in response to changes in technology, demand, and other economic conditions." As his major example, Demsetz cited anthropological evidence that the Indians of
Canada's Labrador Peninsula established exclusive hunting territories for fur-bearing animals
only after the development of the commercial fur trade with Europeans had made the costs
of establishing land boundaries worthwhile. Demsetz's hypothesis predicts that *all* land
regimes evolve in a cost-minimizing direction; this Article embraces the same substantive
prediction, but restricts its compass to the land rules that *close-knit groups* generate. A close-
knit group is a social entity within which power is broadly dispersed and members have
continuing face-to-face interactions with one another. By providing members with both the

information and opportunities they need to engage in informal social control, conditions in such groups are conducive to cooperation. Because the Labradoran tribe that Demsetz discussed was a close-knit group, that particular example supports both versions of the efficiency thesis. However, when a nation-state makes laws, or a strong group overpowers others, Demsetz's thesis anticipates the emergence of efficient land institutions, whereas this Article does not, because the individuals making the rules are not closely knit with those who must obey them. Historical examples such as the institution of slavery and Stalin's dispossession of Ukrainian kulaks pose problems for Demsetz's thesis but not for the one advanced here.

This Article differs from Demsetz's in another significant respect. While Demsetz focused strictly on efficiency, the analysis below addresses other vital human concerns conventionally regarded as noneconomic: liberty, privacy, equality, and community. As Part III's case studies of the kibbutzim and other intentional residential communes make plain, rules of property in land importantly influence nonmaterial aspects of life.

Because the journey has unavoidable convolutions, a rough roadmap is in order. The first three Parts of the Article analyze, in increasing depth, the situations in which it is best to put land in the hands of a "private," as opposed to a "public," owner. This is the issue on which Blackstone and Marx were at loggerheads. These portions of the analysis identify major advantages in private ownership of land, but they also point out desirable attributes of group-owned property that may be decisive in some contexts. In Part IV, the Article addresses the initial bundling of land entitlements . . . and their alienability. . . . The Conclusion summarizes the main propositions and commends attention to the history of land institutions.

# I. The Case for Individual Ownership of Land

The issue that Blackstone and Marx contested – the merits of the institution of private property in land – warrants the priority they gave it. Because the term *private property*, and its counterpart *public property*, are both formless composites, the first order of business is to sharpen the vocabulary of land institutions. Coordination among land users becomes more difficult as the number of users rises; it is therefore useful to subclassify land regimes according to the number of persons who own routine privileges to enter and use a parcel. *Private property* conventionally refers to a regime in which no more than a small number of persons have access to a resource. When more than a small number do, *public property* is present.

## A. THREE SIMPLE LAND REGIMES

Suppose that a close-knit group of 25 adults, identified by letters $A$ through $Y$, was to control the land within the perimeter of [a] large square. . . . Suppose further that this group had to choose to govern this territory either as open-access property, group property, or individual property – regimes that it could establish either by formal rule or informal practice. Recall that under the first of these three alternatives, the open-access regime, anyone at all, including persons other than $A$ . . . $Y$, would be completely privileged to enter and use the land within the perimeter. Both theory and practice suggest that this regime would likely be beset by tragedy.

Under the second alternative, group ownership, the 25 members would jointly own both privileges to use the land within the perimeter and rights to exclude all others from it. The 25 would manage the land collectively by means of some relatively democratic governance system. . . .

To create the third regime, individual ownership, *A . . . Y* would subdivide all of the land within the square into 25 parcels, one of which would be assigned to each member. . . . At this point in the inquiry, an individual owner of a parcel can be regarded as having unfettered privileges of use as well as absolute rights to exclude.

The rational-actor model assumes that an individual calculatingly pursues his self-interest. This implies that a member of a social group will be tempted at times to undertake a land activity that is individually rewarding but socially wasteful. Whatever the land regime, an individual's self-interested, opportunistic act will create a *deadweight loss* whenever the costs it inflicts on others exceed the individual's benefits from the act. When land is group owned, each group member may be tempted to grab too many of the parcel's assets, to pollute the property with wastes, and to shirk from useful work that would enhance the land's value. Conversely, when land is individually owned, a self-interested owner may be tempted to use it without regard to the costs and benefits conferred on neighbors or others. Individuals may be able to reduce deadweight losses by (1) enforcing existing property rights; (2) transferring property rights to better managers; or (3) redefining property rights so as to create better-tailored incentives for appropriate economic activity. Each of these responses, however, would give rise to *transaction costs*. Different land regimes therefore involve different combinations of transaction costs and deadweight losses. A change in land rules is *efficient* when it reduces the sum of these two sorts of costs.

## B. SMALL EVENTS: THE RELATIVE EASE OF MONITORING BOUNDARIES

### 1. The genius of individual land ownership

In his classic work, Demsetz showed that individual ownership of land completely internalizes to owners the effects of what this Article calls small events. In essence, the parcelization of land is a relatively low-transaction cost method of inducing people to "do the right thing" with the earth's surface, the vernacular for avoiding deadweight losses. Compared to group ownership, not to mention an open-access regime, private property tends best to equate the personal product of an individual's small actions with the social product of those actions.

Suppose, for example, that the small event was to be the cultivation of a garden of tomato plants. Under the group ownership regime. . . . the 25 co-owners would be forced to use their internal governance mechanisms to prevent deadweight losses in the growing and harvesting of the tomatoes. They might succeed in doing this, but only by incurring the transaction costs of monitoring potential shirkers and grabbers within the group's membership.

For three basic reasons, monitoring tends to be cheaper under the individual ownership regime. . . . First, self-control by one person . . . by means of his own central nervous system is much simpler than the multiperson coordination entailed in intragroup monitoring. When land uses have no spillover effects, individual ownership directly and precisely punishes land misuse and rewards productive labor.

Second, individual ownership not only greatly reduces the number of instances in which people have to be watched, but it also makes that task simpler when it must be performed. . . . A landowner must . . . be on the lookout for wasteful grabbing by trespassers who enter land without authorization. *A key advantage of individual land ownership is that detecting the presence of a trespasser is much less demanding than evaluating the conduct of a person who is privileged to be where he is.* Monitoring boundary crossings is easier than monitoring the behavior of persons situated inside boundaries. For this reason, managers are paid more than night watchmen. To illustrate, suppose that the 25 owners . . . wanted to deter a deviant member from stealing tomatoes from one of their common gardens. Because each member would have the privilege of entering all gardens, the group might have to assign overseers to scrutinize the minute-to-minute behavior of all persons present in crop-growing areas to guard against pilferage. If the tomato garden were individually owned, by contrast, the sole owner would merely need to watch for an unauthorized entry. Upon seeing a trespasser cross a physically marked boundary, the owner in the usual case could expel him without having to marshal evidence of misconduct beyond the unauthorized entry itself.

[Furthermore], an individual landowner is much more highly motivated than a group member to police boundaries or to carry out any other sort of monitoring function. A sole owner bears the entirety of any loss stemming from his slack oversight, whereas a group member bears only a fraction. The institution of private land ownership thus not only simplifies monitoring tasks, but also tends to ensure that those tasks are in the hands of conscientious agents.

## 2. Technologies for marking, defending, and proving boundaries

Because private property in land necessitates the policing of boundaries, advances in surveying and fencing techniques may enhance the comparative efficiency of the institution. Preliterate societies developed many simple technologies that a landowner could use to detect and deter trespassers. During Hanimurabi's reign around 1750 B.C., pegs were used to mark borders. Cairns, dikes, and stone walls are even more graphic and immovable. In social environments in which neighbors are inclined to cooperate, physically marked boundaries, if uncontroversially placed, are largely self-enforcing. A four year old can understand the convention that one does not cross a marked boundary. By contrast, the internal work rules that govern behavior within group-owned land are not nearly as plain to observers.

For millennia, absentee owners have employed simple technologies such as hedges, moats, and impregnable fencing to keep out persons and animals that do not respect boundaries. In addition, domesticated dogs, especially ones that instinctively bark at or attack strangers, are superb boundary defenders. By contrast, dogs are quite useless in enforcing a group's internal rules of conduct. Can a dog be trained to bark when a familiar person has shirked or pilfered? A modern-day landowner intent on detecting boundary violations can resort, in lieu of a dog, to an inexpensive electronic motion detector. "Shirking detectors" – devices that would sound an alarm when a worker was simply going through the motions – have yet to be invented.

In sum, a shift from group to individual ownership of land substitutes the relatively cheap systems of self-control and boundary monitoring for the relatively costly system of pervasive intragroup monitoring. In contexts where the satisfaction of basic human needs entails the coordination of many small events – such as the planting and harvesting of crops, caring for children and animals, and maintaining dwellings and other structures – the parcelization of land is a major institutional achievement.

Individual ownership does, however, generate some new transaction costs, mainly those arising from the proliferation of boundaries and ownership entities. . . . Disputes may arise over both the location of these boundaries and the identities of parcel owners. Because land boundaries are human artifacts, a group must develop rules concerning adequate means of delineating parcels and proving ownership. Partly to reduce outlays for erecting indestructible boundary monuments, ancient groups that had developed written languages strove to establish authoritative off-site records of boundaries and owners. Some of the earliest surviving human texts, the Mesopotamian kudurrus dating from c. 2500 B.C., record private land transfers on stone stelae about two feet high; these stones eventually came to be kept in temples. . . .

The efficiency thesis predicts that innovations in technologies for marking, defending, and proving boundaries lead to more parcelization because they reduce the transaction costs of private property regimes. According to this view, for example, Glidden's invention of barbed wire in 1874 should have stimulated more subdivision of rangeland in the American West. And this indeed appears to have occurred. . . . Conversely, the viability of group ownership might be enhanced by the advent of inexpensive video cameras or other technologies for monitoring behavior within a group setting.

## C. Medium events: A simple way to promote cooperative relations

A second major argument for private property in land rest[s] on the social dynamics of medium events. Suppose . . . the proposed construction of a small dam. The parcelization of group land . . . would greatly reduce the number of persons concerned with this event. In the democratic group-ownership situation . . . co-owners would have to become knowledgeable about the proposed dam in order to help decide whether it was a cost-justified project. In the parcelized regime, by contrast, only the substantially affected landowners . . . would have to be involved in the externality adjustment process. Embracing the consensus position that transaction costs tend to increase with the number of individuals involved, . . . land parcelization [has] the virtue of increasing small number situations. . . .

Parcelization also relegates the settlement of disputes arising out of medium events to those persons most likely to be informed about the matter in controversy. A sole owner of a land parcel is apt to have better knowledge of its immediate environment than virtually anyone else does. For example, if a dam were proposed for a site on parcel M, $M$ and $N$, the owners of the only two parcels substantially affected, probably could appraise the total costs and benefits of the dam better than could a random pair of members in the $A$ . . . $Y$ group.

In short, for activities that result in mostly small and medium events, individual ownership is better than both open-access and group ownership for minimizing the sum of deadweight losses and transaction costs. According to the efficiency thesis, this insight explains why family farming is ubiquitous, why collectivized agriculture almost always fails, and why virtually no dwelling units are shared by groups as large as 25. Indeed, the historical record supports the following private-property thesis: *a close-knit group virtually always entitles its members to own, as private property, lands used for dwellings, crops, and other intensive activities.*

# II. The Advantages of Group Ownership of Land

The discussion up to this point has given short shrift to the merits of group (and other forms of public) ownership of land. . . . [O]ne can enrich [the] analysis by explicitly incorporating the possibilities of increasing returns to scale and the desirability of spreading risks. The histories of some famous pioneer settlements, presented in the middle of this Part, will illustrate these aspects of land institutions.

## A. WHEN RETURNS INCREASE WITH PARCEL SIZE

Bigger land parcels are sometimes better. As tracts increase in area, the costs of fencing and other forms of perimeter monitoring drop per acre enclosed. This mathematical relationship has prompted many traditional societies to graze livestock on expansive group-owned pastures. A large territory also permits a landowner to use more specialized equipment and workers and to marshal gangs of workers for projects for which returns to scale exist.

### 1. Efficient boundaries

Decisions on where to set land boundaries are fiendishly complex because most tracts of land are suited to multiple uses for which scale efficiencies vary. For example, suppose that the optimal territorial scale of the Coase College campus, given its educational purposes, is 200 acres. But the optimal scale for exploitation of the oil pool beneath Coase is 7,777 acres. And when Coase rents living space to a sophomore, an optimal space is a one-half undivided interest in a 150-square-foot dormitory room. Clearly, a single set of all-purpose horizontal boundary lines cannot be optimally scaled for all purposes.

This sort of conundrum is familiar to organization theorists. A business firm has an organizational perimeter beyond which it shifts from internal hierarchy to external contract. Oliver Williamson refers to the challenge of locating a firm's perimeters as the problem of "efficient boundaries." The identical issue arises, and far more tangibly, when land resources are divided up among the "firms" (landowners) of the "land industry."

In societies that commodify land, the boundaries of private parcels are determined largely by forces of supply and demand. Land rules permitting, landowners can subdivide existing parcels and assemble separate ones together. Of course, governments may constrain this contracting process, for better or worse, with measures such as zoning regulations that set minimum sizes for parcels. Loosely speaking, unconstrained markets can be expected to generate parcels of "middling" size – that is, territorial chunks that are overly large for some activities, too small for others, but not bad on average in light of the range and relative importance of valued land activities.

Because boundary locations are compromises, landowners can be expected to develop internal institutions for coordinating more fine-grained activities as well as external institutions for coordinating matters better handled on a larger territorial scale. Illustrative internal institutions are a household's system for allocating private bedrooms and an employer's system for assigning spaces in its employee parking lot. External institutions designed to deter negative spillover effects of land activities include, for example, norms of neighborliness, common-law nuisance rules, and government land-use regulations. In addition, neighboring landowners may join together by custom or contract to carry out activities that require territories larger than their parcels. Farmers jointly pastured their livestock on medieval open fields. A century ago, Midwestern farm families joined together in "threshing rings" when their grain was ripe.

The term *boundary* usually refers to a horizontal line beyond which a landowner generally switches from internal management to inter-neighbor coordination. *General-purpose boundaries*, the ones described in deeds when land is conveyed, define the territory from which owners typically attempt to exclude unconsented entrants. Other boundaries, while less significant, are also worthy of attention. When a landowner carves out a sub-area within his parcel for special use, internal special-purpose boundaries mark its limits; they define the edges of, for example, dormitory rooms, assigned library carrels, and road easements. When neighboring landowners are joined in a property owners' association or a municipality, the territorial limits of these organizations are external *special-purpose boundaries*.

A landowner who shifts a general-purpose boundary outward increases his burdens of internal management but decreases his burdens of external coordination. Locating boundaries requires sensitivity both to efficiencies of territorial scale and to the transaction costs inherent in a cluster of internal and external institutions.

## 2. Large events

... [A] large event ... [qualifies] enthusiasm for land parcelization. For example, if the large event ... were to be a smoky fire on parcel M, the transaction costs of large-number coordinations might prevent the many affected parcel owners from cooperating to resolve the dispute through some external institution. By contrast, if the governing body of the [collective] group [*A* ... *Y*] already had controls in place to monitor internal small and medium events, it might be able to respond to this large event much more expeditiously than the diffuse group of individual neighbors could. When a group's system of internal social control is itself characterized by increasing returns to scale, the identity of the land regime that best minimizes costs depends in part on what sorts of events – small, medium, or large – carry the highest stakes for group welfare.

The case for private ownership of farms and homesteads rests on the plausible assumption that vital agricultural, construction, homemaking, and child-rearing activities entail mostly small and medium events. For the reasons just suggested, however, industrial activities that cause local air pollution might be better placed on large tracts which, because of the investment required, are likely to be group-owned. Group ownership does not necessarily imply government ownership, of course. The sorry environmental records of federal land agencies and Communist regimes are a sharp reminder that governments are often particularly inept managers of large tracts. Large events are inherently difficult to regulate. Identifying the institutions that govern them best – or, more bluntly, least badly – should be an exercise in experience, not logic. This points up the value of history. Under what circumstances, if any, have pioneers establishing land regimes from scratch chosen to own land collectively?

## B. Three pioneer settlements

Three of the most famous remote habitations in U.S. history were the Jamestown settlement of 1607, the Plymouth settlement of 1620, and the Mormon settlement at Salt Lake in 1847. Each of these pioneer groups journeyed to the frontier laden with cultural predispositions and an ongoing hierarchical structure that had enabled group movement in the first instance. The members of these groups nevertheless possessed a relatively high degree of freedom in deciding how to allocate property rights in the lands they were seizing from the indigenous tribes. In each case, the settlers initially opted for group ownership, but after a few years switched to private ownership of intensively used lands.

### 1. Jamestown

The Jamestown colony, a star-crossed business venture of the London-based Virginia Company, was the first permanent English settlement in North America. Partly because the Company's investors envisioned that group living would aid in defense against enemies, the settlers' first major undertakings after landing in 1607 were a fort and palisade. During Jamestown's early years, the colonists suffered horrendously from starvation, tribal raids, and diseases such as dysentery, typhoid, and malaria. Sixty-five percent of the 108 members of the initial party died within the first year. The Company's efforts to replenish the population were repeatedly frustrated. During the winter of 1609, the most severe period of starvation, the colony's population dropped from 500 to 60. An Indian raid in 1622 killed 347, a minor fraction of the 3,000 deaths at Jamestown in 1619-22.

Jamestown was managed quite hierarchically during its early years, as its investors had intended. Land was held as a collective asset. Although many settlers were bound to the Company by indentures, each was guaranteed an equal share of the common output regardless of the amount of work personally contributed. John Smith, the Colony's most effective leader, organized the settlers into work teams of a dozen or more to erect buildings and palisades, dig a well, and plant 100 acres of corn. When Smith was not in charge, however, the hallmark of the Jamestown colony was idleness. To the puzzlement of historians, the starving settlers shirked from catching fish and growing food. The most enduring image of Jamestown dates from May 1611, when Sir Thomas Dale found the inhabitants at "their daily and usuall workes, bowling in the streetes."

The first settlers at Jamestown anticipated that land would eventually be parceled out to households, and this outcome was indeed gradually achieved over a period of a dozen years. Small gardens appeared within the first year or two. Then, in 1614, Governor Dale began assigning three-acre plots to settlers. According to Captain John Smith, this improved productivity at least sevenfold:

> When our people were fed out of the common store, and laboured jointly together, glad was he could slip from his labour, or slumber over his taske he cared not how, nay, the most honest among them would hardly take so much true paines in a weeke, as now for themselves they will doe in a day, neither cared they for the increase, presuming that howsoever the harvest prospered, the generall store must maintain them, so that wee reaped not so much Corne from the labours of thirtie, as now three or foure doe provide for themselves. To prevent which, Sir Thomas Dale hath allotted every man three Acres of cleare ground. . . .

. . .

Agricultural productivity unquestionably improved at Jamestown as lands were privatized. By around 1620, farmers were energetically growing tobacco, a profitable export crop. Jamestown continued to be severely plagued by disease and Indian troubles, but no longer by laziness. In the 370 years since Jamestown residents first embraced the private farm, they have never reverted to collective crop growing.

## 2. Plymouth

The land story of the colony at Plymouth, Massachusetts parallels the history at Jamestown, except that events unfolded more briskly. To finance their voyage, the Pilgrims formed a joint stock company with London investors. At the investors' insistence, the settlers agreed to pool output, lands, capital, and profits during their first seven years abroad. From this "common stock," residents of the colony were to receive food and other necessities, and, at the end of the seven-year period, the land and other assets were to be "equally divided betwixt" the investors and settlers. The colonists initially complied with the spirit of this contract. Although they planted household gardens almost from the start, they collectivized initial field and livestock operations. The settlers had some agricultural successes, but they were unable to grow corn in their common field. Within six months of reaching Plymouth, almost one-half of the population had perished from disease.

In 1624 the Plymouth colonists deviated from the investors' plan and assigned each family from one to ten acres, depending on the number of family members. This greatly increased productivity.

. . .

## 3. Salt Lake City

In July of 1847 – two centuries after these colonial episodes and well into the industrial age – some 1,700 Mormons arrived at the Great Salt Lake Valley under the leadership of Brigham Young. Especially during the Mormons' first few years at Salt Lake, the theocracy assigned teams to a wide variety of public works projects, including a fort, irrigation canals, roads, and places of worship. . . . [The] settlers started with group ownership of land, but after a period began parceling out plots to individuals and households, a move that improved agricultural productivity. . . .

These events support the private-property thesis, but are unlikely to surprise anyone familiar with the history of collectivized agriculture. It is more intriguing to ask why the settlers declined to establish private property in croplands from the start. The prior section suggested one possibility. The pioneers at the three settlements may have started off with group-owned land in order to exploit returns to territorial scale presented by initial public works such as defensive palisades and, at Salt Lake, irrigation facilities. There is evidence, however, that high risks, not scale economies, were the main impetus for the initial collectivization of land at these outposts.

## C. Group ownership as a risk-spreading device

A sole landowner bears the entire risk that his land will be damaged, devalued, or unproductive. Group ownership, by contrast, pools risk. Because most individuals are risk-averse, the risk-spreading feature of group property is advantageous – even decisive in certain situations.

As alternatives to group ownership of property, a group may employ numerous other risk-spreading mechanisms, including reciprocal altruism within a family or social group, insurance markets, and government welfare programs. In comparison, group ownership of land is in most contexts a mediocre method of spreading losses. It concentrates group investments in a single, highly undiversified, asset. Moreover, for reasons presented in Part I, intensive uses are usually less efficiently conducted on group land than on private land, a fact that makes group land ownership a comparatively costly insurance vehicle.

The efficiency thesis predicts that group land ownership will be more prevalent in situations in which risks are high and a group cannot employ a superior insurance mechanism. The settlers of the three pioneer communities initially faced conditions of precisely this sort. That the risks were acute cannot be doubted. All three pioneer settlements were remote outposts, located weeks or months away from civilization. The first parties of settlers faced lethal dangers, including raids by Indians, infections from exotic diseases, and difficulties in learning how to farm in their strange environments. Remoteness precluded risk-spreading through multigenerational kinship networks, insurance markets, or government welfare programs. The settlers could spread risks only among themselves, and one option was to have a collective economy that guaranteed each member some share of total group output.

Risk analysis also suggests why the pioneers would begin to parcelize their lands after a period of time. Settlers would lower their probability estimates of disaster and be less attentive to risk-spreading as they gradually learned how to prevent tribal raids, avoid disease, and grow crops. Moreover, as the months passed, the settlers could develop more efficient social-insurance mechanisms, such as informal mutual-aid relationships, tithe-supported churches, and tax-supported governments. In sum, after a few years, the risk-spreading benefits of group land ownership would no longer outweigh its familiar shortcomings, such as the shirking that notably afflicted Jamestown and Plymouth. At that point, the settlers understandably would switch to private land tenure, the system that most cheaply induces individuals to accomplish small and medium events that are socially useful.

# III. Parceling Land Among Owners: Liberty, Privacy, Equality, and Community

To most observers, land policy involves much more than the seemingly bloodless considerations of cost-minimization and risk-spreading. The analysis so far misses, or at least submerges, why land tenure is an issue that sends people off to the barricades and into utopian experiments. Land rules literally set the physical platform for social and political institutions. Economists themselves agree that the evaluation of a land regime must go beyond its possible contributions to material well-being.

Commentators who unite in urging a broader inquiry are likely to disagree, however, on the identity of the other normative criteria to be considered. Classical liberals, for example, regard private property in land as an essential instrument for promoting political freedom, privacy, and self-determination. On the other hand, communitarians doubt if humans can flourish in atomized social environments. Communitarians value multi-stranded and enduring social relationships, something that group ownership of land can plausibly be thought to foster. Most communitarians are also egalitarians. Group ownership promises to help reduce differences in individuals' wealth and possibly in their status and power as well. ... In practice, a human group must make trade-offs between individual liberty and privacy on the one hand and community and equality on the other. Land tenure is a major battleground on which this conflict is resolved.

An overview of some notable communes will provide context for discussion of these aspects of land regimes. A commune is a residential settlement that is not kinship based and includes at least a dozen adults. Although a commune may allocate dwelling units to its members for their exclusive use, it carries out agricultural, industrial, and construction activities on group land that it governs through participatory processes. For a settlement to deserve the label, a commune's members must espouse an ideological commitment to community and equality, and, consistent with that ideology, distribute group largesse among themselves according to an egalitarian formula.

. . ..

## A. SOME INTENTIONAL COMMUNES

To give the promise of collective living a fair shake, one should examine voluntary communes, not ones created by state dictates. The two most enduring and robust communal systems in the last 500 years of Western history have been the little-known Hutterite colonies of the Great Plains and the familiar kibbutzim of Israel.

### 1. Hutterite Colonies

The Hutterites are a sect of Anabaptist Protestants. ... In a quest for religious freedom in the mid-1800s, several hundred Hutterites migrated to the northern Great Plains of the United States and Canada. Since their arrival, the Hutterites have prospered. Their current total population of some 28,000 is divided among several hundred scattered agricultural settlements, each on a spread of several thousand acres.

The Hutterites interpret the Bible as requiring the strict sharing of land and almost all products of labor. A Hutterite family has traditionally been allotted, however, some basic furniture, a bedroom, and a share of a sitting room. Hutterites eat meals in communal dining halls and hold church services every evening. By maintaining a Tyrolean-German dialect as their principal language, and by generally forbidding the use of radios and television sets, the Hutterites have substantially insulated themselves from outside influences.

As a Hutterite colony grows toward 120 members (including children), the group bifurcates. Members sign up, seniors first, to join either of two subgroups; lots are then drawn to determine which subgroup is to remain and which is required to leave to found a new colony. The Hutterites' population cap, forged out of centuries of experience, helps to keep their communities closely knit.

Hutterite communities are strongly hierarchical. Women cannot vote in assemblies, and leadership positions are allocated among males largely according to seniority. Six elders are at the apex of authority. . . .

## 2. Israeli kibbutzim

Kibbutzim, although much more widely known, are comparative upstarts dating only from 1909. With 400-500 members on average, kibbutzim are several times more populous than Hutterite colonies. Although almost all kibbutzim are involved in agriculture, many undertake industrial activities as well. The total kibbutz population in Israel doubled between 1951 and 1992, from 65,000 to 130,000. Nevertheless, the percentage of Israel's Jewish population living in these communities had declined by 1986 to 3.6%, well below the 1948 peak of 7.9%.

Kibbutzim were founded on a secular socialist ideology that still undergirds the movement; in some communities, however, religion has replaced socialism as the unifying creed. Kibbutzim vary significantly in their degree of commitment to sharing. The most ideological of the kibbutzim – those described below – are strongly committed to equal distribution of material wealth, a policy they pursue primarily through in-kind transfers.

The State of Israel, which is formally inhospitable to private land ownership, leases land to a kibbutz for a long renewable term at low rent. A kibbutz in turn typically allocates a separate dwelling unit of perhaps two or three bedrooms to each family, while operating a common dining hall and managing collectively the balance of its land. Social controls within a kibbutz support norms of work and cooperation. Agricultural productivity has often been higher on kibbutzim than on private farms in Israel.

All adult members of a kibbutz serve on its governing body, the general assembly, which meets roughly once a week. In sharp contrast to the Hutterites, kibbutzniks espouse equality between the sexes (although they fail to achieve it in practice). . . .

## B. SYSTEMS OF GOVERNANCE OF GROUP LAND ACTIVITIES

These two communal systems have had far more staying power than other intentional communities that have dotted the sweep of American history. An overview of methods of group governance can help reveal why the Hutterites and kibbutzniks have been relatively successful at perpetuating their institutions.

## 1. Hierarchy or democracy?

When many people use the same piece of land, tragedies of shirking and grabbing lurk. A group may of course be able to devise internal institutions for coping with these problems, but, at least according to the analysis in this Article up to this point, these mechanisms are likely to be far more costly than the simple monitoring systems associated with individual land ownership. From a transaction-cost perspective, a commune faces a choice between the Scylla of endless evening meetings and the Charybdis of an ever-increasing pile of unwashed dishes in the sink.

There are many mechanisms for governing behavior within the boundaries of group land. A commune by definition chooses the mechanism of participatory governance. At the opposite pole lies hierarchical governance by an autonomous chief executive. . . . [P]articipatory governance is most competitive with hierarchical governance when members of a group have completely homogeneous interests (as corporate shareholders generally do). When members have heterogeneous interests, they are more likely to delegate power to a manager who is able to act expeditiously and resist lobbying by members with selfish interests. A member may be especially amenable to relinquishing control to a hierarchy in a context where the threat of members' exits helps to keep managers responsive.

Historically, many huge tracts of land have been managed by an owner who hierarchically supervises a multitude of land users. Instances include plantations (such as Mount Vernon and Monticello), latifundia, agribusinesses, landlord-owned multifamily buildings, and corporate manufacturing plants. The survival of these arrangements indicates that, when returns to scale are available, an owner (or homogeneous set of owners) can profitably engage managers to monitor a maelstrom of potentially conflicting land activities. To be sure, these hierarchical forms of land governance have sometimes been oppressive, as slave plantations certainly were. . . .

On the other hand, a homogeneous group of concurrent landowners may well succeed at participatory governance, a process that it may adopt partly to enhance self-respect, equality, and other communitarian values. When the number of participant-owners can be counted on one hand, their decision making is likely to be highly informal. Although Anglo-American law provides standard-form governance vehicles for small groups of landowners, these forms are of little practical importance until the ownership group dissolves. A larger number of participating owners may formally organize themselves as, say, a partnership, corporation, cooperative, or municipality. Even when participant-owners are many, they may govern themselves more by an unwritten "custom of the manor" than by a written constitution.

## 2. Governance of communes

This background helps highlight the organizational difficulties that communards face. To be true to their egalitarian ideals, they must be willing to forego hierarchical governance and to bear the transaction costs of participatory democracy. As noted, the Hutterites hold plenary meetings on a daily basis, and most kibbutzim meet weekly. Both groups prefer to reach decisions by consensus, a time-consuming process. Because their meetings are frequent, the members can readily circulate information about individuals' prosocial and antisocial conduct, and summarily administer organizational sanctions such as negative gossip, ostracism, and expulsion.

The survival of the Hutterites and kibbutzim indicates that a voluntarily organized group may indeed succeed in cooperatively conducting agricultural, industrial, and construction activities on common land. Rather than being beset with shirking, the settlements of both groups are generally beehives of activity.

Has this been the triumph of a self-enforcing ideology? Utopians may dream of inculcating communitarian norms ever more deeply so that communards eventually cooperate in the absence of third-party monitoring and sanctioning. This appears indeed to be a dream. In the kibbutzim, the second generation has proved to be less ideologically committed than the founding generation. After hundreds of years of socialization, the Hutterites have not been able to dispense with their intrusive methods of social control.

... [T]o compete with other land-tenure regimes to which its members might exit, a commune [must] strive to reduce member heterogeneity, and thereby reduce the transaction costs of internal governance. The Hutterites and kibbutzniks both employ a number of devices to this end. Both generally distribute consumer goods on an all-or-nothing basis; either all households get an item, or none do. Efforts are made to keep housing of uniform quality. Tedious tasks are likely to be rotated among members (or, in kibbutzim, assigned to nonmembers such as Arabs or youthful volunteers from abroad). Using seniority or rotation rules to allocate leadership positions side-steps political battles (although it may also lead to less competent management). These strongly egalitarian policies increase homogeneity, but at a price. The absence of material incentives increases the need for pervasive controls against shirking, and may prompt the most skillful workers to consider pursuing greater rewards outside the commune.

To stem exodus, long-lasting communes require a member who departs, voluntarily or as a result of expulsion, to forfeit all, or almost all, of his claim to the group's joint assets – the social-insurance policy to which he may have contributed for years. By deterring exit, this forfeiture policy encourages members to make more conscientious use of voice in shaping community policy. Locking members together also materially motivates members to monitor each other. When group output is shared, the ground for a culture of watchfulness has been sown.

## C. Liberal values versus communitarian values

. . .

The debate over the relative merits of the social atmospheres of the commune and private household is one of the oldest in political theory. The ancient Greeks dwelt in family households on private lands. In the *Republic*, Plato envisioned an ideal state in which the class of guardians would merge both their households and property into a commune. In the *Politics*, Aristotle criticized Plato's scheme in language that foreshadowed the debates between the law-and-economics and critical legal studies camps:

> The hearer receives [Plato's ideas] gladly, thinking that everybody will feel towards everybody else some marvellous [sic] sense of fraternity – all the more as the evils now existing under ordinary forms of government (lawsuits about contracts, convictions for perjury, and obsequious flatteries of the rich) are denounced as due to the absence of a system of common property. None of these evils, however, is due to the absence of communism. They all arise from the wickedness of human nature. Indeed it is a fact of observation that those who own common property, and share in its management, are far more often at variance with one another than those who have property in severalty. . . .

To Aristotle, Plato's assertions of the atmospheric advantages of communal living are utopian. A commune may turn out to be a snakepit, not a love-fest.

. . . .

## D. Inferences from survivorship and migration

A nonparticipant must hesitate before evaluating abstractly the normative merits of a social arrangement as complex as a land regime. The most reliable evidence on this front consists of patterns of migration between different land regimes and of evolutionary changes within them. These patterns reveal how individuals and households actually make the tortured trade-offs between cost minimization, risk-spreading, liberty, privacy, equality, and community.

. . . .

When measured by survivorship criteria, communal regimes have generally fared poorly. Most migrants seem to regard the shortcomings of communes – perhaps too many meetings, or lack of privacy and personal autonomy – as outweighing the advantages of risk-spreading, solidarity, and ideological rectitude.

### 1. Survivorship rates

. . .

[I]n all eras, most communes have fizzled out within a few years. New Harmony, Indiana, dissolved only three years after Robert Owen's arrival in 1825. The Mormon United Order communities in Utah were ephemeral. A majority of the 120 Woodstock-Era communes . . . had lives of four years or less (although attrition rates fell with longevity). . . .

The short half-life of the voluntary commune contrasts sharply with the usual longevity of a farm community or small town voluntarily organized around private land. . . .

. . .

## IV. Standard Bundles of Land Rights: Of Fees and Usufructs

Decisions about other features of land regimes are as momentous as the choice between private and group entities as owners. A group that is willing to recognize private property in land must decide what standard bundle of rights to confer on a meritorious occupier of a part of its territory. By recognizing a standard land bundle, a group can simplify its members' interactions and transactions.

### A. A "BLACKSTONIAN" BUNDLE OF LAND ENTITLEMENTS

Because land entitlements are highly variegated, it is essential to start with concepts whose simplicity strikes the imagination. Because the epigraph from Blackstone invites it, Blackstonian can serve as a shorthand to denote a pristine package of private entitlements in land that involves:

- ownership by a single individual ("that sole and despotic dominion which one man claims . . .")
- in perpetuity
- of a territory demarcated horizontally by boundaries drawn upon the land, and extending from there vertically downward to the depths of the earth and upward to the heavens
- with absolute rights to exclude would-be entrants
- with absolute privileges to use and abuse the land, and
- with absolute powers to transfer the whole (or any part carved out by use, space, or time) by sale, gift, devise, descent, or otherwise.

Some parts of this Blackstonian package are far too draconian to function even as initial default rules that landowners could be empowered to modify. In practice, Anglo-American custom and law have generated the *fee simple*, a standard bundle of private land rights, that is far more nuanced than the pure Blackstonian package. Some of the fee simple's differences have been adverted to above, such as the norms of neighborliness and nuisance rules that diminish a landowner's use privileges. . . . This Part takes up the surprisingly complex issues of how a group might decide to locate the vertical and temporal boundaries of its standard private land interests.

## B. VERTICAL BOUNDARIES

As mentioned, a Blackstonian bundle confers upon a landowner entitlements that extend, from a parcel's horizontal boundaries, ever upward to the heavens and ever downward to the depths. This simple default rule was satisfactory until aircraft opened access to the skies, and mechanized drilling and mining equipment, to the subsurface. These innovations pose an efficient boundary problem in the vertical dimension. Aviation and mining activities are generally most efficiently undertaken over an area whose horizontal scope is much larger than that optimal for agriculture, housing, and other basic land surface operations. Groups have responded by imposing vertical limits on the standard rights and privileges conferred on surface landowners. For example, landowners everywhere are now subject to aviation easements, and, in most nations (but not the United States), to the sovereign's ownership of deep minerals. Dividing space into layers facilitates exploitation of the varying returns to horizontal scale that are available in different layers. Default parcels are of middling size on the ground, but are large, perhaps even unbounded, in the air and under the surface. The creation of a new vertical boundary is administratively burdensome and invites conflicts between owners of adjoining layers. A group is predicted to be willing to bear these costs only in circumstances in which the creation of another layer of ownership interests promises to generate benefits of greater magnitude.

## C. TIME SPANS OF STANDARD LAND INTERESTS

Both the fee simple and the Blackstonian bundle confer upon a mortal person ownership rights that last in perpetuity. Hewing to a commitment to adjectival sophistication, let us call the fee an example of a *long* standard time span. Historically, the usufruct has been the most important standard land bundle of *medium* temporal length. Some preliterate groups have bestowed this time-limited interest on a member household growing a crop on group lands. A usufruct basically entitles its owner to continue his current land use as long as he can. Other aspects of usufructuary packages may vary. To simplify discussion, a *classic usufruct* can be defined as an immutable package of land use rights that are not transferable and that terminate when the usufruct's owner dies or ceases the use, at which time the land is again up for grabs among group members. Finally, *short* standard bundles of land rights which last no more than a few hours are also usufructs, typically carved out of public lands such as parks and streets. A blanket spread on the sand of a state beach creates an interest of this sort.

Temporal transitions in land ownership invariably entail either transaction costs or deadweight losses. Ownership in fee simple, for example, increases the costs of administering the estates of deceased landowners. Classic usufructs eliminate this particular administrative burden and also the transaction costs of land sales, but may stimulate wasteful rent-seeking as would-be successors jockey for position in a usufruct's late stages. The relative magnitudes of these sorts of administrative costs are predicted to influence a group's standard bundling of land rights.

## 1. Land rights at the dawn of history

Anthropological evidence suggests that during the first 300,000 years of the evolution of our species (*Homo sapiens*), people lived in hunter-gatherer bands that moved nomadically as local food sources became exhausted. Then, about 10,000 years ago, prehistoric civilization achieved a great breakthrough. In the Fertile Crescent of the Near East, human groups, which had shortly before begun operating out of permanent settlements, mastered the skills of cultivating crops and domesticating animals. This breakthrough required innovations not only in husbandry, but also in property rights. A prehistoric community had to develop a set of land rules that provided incentives for its members to engage in the small events involved in raising crops and animals. The Promethean invention was likely the classic usufruct.

. . . .

## 2. The usufruct: Some advantages of standard bundles of medium length

In a post-literate society, perpetual private land rights are generally superior to usufructs for governing intensive activities such as crop growing. Owners of usufructs tend to be more shortsighted than owners of fees. A farmer with mere usufructuary rights in a field is unlikely to clear stones from it, and may exhaust its soils too quickly. Empirical studies confirm that usufructs tempt temporary owners to underinvest and to overexploit.

Nevertheless, in certain narrow circumstances, including those that likely prevailed in prehistoric times, intensive activities may be more efficiently conducted on a classic usufruct than on a fee. Three situational variables are particularly pertinent. First, some lands are more susceptible than others to long-term improvement or damage. The more immutable a parcel of land is, the less reason to provide its owner with an infinite planning horizon. A preliterate society, because it has less capacity than an industrialized society to make permanent alterations in land, is more likely to employ the usufruct as its standard time span of ownership. . . .

Second and relatedly, usufructs for crop growing are problematic only when arable land is scarce. When land is plentiful, a group need not be troubled by shortsighted land practices and uncertainties about succession to usufructuary rights.

Third, illiteracy breeds usufructs. A group that recognizes perpetual land interests must develop authoritative systems for proving title to lands whose owners are not currently in possession. A preliterate group may have trouble tracking titles and may prefer the usufructuary system under which, apart from trespassing, what you see is what is had.

Consistent with the efficiency thesis, as land becomes scarcer, technology advances, and literacy improves, a group tends to move away from the classic usufruct and toward the fee.

### 3. The fee simple: The advantages of perpetual land ownership

Although economic historians have only recently begun to give the fee its due, Blackstone was able to articulate many of its benefits two centuries ago. Perpetual ownership rights greatly simplify land-security transactions. But the preeminent advantage of an infinite land interest is that it is a low-transaction cost device for inducing a mortal landowner to conserve natural resources for future generations.

Although the assertion may seem counterintuitive, the key to land conservation is to bestow upon living persons property rights that extend perpetually into the future. The current market value of a fee in Blackacre is the discounted present value of the eternal stream of rights and duties that attach to Blackacre. A rational and self-interested fee owner therefore adopts an infinite planning horizon when considering how to use his parcel, and is spurred to install cost-justified permanent improvements and to avoid premature exploitation of resources. The fee simple in land cleverly harnesses human selfishness to the cause of altruism toward the unborn, a group not noted for its political clout or bargaining power.

. . . [O]nce it develops a written language, a group will almost invariably recognize unending private rights in some of its lands. For example, the ancients in Egypt and Greece, two cradles of Western civilization, conferred perpetual land entitlements on private owners. . . . Perpetual private land rights are most emphatically not a uniquely Western institution, however. Land interests of potentially infinite duration evolved separately among the Japanese, the Ibo of Nigeria, and the Navajo of the American Southwest. In sum, the inherent efficiencies of perpetual private land rights have led to their spontaneous appearance on every continent.

## Conclusion

Too often, the notion of private property in land has prompted a monolithic reaction. Some observers, like Blackstone, have been overly boosterish. Others, like Marx, have been unpardonably hostile. Most contemporary scholars appear to be more pragmatic and should concur with many of the central themes developed here.

The central positive thesis of this Article is that a close-knit group tends to create, through custom and law, a cost-minimizing land regime that adaptively responds to changes in risk, technology, demand, and other economic conditions. In so doing, the group opportunistically mixes private, group, and open-access lands. According to the private-property thesis, a close-knit group virtually invariably entitles its individual members, households, or narrow family lines to obtain exclusive rights to sites suitable for dwellings, agriculture, and other intensive uses. The key utilitarian advantage of private land tenure, in comparison to collective ownership, is that it is far simpler to monitor boundary crossings than to appraise the behavior of individuals who are privileged to be where they are. The Hutterites, kibbutzniks, and others who have succeeded in collectively governing intensive land activities have endured only by developing internal social controls far more pervasive and intrusive than those required where land is parcelized.

As a group becomes literate and its lands become more scarce, its standard bundle of private land rights tends to evolve from the time-limited and inalienable usufruct to something like the perpetual and alienable fee simple. Contrary to the writings of Karl Polanyi, who associated commerce in land with the rise of industrial capitalism, even the most ancient texts document land sales.

But a private-property regime is not always best. To exploit scale economies, and perhaps to spread risks, a group may gravitate toward governing some territories, such as a pasture in a medieval village or a recreation area in a homeowners' association, as limited-access commons. Finally, the public-property thesis asserts that a group invariably embeds its private parcels in an open-access network of public lands that is dedicated to general circulation and social interaction.

... [C]ritics of markets often assert that commodification pervasively corrupts human personalities. This century's tragic collectivizations have stemmed largely from this idea. In light of the horrific record of these interventions, those who wish to disturb indigenous land tenure systems should be required to surmount a heavy burden of proof. A land institution that has evolved over time is far more subtle than the mind of any single individual.

# 29

# Efficient Rules in Highway Safety and Sports Activity

## *Donald Wittman*

### EDITOR'S INTRODUCTION

I show that even such ostensibly non-economic activities as amateur sports and the allocation of the right of way in traffic have efficient rules. For example, sport rules tend to
economize on the transaction costs of allocating rights within the game, as well as the right
to play the game in the first place. This suggests that cultural phenomena more generally can
be explained by the same economic reasoning that has been used to explain formal legal
rules.

Economists have ignored rules of thumb as a method of allocating rights. Yet rules such
as "first come, first served," "the person on the right has the right-of-way," and "majority
rule" are used continually in our everyday lives and are often enforced by legal sanction.
Rules are used as substitutes for ordinary economic markets when the price system involves high transaction costs, and as initial allocators of rights in order to facilitate the
exchange of rights when transaction costs are low. Presumably, those rules which survive
are the efficient ones.

In this paper, I consider a number of rules of thumb and show how changes in technology and
objective determine the appropriate rule. Testable propositions are developed, mainly within the
context of highway safety and sporting activity. These situations are examples of cases where
rights are often not transferable and severely limited in time – sometimes labeled as communal
rights. The basic concepts will be introduced within the context of highway safety rules, while the
main part of the analysis will be devoted to the allocation of rights in sports.

## I. Theoretical Model

If information and decision making were costless, then every decision would involve weighing all the costs and benefits, for example, the decision as to which car should have the right-
of-way at an intersection would depend on which side valued the right more. Because
information processing and decision making is not costless, we may rely on some method

that economizes on these costs. In ordinary economic markets, a price system is very effective in eliciting information concerning relative value. Unfortunately, in many situations the transactions costs involved in instituting a price system outweigh the benefits of demand revelation. This will tend to be the case when the costs of allocating the rights to the wrong person are minor, and when the price system is less successful in demand revelation (for example, when there are public goods). This characterizes the types of situations discussed in this paper. General rules also tend to economize on decision-making costs (not only for the person making the allocating decision, but also for the people affected by the rule). Thus, rules of thumb are a substitute for both a price system and a complete investigation of relative value in each particular situation.

The basic theoretical argument is that only the most efficient rules will be used. Like all of economics, the analysis is based on costs and benefits. Those rules which involve the least costs and provide the greatest benefits will be utilized. This straightforward application of economics provides answers to questions such as the following. Which rule of thumb is chosen? When will rules of thumb be more or less complex? Under what conditions will different groups of people use different rules of thumb?

Different rules of thumb have different properties, thereby encouraging different outcomes and having different cost configurations. Economic efficiency dictates that, other things being equal, the more costly a rule of thumb is to use, the less likely it will be used. Two types of costs are relevant: costs associated with monitoring the rule of thumb; and inappropriate incentives created by the rule. A rule of thumb is by its very nature supposed to save on information costs. If the information costs are very high, the rule of thumb is no longer maintaining its proper function. Furthermore, the rule should not create incentives for costly allocative behavior. We do not want to encourage costly production of an activity whose sole end is allocation rather than an increase in present or future consumption. In a nutshell, we want a system with low transaction costs. In turn, "costs" depend on the problem at hand. For example, when time is at a premium, which is often the case in highway safety, split second rules of thumb are desirable.

The nature and the amount of benefits also determine the kind of rules chosen. Different objectives create different demands. A rule of thumb that encourages safety on the highway is unlikely to be the same rule of thumb that encourages thrills in sporting events. If the benefits are substantial, it pays to have more complex rules or more accurate, albeit more costly, methods.

## II. Highway Safety

### A. FOUR-WAY STOP SIGNS

It is useful to consider the issues within a very clear-cut case – the appropriate allocation of rights at a street intersection with a four-way stop sign. The law states that the first car which comes to the intersection has the property rights; if both arrive at the same time, the car to the right has the right-of-way; and if the cars are facing each other, the car making a left turn does not have the right-of-way. Before explaining why this set of rules is the most efficient method of allocating rights, I will first show why other methods either have high transaction costs or do not allocate the right to the party which is likely to value it the most.

## 1. Price system

In ordinary economic markets, the price system is a very effective method of determining relative economic value with minimal transaction costs. However, in ordinary traffic situations the transaction costs of a price system outweigh by far any benefits of it correctly allocating the rights to individual parties. For example, we might have a toll collector who gives the right-of-way to the person willing to pay the highest price. Clearly, the price system would have very high administrative costs. We cannot get rid of the toll collector and have the participants bribe each other, as the rights have not been established in the first place. Even if they were, it would still involve high transaction costs.

A price system, in the absence of administrative costs, can achieve Pareto optimality as the one individual can buy off the other so that both are made better off; unfortunately, in this case, the administrative costs outweigh the benefits. However, the concept of a pricing system with zero negotiation costs is a useful fiction. Whenever negotiation costs are high, one should ask who would end up with the rights if the transaction costs were low. . . .

## 2. Majority rule

Another method is majority rule. The car with the most passengers has the right-of-way. In the absence of other information, majority rule is a good estimate of greater value. We have no reason to believe that the individual people in the car with fewer passengers value the right-of-way more or less than the passengers in the car with more passengers. In consequence, we would expect the *total* value to be greater in the car with more passengers. That is, where negotiation costs are high and a pricing system is not feasible, granting rights to the majority is a good rule of thumb for determining efficient allocations. Other things being equal, we would expect the majority to bribe the minority and obtain the rights if negotiation costs were low. Because convertibles are not very popular, it is more time consuming to count people than to give the right to the first comer or the person on the right. So majority rule is also ruled out.

## 3. Rank

A third method is rank. A Cadillac might have the right-of-way over a Chevrolet. Again this might be a reasonable rule of thumb for achieving Pareto optimality. If there were a price mechanism for buying and selling rights, even if the right were initially assigned to the Chevrolet, the Cadillac owner would probably purchase it. Rights (privileges) at intersections are likely to be normal goods: that is, higher income will result in a greater demand. Since Cadillac owners tend to be richer than Chevrolet owners, we would expect Cadillac owners to purchase the right. This rule has some drawbacks, however. It would encourage people to buy Cadillacs which involves a social cost. A second problem is that it may take too much time to determine rank. The one ranking we do allow is priority for police cars and ambulances which are readily identifiable (but not unmarked police cars). Again we would expect this to be an efficient allocation of rights.

## 4. Skill

Another method, which is more common in sports, is a test of skill. In this case, better drivers would get the right-of-way. It is plausible to believe that people who are more skilled in an activity derive more pleasure from the activity. First of all, if they enjoy the activity, they will undertake the activity more often and thereby gain greater skill through practice. On the other hand, if a person is naturally more skilled in one area, he will be more productive at gaining utility in that area. For both these reasons, we tend to see individuals undertaking both consumption and production in areas where they are comparatively skilled. If the more skilled get greater utility from the activity than the less skilled, then rewarding the more skilled is likely to increase efficiency. Other things being equal, and in the absence of other information this is a reasonable assumption, we would expect the more skilled to end up with the rights (even if the rights were initially assigned to the less skilled) when transaction costs are zero. . . .

## 5. First come, first served

In the context of a four-way stop sign, first come, first served is a very appropriate allocating device. In the first place, it is very easy to determine. It is also less costly in terms of time. Clearly, it would be silly for the first car to wait a minute or two for the next car to come to see whether it should go first or not according to some other criterion. Even when the difference in time involves only a second or two, we would expect that, in a low transaction cost case, the first person would end up with the rights; the extra cost in terms of time of his going second is greater than the extra cost of the second person going second. . . .

## 6. Random

Another mechanism of property rights allocation is a random allocation – flip of the coin, toss of a racket, etc. In this case, being on the right is a random allocation since in a circle (four-way stop sign) being to the right is not transitive (while being earlier in a first come, first served situation will insure that you have prior rights over all cars that come later).

Of the many random allocators, being on the right is the most efficient because it involves much lower costs than other alternatives, such as flipping a coin. It is also preferable to giving the rights to the person on the left. If the person on the right has the right-of-way and goes straight, he blocks the person on the left when he crosses the first lane. If the person on the left has the right-of-way and he goes straight, he blocks the person on his right when he crosses the second lane. Thus, giving rights to the person on the left involves a more costly allocation. In England, where they drive on the other side of the road, the driver on the left has the right-of-way. With the exception of giving rights to the first person, giving rights to the person on the right involves the lowest transaction costs. Except in comparison to giving the rights to the person on the, left, giving rights to the person on the right does not ascertain relative economic value. Once it has been established that both cars come to the intersection at the same time, the added benefit of determining relative value is outweighed by the cost of determining relative value, thus a low cost random allocator is instituted.

# B. OTHER TRAFFIC SITUATIONS

*List*

Prices; majority rule; rank; first come, first served; tests of skill; and random selection are some of the more common methods of allocating property rights. Different circumstances will result in different rules of thumb being more efficient. Let us now turn toward the issue of predicting which method will be the most appropriate.

First come, first served is a very common rule in highway regulation (for example, the driver proceeding ahead of you in your lane has rights to his space), but it is by no means the only one. Other rules exist when they are either cheaper to administer or better predictors of relative valuation.

## 1. Majority rule used when monitoring costs are low

Majority rule is more likely to be used when it is relatively easy to ascertain. The use of two-way stop signs at a four-way intersection is an example of majority rule. The drivers on the more heavily traveled road have the right-of-way even if they are not first at the intersection. Traffic signals with a longer green light for traffic on one of the cross streets is a compromise between majority rule and first come, first served. As another example, a slow-moving vehicle must pull to the side if followed by five or more cars and it is unsafe to pass but safe to pull aside.[1] Under this circumstance, first come, first served accedes to the more efficient majority rule.

*never heard that*

## 2. Other rules used when they are better estimators of relative value

Both majority rule and first come, first served are inefficient in the following situation: on a narrow road, the vehicle descending should yield the right-of-way to the vehicle ascending and if necessary back up. Why not first come, first served? First of all, it is probably impossible to establish. Should we put a special marker halfway down the road so we can determine who was first? Second of all, an alternative rule provides a quick and better prediction of which party would buy the rights in a zero transaction cost situation. The person in the more dangerous position should be given any advantage. It is more difficult and dangerous to back up and go downhill at the same time than to back up and go up the hill because first is generally a higher gear than reverse, and backing down creates the possibility of accelerating dangerously downhill (both gravity and motor are pushing downhill). Thus, the person going uphill has the right-of-way. This is a better estimator of relative value than either first come, first served or majority rule.

## 3. Skill as an allocator of the right to drive

The decision regarding who has the rights (a license) to drive is based on skill. Again, because of high transaction costs, the pricing system is not a very good rule of thumb. While the transfer of a right to the highest bidder is usually efficient, it is not the case when there are negative externalities. In this case, individual bad drivers might outbid individual good drivers for the right to drive. Collectively the good drivers could bribe the bad drivers not to drive, but the organizational costs would be too high for this to ever take place.

# III. Sports Activity

The methodology developed in Section II can be applied to a variety of other areas including etiquette, sports rules, parliamentary procedure, and business decision making. I will concentrate on sports rules because similar rules of thumb are used in both highway safety and sports (for example, first come, first served), yet the objectives of these two activities are not closely related; and meaningful statistical data can be collected (which may not be the case for many of the other areas, for example, etiquette).

I show how technological aspects of each sport determine which rule is chosen for allocating rights. For each sport, the following questions can be asked. What mechanism is used in establishing who has the right to play in organized and unorganized activity? At the start of play what type of rule is used in granting advantageous rights to one team or another (for example, who gets to serve first)? After play has been initiated, what type of rule is used in granting advantageous rights to one team or another after a point has been scored? And in what circumstances will rules in unorganized play differ from rules in organized play? Both rules that have been codified and more casual rules of thumb will be considered. . . .

## *A.* SKILL AS AN ALLOCATOR

### *1. The right to play*

*Skill will be an allocator of the right to play when skill is relatively easy to determine and skill has a greater payoff to the participants.* Thus professional and organized play will tend to use skill more than nonprofessional and nonorganized play as a determiner of the rights to play. In the first place, spectators will pay more to see skilled playing than nonskilled playing. That is, skill is a derived demand. If there were a market to play in the Stanley Cup Playoff, World Series, or the Superbowl (i.e., places were auctioned off to the team bidding the most), the most skilled team or player would tend to end up with the rights as the rights would be worth more to the skilled team.[2] Furthermore, in organized play, skill rankings for postseason playoffs (as in hockey) or in seeding for tournaments (as in tennis) are relatively easy to determine because the team (or players) have played against each other or against comparable players. Contrast this with three or four people vying to play at a city tennis court. Here skill would be a very costly method of allocating rights. Furthermore, skill would not be as good a determiner of relative value.

*Skill will be less likely to be used as an allocator of rights at the beginning of a game than during the game where skill is more readily determined.* Furthermore, *if skill is used, a special skill task (whose sole purpose is to determine allocation of rights) is more likely to be used at the beginning of play than during the game.* Finally, *skill is more likely to be used at the beginning of a game for those games in which skill is readily determined (at the beginning) than for those games where skill is costly to ascertain.*

## 2. Allocation at the beginning of the game

Starting with the last point first, in many games it is extremely difficult (i.e., costly) to determine skill before the start of the game. Therefore, a skill mechanism is not used. For example, in tennis how does one determine skill starting from a neutral position without actually playing the game? In order to determine who serves first, should we have one play where one person serves first? This clearly makes no sense. At one time it was common in casual play to hit the ball over the net three times before a point could be scored to determine who got to serve first. But unfortunately, this gives an unfair advantage to the person who hits the ball over the third time. In order to determine who shoots first in billiards, each side tries to hit the ball closest to the opposite edge (cushion). The person getting the closest obtains the right to shoot first. In billiards this is a low-cost procedure, but a comparable method in tennis would be impossible. For example, if both tried to see who could serve closest to the back line, it would be very difficult to determine as the ball keeps on moving and the players would be too far away to judge. Thus a random mechanism (spinning the racket) is used instead of a skill device.[3] In contrast, skill is much easier to determine in basketball. In casual play each side may shoot baskets from the foul line in order to determine who gets the ball first. In professional play, the ball is tossed up by a referee. Both sides then jump for the ball.

## 3. Allocation during the game vis-à-vis the beginning

Information on skill is readily obtained throughout the game. Therefore, allocation according to skill is more likely during the game than at the beginning of the game where a test of skill is relatively more costly. Thus football, badminton, and squash use a random method to allocate rights at the beginning of play (for example, in football the winner of the toss receives the kickoff), but a skill mechanism to determine allocation thereafter (for example, in football the side which scored kicks off to the other side).

When there is a tie game and the tie must be broken, skill during the game no longer differentiates and a random device is again likely to be used. In both American football and ultimate frisbee, a coin (or frisbee) is tossed at the end of a tie game to determine who gains possession of the ball or the frisbee. A special skill test to determine the right to receive the ball or frisbee would be redundant for the skill test itself could then be used as a tie breaker.

## 4. Special skill device

(a) During the game vis-à-vis the beginning: If a special skill device is used solely for allocating rights (for example, the tip-off in basketball), it is more likely to be used at the beginning of the game than during the middle of the game. The reason is again on economic efficiency grounds. During the game, skill measures are obtained costlessly as a by-product of play. Thus if a skill measure is used after a point has been scored, it is unnecessary to devise a special method. The cost of a special allocator device becomes prohibitive if it must be used very often. The history of basketball is illustrative. In basketball, at the beginning of a game there is a tip-off (a ball is tossed up in the air by a referee and one player from each side tries to tip it off to another player on his side). Formerly, after a basket was made another tip-off took place, but this rule was inefficient. A tip-off after a basket has been made is redundant because the making of the basket is already a skill indicator. Setting up the players for a tip-off is time consuming, and it emphasizes skills which are not perfectly correlated with skills needed in the rest of the game. This means that scarce resources will be used to succeed in this allocation mechanism that are not appropriate for the rest of the game (in particular, excessive height without other basketball skills). Over time, there was a great increase in the number of points scored in a basketball game, making what would ordinarily appear to be a minor cost into a major misallocation of resources.[4] Therefore, this rule was abolished.

Hockey is a useful comparison to basketball. A face-off (the analog to the tip-off) is still used after every point. But there are two essential differences: the skills needed in the face-off are the same as those in the rest of the game and there are very few points scored in a hockey game (rarely more than 10) so that the costs of redundantly measuring skill are minor.[5]

(b) Property rights vs. communal rights: *A special skill device is also more likely to be used in determining the allocation of rights when the allocation involves an important property right rather than an unimportant communal right.* A communal right is the right to use and not to exclude while a property right involves exclusion. Thus in horseshoes, golf, and figure skating, the sequence of players is a communal right (no matter how skilled the previous players, all others will still get their turn) and is dependent on skill demonstrated in the previous round. A special skill task would be a waste of time for such a trivial right. In contrast, possession of the hockey puck is a valuable property right (it not only provides an opportunity for scoring, but also it reduces the time available to the other team), and therefore a special skill allocation is more reasonable.

## 5. Rewarding skilled or unskilled?

In basketball, American football, and soccer, if a team scores a point, the other team obtains the advantageous rights (possession of the ball). In volleyball and badminton, if a team scores a point, it keeps the advantageous rights (the right to serve, which is a prerequisite for scoring). In high jump and pole vault, if a person has three consecutive failures, he loses the right to jump. When skill is used as an allocator during a game, it is sometimes used to positively reward skill and other times to negatively reward skill. What is the explanation for the differential treatment of skill? The answer to this question is more tentative than the results in the rest of the paper as there are exceptions to the theoretical results. As a consequence, here more than elsewhere in the paper, I emphasize that the propositions are statistical in nature (if *x*, then *y* is more likely). Essentially, the answer depends upon the fact that *many rules are derived demands, the interests of spectators determining the allocation of rights.*

(a) *Objective sports reward skill:* In those games where the teams or players compete in terms of some objective measure (shortest time, highest or longest distance) without interference from the other players or teams, spectators want to see a record broken. As a consequence, if skill is used as an allocator of rights, it will be used to positively reward skill. For example, if there are more than eight contestants in javelin, shotput, discus, or hammer throw, the normal six trials are divided into two parts. Only the eight contestants with the longest distance in the first set of three trials can participate in the second set. As another example, in high jump, pole vault, long jump, and triple jump, a contestant is eliminated after three consecutive failures.

(b) *Offensive-defensive sports reward unskilled:* In sports where the teams work against each other and there is an offense and a defense (such as basketball, American football, and soccer), the spectator obtains relatively greater thrills from a close contest.[6] As a result, in order to make the game closer, scoring points will more likely result in a loss of an advantageous right.[7] This will be especially so when the sport has many spectators (i.e., the derived demand of the spectators is very important) and when the rights granted are more akin to property rights than communal rights. For example, baseball grants communal rights: when a skilled team scores (without an "out" being made) it gets the opportunity to score again. However, no matter how many runs have been scored by a team and how much time the team has taken at bat, the other team still gets its turn. In contrast, in basketball and football, possession of the ball (an advantageous right) by one team reduces the time available to the other team. If the property right of excludability were given to the team which scored, the game would be less close and less exciting for the spectators. The team which scored would tend to be very cautious about losing possession of its advantageous right. Scoring would tend to be more lopsided, resulting in uninteresting final quarters where one team would be so far ahead that the other team would not have a chance to win in the time remaining.

(c) *Historical evidence:* Persuasive evidence for the demand for closeness is found when there are rule changes over time or when the sport is organized along two or more different modes. In offense-defense games, changes over time will be in the direction of giving advantageous rights to the team which has not scored rather than to the team which did. The previously discussed basketball rule change (1937–38) is an example. When the tip-off was no longer used, the team *not* gaining the point was given the right. In hockey the following rule change was made during the 1956–57 season. A player serving a minor penalty was now allowed to return when a goal was scored by the opposing team.

(d) *Differing rules under differing modes of organization:* Many sports have several modes of organization. Automobile racing is the largest spectator sport in the United States. For major events such as the Indianapolis 500, where a major speed record may be broken and the cars are closely matched, the fastest car in the preheat gets the pole position (an advantageous, nontransferable property right). In contrast, in local races the fastest car is often put in a disadvantageous position in order to make the competition more equal because the cars are not so evenly matched and a major speed record is unlikely.[8]

In unorganized neighborhood basketball, the team making the basket sometimes loses the ball to the other side and sometimes keeps the ball. There are no spectators in this sport, so the demand for a close game is not the reason for the variation. But here the demands of the players themselves (including the winning team) are important. For example, the demand by the third team (waiting to play the winner) is for the game to be over as soon as possible (which is more likely if the scorer gains possession of the ball). This is to be contrasted with organized basketball where there are more spectators and a greater demand for a close game and as a consequence the scoring team always loses possession of the ball.

. . . .

## B. THE ALLOCATION OF RIGHTS TO PLAY IN UNORGANIZED PLAY: MARGINAL PRODUCTIVITY AND MAJORITY RULE

Majority rule and first come, first served are commonly used measures of relative value when the administrative costs of a price system make an ordinary market inefficient. Other things being equal, more people would buy out the right from fewer people, and those who come earlier and wait longer would buy out the right to play first from those who come later. Other things are not equal, however, and as a result we have a choice between two imperfect measures of relative value. *When marginal productivity of a player is strongly positive, majority rule will prevail over first come, first served as a method of allocating access to public sports facilities. When marginal productivity is negative, majority rule will be a poor measure of relative value and first come, first served will be the prevailing method of allocation.*

### 1. The marginal productivity of a player in tennis

On public tennis courts, singles generally have priority over a solitary player even if the person was there first; however, doubles do not have priority over singles (although doubles may sometimes be allowed to have the court for a longer period of time), and triples never have priority over doubles. This can be explained in terms of marginal productivity. One person does not gain very much from being on a tennis court alone. The cost to the solitary player in not being able to play on the court is small in comparison to the benefits to the pair of single players being on the court. Thus majority rule prevails over first come, first served.[9] It should be noted that with the advent of serving machines and ball sweeps, the marginal productivity of a solitary player is increased. As a consequence, solitary players in private tennis clubs commonly have the right to the tennis court even when doubles are waiting. Doubles do not have priority over singles, however, even on public courts. First come, first served has priority and is used instead of majority rule. Why? While majority rule is an estimate of a Pareto optimal allocation, it is not a very good estimator in this case, for it is not clear that doubles would buy off a pair of singles. If doubles were given priority over singles, this would create inefficient incentives for people to play in doubles in order to obtain the rights even when they preferred to play singles. Because singles is played harder, the marginal productivity of additional time decreases faster for single play; and thus, there is often a shorter time period for singles.

. . .

### 2. The technology of basketball

In comparing basketball and tennis, we find different technologies and different sets of rules for establishing rights. The technology of basketball allows for greatly varying size teams (from 1 to 5) and varying quality of players. These two attributes often make merger an efficient solution. If four players arrive at a court with only two players, the four players cannot usurp the two players' right to play and often the two players cannot keep the court to themselves. Typically all six players will play on three-player teams. Or, if the court has two baskets, one game can be played at each basket, since the character of the game is only slightly changed when the play is only on half court. In fact, half court is generally preferred when there are very small teams. This is not possible in tennis.

It is very hard to organize six, eight, or ten people to play; so pick up (where players discover other players to play with at the court) is more common in basketball than in tennis where the organization costs are lower. Typically, there are many people coming and going in basketball pick-up games; it is thus very hard to remember who came first. If there are an odd number of people practicing and a game is then organized, first come, first served is not a good rule as it is difficult to determine, and majority rule is meaningless. Fortunately, there is an alternative – shooting baskets from the foul line (not being blocked by the other side). Consequently, we would expect skill to be an allocator of rights to play in unorganized play relatively more often in basketball than in tennis. This is, in fact, the case.

## C. DEGREES OF COMPLEXITY

*Other things being equal, when the costs of making a mistaken allocation are large, rules of thumb will tend to be more complex.* Clearly, vehicle codes are more extensive and complex than pedestrian codes. The same holds true in sports. In both polo and yachting there are very detailed rights of way. In polo the rider going closest to the line in which the ball was hit has the right-of-way. If they both are of equal closeness, the rider to the right has the right-of-way. If both riders are riding along the same line, but in opposite directions, the rider going in the same direction as the path of the ball has the right-of-way. Field hockey does not have these complex rules. The reason for the difference is that the maneuverability of a horse is less than the maneuverability of a person, and the cost of collision is much greater in polo than in field hockey.

Because of the great cost of an accident in yachting, there are even more rules regarding right-of-way. (Yachting, like other sports where players compete in terms of some objective measure without interference from the other team, has rules to prevent interference.) Most of the rules give the right-of-way to the yacht which is less able to maneuver or has less visibility. The capsized boat has the right-of-way and the yacht that is overtaking another must keep clear of the preceding yacht. Thus the "least cost avoider" is the one who is liable, while the other has the right-of-way.[10]

. . .

## IV. Conclusion

First come, first served, majority rule, skill, and random mechanisms are some of the rules which are used to allocate rights in traffic and sports. Despite the disparate nature of these activities, the choice of rules relies on the same economic principles. Differing demands, marginal productivities, and monitoring costs will result in different rules of thumb being chosen.

Rules of thumb are not mere historical accidents; rather they are efficient methods of allocating rights when ordinary economic markets are not viable. This article shows why one rule is chosen instead of another and demonstrates that even "noneconomic" activities such as play can be fruitfully analyzed in terms of economic theory.

## Notes

1. My referent is always the California traffic code.
2. Granting rights to play to the more skilled encourages greater skill.
3. Spinning rackets (in racket games) and tossing coins are inexpensive random allocators. However, many children's games such as hide-and-seek do not have rackets and small children rarely carry money; therefore, rhymes such as "eeny-meeny" are substituted. For small children, the end result of an eeny-meeny rhyme is not predictable and thus appears random.
4. Since basketball is a recent sport, the tip-off during the middle of the game may be seen as an early experiment which did not survive. An increasing shadow price of time may also be responsible for its demise. The following quote from *Illustrated Basketball Rules* is insightful.

   "The elimination of the center jump after a score in 1937–38 was probably the most significant change in the history of the rules. No other rule change has been more experimented with and researched over a longer period of time than this one."
5. Face-offs during the game are still used in other low-scoring games such as field hockey and lacrosse. On the other hand, championship ringers (marbles), pool, English billiards, and carom billiards have a special skill allocator (closest to the line in marbles, closest to the cushion in the other games) only at the beginning of the game. Shooting for the closest ball to the cushion every time a ball was pocketed in pool would be exceedingly costly and unnecessary. It would also be inefficient to repeat a random allocation. Thus in tennis one spins the racket to determine who serves first and then there is an alternation of the service. One does not spin the racket after each game.
6. Spectators also derive financial benefits from betting, which is facilitated by evenly matched teams (the point spread is one method of compensating for inequality).
7. Bullfighting has a number of rules which promote the equality between the bull and the bullfighter. For example, the picador is allowed a second thrust if the bull has injured the horse and is still running forward; reserve picadors are allowed into the game if a picador is injured. Thus increased skill of the bull gives more advantageous rights to the bullfighter, and vice versa.
8. Horse racing and harness racing have handicap and nonhandicap racing. The choice between the two run somewhat along the same lines as automobile racing. For example, the major horse racing events in the United States (Kentucky, Preakness, and Belmont) are not handicapped, so that a record might be achieved.
9. Solitary players who arrive first could be given the rights. Players with partners who arrived later could bribe the solitary players for the right. However, this would be inefficient. A needless transaction would take place. Furthermore, many individuals would come to the tennis court solely to get the right which they would then transfer for a fee. This would increase the inefficiency.
10. It is interesting to compare yachting to automobile racing. In automobile racing, the spectators demand the thrills involved in near misses. Because there are so many spectators, the racers can be adequately compensated for the risks to their cars and themselves that they undertake. Because yachting must take place on the open water, it is technologically difficult to get many people to pay for watching the sport, and therefore the racers are not compensated. Television has overcome some of the technological difficulties. However, at present, yachting does not command a large audience. As a result, payment for broadcast rights is small and typically goes to the yachting clubs to cover the costs of conducting the race. Thus there are no monetary incentives to eliminate all the yachting rules of right-of-way.

# 30

# Rings and Promises

## Margaret F. Brinig

### EDITOR'S INTRODUCTION

Contractors are often required to post performance bonds to insure that they will do as they promised. If they fail to perform, they forfeit their bond. Margaret Brinig argues that engagement rings serve as performance bonds and are a substitute for the civil action of breach of promise which was, for the most part, legislated out of existence in the mid-1930s. According to Brinig, before the 1960s, a woman needed to be a virgin in order to be marriageable. But nearly half the women lost their virginity during the engagement. Without being able to sue for breach of promise, the women would need some other method to insure that a man was not just using the promise of marriage to gain sexual favors. Hence, the added reason for an engagement ring. Engagement rings became quite fashionable after the mid-1930s but became less so after the 1960s when the desire for a virgin bride rapidly disappeared.

I note that the same phenomena can explain why rules of etiquette and law regarding who gets to keep the engagement ring when an engagement has been broken has shifted from the woman to the man (regardless of who broke off the engagement).

## 1. Introduction

... Diamonds were associated in [the United States] with engagement beginning in the 1840s, although they were at first given to men as well as women. ... However, before the Depression, diamond rings were not considered a requisite for betrothal by most Americans. What then made women rather suddenly demand diamonds on the occasion of their engagement, so that by 1945 the "typical" bride wore "a brilliant diamond engagement ring and a wedding ring to match in design?".

The diamond ring rapidly changed from a relatively obscure token of affection to what amounted to an American tradition. It is customary to explain such a shift in demand in terms of an increase in income, a change in relative prices, or a change in tastes. This assumes a stable legal setting – that contracts are enforceable. But if the enforceability of a contract is problematic, what formerly was a relatively costly (hence unused) form of private ordering may become more viable. ..]. This paper looks at the change in America's demand

unenforceable

for diamonds during the period 1930–85, not as a Madison Avenue success story, but rather as a natural outgrowth of economic processes. The event beginning the movement toward diamond engagement rings was the abolition, with great fanfare, of a now relatively obscure cause of action called the "breach of promise to marry."

## 2. The Breach of Promise Action

The breach of promise action entitled a woman whose fiancé had broken off their engagement to sue him in assumpsit for damages, including the actual expenses she had incurred in reliance on the marriage. She might also recover for her embarrassment, humiliation, and loss of other marriage opportunities.[1]

. . .

. . . Many, if not most, women who brought such actions had not only lost a husband, but also their virginity. Particularly during the period between the two world wars, a woman was expected to remain chaste until the time of her engagement (Kinsey, 1948a: 336; 1948b: 364). Once she was betrothed, however, sexual intimacy with her fiancé reportedly occurred nearly half the time (Kinsey, 1948a: 336; 1948b: 364). All this was well and good, but if the marriage never came about, she was irretrievably barred from offering an unblemished self to a new suitor and suffered a loss in "market value" (Feinsinger, 1935a: 983). . . . Because of the importance of premarital chastity, damages in breach of promise actions where seduction (intercourse) had occurred were far more substantial than in cases where no sexual intimacy was alleged (*Paul v. Frazier,* 3 Mass. 71, 73 (1807); Grossberg: 46–47). The trials themselves frequently became public spectacles because of testimony regarding the woman's previous chastity (or lack of the same). By the beginning of the Depression, the breach of promise suit came to be regarded as legally sanctioned blackmail, a threat to marriage and the family (Grossberg: 62-63).

In 1935, a legislator from Indiana sponsored a bill abolishing the heart-balm actions in that state. . . . Almost immediately thereafter, similar statutes were passed in most of the other major urban jurisdictions, so that by 1945, sixteen states had eliminated breach of marriage promise. Today, there are only scattered reported breach of marriage promise decisions from those few jurisdictions where the action remains viable.

## 3. Demand for Diamonds

At the same time the cause of action for breach of promise was being reconsidered, the diamond industry had faced a period of lessened demand and increased supply. For a few years following 1932, diamonds were stockpiled in Europe to prevent a glut on the market. . . .

There was not only a greater supply but also a reduced demand, for sales during the twenty-year period prior to 1939 declined by nearly 100 percent. . . . National advertising was thought of as "vulgar" before the Great Depression, but in 1939, four years after the first states abolished the breach of promise action, DeBeers formed an alliance with a prominent New York advertising agency, Ayers, and prepared to release a significant advertising campaign focused on the slogan that "a diamond is forever." . . .

The advertising agency from the start aimed at a national market. One of its more successful techniques was exploitation of the burgeoning film industry: Hollywood stars were given large and conspicuous diamonds to wear off stage, and special scenes involving the presentation of engagement rings were introduced into popular movies after intervention by Ayers. . . .

The industry enjoyed a phenomenal success during the period following 1935, and by 1965, 80 percent of all brides chose diamond engagement rings . . . . DeBeers attributed the changing market to the Ayers advertising campaign . . . , but, in fact, the market for diamonds began its growth four years before national advertising when the breach of promise action was first abolished in a significant number of important states. . . .

*underlying cause* [handwritten marginalia]

*Shouldn't matter less for reach people* [handwritten annotation]

## 4. Explaining the Change in Demand

The change in demand for diamonds can be studied empirically by analyzing the various factors that might have led to an increased desire for diamonds and observing what turns out to be the most significant. The dramatic increase in demand could be the result of a dramatic decrease in price. Or DeBeers' national advertising campaign could have caused the surge in popularity of diamonds. . . . The hypothesis of interest here, the bond or pledge hypothesis,[2] is that the statutory changes abolishing the breach of promise action explain the increase in the demand for diamonds.

*P↓ – adv.* [handwritten marginalia]

. . .

[A] . . . way of testing the hypothesis that diamond engagement rings serve as pledges is to see what happened to the demand for rings when social mores changed so that sexual intimacy was no longer confined to marriage and engagement. Although from 1965 to 1980 real per capita income continued to increase, the demand for engagement rings leveled off and actually decreased for this more recent period, when cohabitation of nonmarried couples was no longer a curiosity (Koskoff: 273–74, 277).

*natural test* [handwritten marginalia]

There has been a recent decline in the number of marriages as more women enter the job market and more couples postpone marriage until education is complete and careers established. However, since sexual activity by women is not so completely confined to marriage, the current need for a bonding device before consent to intercourse is greatly diminished. Ayers' statistics show that since 1980, and unlike the earlier period, engagement rings have never exceeded 20 percent of diamond jewelry sales (Ayers Research: 6–7). Although diamond sales in general increased, the demand for engagement rings has changed, for the wearing of a diamond symbolic of engagement is no longer a prerequisite to premarital intimacy and because the cost to a woman of a broken engagement is no longer as significant.

## References

Ayers Research. 1987. *The Market for Diamond Jewelry – United States – 1986.* New York: N. W. Ayers.
Feinsinger, N. P., 1935a. "Legislative Attack on 'Heart Balm,'" 33 *Michigan Law Review* 979.
——. 1935b. "Current Legislation Affecting Breach of Promise to Marry, Alienation of Affections, and

Related Actions," 10 *Wisconsin Law Review* 417.

Grossberg, Michael. 1985. *Governing the Hearth*. Chapel Hill: University of North Carolina Press.

Kinsey, Alfred, Wardell Pomeroy, and Clyde Martin. 1948a. *Sexual Behavior in the Human Female*. Philadelphia: Saunders.

———. 1948b. *Sexual Behavior in the Human Male*. Philadelphia: Saunders.

Koskoff, David. 1981. *The Diamond World*. New York: Harper & Row.

## Notes

1. The early action for breach of promise to marry was within the jurisdiction of the English ecclesiastical courts, and in many cases the filing of the action resulted in specific performance of the marriage contract rather than an award of damages since the man was financially coerced into marriage to prevent the suit. One of the reasons given in favor of abolishing the action was that these forced marriages ought not to be encouraged.

2. The utility of a diamond ring as collateral depends upon whether it belongs to the nonbreaching party. Even in Roman law, this was true in the case of engagement rings (*Tulane University:* 501). "The ring is a pledge to bind the contract to marry and it is given on the understanding that the party who breaks the contract must return it" (*Jacobs* v. *Davis,* [19171 K.B. 532).

*examples
of culture
where man
get it,*

*• Prezjy norts*

# Index

*Index compiled by Frank Pert*